ZIMBABWE

Limpopo River

T R A N S V A A L

Pietersburg

MOZAMBIQUE

KRUGER NATIONAL PARK

DISCARD

Sun City
eerust
Mmabatho
TRANSVAAL
WITWATERSRAND

Nelspruit

MAPUTO

PRETORIA
Soshanguve
JOHANNESBURG
Soweto

Potchefstroom
Klerksdorp
Vaal River

SWAZI-
LAND

Welkom

ORANGE FREE STATE

Harrismith
Phuthaditjhaba

Blood River
Nqutu
Ladysmith
Ekuvukeni

N A T A L

BLOEMFONTEIN
Onverwacht

LESOTHO

Pietermaritzburg
Inanda
DURBAN

Umtata

Queenstown

King
William's Town
Mdantsane
Grahamstown
EAST LONDON

Frankfort

INDIAN OCEAN

New Brighton
PORT ELIZABETH

LEGEND

Black "National States"
(Homelands)

▥	Transkei
▨	Ciskei
▧	KwaZulu
▤	Bophuthatswana
▦	Qwaqwa
▥	KwaNdebele
▨	Lebowa
▨	Gazankulu
▨	Venda
▦	KaNgwane

△ Existing "Black Spots"
● Resettlement Areas
□ Black Townships (italic)
⊙ Major Cities
○ Other Cities, Towns

Don Pitcher

Move
YOUR
SHADOW

Move Your Shadow

SOUTH AFRICA, BLACK AND WHITE

JOSEPH
LELYVELD

𝕿imes
BOOKS

All rights reserved under International and Pan-American Copyright
Conventions. Published in the United States by Times Books,
a division of Random House, Inc., New York, and simultaneously
in Canada by Random House of Canada Limited, Toronto.

Library of Congress Cataloging in Publication Data
Lelyveld, Joseph.
Move your shadow.
Includes index.
1. South Africa—Race relations.   2. Segregation—
South Africa.   3. South Africa—Social conditions—
1961– .   4. Lelyveld, Joseph.   I. Title.
DT763.L395   1985   305.8′00968   85-40280
ISBN 0-8129-1237-3

Designed by Stephanie Blumenthal
Manufactured in the United States of America
9 8 7 6 5 4 3 2

for Carolyn

Wena azi lo golof? Mina hayifuna lo mampara mfan.

Have you caddied before? I don't want a useless boy.

Tata lo saka gamina.

Take my bag of clubs.

Tata mabol, yena doti. Susa yena nga lo manzi.

These balls are dirty. Clean them with water.

Muhle wena tula loskati lo-mlungu ena beta lo bol.

You must be quiet when my partner plays a shot.

Tula!

Be quiet.

Noko wena lahlega lo futi bol, hayikona mali.

If you lose another ball, there will be no tip for you.

Susa lo-mtunzi gawena. Hayikona shukumisa lo saka.

Move your shadow. Don't rattle the bag.

—J. D. Bold, *Fanagalo Phrase Book, Grammar and Dictionary, the Lingua Franca of Southern Africa,* 10th edition, 1977

I can tell you the things that happened as I saw them, and what the rest were about only Africa knows.

—Herman Charles Bosman, *Mafeking Road*

CONTENTS

MOVE
YOUR
SHADOW

CHAPTER 1

◼

OUT-KICKED

When they are out to demonstrate their decency and good-will, to themselves as well as others, white South Africa's racial theorists are inclined to lose themselves in a riot of euphemisms, analogies, and fatuous forecasts. A lot of words get spilled as the urge to be understood clashes with an aversion to being understood too well. But when being understood is no longer an issue, language can be used sparingly. The letter informing me I had a week to clear out of South Africa was a model of economy, unencumbered by explanations. "You are hereby instructed," it said, "to make arrangements for yourself and your family to leave the Country on or before the 28th April, 1966."

We had been there for only eleven months, but the message had long been expected, ever since an official had canceled a lunch in Pretoria, privately explaining that he would be compromised if he were seen again with someone the Cabinet had decided to expel. When the snub was finally made official, my immediate reaction was relief. A weight had been lifted, and as we walked out of the terminal at Jan Smuts Airport to our plane for Rome—two days ahead of the official deadline—I had a feeling of lightness, of freedom as a palpable sensation, such as I had never known before. Possibly it occurred to me at that moment to wonder whether I would ever set foot in South Africa again. But since I had now been officially certified an enemy—"one of South Africa's most notorious enemies in the world," an Afrikaans-language newspaper would later say, honoring me beyond my deserts —that would have been tantamount to wondering whether the regime would crumble and fall in my lifetime.

Fourteen years later, when the suspicion that I might be reconstituted as a persona grata in South Africa hatched itself almost in-

3

stantly into a compulsion to return, I could remember the sense of relief and lightness I felt on leaving as vividly as I could recall anything about the place. It was a memory I willed upon myself almost daily to check my headlong flight from Manhattan, where I thought I really belonged, and another uprooting of my family. The white regime hadn't crumbled, and even with the transformation of Rhodesia into black-ruled Zimbabwe, then taking place on its northern frontier, it wasn't about to do so. But the whites' old urge to be understood, coupled with their need to believe their own propaganda about how much had changed, gave me a slight opening; at least that was my calculation. My work as an editor in New York occasionally brought me into contact with South African diplomats who seldom failed to say the diplomatic thing: that my expulsion had been an aberration, or that those had been the bad old days, or that I would be astonished by the changes. Getting carried away, they sometimes seemed even eager to make me a witness. What may have been intended as no more than a civility—or, at most, a suggestion for a brief visit—I took as a sporting wager, even a dare.

I had long had a weakness, amounting to a craving, for going back, not only to South Africa but practically anywhere I had worked as a reporter. There was something irresistible about returning to a story you had once covered; it was like a trip in a time machine, one of the few ways a newspaperman could inject a little coherence and resonance into a vagabond life. To give only one example, a few years before I started to be obsessed again with South Africa, I had gone back to Philadelphia, Mississippi, where three young civil rights workers were murdered in the "freedom summer" of 1964. I had been to Philadelphia only a matter of weeks before I left the first time for Africa. It was the opportune moment when the conspiracy to make an example of James Chaney, Andrew Goodman, and Michael Schwerner was just cracking open. On my return I sat one evening with a white man named Cecil Price. An intimidating deputy sheriff in 1964, when he advised me one afternoon to get out of town, he had eventually spent four years in a federal penitentiary for the central role he had played in the conspiracy. Now, a member in good standing of the golf club, he was only too happy to talk about Cecil junior's experiences with black teachers in an integrated school or his own impressions of the black experience in America as related in the TV series *Roots*, which he rated as only "fair" because, he said, "the violence part was played up a bit too much."

Going back to Philadelphia, Mississippi, for a few days was one thing; going back to Johannesburg for a few years, something else. But as I rummaged through fading memories, I knew as a certainty that no story I had ever covered, no place I had ever been had gripped me as wholly and intensely as South Africa. Remembering in the gray days of a Manhattan winter the scale of the land and its antagonisms, and the vividness of personality that came with them, I felt a pull that was other than nostalgia.

I didn't need to remind myself that there had been places I had enjoyed more; "enjoyment" was definitely not a word I associated with South Africa then. It was a time of silence and fear, when the system of racial dominance known as apartheid was being elaborated as an ideology and the security apparatus, having outlawed and crushed the main black nationalist movements, was stamping out the few sparks of resistance that white radicals had managed to ignite. To a newcomer the supporters of the government seemed a monolith; its enemies, a subdued, if not cringing, mass. The first South African to be executed in the apartheid era for an act of political violence, a white romantic named John Harris who had foolishly imagined he could shake the regime by leaving a bomb in a railway station, had just gone to the gallows singing "We Shall Overcome." Finishing with the radicals, the security apparatus seemed to be switching its focus to slightly larger but nonetheless minuscule coteries of white liberals who still ventured to speak and act on the premise that South Africa was a multiracial country.

Those we knew were the most admirable people we had ever known: brave but often despairing or frightened, or both. Some had been hauled off to prison for solitary confinement and police interrogation; others lived in fear that they would be. Terrible things had happened to their relatives, lovers, and friends, including betrayals under police pressure. They knew their phones were tapped; in one case we knew, the bedroom was bugged as well. If they were writers, they faced the likelihood that censorship would cut them off from audiences they wanted to address. If they were lawyers, they watched helplessly as an increasingly broad range of political offenses was placed beyond reach of the courts. Newspapermen hostile to the authorities expected to be muzzled. Theater people debated whether it was better to perform before segregated audiences or not at all. The thought of going into exile occurred to many, but most carried on in causes they deemed hopeless, partly because they loved their land, also because they were compromised by its comforts and golden climate, but mainly because they knew that silencing themselves would be an unforgivable compromise. The sort of people who would have been civil rights activists in that period in America, they faced dilemmas out of nineteenth-century Russian literature in an environment where most whites were deliberately numb to obvious moral issues. And always there was the awareness that their own suffering, which came from too much clarity, the moral equivalent of a hormonal imbalance, was nothing to that of the blacks; that probably it would be irrelevant in the long run.

All that moral clarity, as harsh in its way as the glare from the South African sun, was a large part of what wore me out in the country. "At least," I would say sardonically, "you won't find anyone saying here that it's a matter of grays, not blacks and whites."* It wasn't the problem of the color bar that gripped me—"the color bore," an English journalist once wrote—or even the great mystery of how it would turn out in the end. Least of all was I preoccupied by South Africa's supposed strategic significance for the West. It was the place itself, its actual workings, its here and now. I had not especially wanted to go there initially; as a fledgling correspondent I had focused my aspirations on Asia. South Africa was an assignment—until I landed there and realized, in something like three hours, that it was already starting to get hold of me.

I had just flown in from what was still called the Congo in transit to what was still called Rhodesia. Five months earlier I had been in Mississippi; a few months before that I had covered race riots in Harlem, Rochester, Jersey City, and Philadelphia. I might even mention, if there is any point in unfurling a curriculum vitae in order to show a grasp of racial complexities, that I had graduated from Booker T. Washington Junior High School on Manhattan's Upper West Side. What I saw looked familiar, yet like no place I had ever been, so startling did it seem in its most ordinary aspects, in the tiny rituals and gaping contrasts of its daily life. My memory has blurred, and I can no longer recall precisely what it was that laid hands on my imagination and made me realize that here was a place in the real world as well as a theme for some of its most boring orators, a weird social order as well as an imminent conflict. It was something commonplace, I'm sure, the

---

*I was eventually proved wrong. On April 9, 1983, the *Star* of Johannesburg declared in an editorial that the South African problem "is not one of stark black and white but rather one of mingled light and shade."

sight of a black nanny with a white child carried as a papoose on her back; a black policeman checking a pass; maybe a white postman with a black caddie to shoulder his mail sack; or beer-drinking blacks sitting on a curbside in front of a segregated bus stop, where whites, who seemed privileged in nothing but their skins, steeled themselves against their human surroundings. Whatever it was, it happened that afternoon in a lower-middle-class white neighborhood called Troyeville.

Up close, apartheid was not only a caste system but a statement about reality amounting to a denial, which then sought to be self-enforcing. That statement insisted, against all the evidence that met the eye, that there was such a place as "white South Africa." It existed as a legal concept, reflecting the solipsism of the dominant minority, but not anywhere in the external world that I could find. The first story I filed from Johannesburg concerned a black choral group that had been denied permission to sing Handel's *Messiah* to a white audience because it had been scheduled to perform with a white orchestra. In the mind of some white official, that constituted illicit race mixing. When the sponsors of the concert proposed as a compromise that the chorus be accompanied by an organist instead of an orchestra, official permission was forthcoming, though the only available organist was also white. "We had to promise that he would play only on the white keys," one of the sponsors wisecracked. Apartheid in those days was often nearly funny; the reality it created seldom was.

In the fourteen years after my expulsion—the headlines in the Afrikaans press had proclaimed that I had been *uitgeskop* ("out-kicked") as if it were a triumph for patriotism and morality—I had lost much of the feel of the place, remembering mainly my own tautness and alertness when I lived there; forgotten, too, its physical and cultural scenery and most of its political rituals and arguments. What had lodged near the surface of my mind, available for ready excavation along with a wad of yellowing clippings, was a series of stark images and, because reporters remember quotes, small shards of dialogue. Two in particular involved blacks in courtrooms.

One was from a visit to a pass-law court, where black men were prosecuted for the crime of being in a "white area" without a stamp in their reference books, the domestic passports they all had to carry, to show they were "authorized to seek work." Then, as now, the "white areas"—as opposed to the former tribal reserves known as homelands—accounted for slightly more than 86 percent of the land.

These trials, which have been taking place in South Africa, one way or another, since 1708, when the first passes were issued to Malay slaves, were fundamental to its way of life, the balance wheel of the political mechanism. The rationalizations could change from decade to decade, but the trials went on. Few blacks could go through a lifetime without an experience of these courts, as either an accused or a relative of an accused; fewer whites cared to know where they were or how they worked, let alone to visit them. The trials themselves could be, still can be, measured in minutes or sometimes seconds. An hour could be long enough to get through thirty or forty cases in open court. The context was something I would have to learn all over again, but one brief exchange was graven in my memory. "Why were you in Johannesburg?" asked the presiding officer, a white civil servant in black robes known in those days as the Bantu commissioner.

"I was looking for my child," the accused replied.

"Where is your child?"

"Lost."

"Fourteen days," the commissioner ruled.

In the other scene of black men in the dock, there had been fifty-six of them, wearing large numbered placards around their necks so they could be identified. Their trial, on charges of belonging to an underground black movement called Poqo, took place in a courtroom in Port Elizabeth on the Indian Ocean coast. It was earlier coverage of trials in that area involving the outlawed African National Congress that appeared to be at the root of my difficulties with the authorities. But it was the Poqo trial that I remembered because of the cynical line of cross-examination the white prosecutor had pursued. The accused came from the same small *dorp,* or rural town, where they represented a significant fraction of the adult black males. In the dock, they were a scruffy, undernourished lot ranging from postadolescent to doddering. The prosecutor's tactic was to demonstrate that they were dissatisfied with their lives and therefore likely "terrorists." In response, the defendants attempted to deny that they could ever be unhappy as black men in South Africa.

"You have no objection to being ordered around by white men?" the prosecutor taunted.

"I have become so satisfied that my health keeps improving," number 23 replied.

"Are you satisfied with your wages?"

"I have never complained, not on a single day."

"Do you want better wages?"

"No, Your Worship."

"Are you satisfied with your house?"

"It's a very beautiful house."

"Are you satisfied with the pass laws?"

"Yes, entirely."

The white prosecutor's scornful questions showed that he knew it was reasonable for black men to rebel, unreasonable for them to claim they could be happy; that they were held in check only by the power of the state, which he represented. Every other white in the courtroom had to know it, too.

The cross-examination of number 23 was a caricature of the political exchanges blacks could have in that period. Conversation was inexplicit, steeped in irony, with kernels of meaning hidden between sardonic throwaway lines. A few weeks before I received my expulsion notice, white South Africans went to the polls to give their leader, Hendrik Verwoerd, the strongest mandate he had yet received to go on building apartheid. Several hours before the returns were due, I went to one of the illegal drinking establishments known as shebeens in Soweto, Johannesburg's black annex, to see if I could elicit some black reflections on the spectacle of white democracy. What I got was typically roundabout. "What were you doing at that polling station this morning?" a black man who said he was an undertaker asked another drinker.

"Voting, of course," came the reply, right on cue.

"Who for?"

"Well," the other man gibed, "that's between my conscience and myself, but if you must know, the candidate's name was Hendrik Verwoerd. He's my man."

What kept conversation in check was the seeming omnipresence of informers, known among blacks as *impimpis*. Invariably, when there was a political trial or wave of arrests, someone discovered the exorbitant price of trust. While visiting Port Elizabeth for the Poqo trial, I met two blacks at the seaside cottage of the playwright Athol Fugard. Because he vouched for me to them, and them to me, we were able to speak with more than normal candor. How was it, I asked, that black security policemen and the state witnesses in political trials were never assaulted in the black townships? "To do something like that," one of the men said, "you would want at least two men, wouldn't you?"

Pausing to indicate that my question was hypothetical and not intended as incitement, I gestured toward the only other person in the room, the man's best friend. "How do I know," came the mumbled reply, "that he is not an *impimpi?*" No one who was not in jail or house arrest under what was called a banning order could ever be immune from that suspicion. So pervasive was it then that the authorities could compromise stalwart black nationalists by seeming to ignore them.

Under the circumstances I had little or no direct experience of black politics in that time and relied largely on intuition and observation for my sense of what it was like to be black in the apartheid society. Many whites never tired of explaining to a foreigner that blacks had their own distinct cultural values as Zulus, Xhosas, and so forth, that it was impossible to try to see the world through their eyes. But it seemed to me a reasonably safe assumption that these cultures did not absolutely require the decimation of black family life that apartheid entailed; that most blacks were aware that they had nothing to say about the shape of the system; that some occasionally wearied of white bossiness; and that when I saw a newspaper photo of nine black schoolgirls in uniform, each holding aloft a placard with one of the letters that spell out A-P-A-R-T-H-E-I-D as part of a welcome to a touring white Cabinet minister, I was witnessing something other than a flowering of indigenous culture.

I got many of my clues to black life from black journalists, in particular Ernest Cole, a remarkable photographer, who had managed with fierce persistence and pluck to get himself reclassified as a colored— a person of mixed race—so he could maneuver more easily as a photojournalist inside the system in order to document what it did to black lives. Other clues came in conversations with servants at the apartment complex where we lived, including a woman of astonishingly serene character and heavy family responsibilities named Dinah Dibakoane, whom we hired to look after our two girls. Shortly before we left, she went back to her own children, for she was due to have another. On a Sunday morning we drove Dinah past Pretoria, following her instructions until she told us to turn left on a dirt road. Then there was a right onto a little track that wound through the veld, becoming increasingly hard to follow until we seemed to be driving across trackless grasslands. I stopped and grumbled that we were lost. No, Dinah insisted softly, this was the way, go on. Soon we reached the top of a slight rise and looked down on a small encampment of shanties knocked together from scraps of rusted metal siding interspersed with brand-new metal boxes that gleamed in the autumn sun. It had a name, Boekenhoutfontein, and it was rising on the veld, apparently out of nowhere, next to nothing, as an officially designated resettlement site for Pretoria blacks, like Dinah's family, who had been deemed "badly situated" because they lived too near the "white areas" where they worked. In their new setting it was hard to believe that they were in the same country, precisely the doubt the authorities wanted to instill. There, with guilty qualms but no alternative, we deposited Dinah with her family.

There was nothing secondhand, and nothing metaphoric, about my most immediate and painful collision with black life in that time, the one that would come to my mind first when I was straining years later to recall what life in South Africa had been like. I never wrote about it because I never could learn anything beyond what I had seen, nor did I know what to say about the role I had played. It is difficult to write about now, although the memory is nightmarishly vivid.

In a driving rain, at night, he came through the windshield. For an interminable moment I thought I had killed him. We were at the end of a 400-mile drive from Durban that had started at the coast, where the Indian Ocean breaking on rocks sent spume into a gray sky, then taken us through the green hills of Natal, mostly shrouded in mist, up to the highveld, through a succession of drab farming towns set off by their churches, their gas stations, and their separate black "locations," until abruptly the openness, the sadness, the sense of the land were lost in the thickening traffic of Johannesburg and we were driving past the movie palaces on Commissioner Street, where overdressed Saturday night crowds came tripping out of the rain.

I had stopped for a light and was shifting out of first gear when I heard a scream, then a thud and the sound of glass shattering. A black man, dressed in black trousers and a black jacket, was lying on the pavement a few feet to the right of the car, which had veered to the left when I slammed on the brakes. I had never really seen him until I bent over to take his pulse, which was strong. I covered him with a blanket from the car and tried to direct traffic around him. A white policeman appeared and started asking questions. White bystanders stepped forward to make sure I was all right, to tell me they had seen the man step out from between parked cars, that I could not have avoided him; in their solicitude for me some even pressed little papers with their addresses into my hand, in the event I needed witnesses.

Black bystanders stood back, watching silently from a distance. By the time I had sent my family home in a taxi, the policeman was bending down to make chalk marks on the rain-slick roadway to show the point of impact and the swerve of the car. No one paid attention to the form under the soggy blanket. The man breathed regularly and occasionally opened his eyes but didn't respond when I tried to put questions to him.

I covered him again, this time with my raincoat, then found another policeman sitting out of the rain in his wagon, reading a comic. Barely looking up, he said the black ambulance had been called. I asked him to call again. "They'll come," he said. The man would die of pneumonia first, I said. "They'll come," he said, returning to the comic. They came an hour and a quarter later. A white ambulance, I knew, would have been there in minutes. Saturday nights were the busiest time for nonwhite ambulances, the black attendant explained. I phoned the emergency room an hour later. "It's nothing serious," the voice on the other end assured me. "Just a knock on the head." I asked for the patient's name. The voice said it was Clifton Roche. Nothing could be done that night, I told myself. It was still pouring, my car had no windshield, and even if I could get there, I wouldn't be able to find the man's family in the township at night. First thing in the morning, I would go to the hospital, speak to Clifton Roche, get his address, and find his relatives. I would also arrange for a good neurologist to examine him.

In the morning the hospital had never heard of Clifton Roche. No such person was in the wards. No records existed of any such person being treated. "*Ja,* it's always like that," a pipe-smoking officer in a cardigan said when I went to police headquarters to ask for help in finding the man I thought was named Clifton Roche. "The hospitals let them go, and we find them dead a few days later." Still, he promised to see what could be done. We called regularly, but at increasing intervals, over the next ten days or so. The officer was unfailingly courteous. "Your Bantu has not been found," he would say. I went off to the Congo to cover a coup, then returned to the hospital to search its records. There was still no trace of a Clifton Roche. "You don't have to worry," the man at police headquarters said the last time we phoned. "No action will be taken against you."

We didn't stop worrying all at once, but Clifton Roche, if that was his name, gradually became a memory, a heavy but unmanageable obligation I would have liked to forget. When it forced its way into my mind, my preoccupation was with what I had done, rather than with his fate, which seemed unknowable. I would ask myself why I hadn't gone with him to the hospital that night or why I hadn't thought of hiring a detective who might have known how to get more cooperation from the authorities than a suspect foreigner could. Only occasionally did I ask myself what would have happened if I had stepped out from between the cars and Clifton Roche had knocked me down. It had been an initiation into white South Africa.

As the incident showed again, this was an idea rather than a place. Clifton Roche may have been there, but he remained an object of indifference. Whites were privileged only in fact, not in theory. They had rights, went the theory, because they resided in the white country. Blacks could be privileged in their own country or, rather, their own countries. While it was all right, if not exactly desirable, for Afrikaners, the dominant white group, to live in the same cities and streets as English-speaking whites, even Jews and Greeks, such intermingling would not do for blacks. So far as possible Zulus and Xhosas and all the other tribal groups had to be kept separate. This, it was to be understood, was not merely for the convenience or safety of the whites but for the fulfillment of the blacks. White supremacy—which had only recently been flaunted under the banner of *baasskap,* from the Afrikaans *baas* for "master" and *skap* for "state of being"—was now said to have been annulled. But there was something called "white civilization" that had to be preserved. Its preservation required that blacks not go to universities attended by whites and that their own so-called universities be located outside the white country, in their own countries, wherever those were. Even there, however, what was taught had to be strictly controlled by whites. To say that "civilization" also required that blacks and whites not cohabit on more intimate terms was hardly necessary, for this had already been spelled out by a law called the Immorality Act. And "civilization" meant the rule of law, didn't it?

It was all very logical and very moral, but only one man, it seemed, could explain it without getting entangled in contradictions. Fortunately the chief ideologue was also the prime minister, who had only recently been preserved for the nation, the white nation, after two bullets had been fired into his head by a would-be white assassin. I never got closer to Hendrik Verwoerd than the press gallery in Parliament, from which I would watch him as he contemplatively fingered the scar that one of the bullets had left next to his eye. At that distance he seemed icy and smug, but those who got near enough to look into his small blue eyes generally found him a kindly man. What they never found there was the slightest glimmer of self-doubt. Verwoerd dealt only in revealed truth, and although he was undoubtedly a humble and pious Christian by his own lights, he made sure that he did the revealing when it came to matters of black and white in South Africa. "He would have made a good impression on the Synod of Dort," Harold Macmillan later wrote in his memoirs, comparing the discourse he heard in Cape Town as Britain's prime minister in 1960 to a seventeenth-century church gathering in Holland, where the doctrine of strict predestination was dogmatically upheld.

I never suspected that much of what I took to be the temper of the Afrikaners derived from the temper of their leader, a self-made Afrikaner who had been born in Amsterdam two years before his family emigrated to South Africa, then educated largely in English schools in Cape Town and Rhodesia. At the time of the Boer War, which erupted ten weeks before the end of the nineteenth century and dragged on for the first two and a half years of the twentieth, the Afrikaners were a frontier people whose nationalism hadn't yet hardened into a doctrinaire creed. The spirit of independence among them was so strong that it proved impossible to maintain discipline in armies that regularly humiliated the imperial superpower in the early months of the struggle. Individual fighting Boers—the word simply means "farmers"—came and went as they pleased, deciding for themselves which battles were worth fighting. "The real fighting Boer is ever a tolerant, good-natured fellow," wrote a veteran of the war named Deneys Reitz, recalling how an uncle spent much of his time at the front arguing that it all was a lost cause, without arousing any resentment in his commando unit. Arriving in the aftermath of the war, Verwoerd's family had tasted none of its bitterness, the concentration camps in which 26,000 women and children died, the loss of farms and sons. But those who could never forgive or forget took him as their leader. It was Hendrik Verwoerd who finally led them out of the Commonwealth, reviving the legacy of the white republics that were crushed when he was an infant in Holland. Verwoerd had no tolerance for dissent, no tolerance even for tolerance. As a result, dissident voices among Afrikaner nationalists were nearly as hard to hear during my abbreviated first tour in South Africa as black nationalist voices.

A soothsayer and visionary rather than a rabble-rouser, the good doctor* set minds at ease. There was a plan, *and* it was moral, *and* it would work: The Bantu would be in his "homeland," and all would be right with the world. He sounded reasonable because he spoke in syllogisms; the premises were batty, but the conclusions were what his audiences yearned to believe. When he was done, they went home congratulating themselves on their Christian generosity. In his first plunge into politics, this immigrant son of an immigrant had resisted Jewish immigration from Nazi Germany on grounds that it was necessary to limit the number of Jews in order to prevent the spread of anti-Semitism. With the same purity of motive, he now argued that blacks could not be allowed a permanent foothold in "white South Africa" because it would be a denial of their rights to keep them there as a disenfranchised majority. Insisting that they belonged in "their own countries"—even if they had never seen them, even if there was not the remotest chance that they would ever go, even if most of these so-called countries existed only in his mind—was actually to champion black nationalism. Thus it was for the sake of the blacks as well as for the preservation of the white nation that no mixing could be allowed in any sphere: not in a boxing ring or on a soccer field; not in a jazz club or a concert hall; not even in the fullness of time in the workplace, where whites had been relying on nonwhite labor since they arrived at the Cape of Good Hope in 1652. True to his principles, his guest Harold Macmillan was astonished to discover in 1960, Verwoerd had no black servants in his official residence in Cape Town.

"So you are left with the taut South African present, which daily becomes more inward, more fragmented, more dreary." That, at least, was my sense of the place as I recorded it in a valedictory article after my expulsion. In September 1966, fewer than three months after that article appeared, Verwoerd was stabbed to death on the front bench of the white Parliament by a parliamentary messenger with a history of incarceration in mental institutions who apparently had none of the political motivations that might easily have been adduced for his act. But by then I was at last heading for Asia, and if I thought about South Africa at all, it was not to wonder whether the spirit of Verwoerd still reigned: I assumed it did. "More inward, more fragmented, more

---

*He had started out as a behavioral psychologist, writing a thesis called *Die Afstomping van die Gemoedsaandoeninge* ("The Blunting of the Emotions").

dreary" remained my sense of the place until a random series of experiences and reflections made me wonder.

First there was my renewed friendship with the photographer Ernest Cole in Manhattan, where he had been living at the very margin of existence for years. When I met him in Johannesburg, Ernest was in the final months of an effort to document black life in South Africa as thoroughly as it had ever been done in pictures. He arranged to have his negatives and prints smuggled out—some actually went in my suitcase when I was expelled—and then left himself, finally bringing them together in a book called *House of Bondage* that had more impact than such books normally have when it was published in America and Europe. Our paths crossed in London and New York and then diverged for many years until I began to hear that he had dropped out and even "disappeared." Friends of his in London asked if I could try to locate him. When I started making inquiries, I was told by one South African expatriate who had put Ernest up for several months that he might now be living on the subways. I left messages wherever I imagined he might show himself, and after many weeks one of them was answered.

It was all true: Ernest was destitute in one of the world's toughest cities, without abode or sustenance or, what seemed almost worse in his case, cameras. For several months I made him my responsibility and saw him regularly. One afternoon we went together to a cheap boarding hotel where he had stashed his few possessions, including negatives and the only picture he had of his mother in Pretoria; the manager took down a ledger and demonstrated that they all had gone in an auction of unclaimed articles, held according to New York's regulations for such sales. Ernest was left with only the clothes on his back.

The last ten years, as he then related his experiences, had been a deliberate retreat into himself. Taken up with enthusiasm by New York's picture editors when his book made its splash, he concluded that most of them had lost interest in him six months later. His sense of rejection reinforced a growing belief that his new surroundings were soulless, which led gradually to a kind of mysticism and a life in the canyons of Manhattan that might be compared to that of a sadhu, a wandering Hindu ascetic, in the foothills of the Himalayas. A human community, Ernest believed, was cursed when nobody noticed the rising and setting of the sun or the phases of the moon. As part of the discipline he imposed on himself when I met him again, he was keeping watch on the heavens for the whole of New York.

My respect for Ernest Cole outweighed my suspicion of sadhus, but I found myself asking, as I could never have asked before, whether it would have been better for him to remain in South Africa, apartheid and all, than to come through our supposed golden door. It was a question he also asked, sometimes with bitterness. I wasn't softening on apartheid, but a blue mold of relativism, I was surprised to find, was creeping into my thoughts on the subject. On a trip to El Paso I sat in a courtroom where aliens from across the Rio Grande were marched through trials in the same quickstep that I had seen in Johannesburg and were then deported; in South Africa, I found myself thinking, it would have been said that they had been "endorsed out." Of course, I realized, it wasn't really their country, at least hadn't been since the Mexican War, but it took a moment or two for me to work out the moral difference, and even then I wasn't sure.

Relativism occasionally crept in as well to my reaction to news reports from South Africa. When there was a new uproar about a political detainee who had died in the custody of the security police, for instance, I couldn't help reflecting that with the advent of the various Latin American death squads and the Ayatollah's Revolutionary Guard, not to mention the Khmer Rouge, South Africa had suddenly slipped into the second division when it came to state terror; that this was so from a global perspective even when you considered the shooting of youthful protesters in Soweto or the vicious killing of Steve Biko, the young black leader who was pummeled into a coma and then hauled, naked and manacled, on a 700-mile journey in the back of a police van to Pretoria, where he died.

Of course, a global perspective is easily used to belittle the sufferings of particular groups, to deny the significance of their history and particular circumstances. If it can be shown that someone in Gdansk or Kampala or Lahore is worse off than someone in Cape Town, then anyone in Cape Town who vents his unhappiness is convicted of a lack of global perspective. I was never impressed by the line that racial tyranny was easier to bear than Leninist totalitarianism. It struck me as an unseemly calculation for anyone who has never borne either. I didn't have to be reminded that I was not South African and not black. Nevertheless, from the distance at which I was following these events, it was the emergence of the student protests and of Biko rather than their suppression that stirred me. Once again blacks were making themselves heard. This was the generation that Verwoerd had intended to educate for a life of meager privileges and low horizons in the "homelands" since, as he put it, there could be "no place for [them] in the European community above the level of certain forms of labor." A system of "Bantu education" had been designed to save the "Bantu" from the frustration that came with exposure to "the green pastures of European society in which he was not allowed to graze." And now it turned out that they had read Frantz Fanon and Aimé Césaire, some of them at least, and were standing up to denounce the legacy of the great white seer and demand their birthright. Without Verwoerd at the helm, the Afrikaners seemed a bit wobbly in their response, uncertain of how to justify the system he had elaborated. They had changed, were changing, would change; so they said. The tenses blurred, and so did the promise, but ideologically, at least, they seemed to be in ragged retreat. More inward? It didn't seem so anymore. More fragmented? More dreary? I couldn't begin to imagine what it was.

On the strength of that uncertainty, I asked my editors if I could explore the possibility of returning. The matter was taken up discreetly in Cape Town by John Burns, who had gone to South Africa a full ten years after my expulsion as the first resident correspondent *The New York Times* had been allowed to station there after me. In that sense Burns was to be both my predecessor and my successor. "Do you think, Mr. Burns," the foreign minister, Pik Botha, asked once my name had been broached, "that a condemned man has the right to choose the witnesses at his execution?"

I took the joke to be doubly ironic, a way of promising that I would be disappointed if I thought I would see the crumbling of white power. But I also took it as an accolade. Five months later my visa finally came through.

My time machine seemed to have landed me in Oz. Or was it Brobdingnag? No, it was Bophuthatswana. This was to be my first weekend in South Africa in nearly a generation, and now, I was given to understand, I was not in South Africa at all. I was in the Tswana "national state," which I had never heard of in my first incarnation because it had not existed except, possibly, as a gleam in Verwoerd's eye. Then there had been something called the Tswana Tribal Authority, but I don't think I had ever heard of that either; if I had, I certainly had not thought of it as a place. Bophuthatswana—now alleged to be a sovereign and independent nation for the 2 million black South Africans of Tswana origins who, by virtue of its existence, were no longer deemed to be South Africans—was not exactly a place either. It was at least seven places, scattered across three South African provinces, surrounded on nearly every side of each fragment by the huge holdings of white ranchers and farmers. Three times on the drive from Johannesburg I had crossed its border without running into anything that remotely resembled a border post. There were small "Bophuthatswana Border" signs, but they were superfluous; a glance out the window could always tell you which country you were in. If you saw fields that were empty except for cattle and grain, it was obviously South Africa. If they were full of people in tribal villages and desolate shantytowns, it was the "national state." But now I was in neither a village nor a shantytown. I was in a glossy casino resort called Sun City that seemed to have taken some of its decorative cues from the Peachtree Plaza Hotel in Atlanta. Here, where whites and blacks mixed as freely as they might there, a black and a white were to fight for one of the world's two heavyweight championships. Hendrik Verwoerd, I wondered, where is thy sting?

From ringside it seemed likely that Verwoerd was revolving in his grave over this bizarre fulfillment of his vision, which nonetheless was turning into a festival of white South African, mainly Afrikaner, patriotism. Gerrie Coetzee from Boksburg, South Africa, was to fight Mike Weaver from the wrong side of the tracks in Gatesville, Texas, and a crowd of about 17,000, who had consumed about 100,000 cans of Castle or Lion Lager, screamed in good-natured frenzy as the theme from the movie *Star Wars* blared over huge quadraphonic speakers and a chorus girl from an ensemble called the Sun City Extravaganza, dressed mainly in orange ostrich plumes and sequins, danced down the aisle, bearing the South African flag as honor guard to the contender. Another chorus girl brought Weaver and the Stars and Stripes. These were followed by chorus girls with the Bophuthatswana flag and even a flag for Sun City itself, until finally there was a lineup of eleven Extravaganza dancers, mainly but not exclusively white, swinging their bottoms and kicking their heels in the ring. Floyd Patterson, the last black heavyweight champ to be defeated by a white, got a cheer as he climbed through the ropes wearing a T-shirt that advertised Old Buck Gin, a local distillate. Then came the anthems, including that of Bophuthatswana, with the thousands of whites standing at solemn attention. Finally, when the chorus girl holding their flag gave the signal by thrusting its staff into her navel and raising it high, they burst

into a full-throated and passionate rendering of their own "Die Stem"
("The Call") so that Coetzee would be left in no doubt of his duty:

> *At that call we shall not falter,*
> *Firm and steadfast we shall stand,*
> *At thy will to live or perish,*
> *O South Africa, dear land.*

The poor lug perished in the thirteenth, dropping with a thud in a
stunned and suddenly silent arena. To those of his countrymen who
had been intent on viewing the fight as a racial allegory, he had presented a chilling foreshadowing of their destiny. For eight rounds their
hero, their white hope, had seemed cruelly invincible, but the black
man proved to be more patient, more determined, and finally just
stronger. In far-off Soweto blacks were rejoicing over the Afrikaner's
defeat. A mood sodden with anticlimax and regret descended on the
casino resort in the independent homeland. Yet there was no apparent
bitterness of a racial kind as Afrikaners and Tswanas brushed shoulders
at the slot machines and fast-food stands. On the platforms cantilev-
ered over small lagoons in the dimly lit lobby, a few voluble young
whites threw themselves into earnest, boozy colloquies with young
blacks, which gathered intensity as the evening wore on but seemed to
be largely one-sided. Out on the patio a middle-aged Afrikaner tried to
catch the eye of a black barmaid. "Mrs. Weaver, Mrs. Weaver," he
called in a bantering tone. She took his order with a wary smile that
seemed to show there had been no offense.

The nearest thing to a confrontation occurred at the entrance to the
casino when a uniformed black security man informed a leather-jack-
eted young Afrikaner that he could not proceed farther in running
shoes. It was not farfetched to imagine that it was the young man's first
encounter with black authority.

"Why can't I?" he demanded, asserting his whiteness but looking
around with noticeable uncertainty for support from his friends.

"That's our rule," the black man said.

"What's the reason for the rule?"

"Look," said the guard, who was trying to unclog the entrance and
get the line moving, "I don't want to talk."

Not knowing how to step back without humiliating himself, the
young white persisted. "What did those shoes cost?" he asked, pointing
to the cop's brogans. "Mine cost nineteen rands."

"That's cheap," said the black.

"What do you mean cheap? What did yours cost?" And when that was met by silence: "Don't you want my money?"

The man in uniform was now insulted. "I don't need *your* money," he replied. "I get paid."

The kid in the leather jacket was now as beaten as Gerrie Coetzee. His forefathers had fought blacks for half a century and built one of their frontier republics in this area on a constitution prohibiting "any equality . . . either in church or state," then had been ground down in a filthy war with the British and lost their republic, but had clung to the principle so hard and nurtured their grievances and sense of destiny so fiercely that decades later they reversed the tide of history. "The blindest heathen and unbelieving creature," the patriarchal Paul Kruger said in the nineteenth century, "must acknowledge that it is God's hand." But now the long struggle had brought the Afrikaners to the point where a fairly upstanding, at least erect, young member of the tribe could be turned away from a casino entrance by a black cop. Was that also God's hand?

If I had paid more attention to the designer emblems and signatures that many of the whites in the casino were flashing on their sleeves and pockets, I might have realized that there was a sumptuary code operating in reverse throughout the land. "Dress Smart Casual," warn signs at the entrances to most drinking and eating establishments that aspire to be more than commonplace. Or, absurdly, "Elegant Casual." Or, packing all the anxieties of a class of arriviste Puritans into three words, "Strictly Smart Casual." Independent Bophuthatswana, the borders of which could not be guessed at in the darkness as I drove back to Johannesburg in the early hours of the morning with Allister Sparks, aspired to be "smart casual," too. Sparks, a fellow journalist and old friend, lost his way in the vicinity of two Transvaal hamlets, Hartbeespoort and Hartbeeshoek. It was three in the morning; there was no traffic, and we had no map. The authors of the highway signs that appeared in our headlights every thirty miles or so had obviously never heard of Johannesburg or Pretoria, only towns named after antelopes, either hartebeests or elands. In my mind they all merged into a mythical Hartbeespoortfontein. The points on our wayward compass made us laugh all the more as we pronounced them. "I think this is Hartbeespoortfontein now," I would say. "No," Sparks would say, "I think it's Bophuthatswana." So one blind heathen laughed most of the way back, as he had never laughed before in South Africa, without being able to say what was really so funny.

CHAPTER 2

■

SPEAR-SHIELD

The black room service waiter who brought my breakfast in the Carlton Hotel in Johannesburg late on the morning after the fight managed to "sir" me four or five times. The servility got under my white skin; for the first time in years, I felt the urge to protest, "I'm not from this place." Instead, I grabbed the check. As I did so, the waiter dropped his patter and spoke up in a natural voice, forgetting the "sir." He was saying something real, but I didn't get it. "Look there," he said again, pointing to a rooftop a block and a half away and a dozen or so stories lower. "They're making an arrest."

Once I had my glasses on, I could make out three blue figures, policemen obviously, facing three blacks while several other blacks looked on from a distance of maybe twenty yards. One of the policemen seemed to be studying something at chest height. I knew, or thought I knew, that it was a reference book.

"Is it a pass-law arrest?" I asked.

"Must be," the waiter replied, over his shoulder, sounding suddenly neutral as if it could be no concern of his.

I suppose I then had some breakfast. The next time I looked two of the policemen had one of the blacks against a wall. Slowly and methodically they were beating him on the head and shoulders, seemingly with their fists. The blows came one by one, not all in a rush. When the man ducked, they waited till he raised his head; then one of them would slam him again. At that distance, in the glare of the morning sun, the scene had a surreal quality as if I were a character in a dream sequence peering through blinds at a medieval square where something sinister was happening. Except for the faint beep of a distant horn and the hum of the air conditioning, there were no sounds; on the streets below, the light Sunday morning traffic moved quietly, and quiet family groups, black and white, dawdled by shopwindows. I didn't have to move my head to shift my glance from them to the quiet bashing beyond their view on the rooftop. Seen in this way, the bashing no longer looked surreal but normal.

Finished with the man by the wall, the three figures in blue turned to the others. One of the policemen ambled over to a man standing by what looked to be a laundry tub. Maybe he spoke, maybe his expression spoke for him, but I could see only the action of his arm as he struck the man on the side of the head. The other two were chasing a third black to the far side of the roof. Their prey tried to dodge, then crouched with his arms over his head near the parapet. Together they hauled him to his feet. Then one held him while the other aimed three sharp blows at his face. The one who was doing the holding got in an awkward backhanded left before they dropped him, returning to the laundry tub, if that's what it was, to slug the man there, who had made the mistake, it seemed, of remaining upright. Then the policemen left, taking no one with them.

I showered, dressed, and went downstairs. The Carlton is what is known as an "international" hotel, a euphemism meaning it serves whites and the relatively small number of blacks who are affluent enough to go there and eager enough to laugh off the insinuation in the word "international" that they are foreign. A fashionably dressed black couple was looking at a "What's On in Johannesburg" guide. A black was on duty as a desk clerk. A lobby in Detroit would not have looked much different. I crossed the street, walked a block, and went to the rooftop I had been watching. There I found a half dozen or so men crowded into a little room with bunks, watching another two who were playing checkers with Pepsi and Coca-Cola bottletops. My appearance provoked no discernible surprise or interest. Awkwardly I mentioned that I was an American staying at the Carlton and that I had witnessed their encounter with the police. A large silence was the reply. It was obvious that everyone in the little room already had had his fill of interracial communication and that my interest was at best gratuitous. Still, I tried to chip away at the silence with questions. A compact man with a shaved head and pencil-line mustache spoke for the group, furnishing minimal answers. Yes, the police sometimes came to check their reference books. Yes, they were in order. Yes, they worked in the neighborhood. Downstairs at a restaurant called Chez

André. No, they were not normally assaulted like that when the police came. No, the police didn't shout while the beatings were taking place. No, they didn't curse. They said nothing at all. No, the men were not surprised it had happened.

I had just about run out of questions and hadn't gotten anything like an explanation. What was it all about? "Maybe," the spokesman replied, without showing the least sign of feeling or lifting his eyes from the checkerboard, where play was continuing, "they didn't like the way their brother was beaten last night."

Less than an hour later, at an elegant lunch in a green park of a garden in the white suburbs, I mentioned the random vindictiveness of this epilogue to the Coetzee fight to my hostess. I was back now in Johannesburg's Chekhovian precincts, where great privilege and great social conscience occasionally converge. My hostess was Helen Suzman, a liberal member of the white Parliament who had battled against every apartheid law and expansion of arbitrary state power for nearly three decades; in the darkest period, for thirteen consecutive years, as a tireless minority of one speaking for all those who had been silenced. A woman without illusions, she understood immediately why the victims had no interest in lodging a complaint. The police would testify for each other, she said, and the blacks would be lucky not to be jailed for assault; not just their jobs but their status in the urban areas as migrant workers could be made to depend on their taking their lumps quietly. It had been, after all, a lesson in helplessness.

That did not mean they took it meekly or with resignation, I thought later, trying to work out their attitude on the basis of the terse answers I had gotten. Being unsurprised meant being unforgiving, it seemed to me. It meant keeping score.

It may have been useful, from a didactic standpoint, to have been reminded of the basic conflict in so raw and unsubtle a manner on my third morning back in the country after nearly fifteen years. But obviously it was not a discovery. I knew, the whole world knew, that there was a problem of racial dominance there. Yet for the next three years I was regularly surprised and often astonished by South Africa. It was a particular kind of sensation, a cheap thrill maybe, available to outsiders and voyeurs who can maintain access of a kind on all sides of its various racial and political divides—as few South Africans can—experiencing the huge evasions of the whites and the helpless knowledge of the blacks, the willful denial of reality as well as its crushing weight. South Africa was much more open to an outsider's inquiries than it had been in the ice age of Verwoerd; in that sense, it had changed more for me than for itself. In a day I could travel through several worlds, could look at the same landscape through several sets of lenses. Often I would fill up, reaching a state of supersaturation in which I felt I couldn't absorb another impression. Sometimes my head would throb from having heard too many discordant views earnestly or bitterly argued; other times, especially when talking to the sorts of whites who seemed complacent in their privilege, I could taste the small and possibly snide satisfaction of knowing that in my short time there I had traveled far more deeply into their country than they would in their entire lives.

In its spaciousness and harsh beauty, South Africa was still gripping as a land. It was still absorbing, too, as a political conflict. But what made it different from other gripping lands and absorbing conflicts was its many ways of looking at itself: of explaining, rationalizing, and forgetting. And it was there—on the level of perception and expression —that South Africa seemed new when I returned. Something had definitely slipped loose, but whatever it was, it wasn't political power.

In the years that elapsed between my two lives there, the white settler or colonial regimes in the key buffer states of Rhodesia, Angola, and Mozambique had collapsed on its borders, and the black population inside had risen by 90 percent, compared to only a 30 percent rise in the number of whites (whose share in the total of about 32 million had thus dipped from 18 to 15 percent). Those were fairly conspicuous facts. Yet white power seemed more entrenched and happy with itself, with its own devices and cleverness, than ever. The old Verwoerdian trick of changing attitudes without changing practices, of annihilating white supremacy in theory without losing its advantages, had been marvelously refined. Ways had been found to change practices as well as attitudes without losing the advantages of white supremacy. Black trade unions were getting legal rights. The brown-skinned minorities, the mixed-race coloreds and the Indians, were being offered a junior partnership in a national government that would continue to exclude blacks. Now Verwoerd loomed as a tower of intellectual honesty; he had told blacks at least that they had no chance in the white world, that they belonged somewhere else.

His successors continued to send blacks somewhere else—to the "homelands," where they could now be legally defined as foreigners—while arguing that blacks, or at least some blacks, have to be given every chance in South Africa; that blacks are, or will soon become, essential as consumers, skilled workers, even managers. In the evolving white ethos, therefore, South Africa had already transformed itself into a meritocracy, whatever its laws say. If it also happens to be a racial hierarchy, that isn't a problem, a reflection of what might be seen by naïve outsiders as a grotesque imbalance of power. Instead, it should be seen as an outgrowth of history and culture, of natural selection in that sense and maybe also biological destiny, although that thought can no longer be spoken out loud in polite company; a reflection, anyhow, of what is needed to keep the country running, what the blacks need and would really want if only they knew, if only they could absorb the lessons of postcolonial Africa's assorted disasters, which most whites know, or presume they know, by heart.

The word "apartheid" (literally "separatehood," with the same suffix as "brotherhood") was coined as an election promise in 1948 by the political party that has governed ever since. But now that word is shunned, even resented by the party's high priests as if it were an epithet fashioned by the country's enemies. "Apartheid, whatever that is supposed to mean," sneered an editorial in *Die Burger*, the party newspaper in Cape Town. As if Daniel F. Malan, the paper's first editor, had not become prime minister on the apartheid platform. As if he had not promised "to make South Africa a white man's land." As if, in pursuit of that dream, apartheid had not transformed Cape Town. As if it did not now operate there more harshly than anywhere else. "Apartheid, the propaganda concept of the past few decades," grumbled *Rapport*, another pro-government newspaper.

Yet the promise of 1948 has been faithfully kept, sculpted into the landscape. The areas in which whites, browns, and blacks once lived in proximity have nearly all been cleared and sorted out. Before apartheid one-third of Cape Town's whites lived in neighborhoods where coloreds also lived. Now the exceptions to the rule of racial exclusion are so few as to be statistically invisible. There is still some tidying up to be done—"black spots," meaning black-owned land in legally proclaimed "white areas," to be expropriated—but the racial checkerboard is firmly in place.

"They don't need their laws anymore!" exclaimed J. N. Singh, a fiery leader of the resistance to apartheid in the forties and fifties, after taking me on a tour of neighborhoods in Durban from which Indians had been driven. "They've done it! Whoever comes into power will not be able to change *this.*" His gesture took in a major Indian township called Chatsworth in which the racially displaced of Indian origins had been regrouped. In another part of the city, close to the seafront, the lot on which his family's home once stood was now the corner of a shopping center parking lot in a white neighborhood. Across the street were a white gospel church and an Afrikaner high school. Real estate speculators were cashing in on high-rise apartment houses for whites that had shot up nearby, within view of the Indian Ocean surf. The only evidence that the land had been taken away from Indians—in truth, when you considered the money that was now being made, stolen from them—was unattended groves of mango trees on an overgrown hillside where Hindu and Muslim merchants once lived and, over the next hill, a whitewashed mosque that, as a small mercy, had not been razed.

I took that same tour in many South African towns and cities, visiting neighborhoods from which blacks and browns had been hounded on no basis other than skin color. The ripples from these dislocations quickly vanish from the memories of whites the way a pond recovers its glassy surface after a stone has been thrown, so the resentment in the depths, among blacks and browns, is beyond their comprehension. In Johannesburg the old black section called Sophiatown had been renamed Triomf ("Triumph") when whites took over. Years later in Johannesburg, the bulldozers were still at it, plowing Indians out of a district called Pageview, where they had lived since Gandhi's time. In Cape Town there was the naked wound of District Six on the lower slopes of Table Mountain; a teeming, predominantly colored neighborhood when I first came to South Africa, it was now a wasteland in the heart of the city.

In the eastern Cape industrial town of Uitenhage, the Reverend Allan Hendrickse, a Congregational minister who was head of a colored political faction that had decided to accept the new constitutional order as a Mephistophelian bargain, drove me past the ruins of the church his father had devoted his life to building. When the bulldozers came to knock it down after the neighborhood had been declared "white" under the notorious Group Areas Act, the elder Hendrickse went into a decline and soon died. Now only a chunk of the belfry remains standing to mark the site. What happened, Allan Hendrickse explained with grim satisfaction, was that this last portion of his father's church miraculously withstood the chain that had been wrapped around it and hitched to the bulldozer. And the chain had not broken after the bulldozer had been put into gear and driven to the end of its tether. Instead, the heavy machine stopped short, and its white operator went flying, broke his neck, and died. This was taken as a sign from God, and the bulldozer never returned to finish the job. In the Reverend Hendrickse's new church in a segregated township there was a memorial fixed to a wall built of bricks from the old church that read: "To the memory of the Rev. C. W. Hendrickse and all other victims of the Group Areas Act."

In Oudtshoorn, yet another town in the Cape that had been reordered on a racial basis under the Group Areas Act for the convenience of whites, a young colored official who had been detailed by his white superior to show me how well his people lived in their new township extended the tour to show me where they used to live before they were displaced. Every weekend, he said, you can see coloreds from Port Elizabeth or Cape Town or Johannesburg driving slowly through the old neighborhood in Oudtshoorn where they grew up. "And then the sorrows come," the young man said.

Apartheid ("whatever that is supposed to mean") is thus no longer a concept. It is there to see, or, rather, not see, for it is the screen that hides the vast reality of black South Africa from the vision of most whites. (By "reality" I mean simply human experience. By "black South Africa," I refer not to the nationalist idea, which was copied in part from the whites, but to something even deeper, approaching an existential truth, that Anthony Trollope may have been the first white to express. "South Africa," he wrote, "is a country of black men—and not of white men. It has been so; it is so; it will be so." Being basically a naïve democrat who believes in what a South African Cabinet member dismissed as "simplistic Western solutions," I prefer to be statistical in these matters; say, rather, an existential three-quarters or four-fifths truth.) Hardly anywhere do whites now have to live near blacks —excepting those blacks, 120,000 in Johannesburg alone, whom they keep in their backyards to tend them as servants—and hardly anywhere is it ever necessary for them to see where blacks live, except occasionally at a distance from a passing car. Whites still require permits to enter black townships. (The one I had for Soweto carried a warning that it could "be withdrawn at any time without any reason given.") And blacks require authorization to be in "white areas." Yet on the screen of apartheid—this, it may be said, is its sinister beauty—whites can project any version of reality they please, including their own fantasies of life in a society where apartheid does not exist.

This reinvented South Africa is ever-absorbent, defiantly open to the world that periodically menaces it with sanctions and boycotts. Now the threat can be turned on its head. Revolution is a brand name for jeans. "Freedom is the pulse of living" doesn't mean black power. It's the slogan for a new Datsun that is available, of course, to blacks and whites alike. *The Rocky Horror Picture Show* goes on uncut, including its serenade to "a sweet transvestite from Transsexual, Transylvania." (That is a little daring, but then it shows only in a segregated theater.) Bob Marley is fine; so was Stevie Wonder, until he voiced his support for Nelson Mandela on a TV program that was due to be beamed from Hollywood to South Africa by satellite. My wife heard him singing:

> *Peace has come to Zimbabwe*
> *Third world's right on the one*
> *Now's the time for celebration,*
> *Cause we've only just begun*

in the record section of the O.K. Bazaar, a big department store in Cape Town, at a time when the South African Army was widely presumed to be infiltrating undercover units north of the Limpopo River into Zimbabwe on missions that were calculated to reverse the meaning of the song's title, "Master Blaster."

Pressure from whites, mainly Afrikaners, seemed to be turning the tide of censorship after the banning of some 15,000 books, magazines, pamphlets, calendars, and posters. The old joke was that *The Return of the Native* and *Black Beauty* had sounded dangerous to the censors. Now, rushing into the 1960's, they unbanned *Lady Chatterley's Lover* in 1982. More to the point, a revamped Publications Appeals Board also canceled bans on novels that portrayed torture at the hands of the South African security police. One of these, *Store Up the Anger* by Wessel Ebersohn, contained a clinically detailed description of a death in detention that closely paralleled Steve Biko's. That was now all right, but any words that Biko ever spoke or wrote were still banned. Like so much else in South Africa, the distinction was complicated without being subtle: Blacks still have to be insulated, as far as possible, from radical and revolutionary points of view and their own tradition of resistance, but even if torture has to be practiced, it does not have to be condoned. In other words, the state and its censors should be seen to be "reasonable." So Karl Marx sells openly, but not Lenin or Mao or Frantz Fanon. Women's liberation and gay rights pass muster, but not black nationalism. With wild unpredictability, a constantly changing farrago of American periodicals, including the *New Republic, Texas Monthly, Village Voice,* even *Black Enterprise,* shows up in bookshops and at airport newsstands. The impulse seems to be much the same as that which fills the food hall at Stuttafords, a department store, with imported delicacies ranging from Greek quince to Hong Kong almond cakes; from Wensleydale and Tête de Moine, among a plenitude of imported cheeses, to sixteen varieties of Scandinavian herring.

Stuttafords is one of only 200 or more stores, boutiques, and fast-food stands in the huge new Sandton City shopping plaza, which is Dallas-on-the-veld. Look at the directory and storefronts; the names are seldom homespun: Amalfi, Céline, Christie's, Dunhill, Enzo of Roma, Gucci, Lalique, Lanvin, Laura Ashley, not to mention La Baguette for croissants and Señor Pico for tortillas. *Das vingerlek lekker* ("It's finger-lickin' good") is one of many imported mottoes on apartheid's escutcheon, proclaiming that autarky is no kind of cultural ideal. Avis, Budget, and Hertz flash Aquafresh smiles at every airport. Sufi, Scientology, Raja Yoga, and something called Niagara Therapy—these could also be freely promoted at a Festival of Mind, Body and Spirit, open to all races, that was held in the showground where Verwoerd was shot in 1960.

The South African state is still authoritarian for most of its people, but it can tolerate any amount of kinkiness. Of all known movements, only communism and black nationalism seem to be subject to intensive police quarantine. It is unclear whether the authorities have learned to draw sophisticated distinctions between words and deeds or are so preoccupied with deeds that speech has become relatively easy, at least when it is a matter of whites talking to whites or even blacks talking to whites. Seemingly liberal opinions sprout in the most unlikely ground, like succulent plants on the arid fringes of the veld: in slick magazines intended for the coffee tables of corporate executives who find it helps to be known to their foreign bankers as "equal opportunity employers" or even in the pro-government Afrikaans press. No longer does it make sense to talk of a white monolith; a little promiscuity in the realm of opinion is not a dangerous thing after all. It's good for the image, good for self-esteem. So the various white elites are constantly talking, talking, talking about their future and the country's through a network of incestuous discussion groups that pride themselves on their openness and regularly now solicit opinions from browns and blacks. These are drawn from a roster of 15 or 20 names among the 27 or 28 million, those mainly who can be counted on to be "responsible," plus a few who carry verbal whips and chains to satisfy an occasional white urge for flagellation.

Starting on the white side of the racial boundary, I found it took a while to learn the limits of this new openness: to understand that nonwhites are normally heavily outnumbered in such interracial encounter groups; that they tend to be invited mainly when whites want to show off to foreigners; that the whites aren't all that interested in what they have to say; that few of the whites who attend such meetings have ever imagined that worthwhile communication could occur at a gathering where *they* could be outnumbered and talked down. Searching for a middle ground where their scope and power won't be diminished, the whites are prepared to admit selected blacks to their circle. But even those chosen few, knowing that they are being patronized, tend to drive the conversation further than the whites want to take it: to talk of ultimate solutions. At one of the little symposia I attended, an establishment colored, a man who mixed freely on a first-name basis with corporate moguls, brooded silently for two hours as the whites ran through their usual clubby debate about the immediate future, then exploded: "I wonder if it worries you that I haven't heard a word you've said." When he stormed out moments later, the discussion missed a beat, then continued as if nothing had happened.

It took a while to realize, also, that the rules are entirely different when blacks talk to blacks. Here, too, something had slid loose, in that the danger of informers no longer stifles the expression of opinions in private conversation. But opportunities for public speech remain strictly limited, and the informer network still spreads mistrust; in any serious political gathering where action is on the agenda, the calculation has to be made that there probably is a police agent present. A black political figure needs no permit to go to an "international" restaurant in a "white area" to discuss the revolution with a foreign journalist or other interested whites over an expense-account lunch. But if he tries to call an open meeting in the township to protest a rise in bus fares, let alone some detentions or an army raid across the border into a black state, it is almost sure to be banned as a potential "riotous assembly" under the Internal Security Act. At the same time that the authorities eased up on censorship, they enacted a law authorizing the police to forbid political pronouncements or songs at black funerals, which had become forums because the cemeteries were virtually the only places left where blacks could gather freely.

South Africa sates you with paradox. A black poet can say almost anything, it seems, as long as he is sparing in his use of proper nouns. Here is a passage from a poem called "Time has run out" by Mongane Wally Serote, a black writer living in exile, whose work sells openly in Johannesburg:

> *after these deaths*
> *our staring silent eye*
> *speaks of national revolution which we make . . .*
> *we learned by losing children and dying terrible deaths*
> *how to hold a gun and grenade*
> *we know now*
> *how to make fire fire fire*
> *inside this hour*
> *of intensely long and dragging movement . . .*
> *this is our land*
> *it bears our blood*
> *it must bear our will*

But Thabane Ntshiwa, a twenty-three-year-old diesel mechanic who scratched some slogans on a stainless steel mug that he used on lunch breaks at a factory near Johannesburg, not only had his mug confiscated but was himself arrested by the security police and charged under the Internal Security Act. "P.W.," one of the legends on the mug exclaimed, addressing the prime minister by his initials, "We want our land." Another said, "Release our leaders, release Nelson Mandela." The actual inscriptions were invisible from a distance of four feet and barely legible close up, but Ntshiwa had used proper nouns. I was allowed to handle the mug and talk to the prisoner in a small magistrate's court in Krugersdorp the morning he was sentenced. The magistrate noted that Ntshiwa had been fired the moment the mug was discovered and had already spent more than four months in jail, then spoke sententiously about his own obligation as a Christian and officer of the law to show compassion. But the statute's provisions did not allow him to overlook the fact that Ntshiwa had carried the mug on a daily basis into a canteen used by 135 other blacks whose passions might easily have been "whipped up." On the one hand, on the other hand; a judicious balancing of these various considerations yielded a sentence of eighteen months in jail, more than Ntshiwa had gotten on a previous conviction for culpable homicide.

The capriciousness of a system that can ban a mug and release a poem, torture one activist and seem to ignore another, keeps its enemies constantly off-balance while enticing potential collaborators, both at home and abroad. If it cannot be all things to all men, it can at least have the Promethean experience of being all things to itself. The zigzag pattern can be relied upon to confuse. Western bankers and diplomats, Americans especially, who want to believe in a meliorative dynamic seldom make the fairly obvious calculation that blacks are left with less political freedom than they had thirty years ago, before their main nationalist movements were banned.

If there is a mastermind behind all this, I remarked one day to Zwelakhe Sisulu, he must be a genius. Sisulu, a young black who might have an enormous following if he were allowed to lead, knew all about official capriciousness. In the three years since I had met him, he had been successively an editor and union leader; then, by official decree, a nonperson under a banning order that made it a crime for him to enter a newspaper or union office or be in a gathering of more than two persons; then, for nearly a year, a prisoner held incommunicado without charge; then a banned person again; and, finally, as if completing one lap in a marathon, a union leader and journalist all over again, accredited to go to the Union Buildings in Pretoria and put pointed questions to the prime minister at a news conference. His mother in that same period had been banned, unbanned, banned again, and jailed. (His father, a former secretary-general of the outlawed African National Congress, had only been jailed, for he was serving a life sentence with Nelson Mandela.) Sisulu was prepared to agree that the system worked very effectively and that it was run by people who were certainly not stupid and probably quite shrewd. But he didn't think there were any geniuses among them. "A system like this can only evolve," he said, taking the long view—the only view available to blacks.

If whites took the long view, they would be in a panic. This is one reason that white reality and black reality can be regarded as so different that newspapers that editorialize regularly about the evil and futility of apartheid find it perfectly natural to make up different front pages for blacks and whites. Most news is either black or white after all. In Johannesburg the black edition of the *Star* is called the Africa edition, underscoring the conviction of most whites that they are somewhere else. A Saturday morning's choice of front pages from the relatively liberal *Rand Daily Mail* nicely illustrates the assumptions made, on a commercial basis, about the conflicting preoccupations of whites and blacks. On the white front page there is a large color picture of a little blond girl sitting on a bed, propping on her lap a book entitled *Best Loved Horses of the World.* The caption explains she is "making herself at home in the luxurious surroundings of one of the Rand Daily Mail Ideal Homes Exhibition showhouses." The headline on the paper's lead story warns:

SUMMER STORMS
ARE ON THE WAY

On the black front page the color picture shows a black nurse attending a black servant who survived a five-story fall from a fire escape. The main story concerns a magisterial order banning a series of political meetings by what is known as the Black Consciousness Movement:

ALL WEEKEND BC
MEETINGS BANNED

In Chinese the two characters used in the common term for "contradiction" separately represent a spear and a shield. Spear-shield is everyday South African reality, a feature of the land whites grudgingly share with blacks in their increasing millions. The whites have learned to make small adjustments; they have lately become accustomed to standing in line behind blacks at banks where they may even be served by a black teller. But the system tries to minimize such discomforts. At one corner you see the world the way whites want to see it; at the next, the world as blacks experience it. The difference can be between an "international" hotel and a squalid rooftop barracks for black migrant workers that is periodically raided by the police. Or it can be between white bus stops conveniently located near the main shopping areas and black bus stops hidden away at the edge of town.

Nowadays a certain understatement amounting to deception is practiced so as not to call attention to discrimination. The mass arrests of "illegal" blacks that used to be heralded in the press as police "swoops" still take place but seldom in daylight in "white areas." The blatant "Europeans Only" signs that used to be constantly in view have mostly come down, but the signs that replaced them sometimes say the same thing in code. The sign at a white bus stop in Johannesburg, for instance, just says "Bus Stop," but it says it with black letters on a white background; at black bus stops the letters are white on black. The benches at the white bus stops no longer say *Net Blankes* ("whites only") but *Net Bus Passassiers* ("bus passengers only"), the catch, of course, being that only whites can be passengers on the buses that use those stops.

The motives for such changes are worth pondering. Is it that whites think apartheid can be made more acceptable if it is less insulting? Or since it is impossible to conceal the survival of apartheid from blacks, is it a matter of hiding it from gullible foreign visitors? Or is it that the whites need to hide it from themselves? Whatever it is, Prince Potemkin would have had nothing to teach Verwoerd's heirs.

But islands and bridgeheads of genuine multiracial endeavor also exist, side by side with the central institutions of the apartheid state. Spear-shield is visible in the Johannesburg skyline. The nondescript cement-block building near the railway yard where I once watched pass-law cases has long since been torn down and replaced with a fortresslike structure on reinforced concrete pillars, a gloomy monument to the system's survival and ruthlessness. Looking out a window in a corridor there, you can hold John Vorster Square and the Market Theater, two buildings that represent antithetical forces and endeavors, in a single mental snapshot. The one is the headquarters of the security police; looking at it, I would always count the floors till I picked out the notorious tenth, where many blacks and some whites have been tortured as a matter of routine. Two blocks away, in the city's old produce market, stands a complex of theaters and galleries where the country's racial conventions are ignored except as a subject for ridicule and condemnation, where torture frequently becomes a theme for moral inquiry. There is little that Athol Fugard or anyone else has ever thought to say on a stage about South Africa that has not been said there. Fugard's passion and pain; the triumphant mockery of *Woza Albert,* a black satire that later went to London and New York; or the comic revues of Pieter-Dirk Uys, a writer and female impersonator who wickedly takes off the Afrikaner establishment in drag ("Democracy is too good to share with just anyone," a favorite Uys character giggles, vamping her audience)—they all get played in integrated theaters in the shadow of the security police.

That is also South Africa, and so, on the other side of the pass-law court, are the offices of the major banks and insurance companies where, increasingly, whites, browns, and some blacks perform the same white-collar jobs side by side for equal pay, at least at the clerical level. So, too, even nearer the pass-law court, is a vainglorious glass structure that the mammoth Anglo American Corporation has erected next to the Stock Exchange. It's a small embarrassment that the new building, a monument to the country's nonrevolutionary future, has to stand on land expropriated from Indian traders under the Group Areas Act, which the corporation's directors periodically decry as contrary to free-enterprise principles. But the structure, intended as the most prestigious corporate address in South Africa, seeks to soar beyond contradiction. Pointed as if for takeoff with gaudy flying buttresses, it seems to have been conceived as a cross between a Concorde jet and a Gothic cathedral. But it never gets away from apartheid, for its large reflecting panels stubbornly mirror an unchic and supposedly bygone reality. On one side there is a row of what once were officially licensed as *Bantoe winkels* ("Bantu shops") selling spices and herbs, the potions and powders that witch doctors prescribe, also halal meat for Muslims: Indian-owned emporiums that have survived in a shrinking enclave despite the harassment of the Group Areas authorities. On the other side, the new building catches the squat, implacable image of the Commissioner's Court, the scene of the daily judicial carnage for hundreds of "illegal" blacks. Anglo American's agents sent decorators and restorers to paint and prettify the derelict two-story buildings that house the Indian shops, tempting the merchants to regear them as boutiques. Their future was now assured, for the government was conceding the case for the lifting of Group Areas restrictions from downtown business districts. But no amount of retouching could prettify the pass-law court, which fixes itself like an evil sign in the reflecting panels. Spear-shield.

For whites the contradictions can be taken as an expression of the country's undeniable vitality. For blacks they are only relatively less humiliating than the old, straightforward style of apartheid. Blacks are still ghettoized in their townships. Even if portions of these are being upgraded for a small, emergent middle class, they are nearly always set

off by buffer zones—highways, railway yards, factories, mining dumps
—in a manner that plainly reflects meticulous preparation for a military
siege. South Africa never achieved the absurdity of segregated flights
on its airline, but the trains and buses, the services the mass of blacks
require, are still demarcated by race. Legitimate theaters, which blacks
are unlikely to attend in large numbers, have been allowed to desegregate. But movie theaters outside the townships are still for whites only,
although an official commission has raised the possibility of desegregat-
ing some of them. Swimming pools at "international" hotels are supposed to be open to blacks and other nonwhites, but beaches remain
segregated. Restaurants are a matter of guesswork. Where a "Right of
Admission Reserved" sign is displayed, the guess is not difficult. Most
are for whites only, but some allow whites to take blacks; a handful
allow blacks to take themselves. It is this crazy-quilt pattern of devious-
ness, manipulation, and control that whites call progress. Some blacks
allow themselves to share the illusion for minutes at a time, but most
know it for what it is. They call it apartheid.

Provoked by an article on an attractive new country restaurant in the
women's pages of Cape Town's afternoon English-language newspaper,
the *Argus,* a reader signing herself "Classified Colored" wrote in to
inquire, "May colored people go there?" The newspaper owed its
nonwhite readers that information as a basic service, the letter maintained. "We of color," it said, "always have to carry a coolbag, folding
chairs, bowls of prepared food and loo paper because we do not know
on long trips where we can obtain something to eat and drink, or even
where we may use a toilet." The italicized reply from the newspaper
came in a voice that identified itself as white by its patronizing tone.
"This situation distresses us at ARGUS WOMAN as much as it distresses
you," it claimed. But the reader's reasonable suggestion that restaurant
listings and ads be required to specify whom as well as what the
restaurant serves was brushed aside. Instead, the newspaper offered this
tip: "We think you should telephone a restaurant beforehand, if you
can." ARGUS WOMAN was silent on the etiquette for such inquiries. After
a rebuff does the nonwhite caller say, "Thank you anyway," or something unprintable?

The least sign of black impatience vexes whites. Yet whites need
blacks to validate their belief that apartheid has now ceased to matter
—ceased, that is, to matter to them. Sun City, I was told, was ready
to pay a black superstar, a Diana Ross or Sammy Davis, Jr., or Lena

Horne, as much as the $1 million it supposedly showered on Sinatra to get that cachet. (The bait wasn't taken, but Shirley Bassey and George Benson, two black stars of lesser magnitude, came for less.) For much the same reason, I think, blacks have their place in the cosmopolitan fantasy that is constantly being marketed to whites. Ad agencies have different techniques for slipping them into promotions without denying outright the crude facts of South African life. Sometimes an interracial theme is presented as patriotic. (An ad for British Petroleum shows a white and a black side by side in a coal mine. "Shoulder to shoulder in the search for energy," it says.) Sometimes it is futuristic. (A Johnnie Walker ad has a black couple drinking with a white couple in costumes out of *Star Trek* or the twenty-fifth century. "Good taste doesn't change with the times," it says.) And sometimes it is a matter of geography. (A black couple cavorts in the transparent green waters of a tropical lagoon with two white couples as part of the promotion for a cane liquor. Small print reveals that this interracial idyll was photographed on Fiji. "Break Away with Mainstay," the big print urges.)

The variation on this theme that first grabbed my attention was a fashion spread that I came upon in the waiting room of Joshua Nkomo, the Zimbabwean political figure, which had unaccountably become a repository for a pile of old South African women's magazines. What caught my eye was a two-page picture of a black South African model in what was described as a gold bouclé jacket. She also wore gold slacks, gold shoes, gold gloves, and a feathered gold beanie, and she was reclining on a parapet above El Greco's Toledo in order to display these garments from South Africa to the mainly white readers of *Fair Lady*. "Lady in Spain," the article was called. On subsequent pages the South African model was on her feet in other South African glad rags in Madrid and in Segovia at the Alcázar. On the steps of the monastery of El Parral, also in Segovia, she was again recumbent. "The Fair Lady team" had been flown to Madrid from Johannesburg, a caption said, by Iberia Airways.

Although I tried several times, I never succeeded in explaining to white South Africans why I found this remarkable. *Fair Lady,* the most successful magazine in the country, was published in English by the major Afrikaans press group, Nasionale Pers, which is intimately associated with the governing party. The prime minister was once on its board; its senior executives are reputed to be his confidants. Certainly Nasionale Pers would never show a black model recumbent on a parapet above Pretoria or on the steps of the Dutch Reformed church in Graaff Reinet. Nor is the government it supports closely identified with the principle of free movement for blacks. I showed the article to Piet Cillié, then the board chairman of Nasionale Pers, and asked whether he didn't find it a little strange. He could not see what I was getting at. "It's an article on fashions," he said. "Very nice."

My point was extremely unsubtle. If I were the contentious sort, I might have made it more vivid by contrasting the model in Segovia to a black woman I had seen standing in the dock at the Commissioner's Court in a Cape Town black township called Langa, about six miles from his office. Her name was Virginia Nqanulyo, and her ensemble included a knitted white hat, a pale blue turtleneck jersey, and a baby wrapped in a yellow knitted blanket. The baby had been with her in Pollsmoor Prison, where she had been taken on a charge of having traveled illegally to Cape Town from a homeland called Transkei. The baby gurgled while the mother answered the questions of the white official on the bench, telling him a story that is repeated in the Langa court dozens of times daily, year after year: how she had lived for years in Cape Town, had met her husband in Cape Town long before Transkei achieved its bogus independence, had given birth to her children in Cape Town; how there was no livelihood for her in her "homeland." While she was being cross-examined, the baby started to squall; dropping a shoulder, demurely turning her torso away from the public gallery, and tucking the baby's head under her jersey, Mrs. Nqanulyo gave it her breast to quiet it. The commissioner gave her a suspended sentence of sixty days in jail on the condition that she leave Cape Town immediately. A few days earlier he had told another woman who said she would starve in Transkei, "We are starving in Cape Town. You can rather starve at home."

Lady in Langa, "Lady in Spain." Of course, they had nothing to do with each other. The one was a part of black reality in South Africa, the other a part of white fantasy. To do it justice, *Fair Lady* has a social conscience that periodically permits it to slip in an article about hunger in the black rural areas. But when it hands an Iberia ticket to a black model, it is imitating *Vogue*, showing its readers that *they* have risen above apartheid and joined a wider world. It's a characteristic South African disjunction.

SA'S PRISON
POPULATION
HIGHEST IN
FREE WORLD

exclaimed a headline in the *Star*. The boastful tone may have been unintentional, but not the assumption that South Africa stands for something other than an isolated and beleaguered white oligarchy at the tip of Africa. Better to believe that it is a sane precinct of the world, a place like other places; maybe no better but maybe not much worse.

At a disco called Q's, I met a black American known as J.J., who had moved into this cozy warp in white perceptions and made a home for himself in Johannesburg as an honorary white. An ex-marine from St. Louis by way of L.A., he had come to South Africa as a dancer in a group called Skintight that had played Sun City, then found himself stranded after he had rebuffed a demand from the South African agent that he perform in Johannesburg cabarets that offer tame striptease and seminude pas de deux (or trois) on sadomasochistic themes at lunchtime. So J.J. (he was Donald Givens on his passport, Jay St. Jerome on his professional calling card) had found work as a model for ad agencies in Jo'burg. Soon he was in demand for TV commercials; finally he found steady employment as the DJ at Q's, a club that practiced a kind of demiapartheid: Blacks were permitted to wine and dine there but not to dance.

J.J. was now banking more money than he had ever earned as a dancer and getting experience as a DJ that he would have found difficult to acquire at home. He lived in an "international" hotel in Hillbrow, a faintly bohemian and more than faintly sleazy section of town that can be loosely characterized as Johannesburg's answer to Greenwich Village, and even found he could ride the segregated white buses without incident. Once they discovered he was from Los Angeles, not Soweto, the club's young clientele, Afrikaners as well as English-speaking whites, were eager to befriend him, to explain at interminable length how he was different from "our blacks." Among the women who came on Thursday nights, when male "exotics" were presented, there were even some who he thought might consider an invitation to his hotel. But J.J. had his own timetable for how long he wanted to stay in Johannesburg, for how much cash and experience he needed to bank; he did not, he said, want to tangle with the Immorality Act, which forbade sexual relations across the color line. Nonwhite women, like the whites, seemed to be interested in him only when they found he was from America, and that, he said, turned him off. So living what he portrayed as a sober and celibate life in the "smart casual" fantasy world of white South Africa, where acceptance for him was not really an issue, J.J. managed to experience Johannesburg as if apartheid were only a rumor and to feel a degree of empathy for whites striving so earnestly to appear and feel uninhibited.

In the glass control booth where he operated two turntables and spun the dials on a range of amplifiers and lighting controls, J.J. made his own compositions, mixing bits of "Puttin' on the Ritz" with a little of "Last Night a D.J. Changed My Life." The lights rotated, flashed, and struck like lightning; the music throbbed, sliding into a diminuendo, then leaping out. Through it all, the couples on the floor seemed to be battling with invisible bonds, looking glassy-eyed in some cases to the point of autism, as they performed their mechanical two-steps. "They're really enjoying themselves," my black friend from St. Louis explained. "You can't tell it, but they are. They're just so tight."

Perhaps J.J. would know how to explain, if any explanation were necessary, the tendency of the cosmopolitan fantasy of the whites to turn a shade or more licentious. For a time most whites seemed to acquiesce in the notion promoted insistently by the state broadcasting monopoly that the rest of the world was hurtling to perdition. Now it is fashionable to imagine going along. Of the two kinds of repression South Africa experienced at the start of the apartheid era, the Freudian kind is giving way, ostensibly, to a diligent pursuit of whatever is passing as new and spontaneous in California and New York. The promotion of foreign brand names seems to have everything to do with the dropping of restraints. Denim cologne is offered in Afrikaans *vir die man wat nie te hard hoef te probeer nie* ("for the man who doesn't have to try too hard"). Wranglers are "the pants most women want to get into." The man's shirt is unbuttoned; so are his jeans; the blonde's head, resting on his thigh, has an expression that can reasonably be interpreted as postcoital. Another blonde, in an ad for a Japanese cassette deck, sits in a sports car with her legs spread and her skirt hiked up above the top of her stockings. Her head is thrown back. "Fill her with power," the ad says.

One evening shortly after my arrival, I was mildly astonished to discover under a windshield wiper an invitation to a salon called Extrav-

aganza, promising "Jacuzzi, sauna and body rub" until 2:00 A.M. "Are
you allergic to water and girls?" it asked. The Immorality Act seldom
seemed to be mentioned when the vice squad busted a massage parlor
for offering "extras," but a raid on the Sauna K.O. in Durban produced
this report in the *Natal Daily News*:

EMPLOYEE
TELLS COURT
OF SAUNA SEX

A colored woman employed at a sauna parlor told a Durban
Regional Court today that she saw the wife of the [white] co-
owner having sexual intercourse with an Indian man in a cubicle. . . .

The woman told the court that she had been told by Mrs. Zelna
Swanepool (25) how to give pelvic massage when she was first
employed at the parlor.

The employee said that an Indian friend of hers called Joe had
visited the parlor on one occasion. He had gone into a cubicle with
Mrs. Swanepool. The woman said she had peeped through the
curtains because she wanted to tease Joe afterwards. She saw Joe
having intercourse with Mrs. Swanepool. . . .

When the Elegance Sauna was hauled into court in Johannesburg,
it became evident that it had also attracted a multiracial staff and
clientele. A white attendant named Dawn Hart testified, the *Citizen*
reported, that she told the manager she would charge fifty rands for
sexual intercourse; he then asked "whether she was prepared 'to do'
Indians." A deacon of the Dutch Reformed Church, who testified for
the prosecution on the understanding that he would not be named, said
under oath that he had been "attended by a woman whom he did not
notice was not white"—so the *Rand Daily Mail* reported this awkward
mea culpa—"because it was dark inside the cubicle." I was tempted
at first to read these reports as omens of apartheid's slow demise, but
then I arrived at the obvious reflection that whites in South Africa had
been crossing the color line for sex for three centuries before their
elected representatives got around to enacting the Immorality Act.

A more unbuttoned attitude to sex seemed to have only a tangential
connection to other kinds of liberation. Nonwhite contestants did not
appear to be welcome at the Plumb Crazy nightclub in Johannesburg
on "ladies' nights," when young studs were invited to participate in
what were called "the finals of South Africa's first wet underpants

competition." And Suzy's "Strip Er Gram" in Durban specified that it was for "Europeans only." This was apartheid, but not the apartheid I remembered. Increasingly the system seemed to inspire burlesques of itself. At the hairdresser's on a Saturday morning, my wife was informed that it was "Turnaround Day." Everyone working in the shop —the white males, the white females, and their black female assistants —had come to work in drag as part of a sendoff to one of the men, who was taking a trip to America. Carolyn's hair was cut by a man wearing leotards, falsies, and a shawl. At the next chair a Jewish grandmother was having hers done by a man who wore bikini panties and a bra with nipples painted on it under a see-through nightie and a red wig. The black women were garbed in the sort of coveralls black workmen usually wear, with mustaches smudged on their faces. An election was held on strictly apartheid lines to choose the best white man dressed as a white woman, the best white woman dressed as a white man, and the best black woman dressed as a black man. Balloting was limited to customers, meaning it was for whites only.

"This morning, when I came down in the elevator at my building," Carolyn's hairdresser said, "I was praying that it wouldn't stop so no one would see me like this. But it did stop. It stopped at the seventh floor, and my heart stopped, too. But it was only for a black girl, so it was all right."

The gap between black reality and white reality is huge and roughly quantifiable. It can be shown that the 4.5 million whites have more than 250,000 swimming pools and 800,000 servants; that the per capita white income may be as much as fifteen times higher than that of blacks; that the white 15 percent of the population has reserved more than two-thirds of the land for its own use (leaving the other one-third to the blacks, the browns, and the animals in the game parks). There are various ways of demonstrating that this gap is narrowing (or widening) as a result (or in spite) of a general rise in the wages of urban black workers. But I never knew how to calibrate the gap between white fantasy and black reality, or white fantasy and black fantasy, or to justify my impression that these were widening all the time. Whites insist this is a matter of "culture" and "civilization," as if these were static and immutable, when it is evident that for both themselves and the huge majority whose existence they all but deny, values and standards are churning crazily.

At one extreme there is the decadence epitomized by a magazine called *Style* that emulates, or sometimes seems to parody, the slick life-style magazines that litter American coffee tables with bulletins from the front lines of gluttony and display. "Nouveau riche is better than no riche at all," *Style* assures its readers, who are presumed to aspire to Johannesburg's fancier suburbs. What it promotes is less a style than a syndrome that reeks of narcissism, aggression, and greed, equating insatiability with power. Thus this blurb for an article on the "social stamina" of the corporate striver: *Today's executive supermen are more than just boy scouts with good teeth. They're an alternate breed, a new genetic force, a threat to the norms of menopause.* Or this: *You're the sophisticated product of a fast-moving, permissive era. You live in an achievement-oriented society where anything that stays static soon begins to seem stagnant. No wonder your steady old marriage seems a little out of synch.*

"Still Married and Feeling a Little Passé?" that article is headed. In the South African montage, it should be pasted next to the following item from the *Star:*

FINED FOR
LIVING WITH
HER HUSBAND

A domestic worker, Mathilda Chikuye, was this week fined 30 Rands (or 15 days in jail) for illegally harboring her husband in her room at 20 Talbrager Avenue, Craighall Park. . . .

Mrs. Chikuye does not live in an "achievement-oriented society." She is only physically present there to perform a service. The insatiability of the whites and the craving for security of the blacks are in fundamental tension. While the up-market white magazines counsel their readers on how to have affairs, the advice to the lovelorn columns in magazines directed at urban blacks dwell constantly on problems of infidelity, unwanted pregnancy, and the difficulty of achieving a stable married life in the overcrowded conditions of the townships. The black fantasy, it seems, is of something like the drab middle-class reality that can't seem to satisfy the appalling white hunger for more. This could be spear-shield with a vengeance.

Still, the white fantasies of a cosmopolitan life remain largely fantasies, while the black fantasy of a householding nuclear family in which grandparents, children, aunts, and uncles all don't have to bed down in the same room is beginning to be a reality for a tiny bourgeoisie. It is a trend the authorities feel constrained to encourage, but only up to a point. If the black fantasy started to merge with the white reality, what would be left of apartheid? And who then would rule?

The problem of segregating fantasies as well as people confronted the authorities when they initiated a television service for blacks. The theoretical justification for apartheid is essentially Jungian: that each of South Africa's racial, ethnic, and linguistic groups has its own collective unconscious that must not be disturbed. TV threatened to make them mutually permeable, forcing the whites to live in McLuhan's "global village" with everyone else. The state broadcasting monopoly sought to tame the monster by decreeing that all programs "targeted" at blacks had to be exclusively in one of five African languages—Zulu, Xhosa, Tswana, Sotho, or Venda—with none of the mixing of dialects or flights into English and Afrikaans that are common in real African speech. Thus there can never be a program in English directed at blacks, though they have used English as their political lingua franca for decades; programs in which whites and blacks talk to each other, as if they inhabited the same country, are also likely to be ruled out unless the whites are dubbed. In addition, the monopoly laid down strict rules governing the appearance of blacks in commercials or programs on the English and Afrikaans channel or whites in commercials on the black channels. They could be shown together on their feet at a Kentucky Fried Chicken stand, but not sitting in the same establishment.

Black appearances on the channel aimed at whites have to be carefully rationed so as not to disturb viewers in their dream of a white South Africa. But the broadcasting monopoly's authority is not powerful enough to keep black fingers from straying a quarter of an inch to the white button on their sets. One evening we took our college-age daughters to visit their former nanny, Dinah Dibakoane, who was still living in the area outside Pretoria where we had deposited her in 1966. Now it was no longer a collection of tiny metal shacks in the veld; also, it was no longer supposed to be South Africa. The township had grown and obliterated the veld, and most of it had been gerrymandered into Bophuthatswana. The racial planners who had seemed so weirdly out of touch with reality had achieved their vision, except for one thing. Dinah, who like most urban Africans was competent in at least four languages, was watching Afrikaans rather than Tswana TV.

And that wasn't the worst of it. What she was seeing on her black-and-white screen was an old American sitcom, dubbed into Afrikaans, about a basketball team at a high school where there was at least one black teacher. She could also see the mystery series *Quincy* in Afrikaans, and even when she switched to the black channels, there was a fair chance that she would end up watching dubbed American shows there as well, *The Jeffersons* in Zulu or *Spiderman* in Xhosa.

It is hard to say whether this is the global village or the South African Babel, but if the Afrikaans and Tswana cultures can be preserved from mutual contamination only by dubbing American sitcoms, the question of what it is that is being saved is at least raised. Possible answers include white dominance and white illusions, or both since they go together. When Afrikaners spoke in the past of an identity and culture that needed to be fenced off and preserved from the ravages of Africa, they seemed to be referring to their language, their separate schools and churches, their enduring love of the veld. Now Afrikaner identity has bellied out to include country music with a panhandle twang, pizza, the latest doctrines in counterinsurgency, under-the-table oil deals with Arab sheikhs or their middlemen, saunas and Jacuzzis, arms smuggling, fast cars, Italian silk shirts, package holidays in Rio or Bangkok, and, for some in the new elite, secret overseas bank accounts. Even the coruscating black American comedian Richard Pryor. A detribalized Afrikaner took me and a couple of South African newspapermen to a rugby test match in Pretoria, the first I had ever seen, as vital a cultural initiation as one could have in South Africa. On the way back, with great pride and mirth, he played a cassette of a scatological Pryor monologue as we drove at dusk through the veld, past the Voortrekker Monument, the national shrine.

Finally, for some, Afrikaner identity has come to be equatable with power, for the one can seldom be imagined any longer without the other. Their interior world, where the old pieties and racial doctrines cohabit with the new cosmopolitan ideal and cult of power, seems to the outsider trying to imagine its contours and feel like an exhibition house in which each room is furnished in a different style: Colonial or Empire, rustic or high-tech, Vegas or Valhalla—you name it. Of course, many inhabitants stay put in one room or wing. For them the old pieties hold true: The Afrikaner is still on his pilgrim's progress in an impious world and can achieve salvation only by being more self-disciplined and devoted to duty than everyone else. Others, the real powermongers, are constantly on the move, quick-change artists priding themselves on their ability to refurbish their minds and conversation each time they change their masks.

In Pretoria a nondescript office building attached to a shopping mall seemed to me to house the Afrikaner antipodes. The Parkade Building it is called. I visited it twice, once to chat with Hendrik Verwoerd, Jr., the son of the martyred prime minister, in a crowded, little office on the fifth floor; the next time to get a look at the lunchtime cabaret at a popular disco called Jacquelines, a cosponsor with Plumb Crazy in Johannesburg of the "wet underpants competition."

Upstairs Dominee Verwoerd, an ordained minister in the Dutch Reformed Church and former missionary, wrestles with what he takes to be the central dilemma facing his people: their continued dependence on black labor, which will ultimately force them, he fears, to concede political rights to blacks and relinquish their hard-won nationhood. The younger Verwoerd's solution is a strictly logical extension of his father's formulations, even if it appears to represent a retreat. The whites must carve out their own "homeland," an area of South Africa that will conform to the original Verwoerdian ideal: Not only will no blacks reside there on a permanent basis, but black labor will be largely excluded. The dominee, who manifests all the kindliness that visitors attributed to Verwoerd *père*, hastens to add that blacks will always be welcome as tourists or guests. The white homeland would not want to be isolated in Africa, he says. However, there are a couple of conspicuous obstacles to the realization of his scheme, Verwoerd concedes. One is that most whites are unused to doing menial tasks for themselves; another that there is no habitable region of the country where whites are in the majority.

To overcome these obstacles, he has organized a movement called the Oranjewerkers (Society of Orange Workers), which hopes to exert leverage on the Afrikaner government similar to that exerted on the Israeli government by Gush Emunim when it started to establish Jewish settlements on the West Bank of the Jordan River. Gush Emunim was dismissed as a fanatical fringe group but came much closer than anyone imagined to working its will. The Oranjewerkers are still dismissed as a joke, Verwoerd acknowledges, but they are forming property and construction companies to amass the capital and work habits their scheme will require. It will be an example, an inspiration to others,

Verwoerd says, when the movement's white members start to carry bricks on construction sites. All they ask of the authorities at this stage is the right to set up local enterprises employing only whites. Since the South African interpretation of free enterprise preserves the freedom to discriminate, that should come easily. At a later stage the Oranjewerkers intend to demand that their "white growth points" be proclaimed "white labor preference areas" so that no nonwhites can be hired in preference to a white for any occupation. Instead of building apartheid from the top down, as his father tried to do, Verwoerd wants to build it from the ground up, or halfway up, for he is not in favor of dismantling white power at the top any sooner than necessary. His aim is to create something that could endure, something that has never existed in South Africa: a self-sufficient white economy. In 1797 a prominent Dutch burgher named Van Ryneveld expressed the fear that it was already too late. "A peasant who has always been accustomed to have his work done by slaves and has therefore done nothing but superintend it will not always be brought to perform every kind of rural labor," he wrote. But if latter-day Zionists could attempt to build a true Jewish state after two millennia, Verwoerd reasons, maybe it is not too late for the Afrikaners after only three and a half centuries.

Of the 2.8 million Afrikaners, who represent 60 percent of the whites but only 8 percent of the overall population, 1,200 had joined the Oranjewerkers in three years. Had they all dispensed with black labor? I ask. "Not everybody immediately," the dominee concedes with a shy smile that lights up his honest blue eyes, "but everybody in the long run. They are all committed to the ideal." True to their principles, the Oranjewerkers seek to make use of no black services. It is not their fault that black cleaning women are used to scrub the corridors of the Parkade Building, but at least when they moved in, Dominee Verwoerd tells me proudly, all the furniture was carried by whites. It is also a point of pride that no black messenger is employed to carry the society's mail to the post office. The proof is before my eyes: Envelopes are piled high on Verwoerd's desk and nearby counters, waiting for white volunteers to show up and dispatch them; the mail has obviously not moved for days.

Downstairs at Jacquelines, black labor is costumed and highlighted as part of a tropical motif: The waiters wear not only tropical shirts but battery-operated eyeshades studded with little bulbs that flash red and green, streaking eerily as these bearers beat a path between bar and tables. The customers are all white and nearly all male: hefty young men, who enter in three-piece suits, then hang their jackets over the backs of their chairs, or wear safari suits, the traditional summer uniform of the civil service. There are ice buckets chilling wine at nearly every table and slabs of beef, with an optional spicy ooze known as monkey gland sauce, on nearly every plate. At one table there is a party of three young women, self-consciously overdressed in a manner that is characteristic of Pretoria, without a hair out of place above their Estée Lauder faces. Nursing a bloody mary, I watch from behind a picture window in a bar that is set, one flight up, above a small stage. The background music, astonishingly, is made up at first of the same folk staples of the traditional *boeremusiek* ("country music") that are still nostalgically sung in unison before Afrikaner political rallies, tunes like "Sarie Marais" and "O, Boereplaas," only here they are given the tinkly, upbeat treatment of a cocktail medley.

Many of the tables have switched from wine to Irish coffee by the time the lights go low and the music changes to a pulsating Hollywood fanfare. Four white dancers in cowboy hats and red tights, three women and one man, appear on the little stage. The man is bare-chested; the women wear halters with cutouts that appear to expose their breasts, which nevertheless are covered in the transparent gauze of body stockings, with sequined stars serving as nipple caps. The women slink sinuously around the male dancer, winding their legs and arms around his and clutching at his flesh in an unconvincing mime of desire. The man, who has a small mustache and short haircut, like many in his audience, preens and plays hard to get. The scene changes; the girls bump but don't grind. Then a dancer laboriously mouths the words to the original recording of the song "Tits and Ass" from the Broadway musical *A Chorus Line,* pointing to the apposite parts of her anatomy whenever she comes to the refrain as if she were giving elementary language instruction. If there is any turn-on at all, it seems to be in the lyric and the brassy imported voice with its suggestion of an uninhibited, ready-for-anything female. The man, always the cynosure when he is onstage, always an object of glorification, strips down until finally he is in his Tarzan briefs, writhing on the floor with a flaming torch, which he applies to the soles of his feet and the hair on his chest before plunging it into his mouth.

By this time I feel embarrassed for Pretoria, for this audience at least, hoping that it feels cheated, that it rejects what seems to me a cruel

and cynical rendering of its fantasies. I can see that this sordid little
ballet, with its mouthing of imported lines and emphasis on male
dominance, reflects something in the world outside the Parkade Building. But it was for this kind of display that the show biz expression
"over the top" was coined. It is just too weird. But no, the Pretoria
audience looks relaxed and cheerful and even entertained right up to
an inspirational finale, which is another mouthing of an American show
tune, one that might be interpreted, in context, as a satire on the
Afrikaner's dream of omnipotence on a black subcontinent. I find it
hard to believe, stupefying in fact, but the dancers, dressed now as
harlequins, move their lips and the audience actually hears:

> *Gonna build a heaven from a little hell.*
> *Gonna build a heaven and I know darn well.*
> *If I build my mountain with a lot of care*
> *And take my daydream up the mountain*
> *Heaven will be waiting there.* ©

CHAPTER 3

■

BLANC DE NOIR

Johannes van der Linde did not seem to have even a nodding acquaintance, when I met him in 1965, with contradiction and moral ambiguity. It was one of those encounters when an opportunistic reporter represses a shudder of embarrassment and sympathy for his prey, knowing that the words being so earnestly expended on a self-portrait are bound to make exactly the opposite impression from the one intended. He was a major then in the army's ready reserve force who devoted the nonmilitary portion of his life to increasing the size of his dairy herd and his farm in the Orange Free State, which was east of Bloemfontein in softly rolling country spectacularly punctuated here and there by steep hills the tops of which have been flattened like the deck of an aircraft carrier. A hospitable, candid, thoroughly likable man, he patiently explained his theory of labor relations, using the paradigm of a father and his children: how, for instance, he had built a schoolhouse for the boys of his "boys," his black laborers of all ages, not because any outside authority had required it but because he thought it only right. "The white man won't get the benefits of doing right by the native if his only motive is self-preservation," he said.

On Sundays the school was made available to itinerant black preachers from the mission branch of his own church, one of whom, he was astonished to hear, started preaching "communism." It was his faithful "boss boy," Ou ("Old") Sam, who had called this to his attention. Sam was an elder in the church who sometimes left the farm to travel to synods. "It's very good to have black people like that," Major van der Linde said. "You meet white people who don't have the same quality. Of course, every now and then Sam will get cheeky or something."

The reporter could not refrain from asking what happened when one of the "boys" got "cheeky." The major replied: "It's very like the way

51

you treat your own children. You don't want to be too tough, but if you're not firm, you won't have your farm long. I have to clout one every now and then in the stable." Needing no further prompting, he told me how black fathers with unruly sons sometimes asked him to cane them, how the discipline he provided was necessary to contain the ever-present menace of cattle theft. Major van der Linde had heard that Afrikaners were often misunderstood in the world at large. For the first time a note of wariness crept into his voice. "Do you really think they'll believe this in New York?" he asked.

The interest of outsiders mystified him. "There's a lot of talk about these natives in the world today," he commented in a voice that expressed wonder and curiosity rather than the resentment other Afrikaners would have vented. "I ask myself why. Is it something in this century? It wasn't always so."

Before Hendrik Verwoerd, Afrikaners never theorized much about the status of blacks or dreamed of a white nation in which only whites would live. The blacks and browns were simply there, part of the natural order: to be used, when there was a use for them; treated fairly, on a sliding scale of fairness, so long as that did not compromise the status of the poorest whites; possibly "uplifted" by regular readings from the Bible but never conceived of as individuals made from the same clay, responding to emotions and values that were more than remotely fathomable—let alone thought of as social and political equals, not before the kingdom of heaven anyhow.

The worst thing that could befall a white was to sink to the level of blacks, to become a "white kaffir." The worst kind of black was one who was *te wit* ("too white"). Academics argue now that the main theme of the Afrikaner's long tribal saga has been not racism but ethnocentricism, a preoccupation with preserving a cultural identity that must often have seemed fragile or easy to misplace. Self-involved the Afrikaner certainly is, but such interpretations tend to turn on brittle definitions of terms and away from history. The sense of an ordained racial hierarchy came very early, when the whites collectively amounted to less than a speck at the tip of the huge, unknown landmass; if it wasn't there from the start, the idea of hierarchy was certainly there long before the Afrikaners knew themselves as Afrikaners, a people of Africa, rather than as Europeans. And inside that idea the urge to dominance was always incubating, waiting to sprout.

Jan van Riebeeck, the Dutchman who established the first white settlement at the Cape of Good Hope to provide fresh vegetables and meat to ships of the Dutch East India Company as they turned east to Java, set the tone when he described the local inhabitants as "a dull, rude, lazy and stinking nation." He was referring to the brown-skinned people who came to be known as Hottentots or Khoisan. Pastoralists or hunters, these aboriginals did not leap at the opportunity to indenture themselves to the newcomers, so the company hauled in slaves and convict labor from Madagascar, India, Ceylon, Malaya, and Java. Van Riebeeck, the founder of "white civilization" in Africa, was evidently not tempted to settle; after nine years he left his torpid little way station and headed for the East Indies himself. By then miscegenation between whites and slaves, also slaves and aboriginals, was starting to produce the people now called coloreds who still mainly speak Afrikaans, which evolved from the Dutch of their most privileged progenitors. In the early days a dark skin was not invariably a bar to white society, but the identification of color with class gradually hardened. Nevertheless, it took nearly two centuries before the idea of nationhood started to dawn on the whites, who were always small in number, scarcely 20,000 by the end of the eighteenth century, when most families were already into their fourth or fifth generation in Africa. Latter-day nationalists traced the idea somewhat romantically to the decisive event in Afrikaner history, the Great Trek, when some 5,000 whites put the Cape behind them and journeyed into the interior in ox wagons.

But the trekkers never imagined they were getting away from blacks and browns. If their departure was a bid for self-sufficiency, it was self-sufficiency of a peculiarly South African kind, for they were all but outnumbered by the servants and former slaves they took along. They knew, too, that there were more blacks where they were going than where they were coming from, that they might have to bargain or even fight for their place in Africa. What they were fleeing was British colonial authority, with its weak-kneed susceptibility to philanthropic opinion in London, which pressed first for the abolition of slavery in the colonies and then for the easing of other forms of coercive labor. Just as there is a connection by lineage between today's antiapartheid movements and the antislavery lobby that existed then, the resentment of interference and sense of being misunderstood that propelled the trekkers have had a century and a half to shape themselves into a cultural reflex. Their most specific grievance was over the imported idea that whites and nonwhites could sometimes be placed on an equal footing before the English courts. They called this "equalization," but it was really only a highly qualified legal concept, nothing more than the germ of an idea of equality, simply holding that there was an external authority that could, under certain circumstances, regulate the relations between master and servant. Even this, in their rough-and-ready view, was the antithesis of "justice" in the circumstances of Africa. It was a radical idea that, as one matriarch expressed it, obviously was "in conflict with the laws of God and the natural divisions of descent and faith."

Later, when they fought their two wars with the British to preserve their frontier republics, the Afrikaners relied on blacks to drive their wagons, tend their horses, dig their trenches, and scout enemy positions. They thought it immoral, however, for the British to put guns in black hands. Guns could make blacks a factor in political disputes which could damage "the cause of civilization in Africa," said Jan Christiaan Smuts. In all this there was a consistent view of race relations that was succinctly put a century after the Great Trek by one of the founding spirits of Afrikaner nationalism, General J. B. M. Hertzog: "Whatever the rights of the native may be, they have no right to call on us to do anything that might jeopardize our supremacy." Dressing it up in ideological terms, Verwoerd had the tact to substitute the term "self-determination" for "supremacy." But he always made it plain that "white self-determination" came first, that whites set the rules by which peoples of other hues might have a little self-determination, too.

Thus, at the heart of the struggle by the Afrikaners for their cherished "identity," there lurks an obvious and huge contradiction that has never been resolved: The freedom they sought for themselves from externally imposed laws meant, of necessity, the freedom to impose their laws on others. They even came to see it as a duty, one that defined their role, so the Afrikaners who fled British law took on the Mosaic mantle and pictured themselves as lawgivers. In fact, in a country that is 85 percent nonwhite, "white self-determination" is impossible without supremacy. And so a people who are widely credited with having fought Africa's first anticolonial struggles, who are native to the land and not colonists in any normal sense, have come to establish one of the world's most retrogressive colonial systems. Sometimes this is presented as a paradox, but nothing in the traditions of the Afrikaner suggests that there could be anything paradoxical about whites telling blacks what to do.

Earnest and sophisticated Afrikaners, of whom there are many, realize that it is necessary to avoid using or even thinking provocative words like "supremacy," which have a tendency to backfire practically as well as ideologically. But it is also necessary, they believe as an article of faith, to keep control of the country. For many white South Africans, control seems to be more than a concept or political outcome. It is almost a physical sensation, habitually expressed in images of grip and stress. "You can't force them down all the time," an Afrikaner teacher in an industrial town called Benoni told me, explaining why he was supporting constitutional changes that would give browns, but not blacks, a token role in national government for the first time. The extremist opposition to this so-called reform adopted a slogan that was not just tactile but prehensile. "Don't let go," it urged. Conversely blacks experience white power in physical terms as a force pressing down or squeezing. The raw reality of that power can be veiled for the sake of the whites, but it cannot be hidden from blacks. There is nothing coy about the plainclothes white security cops who cruise around the major black townships in big Fords and Datsuns. Guns are usually conspicuous when these officers are outside their cars. Obviously it serves their purpose to have it known that they are there and they are armed.

Elsewhere white power sometimes hides behind a black façade but seldom very far. There are a handful of blacks with doctorates in education working for the Ministry of Education and Training (alias Bantu Education), but they never are assigned to the headquarters in Pretoria, from which control is exercised, directly or indirectly, over the entire educational apparatus for blacks. There the only black faces belong to messengers and tea "boys." If blacks could have a hand in shaping the curriculum their children are reared on, in shaping their view of history, society, and Africa, in addressing the fundamental questions of citizenship and equality, then "white self-determination" would be on its way to extinction. Instead, "white self-determination" seeks to determine in an authoritarian manner what blacks may learn. Significantly, books by African authors such as the Nigerian novelist Chinua Achebe that are occasionally approved for white schools—presumably because they satirize black politics—are never used in black schools, where *Silas Marner*, that all-purpose universal set text, still is assigned. Serious writing by black South Africans is even less welcome.

There is no such thing, either, as a black official at the headquarters of the Byzantine and secretive bureaucratic structure euphemized as the Ministry of Cooperation and Development. It would more accurately be known as the Ministry of Control, for that is its function in relation to black lives. Formerly called the Ministry of Plural Relations —and before that Bantu Affairs, and before that Native Affairs—it seems to require a new name every five or six years to sanitize and mask its real role, which is to regulate the movement of blacks and rationalize the pattern of black habitation in South Africa so as to minimize any threat or inconvenience to whites. It is this vast warren of white racial ideologues, constantly fine-tuning the huge corpus of apartheid law, that is responsible for telling millions of blacks whether, where, and when they can live with their families. Only when it disbands or has its policies set by blacks will it be possible to start speaking seriously about the phasing out of apartheid. Barring an upheaval, that won't be soon.

At this ministry's headquarters in Pretoria, black menials had a sign-in book where they were expected to put their X's next to their Christian names—Absalom, Samson, and John were the first three— in accord with the South African tradition that whites cannot be bothered to learn African names. At the Port Natal Administration Board, an arm of this bureaucracy that administers blacks who want to get a foothold in employment in Durban, I spied an organization chart for what was clearly labeled "The White Establishment" of one of its bureaus: The top 361 boxes all were color coded on a racial basis and plainly reserved for whites, down to the level of assistant typist; underneath were 168 boxes for black employees. As both graphics and social fact, the chart represented a white lid clamped on a black mass.

Again "white self-determination." So was a revealing scene at one of South Africa's top security installations, the uranium enrichment plant at Valindaba, which is nestled behind some impenetrable fences in lovely hill country outside Pretoria. The name of the place comes from the Sotho language and means, I was told, "about this we do not talk." South Africa has always denied that the enterprise was part of a nuclear weapons program but refuses to sign the nonproliferation treaty because that would mean admitting international inspectors to Valindaba. I had gotten on the premises for an interview with the man who named the place and headed the state corporation that runs it,

Ampie Roux. A shortish man nearing retirement after a quarter of a century as the "father" of South Africa's nuclear programs, he showed his suspicion of a foreign journalist by keeping his head down like a bulldog and glowering. But he was eager to make a case about the failure of successive American administrations to supply nuclear technology and fuel. Having registered his points, he lowered his guard slightly and invited me to lunch in his private dining room. There, after soup and wine had been served by white stewards, he apologized for having to leave me for a few moments, explaining that he was due to make a brief address to the Valindaba work force on the subject of pay increases; there would therefore be a short intermission before the main course. The dining room had a balcony, and I stepped outside into a strong autumn sun. Below, dozens, then hundreds of staff members were gathering on a perfectly tended lawn in front of a rostrum. By the time my host rose to speak, there were more than 1,000 persons beneath the balcony, and it was conspicuous that there wasn't a single nonwhite among them. Later, as a steward served overdone beef, Dr. Roux reluctantly confirmed that his staff was all-white. Initially it had been a matter of apartheid principles, he said. It was decided that separate decontamination rooms would have to be built if any nonwhites were hired.

"And decontamination rooms are very costly, you know," he explained with the resigned sigh of a visionary who has been forced to accept practical restraints.

The explanation was put in the past tense, where apartheid was now supposed to belong, but the staff was still all-white. "There must be security reasons, too," I ventured. Dr. Roux gave the smallest of nods. The only blacks allowed on the site, he said, were construction workers, and these were subject to strict security checks. Later I happened to meet a black who worked as a cleaner at a factory where artillery shells were manufactured for the state arms corporation. No blacks there, he told me, were allowed into the room where the shells were assembled. Of course, this would not have been apartheid either in the official view. But what is it? How do the white elite groups that plan such installations express the need to exclude blacks when they are speaking among themselves? Do they continue to rely on euphemisms, or do they say, "Of course, we can't have any blacks"? At what point do they acknowledge that their aim is to keep power in white hands? Do they ever admit that they are preparing for an unambiguous racial struggle?

At times I would go around and around asking myself such questions. At times the answer seemed all too obvious. There was the morning in an amphitheater adjacent to the Voortrekker Monument, a lugubrious granite temple placed on a hilltop outside Pretoria on an angle that was precisely calculated so that every year, precisely at noon on December 16th, the Day of the Covenant, a ray of light will shine through the dome and fall on the inscription on a cenotaph: the symbolic resting place of Piet Retief, a trekker leader who became Afrikanerdom's first martyr when he was treacherously slain on the command of Dingane, a Zulu king. The temple, opened to the public on a segregated basis in 1949, was thematically conceived to portray the epic struggle between "civilization" and "barbarism." On a marble frieze inside its Hall of Heroes, civilization is always depicted as white, barbarism as black. But the gulf is not shown to be absolutely unbridgeable: Though attired in only a cape and a codpiece, a chief of the Barolong tribe is portrayed in honorable negotiations with one of the white chiefs by the sculptors, who, we are told, had a mandate to model their style on Verrocchio and Donatello and, simultaneously, "to guard against any un-Afrikaans elements creeping into the work." Perhaps that reference, in an early, unsanitized edition of the official guide to the monument, is not to the Renaissance sculptors but to some homebred Willie van Verrocchio or Hendrik Donatello. Or perhaps this was one of those occasions when "Afrikaans" could be equated as a cultural modality with "European." The Barolong chief, that same guide makes clear, was exceptional. For the most part, "The Bantu was not amenable to reason. He respected one thing only and that was force."

And it was force that was now on display in the amphitheater, white force. The occasion was a military parade in honor of Prime Minister Botha, who had stepped down as defense minister after fourteen years. The Pretoria skyline shimmered in the distance with more monuments, pompous structures thrown up in the apartheid era by the descendants of the trekkers in tribute to their own power. There stood fortresslike government ministries turned inward on themselves in great slabs and hunks, as descriptive, in their own terms, of a mental outlook as the Stalinist monstrosities of Eastern Europe. And there, studded among these, stood the corporate citadels of Afrikaner *volkskapitalisme* with pastry chef trimmings intended to be at least slightly ingratiating. As a skyline it might be called sterile, even decadent, but it made an assertion that morning that was softened only slightly by thousands of jacaranda trees in full flower, a profusion of purple leading up to a more distant view of the stately Union Buildings that Sir Herbert Baker designed after the Boer War, the seat still of the Cabinet, whose members were now arriving in convoys of silver Mercedes limousines. Perhaps 2 or even 3 percent of the 10,000 or so troops who marched through the amphitheater had brown or black faces. But its location at the national shrine made this unmistakably an Afrikaner consecration. The New Testament selection read out by a chaplain resounded to the spirit of the surviving trekkers who had their revenge against Dingane at a site in Zululand that thereafter retained the sanguinary name Blood River. From Paul's Letter to the Ephesians he read: *Put on all the armor that God gives you that you may stand up against the devil's evil tricks. For we are not fighting against human beings but against the wicked spiritual forces in the heavenly world, the rulers, authorities, and cosmic powers of this dark age. So put on God's armor now!*

Mirage jets streaked low over the amphitheater, trailing stripes of colored vapor, then over the Palace of Justice in the center of Pretoria. About an hour later there, I watched as a white judge condemned three members of the underground African National Congress to the gallows for the parts they played in an attack on a rural police station where one black sergeant was slightly wounded.

The thought of how far the Afrikaners had come since Paul Kruger abandoned his capital to a British army under Lord Roberts at the turn of the century must have occurred to many at the monument that morning. In the courtroom the opposite thought seemed to have occurred to an Afrikaner professor who stood next to the dock with a stricken look, expressive of grief and shock, as the judge swept from the bench in his red robes and the blacks in the public galleries defiantly thrust their fists in the air and joined the condemned men in singing "Nkosi Sikelel' i-Afrika" ("God Bless Africa"), a Methodist hymn that has long served as the black anthem. To Frans Maritz, a sociologist who had testified on behalf of the young blacks when the time had come to plea for mercy in sentencing, the clash of nationalisms seemed in that terrible instant to have destroyed the middle ground where he had tried to take a reasoned stand. Just before the sentencing Professor Maritz had assured me that the three would be spared, that the court would have to take account of his testimony, based on interviews with them in their cells, that they were essentially passive young men who had been caught up in the wave of fury and despair that engulfed urban black communities at the time of the student protests of 1976 and 1977, when nearly 600 blacks lost their lives in confrontations with the police. In his view, they were victims of a sociological accident, neither hardened "terrorists" nor committed "freedom fighters." It was the professor's thesis that the authorities—the same elite I had just seen at the amphitheater—now recognized that something had to be done about black grievances and that understanding this, they would perceive the injustice and even recklessness involved in turning the likable, mild-mannered youths he had gotten to know into martyrs. But I noticed that the professor had brandy on his breath, though it was still midmorning, that he had apparently found it necessary to fortify himself just to be in court. Once the sentence had been passed, with the incantation of the fierce and palpable image of hanging "by your neck until you are dead," the blacks had their solidarity, their sense of righteousness and inevitability, and it was this rumpled middle-aged white man who suddenly looked bereft.

Shortly after the trial, the professor's office at the University of South Africa was bombed by white extremists who thought he had committed racial treason by testifying for blacks. But by the time I visited him several months later, his sense of vulnerability had receded. The three young men had not yet been spared—their sentences were later commuted as a result of international pressure, rather than the sociologist's arguments—but he had already recovered his optimism and sense of being in the mainstream. Now he could talk comfortably about how far the Afrikaners had come in their attitudes. In his view, they were pragmatically looking for solutions, inhibited only by their lamentable ignorance of the facts of the black man's situation in their country and their understandable fears, brought about by the failure of blacks to adapt to the capitalistic society whites want to preserve.

Blacks weren't really interested in freedom "and all that sort of thing," the professor said, but in economic advancement; if whites could help them gain that much, then violent pressures for changes in the legal structure might be deferred. The issue thus became how whites could overcome the passivity of blacks, which was inhibiting their advance. Professor Maritz was obviously a man of decency; of courage, too, considering his willingness to testify on behalf of three young "terrorists." He did not deserve to be glibly judged. But like many Afrikaner intellectuals of apparent goodwill, he seemed unable to hear how remote and patronizing he sounded when he talked about blacks. The concept of black passivity was so central to his understanding of his world that he could not seriously consider the possibility that young blacks who went into exile, received military training there, and then returned to their country on dangerous, practically suicidal missions may act, at least sometimes, with deliberation and commitment; or that black adaptation to free-market economics was strictly regulated in a system that placed severe legal restraints on the most ordinary forms of initiative such as the search for a job, setting up of a business, or purchase of property; or that, from a black perspective, the problem was the cultural attitudes of whites, which took for granted the proposition that black advance was possible only under white tutelage. He understood but did not seriously consider the proposition that it was white power, the power of the guns displayed at the Voortrekker Monument, that accounted in large measure for the mysterious survival of a lopsided social structure.

It is a favorite parlor game among Afrikaner elites, this search for some explanation of the black man's backwardness and supposed lack of initiative. Implicitly it is a ritual of self-congratulation, a way of saying how benevolent and advanced the dominant racial caste is, how undeserving of condemnation. On an unconscious level it says something more: how close the Afrikaner elites have come to absorbing the style and arrogance of their old adversaries in the English-speaking elites, which kept alive the colonist's fascination with pseudoanthropological theories explaining the differences between "them" and "us," an explanation that Afrikaners found in the biblical story of the curse on the descendants of Ham on the rare occasions that they found it necessary to seek any explanation. Once perilously close to being "them," the Afrikaners are no longer content with Divine Providence as the reason for how they got to be "us." In speculating about blacks, they thus reach for stereotypes that several generations of English writers and officials used, including some that were used to explain the quirky survival of Africa's white tribe.

As early as 1835 a British journal found the Dutch inhabitants of the Cape to be notable only for their cunning. "No people can trick or lie with more apparent sincerity," it said. In 1842 an English newspaper in the Cape commented on "the profound and rayless ignorance" of the Boers on the frontier. (Viewed in the same light but through a racial prism, the blacks came off even worse. "They are crafty and cunning; at once indolent and excitable; averse to labor; but blood-thirsty and cruel when their passions are inflamed," an official commission drawn from the first generation of English settlers in Natal reported in 1852.) Writing on the eve of the Boer War, Lord Bryce said the Afrikaners had "neither the taste nor the talent" for industrial activity. Lord Kitchener, the last British commander in that conflict, described them as "uncivilized Afrikander savages with a thin white veneer." Lord Randolph Churchill, shortly before he was unhinged by syphilis, portrayed the Afrikaner farmer as the personification of "use-less idleness." His portrait of the Boer established a benchmark for sheer bigotry that no Afrikaner has surpassed:

> It may be asserted, generally with truth, that he never plants a tree, never digs a well, never makes a road, never grows a blade of corn. Rough and ready cultivation of the soil for mealies by the natives he to some extent permits, but agriculture and the agricul-turalist he holds alike in great contempt. He passes his days doing absolutely nothing beyond smoking and drinking coffee. He is perfectly uneducated. . . . His simple ignorance is unfathomable, and this in stolid composure he shares with his wife, his sons, his daughters, being proud that his children should grow up as igno-rant, as uncultivated, as hopelessly unprogressive as himself.

Pauline Smith, a novelist now neglected outside South Africa, por-trayed Afrikaners with sensitivity and sympathy, but in her chef d'oeu-vre, *The Beadle,* which is *Tess of the D'Urbervilles* transplanted from Hardy's Wessex to the Cape, she dwells on their "slow-moving thoughts," their "fatalism," the absence among them of any "craving for mental excitement." They are, she concludes, a "simple race." The epithet "childlike," which Smith uses repeatedly, recurs more than thirty years later in descriptions of Afrikaners in Doris Lessing's 1957 memoir, *Going Home.* There is more positive feeling in "childlike" than colloquial epithets for Afrikaners still used by English-speaking white South Africans, such as "hairies" and "crunchies" and "ropes" (i.e., thick and twisted), but its survival over decades as a stereotype is clearly not unrelated to the bitterness that fueled Afrikaner nationalism in the same period, ultimately carrying this "simple race" to a position of such dominance that the custom of patronizing others could be elevated into ideology and law.

Few Afrikaners hear these echoes when they speak about blacks.

The practice among them of intellectualizing about the black man as a racial type may have been initiated by Jan Smuts, the Boer War hero who came to be viewed as a turncoat by many in his tribe as a result of his later Anglophilia. It is striking that Smuts saved his weightiest theorizing about the black man and his destiny for elite audiences in Britain, rather than Afrikaner audiences in the *platteland* (rural districts) of the Transvaal or Free State. What he had to say was seldom raw enough for them. But given his passion for letting bygones be bygones as far as the English were concerned, he had no hesitation about accepting an invitation to deliver the Rhodes Memorial lectures at Oxford in 1929. "The negro and the negroid Bantu form a distinct human type," he said there. "It has largely remained a child type, with a child psychology and outlook." That sort of line evidently went down well at Oxford in 1929; Smuts's lecture, which strongly suggests that his contributions to the theory of what came to be known as apartheid have been seriously undervalued, was later published in a collection of his talks by Oxford University Press. Of course, Smuts was eager to express his affection for blacks as a politician who wanted to be known as a *ware* ("true") Afrikaner would not have done in those days, or even now. "A child-like human," he told his English audience, some of whom might have said the same for Afrikaners, "cannot be a bad human, for are we not in spiritual matters bidden to be like unto children?"

Gradually, as they became accustomed to power, other Afrikaners began to feel a need to be recognized as magnanimous and Christian in their attitude toward blacks. "They are very like children," Johannes van der Linde said of his laborers on my first visit to his Free State farm. "As the parents of the black peoples of South Africa," the white minister of cooperation and development found it possible to tell a black assembly in one of the most wretched homelands a generation later, "we are aware of these peoples' aspirations and ideals and would like to help our children make their own way as adults."

It may be an advance that black backwardness can now be viewed as a problem, rather than predestination, but most white theorizing on the subject lacks integrity, for it departs from the self-regarding assumption that it is a problem only whites can solve. In other words, it departs, travels in a little circle, and returns to its premise. Verwoerd gave the Afrikaner a picture of his place in the world similar to the diagram of the heavens that the ancient astronomer Ptolemy provided:

He was at the center. Present-day theorists bear comparison to the sixteenth-century astronomer Tycho Brahe, who recognized that the prevailing movements of the planets did not sustain the theory that they all were revolving around Earth and then, instead of questioning the central premise, recharted the movements. With a mighty expenditure of energy and ingenuity he thus managed to preserve the theory for a few decades by imagining that the paths of the planets followed a series of detours and curlicues known as epicycles. South Africa's new theorists even speak in terms of a "constellation" made up of the "homelands" and other black satrapies revolving in little epicycles around a white center of power. The Copernican view that it is all too complicated to be real, that sooner or later blacks will have to be at the center, remains heresy.

In search of concepts and jargon they can use to make their world make sense, the Ptolemaists regularly commit a kind of intellectual rape of the literature and journals of Western, mainly American, social science and economics. Listen to Professor J. L. Sadie, an economist at Stellenbosch University, discoursing on "Socio-Political Requirements for Stability and Growth." Professor Sadie is nobody's idea of a Marxist or neo-Marxist, but he chooses to speak in terms of classes rather than races. These he numbers I (for the executive class), II (for the highly skilled), III (semiskilled), and IV (unskilled and unemployed). Classes I and IV, he finds, are in drastic imbalance in South Africa, making it an undeveloped country and thus inherently unstable. The removal of some discriminatory laws won't change these facts, although it is worthwhile for what he calls the "international marketing of this country." A political settlement won't change them either, for it is likely to remove power from "responsible people" who understand that economic growth is not "an abiogenetic process to be had for the asking," people who understand how dangerous it would be "if all economic issues were to be politicized, with redistribution of national income given a priority rating." The causes of instability can be addressed only by increasing the supply of Class I—that is, by producing *"NEW MEN* of bold imagination and energy" with an "eta-achievement or need for achievement" that can only be acquired early in life. "Parents do not transmit to their children motivational characteristics which they themselves lack." Here we get down to race: Blacks with what Professor Sadie obtusely or perhaps boastfully terms their "built-in custom" of migratory labor remain mired in a traditional society, and therefore, "very few would qualify for the description of *NEW MEN.*" Thus they cannot provide the energy for development "in the Schumperterian sense" that South Africa needs. They are not open to the challenge posed by "the Toynbeean thesis." There is a regrettable problem here of "national character." Unlike the Japanese, the blacks have characteristics that are "inimical to growth." The article then trails off. Nothing specific is said about dismantling what is "built in," but something, Professor Sadie suggests, will have to be done about education in the homelands. In the meantime, it goes without saying, the overburdened and unappreciated whites who account for 96 percent of Class I will have to continue to shoulder "the sizable disutilities" such as "a 16-hour working day, chronic stress, psychosomatic disorders, ulcers and heart failures" that are the price of leadership in order to provide "the maximum economic welfare . . . for the maximum numbers of people." There you have it: the white man's burden.

The possibility that his missing *"NEW MEN"* may be well known to the security police, that they may be either in jail or in exile plotting new sabotage attacks, is not one that interests Professor Sadie because such cultural mutants among blacks are obviously not going to promote stability or capitalism. Unlike the "responsible persons" who now govern, they show through their reliance on the gun that they are "power-hungry." The key then to stability, evidently, is to cultivate *"NEW MEN"* among blacks who won't be power-hungry.

Corps of Afrikaner pedagogues, in preparation for this great task, have pored over the studies that have been done of school integration in the United States and of educational programs in the third world generally. The scientific method, as they practice it, has reduced itself to the technique of selective quotation. There is a giddy enthusiasm, even innocence, about the strenuous efforts they make to translate old racial doctrines into current academic jargon that will advance the "international marketing of this country." Fortified by their new vocabulary, they then declare with patent sincerity that they are not peddling apartheid. Far from it; they are only paying prudent heed to findings in the *Journal of Negro Education* or a study done for the U.S. Civil Rights Commission. A former rector of Pretoria University, C. H. Rautenbach, cites the Reverend Jesse Jackson as his authority for the argument that school integration is an "antiquated concept." Daniel J. van den Bergh, author of "A Pedagogical Study of the Black Man's Mathematical Ability," assured me that "very in-depth research" had clearly demonstrated the need for separate technical education for blacks. For instance, he said, data collected by the Human Sciences Research Council in Pretoria pointed to the conclusion that blacks and whites learn at different optimal temperatures. Blacks, it appeared, needed classrooms that were several degrees warmer.

There were many more reasons: Blacks come from a culture that is static rather than dynamic; they are strongly oriented to group rather than individual effort; they are not given to detachment or objective thought; they have a different concept of time. Eagerly, his eyes glowing with the excitement of his discoveries, Dr. van den Bergh cited Kenneth Kaunda as one of his many authorities. I found it unlikely that Zambia's president had really argued that blacks could learn only in segregated institutions controlled by Afrikaners but refrained from injecting politics into an elevated, scientific discourse, especially as Dr. van den Bergh went on to expound some of the pedagogic consequences of these principles, assuring me that the "problem of Africa" was on its way to being solved.

The conversation was taking place in a $100 million technicon, established to train blacks in civil and mechanical engineering, analytic chemistry, public health, and various other technical fields; a separate course, including instruction in "speech and deportment," prepares black women to function as secretaries. It is the Sun City of Bantu Education; you could mistake it for a campus of the University of California—all exposed brick, skylights, and hanging plants—unless you allowed your gaze to wander beyond its perimeters to the squalid Pretoria township in which it is situated. In the harsh light of day, the technicon can then be seen as a monument to the conviction that a common society is unthinkable: not only for whites but for blacks. This township is called Soshanguve, which is not an African word but an acronym fashioned by white administrators for the various black ethnic groups (*So*tho, *Sha*ngaan, *Ngu*ni, *Ve*nda) that are officially deemed to be foreign to an adjacent, virtually indistinguishable township in the supposedly sovereign and independent Tswana homeland, half a mile away. Whether Tswanas and Vendas can learn at the same temperature is never explained. Apartheid is profligate—only a country with half the world's production of gold could afford to quadruplicate bureaucracies and facilities on racial lines—but the ideal of a separate technicon for each black ethnic group is too expensive even for South Africa. The mind boggles on such visions, so you lower your gaze and try to concentrate on what Dr. van den Bergh is saying about the institution's approach to teaching. And surprisingly, even alarmingly, he is beginning to sound sensible because either you have now been sufficiently softened up or the whole theoretical windup has been necessary to demystify the process of learning for the instructors even more than the students.

Education for blacks should go from the concrete to the abstract, so the students are shown how to make things before they are taught the theory behind them. They are encouraged to work in groups and even take tests in groups, rather than pitted against one another. They may talk all they want in class so long as they are talking about the subject. The school is geared for success; they have the time they need to learn. I comment that roughly such an approach was called progressive education in America about half a century ago. Is there any reason, I ask, why it wouldn't also be good for South African whites? It is a question that Dr. van den Bergh has apparently never considered. "There is no such thing as black education and white education," he replies, crisply nullifying everything he has been saying for an hour. "There is only good education."

But why then a black technicon in a place called Sotho-Shangaan-Nguni-Venda that must be conceived to be in another galaxy rather than where it really is, on the outskirts of Pretoria, scarcely fifteen miles from the prime minister's office? A small but important clue can be found in the elaborate arrangements that have been made to control political expression by the students. To be admitted to the technicon, I am told, a student has to be sponsored by a corporation. "If there is any disciplinary problem," an official says, "all we have to do is lift the phone." South Africa needs blacks with technical skills. But blacks with political aspirations as well as technical skills are emphatically not needed. That is the message.

The serviceability of the jargon generated by American political scientists for this kind of approach to the renovation of apartheid was always marvelous to behold. Just as fast-food chicken has now been domesticated as *vingerlek lekker,* the ruling National party can hold a mirror to itself and discover that it has the potential to become, in the words of Professor Robert Rotberg of MIT, "a model modernizing oligarchy." Terms like "parameters" and "legitimacy" float in the conversations of white politicians and officials like slices of exotic fruit in a highball. A Stellenbosch professor told me of the party's efforts to engineer a "paradigm switch." The first major document on the new approach to constitutional change, a report by a committee of a multiracial advisory body called the President's Council, was written by an in-house academic with a Cornell Ph.D. who managed to append a bibliography with citations to about thirty American political scientists: all to dress up an argument that brazenly hinged on the honest declaration of a corrupt calculation, that blacks could not be included in "a successful democracy in current and foreseeable circumstances" because of "their cultural differences, relative numbers, conflicting interests and divergent political objectives." In other words, there was a danger that the majority might abuse democracy to serve its own interests. The report then called for "limited consociation" among whites, coloreds, and Indians based on "segmental autonomy," which it promised "would not in the least disturb existing power relations."

Professor Samuel Huntington of Harvard, who had the dubious honor of being cited more frequently than any other American in this document, had flown to South Africa to deliver a paper in which he considered the abstract proposition that increased authoritarianism might actually be necessary for reform. "It is not inconceivable," he declared loftily, "that narrowing the scope of political participation may be indispensable to eventually broadening that participation." Professor Huntington left himself an out with words like "not inconceivable" and "eventually." It was hard to tell whether his oracle referred to white movements, black movements, or popular movements of any description. But he was refining one of the standard rationalizations for clamping down on dissent and installing martial law. He went on to offer a possible rationalization for police state methods: "The centralization of power may also be necessary for the government to maintain the control over violence that is essential to carry through major reforms." To advance such a thesis in Johannesburg without considering the actual methods by which "control over violence" is maintained in South Africa—indefinite detention without trial, solitary confinement, humiliating interrogation sessions often including torture —was to offer a form of unction, to say, man to man, that we all know how difficult reform can be.* Finally the visitor from Harvard observed

*Writing a year later in a magazine called *Servamus* that is published for the South African police, their commander, General Johan Coetzee, gratefully cited the "Huntingdon [sic] thesis" as if it were on its way to being recognized as a law of nature.

that the "reform process" requires "substantial elements of duplicity, deceit, faulty assumptions and purposeful blindness."

That may be disinterested analysis. It may even be an accurate description of how a socialist party came to power in Spain without violence in less than a decade after the demise of General Franco. It proved to have some bearing on the process by which representative institutions were phased back into being in Brazil. But such analogies remain only analogies. They beg the question of what it is that is being reformed. In South Africa, the essential question about reform is whether it aims at eliminating, or simply renovating, the racial system. If reform can be deduced from narrowed political participation, centralization of power, duplicity, and deceit, then apartheid has always been a reform movement. And in fact, it has always presented itself as one. No one has to teach Afrikaner politicians the lesson that words can be weapons. Their grasp of that point is the reason they are forever renaming things, inventing new euphemisms for old realities. The "native reserves" became "Bantustans." Then they became "homelands." Then they became "national states." The level of human misery within their borders rose in the process. The level of "purposeful blindness" rose, too.

At the risk of indulging in stereotypes myself, I found that it helped to think back to the Boer War and remember that Afrikaners were the century's first guerrilla fighters, that tactical flexibility could be their end as well as their means. In that perspective there was a temptation to compare the professors and out-of-office policy makers who flock to the seasonally recurring symposia on change and reform in South Africa to the "foolish English Generals" derided by an officer's Sikh orderly in the Kipling story "A Sahibs' War." The generals, the Sikh complains, distributed *purwanas* (permits) to Boers who promised to put aside their arms and return to farming. "But these people," he exclaims, "were as they were in Burma, or as the Afridis are. They shot at their pleasure, and when pressed hid the gun and exhibited *purwanas*, or lay in a house and said they were farmers. Even such farmers as cut up the Madras troops at Hlinedatalone in Burma! Even such farmers as slew Cavangari Sahib and the Guides at Kabul!"

It is no insult but a tribute to the Afrikaner's tenacity and ingenuity to suggest that he still sometimes shoots from "houses adorned with a white flag." The whole enterprise of constitutional reform, as it has been experienced so far in South Africa, amounts to little more. On his own terms this same Afrikaner is indulging simultaneously in a measure of soul-searching, which is really quite new, on his racial attitudes and relations to other groups in the land he has been reared to think of as his own. This leads him to reflections that are so surprising, so unlike those of his father, that he sometimes imagines the revolution has already occurred, not realizing that the most dramatic changes have taken place in his own armchair and his own head. In the real world Afrikaners who make an effort to speak to blacks and examine the circumstances in which blacks live remain rare specimens. That is still a job for surrogates, the police and minions of the multiple apartheid bureaucracies. But the plea that white safety entails a rise in black living standards and a new etiquette for communication across the color line has become a staple of the intensely inward discussions that Afrikaner elite groups ceaselessly pursue. It is a theme that politicians in the governing party preach with evangelistic fervor, sometimes movingly. But it is the style of politics, not the essence of power, they are talking about. South Africa will be easier to govern if whites can get over the assumption that all blacks are servants and all servants are infinitely disposable. When that message is not grasped, some Afrikaner politicians feel a genuine frustration and even anguish. But it is anguish on behalf of their own people, not the blacks.

The difficulty of reconciling the continued existence of white authority with the promise of reform produces some instructive and pathetic examples of political syntax, sentences that not only are geared for ambiguity but totter on the edge of nonsense in an effort to communicate different meanings to different audiences. The minister of cooperation and development went around the world declaring South Africa's intention to abolish "unnecessary and hurtful discrimination." When I asked him what discrimination wasn't hurtful, he brushed the question aside. "That's semantics, that's absolutely semantics," he replied, as if his sense of his own good intentions should be enough to satisfy anyone.

Here is the minister of national education toiling to impress an impressionable audience in Washington, D.C., without raising a furor in his white constituency at home: "Separateness is no longer recognized as the total answer to the problem of accommodating a multiethnic society; while separateness is recognized as still an essential ingredient, it is accepted that it should in many cases be combined with an inevitable measure of togetherness." Parse that if you can; I think it means, "We will have as much separateness as we can get, but we realize that we can't have as much as we want." Here is the same minister speaking to the white Parliament: "Differentiated cultural promotion must be exercised within the different communities but this must be done with flexibility." In plain and honest language, that would become something like this: "We are going to hold on as long as we can and retreat, if we must, inch by inch, taking as many of our people with us as we can."

In private conversation the minister of national education once expressed himself in simple terms for my benefit. Afrikaners were not racists, he said. They were simply revolted by the way some blacks sneeze and spit in public. When black manners improved, so would the willingness of whites to seek political accommodation. This was offered as a clinical judgment on both communities and as realistic political analysis. But I sensed that it reflected a mean little anxiety and primness in the minister as well, a physical tension left over from the days when the aim of Afrikaner politics was to keep poor whites from sinking to the level of even poorer blacks. "Togetherness" remains a frightening idea.

The minister of national education was a model of lucidity in his public pronouncements compared to the minister of constitutional development,* who also traveled to Ronald Reagan's Washington to deliver a speech. What he offered there as an explanation of reform in South Africa had all the moral force of the small print in a dubious contract; the government, he said, planned:

> to restructure the historically determined hierarchical political system of apartheid into something based on the premise of divided power and joint structures in which discrimination—and this goes without saying—will have to go, but without jeopardizing the non-negotiables of the maintenance of group interests and aspirations within the wider context of security and stability.

Just as that illumination was fading on the banks of the Potomac, an official circular was issued in Cape Town that contained some clues to

---

*South African Cabinet ministers are generally interchangeable when it comes to illustrating trends in bombast. But for the record, the three quoted here do have names. The minister of national education in this period was Gerrit Viljoen, an owlish former classics scholar who once specialized in Pindar. The minister of constitutional development was J. C. Heunis; and the minister of cooperation and development, Piet Koornhof.

the nature of this "restructuring." It had to do with the courts, and it said: "All new buildings to be erected in the future will be planned without segregation facilities except as far as toilets and waiting rooms are concerned." I can carry the exegesis a step further. This circular caught my eye because of an encounter I had just witnessed at a Pretoria courthouse. I happened to be standing outside the men's room there when my friend Chabani Manganyi—university professor, clinical psychologist with postdoctoral training at Yale, author of several books highly regarded for their originality and force, and that day expert witness in a political trial—was told to use the toilet downstairs that "the other boys use." That may not have been what the minister intended, but it was the end of the causal chain linking theory and practice. That, finally, was what it meant to protect group aspirations within the wider context.

It is easy to lampoon official double-talk, but hidden here and there in the acres of verbiage are kernels of real meaning. Consider the minister of constitutional development. On home ground he once explained in a brief spasm of candor why there could be no place in the parliamentary structure for blacks, even on the segregated basis of the new constitution, which gives coloreds and Indians a subordinate role in the national government. Blacks would outnumber whites, coloreds, and Indians, he said, by a ratio of 36:9:5:2; if only those classified as urban blacks were counted, the ratio would still be 16:9: 5:2. "And what would remain of the principle of maintaining civilized standards then?" he asked. On another occasion he went so far as to explain how civilized standards have to be maintained. "It is in the long-term interests of South Africa," he said, "that the Afrikaner should always have the privilege of the leadership role." Not for just a day, not for just a year, but *always*.

That is the only premise on which orthodoxy is still demanded. An Afrikaner can go surprisingly far these days without reading himself out of the establishment. He can theorize on issues such as land reform or income distribution; he can draw constitutional models that look like chandeliers or DNA molecules; he can take his crayon to the map and find new borders for partition. He can even theorize about the likelihood of negotiation one day with the banned black movements. Those are all legitimate gambits in the intellectual game. What he cannot do is question the Afrikaner's "leadership role" or attack the government's policies on criteria other than utility. He cannot appeal to values such as justice and equality. He cannot argue that the survival of the Afrikaner's culture depends not on power but on the willingness of individual Afrikaners to demonstrate, as Professor André du Toit of Stellenbosch expressed it, "that Afrikaner culture can be a creative and liberating force in the wider South African society . . . to stand and work in solidarity with non-Afrikaners in common causes even and especially where this might involve supporting black movements on their own terms." Only then does he become a renegade. It was "politically quite immoral" to appeal to justice and the "fairness factor," the newspaper *Die Transvaaler* retorted without any apologies or the smallest trace of irony, because that could only mean "surrender to black power." Justice might demand that the door be opened to black power, the newspaper was saying, but black power would be inherently evil. Therefore, justice was immoral.

Before long I came to find conversations with most middle-of-the-road, so-called enlightened Afrikaner thinkers anesthetizing. They seemed to last for hours and to float free above the land, beyond all gravitational pulls except those of career and influence. Most of all, I hated the sound of my own voice in these encounters, so calm, so neutral, so reasoned. I was not pretending to be detached as a journalistic stance. I really was. Maybe the torpor was mine alone, but I thought it was in the air, that there was a whiff of something more enervating than doubt, an acknowledgment that Afrikaner power would go on trying to justify itself without ever succeeding. In czarist Russia, conversations in French around the samovar in the houses of the landed intelligentsia must have had the same high-minded inconsequence when the abolition of serfdom was looming as a possibility. "We can only define what we're against, not what we favor," one professor said.

Drifting along with the conversational current, I would reflect that these were not evil men, that they were no more opportunistic than I. Or I would toy with the thought that they were victims, too, that the best of them were shackled to the obsession with power, unable to find a satisfactory way of committing themselves to the country they loved. Every now and then I would bump against a comment that would jar me out of my reverie. There was the Stellenbosch political scientist who became bored with his own discussion of "confederal" and "consociational" forms of government and abruptly asked whether I had ever noticed that the male was usually black and the female usually white in racially mixed couples on American campuses. I hadn't noticed, I said, ending that discussion. Later I was sorry I hadn't shut up or even baited him a little with a speculative remark about black sexual prowess. At Potchefstroom the flash of self-revelation came in a description by another political scientist of a day trip he had recently taken to Soweto with a fifty-year-old colleague who was setting foot in a black township for the first time. "I hope I see you tonight," the man said to his wife, nervously joking as he kissed her good-bye. My host chuckled condescendingly. He went on these excursions to Soweto twice a year as a pedagogic exercise. "We drink tea with them," he boasted. "No problem." He was saying, I realized, that the whites managed to drink from cups that blacks must have used, as they would never knowingly have done before.

We were sitting in a living room that was like many Afrikaner living rooms in which I had been entertained. An obvious thought that had eluded me before now registered. For a people obsessed with their cultural identity, Afrikaners have surprisingly few cultural artifacts they can call their own. Only the rich can now afford authentic pieces of Cape Dutch furniture, the best of which were bought up long ago by English-speaking businessmen and foreigners. Occasionally there is an old rifle of Boer War vintage, the head of a kudu, a family Bible, or a sentimental landscape of the Drakensberg Mountains bathed in an ambiguous pink light, either dusk or dawn. More often the Afrikaner shows himself to be a cultural hybrid, displaying cheap souvenirs from Europe and Africa: porcelain figurines and pictures of windmills beside carvings of grizzled Africans or their daughters. This one had a drawing of the canals in Amsterdam and a small tapestry showing a tribal maiden in a rural setting. My host's son walked through the room in army fatigues. Now and then we could hear the echoes from the artillery range on a nearby army base. Only about 10 percent of his students, the professor was saying, had been into the black townships nearest their homes. It was impossible to discuss contemporary issues without showing them a bit of their country. That was why he took these field trips to Soweto. It wasn't for his own benefit.

"What do I need to go to Soweto twice a year for?" he asked.

A full eighteen years had passed before I paid my second visit to the Van der Linde farm in the Free State. The idea hadn't occurred to me until I visited the Pretoria Art Gallery to see a retrospective exhibit of the work of David Goldblatt, South Africa's most original and sensitive photographer, who had accompanied me on that first visit. There, in a photograph I knew well, was the young major in khaki trousers, a tweed jacket, hair shaved short at the sides, talking to Old Sam, who wears a floppy hat and stands at slightly more than an arm's length, responding with a mild smile. In between the two, standing several paces farther back at the edge of a muddy field, is the figure that gives the picture a tension that is more than formal: a younger black in a striped beanie who seems to be about to light a cigarette. The angle of his body shows how alert he is to the presence of the *baas,* but his face wears a mask of unconcern.

I thought of bringing a copy of the picture to the Van der Lindes, assuming that they wouldn't have seen it. It was fortunate that I arrived empty-handed, for they knew the picture well, and Mevrou ("Mrs.") van der Linde didn't like it at all. "It's the *pointing,*" she explained, making a face and shooting her index finger out in a couple of sharp gestures, expressive of overlordship. I knew immediately what she meant; her husband had been shown as a figure of authority, and the image was not necessarily flattering. The modern Afrikaner does not want to be seen as a feudal figure. Only later, when I looked at the picture again, did I realize that her keen intuition of meaning had played a trick on her memory and mine. No one was pointing at anything. The major stands with his hands to his sides, much as he would if he were standing at attention.

Now he was a colonel, and—while he indicated that he harbored no grudge over the way he had been portrayed in print after my first visit, that after the passage of so many years he might even count it as a worthwhile lesson—he was no longer naïve about what was believed in New York, or, for that matter, in Pretoria, where he was on friendly terms with the chief of the Defense Force. In fact, he had just returned from New York, where he had stopped after a tour of the American Farm Belt, on which he was one of a group of South African farmers who had been guests of the Allis-Chalmers Corporation, the makers of the huge tractor that stood in a shed next to his Mercedes. The passage of years had turned his hair gray and thickened his gut, which poked out over jeans that had the words "Better by Design" stitched on a rear pocket. With the addition of more land, better cattle, and more black laborers, it had transformed him into an agribusinessman, and it had enriched his sense of humor. Broadly speaking, it had thus done for him everything it had done for Afrikanerdom as a whole.

As we rode out to inspect some nutritious rye grass on which he had managed to keep his dairy herd fat during the century's worst drought, he entertained me with tales of his American tour: the night he spent drinking in Milwaukee with a black accountant who asked whether blacks had rights in South Africa ("No," he said he replied, "but we're working on it"); the farmer from the Transvaal who somehow got separated from $1,500 at a bar called the Mardi Gras off Times Square in Manhattan; the Cabinet minister's son-in-law who exploded with loathing of American decadence in order, or so it seemed, to cover the tension and guilt he felt after an afternoon at a pornographic movie house. Colonel van der Linde himself had not felt undermined by New York but had liked it for good reasons: the mixture of people, the smart way they dressed, the verve, the pace of life.

"You know, I should never have said that thing to you about hitting the boys," he remarked with the same good humor. "That was the old way. There are farmers who still do it—my neighbor over there does —but they are the farmers who can't keep their labor."

Old Sam had died and been buried on the farm while the colonel was on active duty with his tank corps in Namibia. In 1965 he told me he had four families that had been on his farm for more than twenty years and six that had been there for more than ten. Now there were twenty-five families in all, about 120 individuals, but fewer old hands. The old feudal relationship was less attractive to blacks. He gestured to the east to show me a cause of their increased mobility. There, like an extrusion of living substance, of protoplasm from some giant amoeboid growth, a dense human settlement could be seen extending over the nearest hillside. It hadn't been there eighteen years ago, or even five years ago, but it was already the biggest black settlement in the Orange Free State with a population approaching a quarter of a million, and it was sopping up the surplus population from the farms because it had at least opened the door to the theoretical possibility of menial employment in Bloemfontein, thirty-five miles away. Onverwacht it had been named initially after one of the white farms the authorities had hurriedly purchased when they realized that the only way to avoid the infiltration of Bloemfontein's nearer black townships by so-called illegals was to start a new settlement.

Onverwacht means "unexpected" in Afrikaans. Colonel van der Linde, at least, hadn't expected it, but it was now less than two miles, at its nearest point, from his land, occupying roughly the same amount of space he did. In between was a large dam, functioning as a kind of moat, and on that dam this Saturday morning young whites were windsurfing and speedboating in a segregated recreation area that was fenced off from the black settlement. No lens could quite capture the picture, but it was the image of South Africa: in the foreground, the rich white farm; at a middle distance, the water sports, also for whites; in the background but clearly visible across the veld, the overcrowded black settlement in all its squalor. As one of the top officers in the reserve force in the Free State, my host must have been familiar with the contingency plans the military and police would have drawn up to keep Onverwacht within its designated perimeters; he did not appear to be worried. But he realized he would now have to be competitive in wages and living conditions to keep his laborers. There is a regulation that bars black farm workers from urban employment unless they can produce written approval by the white farmers' union in their area, but Colonel van der Linde was not going to rely on that. Already he had two brick houses built for his most valuable laborers, replacing the traditional mud shanties in which they had always been left to house themselves. It was just the start, he said.

The living conditions in his own house had changed more conspicuously than those of his workers. I dimly recalled being struck by the sparse furnishings of the brick farmhouse on that first visit, especially by the presence of a new refrigerator in the dining room as if it were a luxury to be shown off. Now there was a color TV, a videocassette recorder, an elaborate stereo system, an electric organ, and a liquor cabinet. The Van der Lindes had skipped several generations in taste. Their living room was smartly furnished with a sofa and matching chairs in brown velvet. On the walls, there were ceramic plates from Greece. But as her husband poured Boschendal blanc de noir, Mrs. van der Linde confided that she had not liked Greece. "It's so poor," she said. "So dirty." Later I asked whether she had ever been to the settlement next door. It was like asking a hostess on East End Avenue in Manhattan whether she has ever been to Spanish Harlem. She grimaced and said no.

The colonel then told a story on himself, how he had lost his temper after being stopped by a black traffic cop for entering a black township without a permit. But as he told it, its point seemed to undergo a subtle change. Originally, I guessed, it had been a yarn about the "cheekiness" of a black officer and the way embarrassed white officials were then made to jump through hoops to placate an influential farmer with impressive connections in the military, the party, the government, and (if they bothered to check the membership list included as an appendix to an exposé published a few years ago) the secret society of Afrikaners known as the Broederbond that is pledged to "the eternal existence of a separate Afrikaner nation." In defiance of the black officer's orders to halt, the colonel had roared away and then phoned "someone very high up," who assured him that blacks were not supposed to give summonses to whites, that they were expected to call a white officer if they thought there was a problem. But now, as he reached that point in his narrative, the colonel seemed a little uncertain about where to put his comic emphasis. Maybe he was thinking about how it would sound in New York or how he might have had to tell the story to his accountant friend in Milwaukee. Anyway, a small critical voice seemed to be warning him to tread carefully. Improvising a new punch line and laughing at himself, he conceded that he had probably been in the wrong. "The real fight," he said with unimpaired good humor, "is the one you have with yourself."

He sounded just as flexible when he reflected on the history of his people. "You can argue about history, whether the Great Trek was really necessary, or the Anglo-Boer War, or whether we were wrong in 1948, when we brought in apartheid," he said. "But you can't change it. That's reality. We must do what's right now." On its face it seemed a startling reflection for a farmer in the Free State, where blacks had never been permitted to own land since white authority was first established and where Indians, supposed beneficiaries of the new reform, were barred from residing under any circumstances. But as I thought about it, it became less startling. It wasn't really so different from what he had said in 1965, that "the white man won't get the benefits of doing right by the native if his only motive is self-preservation." Basically it was a case of if at first you don't succeed: He had been doing right by his lights for a generation and he had certainly reaped the benefits, and what was new on the horizon was Onverwacht.

By road the entrance to the settlement was twenty-five miles from the Van der Linde homestead; in a straight line it was probably about eight. Since my previous visit to Onverwacht, the part that could be seen from the highway had received a Potemkinesque face-lift. There were bright new hoardings, metal sheds for what was said to be an industrial park, and rows of model houses. There was also a paved road with tall curved lighting fixtures lining it, but the paving and lights stopped abruptly almost as soon as the road wound out of sight from the highway. The biggest expanse of population was about six miles in, where there were rows on rows of little metal latrines awaiting the next influx. In the older sections, those that had been there for two or three years, cinder-block houses of a reasonable standard were regularly interspersed among the metal hovels and shanties; in the newer sections it was shanties all the way. It could have been a refugee camp in Pakistan, Honduras, Eritrea, or anywhere poor and "third world," a term white South Africans have come to use routinely to describe the black areas of their country. As a metaphor it beats "homelands" because it says they are not only in another country but in another world; cholera epidemics or children dying of hunger in a wealthy land are not therefore a disgrace but examples of chronic "third world" problems. South Africa can even be pictured as a "microcosm" of the whole North-South dichotomy, an image that provides several kinds of psychic balm: The whites can identify themselves then with the first world, which they tend to think of in racial terms; they can find support for the view that their country's problems are not susceptible to short-term resolution or even assert, as a Cabinet minister once did, that South Africa (meaning the mythical white country) was forking up more aid to the third world (meaning the majority of its people) than any other developed country.

It is only an argument meant to stifle other arguments, a debating point rather than an insight, but it can sound a little plausible until you drive into an Onverwacht. Many third world countries have irresponsible oligarchies that have as little conscience about their landless and unemployed as South Africa's white elites; sometimes, in truth, much less. But none of them, while preaching reform, creates refugee camps in the midst of prosperity as a matter of state policy. The people in the shanties I was passing were there not because they were poor but because they were black; no amount of money could legally purchase for them the right to move the thirty-five miles into Bloemfontein or a piece of land to till nearer at hand. I drove on until I could look back across the dam to the Van der Linde farm, where I had been sipping blanc de noir an hour before. It was midafternoon, but the light was failing rapidly as in an eclipse, and I could barely make it out. When I turned around, I saw that the northern sky had taken on a deep and ominous terra-cotta color. The drought had made the Free State vulnerable to dust storms, and valuable topsoil was now swirling up hundreds of yards into the sky in great, gritty clouds that were gusting toward Onverwacht and the Van der Linde farm without distinction.

A young couple I had seen walking hand in hand as I drove into the settlement were huddling against each other and walking backward into the wind as I drove out. Before I reached the highway, I had to turn on my headlights. Again I found myself thinking that it was over the top, that the dust storm was exactly what the producer of a second-rate TV documentary might have seized on for his fade-out on such a day. But I had grown mistrustful of all South African metaphors. The thought of an inevitable catastrophe was frightening, but even more frightening was the thought that it could be indefinitely deferred, that the whites would go on windsurfing and trying to do right, the blacks would go on moving into squalid encampments, and the dust storms would just be dust storms.

CHAPTER 4

■

RULE OF LAW

I t's time to talk law. Where other regimes have no difficulty
tyrannizing their citizens under the cloak of constitutions guaranteeing
universal human rights, South Africa's white rulers have been unusually
conscientious about securing statutory authority for their abuses.
When a right, even a birthright, such as citizenship, is to be annulled,
it is always done with a law. Most whites are uncomprehending of the
argument that law is brought into disrepute when it is used to destroy
habeas corpus, the presumption of innocence, equality before the law,
and various other basic freedoms. Law is law. It's the principle of order
and therefore of civilization, the antithesis advanced by the white man
to what he knows as a matter of tribal lore, his own, to be Africa's
fundamental thesis: anarchy. Excessive liberty, in his view, is what
threatens civilization; law is what preserves it. The opposing view that
law might preserve liberty is thus held to be a contradiction; in Africa,
a promise of surrender. On this basis it has been possible to build
apartheid not simply as the sum of various kinds of segregation, or the
disenfranchisement of the majority, but as a comprehensive system of
racial dominance. A decade after the South African authorities announced their intention to move away from "hurtful and unnecessary
discrimination," I thought I would get the feel of the basic statutes by
holding them in my hands as you might if you were apprizing an
eggplant or a melon. Some laws, especially those reserving the best
industrial jobs for whites, had been repealed. Others, such as the
Prohibition of Mixed Marriages Act, seemed destined for repeal as part
of a calculated effort to lower the level of ignominy attaching to the
system. I wanted to feel, literally to weigh, what remained.

What remained weighed slightly more than ten pounds when I

stepped on a scale with an up-to-date volume of all the laws in South Africa that relate specifically to blacks—laws, that is, that can normally be broken only by blacks (or by persons of other racial groups only when they interfere with the state's master plan for blacks). The figure of ten pounds had to be halved immediately because the volume of 4,500 pages contained both the Afrikaans and English versions of sixty-four basic statutes that regulate the lives of blacks. These then amounted to about 2,250 closely printed pages, weighing about five pounds. But the small print that followed the statutes indicated that they had given rise to some 2,000 regulations, adding two or three pounds at least. These, in turn, would have given rise to hundreds or maybe thousands of official circulars that were not in the public domain but were treated as law by the officials who regulate blacks. And that was only the racial law for blacks. There were also laws, regulations, and circulars for coloreds and Indians, running to hundreds of additional pages and another couple of pounds. And there were the laws, regulations, and circulars relating to the administration of the Group Areas Act, the basic statute guaranteeing absolute residential segregation. Gathering all the materials for a precise weighing was more than I could manage; but the basic corpus of South African racial law still ran to more than 3,000 pages, and when all the regulations and circulars were added in, its dead weight was bound to be well over ten pounds. Apartheid was not wasting away. For argument's sake, there was enough of it left to give someone a concussion. And this still did not include the mass of draconian security laws and the other legislation restricting political association and expression, which are certainly oppressive but not as distinctively South African.

Of course, the impact of apartheid cannot be measured in pounds. A South African Gogol may contrive a way someday to measure it in "dead souls." But I could measure it only by trying to witness the system in operation, at the points where it impinges on individual lives, especially in the mazelike structure of courts and official bureaus it has established to channel black laborers in and out of areas of economic opportunity while minimizing their chances of establishing permanent residence with their families. If this structure were suddenly dismantled, if whites stopped regulating black lives, there would still be migrant workers by the hundreds of thousands in South Africa and millions of impoverished blacks. There would still be wealthy suburbs, huge ranches, black townships, and squalid rural areas. But it would then be possible to think of the society as a whole and talk rationally about its needs. Apartheid ensures that the language for such a discussion hardly exists. It does so for its own cunning reasons. Once you think of the society as a whole, it is impossible not to think of the distribution of land—50,000 white farmers have twelve times as much land for cultivation and grazing as 14 million rural blacks—or of the need to relieve the pressure in those portions of the countryside that have been systematically turned into catchment areas for surplus black population.

If South Africa were viewed as one country, it might be possible to recognize a glaring fact about its social geography: the existence of an almost continuous scimitar-shaped belt of black rural poverty, stretching for more than 1,000 miles from the northeastern Transvaal through the Swazi and Zulu tribal areas and down into the two "homelands" for Xhosa-speaking blacks in the eastern Cape, a belt that is inhabited by about 7 million people, amounting to nearly 30 percent of the black population. Instead, in the layered, compartmentalized consciousness that apartheid insidiously shapes, these blacks are dispersed in Venda, Gazankulu, Lebowa, KwaZulu, Transkei, and Ciskei: foreign places, hard to find on maps, another galaxy.

In apartheid's terms, it is revolutionary or at least eccentric to think of this band of poverty as South Africa's problem. Apartheid thus raises the stakes, deliberately compounding mass rural poverty in order to preserve white privilege and power. It is the ultimate divide-and-rule strategy, dividing the land into racially designated areas and bogus homelands and the population into distinct racial castes and subcastes of which I can count at least eight: the whites, who are free to do anything except move into an area designated as nonwhite; the coloreds and Indians, who can move freely in the country but are barred from owning land in more than 95 percent of it; and the blacks, who are subdivided by law into six distinct impermeable or semipermeable categories.

The broad distinction between urban and rural blacks is only the beginning of this process of alienation. The urban blacks come in two subcastes: the "insiders," as they are now sometimes called, and the "commuters." The insiders are conceded to have a certain immunity to arbitrary expulsion, amounting to a right of permanent residence in what is acknowledged to be South Africa. The circumstances of the urban commuters appear to be exactly the same, except that the townships in which they reside are now deemed, as a result of gerrymandering, to fall within the boundaries of some homeland. Although they may be only a short bus ride from a South African city such as Pretoria, Durban, or East London, no farther than the blacks of Soweto are from Johannesburg, they are regarded by South African law as foreign or on their way to becoming foreign. But such commuters can still get "special" licenses of limited duration making them "authorized work seekers" in an urban area.

This means they are still far better off than a second group of commuters who must be regarded as a separate subcaste because they commute to the industrial centers from homeland areas that remain essentially rural. These rural commuters are on a distinctly lower level of the hierarchy, but it can be argued that they are the most privileged or, rather, least abused of the four distinguishable subcastes of rural blacks. The rural commuters generally travel much longer distances to work than the urban commuters, live in officially designated "closer settlements" without such amenities as running water or electricity, rather than organized townships, and get their jobs through the state's network of labor bureaus. They generally work on annual contracts like migrant laborers, but at least they come home to their families at nights and on weekends.

The migrants, the next subcaste, live in urban townships or on the mines and sugar plantations in barrackslike single-sex hostels, usually for eleven months of every year; it is theoretically possible for some of them to acquire a right of urban residence after ten or fifteen years but practically impossible for them to acquire a house in which to exercise it.

Blacks who live in the white rural areas as farm laborers make up the next subcaste; by tradition they receive more of their compensation in kind—sacks of mealie (corn) meal usually—than in cash, but wages are gradually coming into vogue. And finally, there are the homeland blacks, who live their whole lives in the black rural areas. Of these, a tiny elite is employed by the homeland governments as officials, teachers, or police; others are employed as menials. But overall the former tribal reserves provide gainful employment for fewer than 20 percent of the young blacks reared within their borders, only 12 percent, according to a statistic let slip by a white Cabinet minister who was trying to counter extremist arguments during a political campaign that too much was done for blacks. The rest of the homeland blacks—those who cannot become migrants themselves—are mainly dependent on the wages of migrants, or scratch out a meager existence as subsistence cultivators on exhausted soil, or are unemployed and wholly destitute. The life-threatening protein deficiency known as kwashiorkor and the starvation condition known as marasmus are endemic among children in this group. Reliable statistics are spotty, but in some black rural areas in a country that has been aptly described as the Saudi Arabia of minerals, it appears that scarcely 50 percent of the children who are alive at birth survive past the age of five.

A lopsided social structure is not peculiar to South Africa. What is peculiar is the fact that it is legally mandated and rigorously imposed on the basis of race. It is impossible to change caste without an official appeals board ruling that you are a different color from what you were originally certified to be. These miraculous transformations are tabulated and announced on an annual basis. In my first year back in South Africa, 558 coloreds became whites, 15 whites became coloreds, 8 Chinese became whites, 7 whites became Chinese, 40 Indians became coloreds, 20 coloreds became Indians, 79 Africans became coloreds, and 8 coloreds became Africans. The spirit of this grotesque self-parody, which results from the deliberations of an official body known as the Race Classification Board, is obviously closer to Grand Guignol than the Nuremberg Laws; in other words, it's sadistic farce. "Look, man, it's all a game, it's all a big joke," I was assured once by a Cape Town colored who had managed to get himself reclassified as a white, a transformation sometimes described in Afrikaans by the term *verblankingsproses* ("whitening process").

"When you're in Rome," the man said, "what are you? A bloody German? Hell, no, you're a Roman! Self-preservation is the only rule."

The legal definitions that attach to the various categories of racial caste are vague, overlapping, and sometimes contradictory. A white, by one of the definitions, is "any person who in appearance obviously is or who is generally accepted as a white person, other than a person who, although in appearance obviously a white person, is generally accepted as a colored person." In other words, a rose is a rose is maybe not a rose. "A colored person," this same statute holds, is "any person who is not a member of the white group or of the black group."* But a colored

---

*Unless, of course, he is an Indian, who may be the same color but is legally set apart on the basis of ethnicity, most of the time, anyhow.

can also be any woman "to whichever race, class or tribe she may belong" who marries a colored man, or a white man who marries a colored woman. Mixed marriages may have been illegal throughout the apartheid era—as they were, lest we forget, in a majority of American states within living memory—but even when the South African law prohibiting them is finally repealed, there will still be this other racial statute to bar mixed couples from living in white areas.

Apartheid never concerned itself with mixed marriages between browns and blacks. They remained legal. It was only the white race that had to be preserved. Carel Boshoff, a theology professor at Pretoria University and son-in-law of Hendrik Verwoerd, informed me as if it were a matter of incontrovertible fact that a group could be diluted by 6 or 7 percent and still maintain its "identity." In fact, Afrikaner researchers in this esoteric field have concluded that 6.9 percent is the probable proportion of "colored blood" in their veins. Racism, it then may be deduced, is no more than 93.1 percent of their doctrine. Nevertheless, classification remains the essence of the system. No one —least of all a black—has the right to classify himself as simply a South African. Thus the single most important determinant of status and rights in South Africa remains the accident of birth. Most white South Africans would dispute this assertion, but then most white South Africans have insulated themselves from any knowledge of how the system works.

Viewed even on its own terms, South African racial law is the opposite of elegant. It is not a body of law really but a tangle of legalisms designed to maximize the power of officialdom and minimize the defenses of the individual, a labyrinth of words the meanings of which are determined by the white functionaries who administer it. Thus blacks are either "qualified" or "disqualified" for residence in "prescribed" urban areas. Even if they are "qualified," they must have "authorized accommodation" in which only their "bona fide dependents" are eligible to live. Officials qualify, disqualify, authorize, and prescribe, and ultimately decide what all these terms mean. Even if she is "bona fide," a wife can be "disqualified" simply because the authorities have not chosen to "authorize" an accommodation. It is a crime for a "disqualified" black to be in a "prescribed" area for longer than seventy-two hours. Definitions and statistics are elastic, impossible to pin down, but it is indisputable that most of the land is "prescribed" and most blacks are "disqualified." The definition of a "qualified" person is revised every few years, but the most recent version provides a fair sense of the status of the most privileged blacks in South Africa today. According to the Black (Urban Areas) Consolidation Act,

> [A "qualified person"] means a Black referred to in section 10 (1) (a) or (b) who is not a Black referred to in section 12 (1), and any descendant of such a Black who is a Black referred to in section 10 (1) (a) or (b), and . . . also any Black who is not a qualified person but falls within a category of blacks recognized by the Minister by notice in the Gazette as qualified persons for the purposes of section 6A and 6B and the regulations relating thereto, or who has in any particular case been expressly recognized by the Minister as a qualified person for such purposes, as well as any person who has in general or in any particular case been expressly recognized by the Minister, subject to such conditions as may be determined by the Minister, as a qualified person for said purposes: Provided that the said conditions may also provide that a person shall be recognized for a particular purpose or for a particular period or until the occurrence of a particular event only.

Some South Africans speak of blacks with "residence rights" in urban areas, but the term "rights" appears nowhere in the law. The most privileged blacks have a limited, conditional immunity to arbitrary actions that all other blacks must endure. Even then, they can be removed if some official deems them to be "idle and undesirable." The law provides that "the onus of proof" that a black is legally in an urban area "shall be on the accused." It provides, too, that "a Black who is at any time found in any building under any circumstances giving rise to a reasonable suspicion that he resides in that building shall be deemed to reside there." That reasonable suspicion is enough to send him to jail if he fails to prove that his presence has been "authorized." The proof must be recorded in his reference book, the domestic passport all blacks over sixteen are required to carry when they are in "prescribed" areas. Failure to have the reference book, or failure to produce it, normally means jail. No writs are required for this inspection. It can happen to any black, anywhere, anytime, including in his own home in the middle of the night. The law says flatly: "Any authorized person may at any time call upon any Black to produce to him a reference book."

In addition to his legal status, the reference book must spell out the circumstances of a black person's employment. "No person shall employ any Black if it appears from such Black's reference book," the law says, "that he entered into a contract of service with some other person and such other person has not recorded in such book . . . the fact that such contract has terminated." In effect, a black needs his employer's permission to quit; if he is not a "qualified person," his right to be in the "prescribed area" will end automatically with his job. Finally, a law called the National States Citizenship Act requires that all blacks be designated as citizens of one or the other black "national states," even if they have never lived in them or seen them. The decision on which state a black will have his citizenship in can be made by "any officer or person designated by the Minister," and "it shall be binding on that Black person and the territorial authority concerned." The implication of this provision was spelled out in 1978 by a Cabinet minister who looked forward to the day when all the black states would have accepted the ambiguous sovereignty South Africa offers and who pointed out that then, "There will not be one black man with South African citizenship." Four of the ten black states are already held to be sovereign, and as a result, their supposed citizens—all but the youngest of whom were citizens of South Africa by birth and most of whom still reside in what is held to be South Africa—are vulnerable to deportation under the Admission of Persons to the Republic Regulation Act without right of appeal.

Those are some of the basics of South African racial law. There are plenty of wrinkles. Heedless of overkill, the legal draftsmen have sought to arm the multiple white bureaucracies with powers of control in just about any circumstance in which blacks might seek to act of their own volition in a white area.* Blacks and browns have never had anything to do with shaping this code. And even though this is supposed to be a period of "reform" in South Africa, enforcement of the laws relating to the entry of blacks to "prescribed" areas has been made steadily

---

*In what other professedly Christian country, to cite a relatively obscure example, could you find a law restricting Christian worship? In South Africa the danger of uncontrolled black worship in white areas has been fully anticipated. The Black (Urban Areas) Consolidation Act provides that "the Minister may by notice in the Gazette direct that the attendance by Blacks at any church or other religious service or church function on premises situated within any urban area outside a Black residential area shall cease from a date specified . . . and any Black who in contravention of a direction under this paragraph attends any church or other religious service or church function shall be guilty of an offense." The provision is seldom, if ever, enforced against established white congregations that admit blacks to worship, but it ensures that there can be no black churches in areas deemed to be white.

more stringent. There are two apparent reasons. The first has to do with security: The tighter the controls, the more computerized information there is on what blacks are "authorized" to be where, the easier it is to trace infiltrators dispatched by underground movements. The other has to do with politics: Should it prove impossible to achieve the ideal and make all blacks foreigners, then political rights of some description may have to be conceded to blacks in urban areas that cannot be fitted into a homeland, making it all the more crucial, in the calculations of official planners, that there be as few blacks as possible who are even potentially eligible for those rights. "Reform," in other words, means stricter controls for most blacks.

At the same time the authorities try to avoid brutalizing those with whom they are trying to make tactical alliances across the color line based on common class interests: coloreds, Indians, middle-class blacks. The law actually provides that reference books may be issued with covers of different colors so the police can tell at a glance when they are dealing with a black—a clergyman, perhaps, or physician or functionary within the apartheid system—who should be handled with common courtesy. But the system cannot refrain from functioning like a system, from crushing and humiliating those it is supposed to entice. A brown-skinned person may now be allowed to cast a ballot for persons of the same racial classification, who will then sit in a segregated chamber of Parliament, where they can always be outvoted by the separate white chamber, but neither the brown-skinned representatives nor the voters can legally reside in an area that has been proclaimed "white" under the Group Areas Act. In the major cities it is only in such areas that there is readily available housing, for white greed and white fear combine to ensure that there is a permanent shortage of housing for browns and blacks. The law is then broken by the very people the ruling white elite has identified as potential allies, the upwardly mobile coloreds and Indians who move into white fringe neighborhoods, where, because of their legal vulnerability, they pay exorbitant rents for deteriorating dwellings. For this criminal act they are charged by the section of the police detailed to follow up any anonymous complaint of a nonwhite breaching white residential citadels.

It happened every day in Johannesburg. Cheryl and Michael Noel were the sort of people who turn up in the advertisements South Africa puts in *The Wall Street Journal* and the *Financial Times* of London to show the new opportunities opening up for nonwhites under the revised labor laws. Their values were indistinguishable from those whites with whom they brushed shoulders at work or in the shops, but they had experienced a kind of desperation that whites couldn't imagine. So, although they were not politically involved or militant, they were full, when I met them, of the pure, moral revulsion the powerless are forced to swallow when they hear the deceitful rationalizations of the powerful. You could call it disgust.

Michael Noel was a skilled artisan in a plant that built armored personnel carriers for the South African Army. If he had been white and born in the English midlands, his company would have paid him to emigrate to South Africa and would have established him in a comfortable home. Since he had been born brown in Durban, it took no responsibility for his housing. Cheryl Noel held a supervisory position at Barclays Bank, which would have given her a mortgage on favorable terms but could do nothing to help her find a house or piece of land she would be eligible to occupy under the law. So the Noels were living illegally in a grubby one-room apartment in Hillbrow, where their rent had been raised three times in eight months and their complaints about a clogged toilet ignored. They were also facing criminal charges under the Group Areas Act. Ismail and Marlene Jeena had virtually the same story. He was a garage manager. She was a clerk in an insurance company. They had lived in five Hillbrow apartments in five years, staying just a jump ahead of the Group Areas police until finally they were charged.

"We are not living here because we want to be white," Cheryl Noel said.

"We don't care where we live as long as we live happy," Michael Noel said.

"I've got insurance policies. I've got everything in a straight line of living for a normal human being," Ismail Jeena said. "I can afford to buy a house or a plot, and I'm South African-born. Do I have to be a criminal for no reason at all?"

The minister of law and order condemned those who make *strydpunte* ("strife points," or issues) out of little *knelpunte* ("pinch points," or predicaments) like these. They were hostile to the state, he said. But it is the state that does the pinching, that hauls people into court on the basis of race and there harangues and cross-examines them to make them confess that in their search for livelihood or shelter they had become criminals. Cynthia Freeman had white skin, blond hair, and blue eyes, but as the daughter of a white father and a colored mother, she was classified colored. When she moved to Johannesburg from Natal, she lived in a hostel for coloreds, then moved into a Hillbrow apartment, where she stayed for a time with a white man, who left her with a baby that also looked white. Her employers, a small construction company specializing in swimming pools, presumed her to be white. When she was charged under the Group Areas Act, she did not deny her racial classification but partly rested her defense on a loophole discovered by her lawyer, who contended that the definition of "colored" in the law under which she was charged was different from that of the classification system. As a person who was obviously white and generally accepted as white she met its racial standard, he said. She had a necessity to house herself and her child, he also maintained, and could not be convicted if no other housing was available.

In rebutting those arguments, the prosecutor had no choice but to expose the contempt and racism inherent in the system. His tone was derisive, inquisitorial, unapologetic. Why hadn't she moved back into the colored hostel? he wanted to know. "I've got the child to see to," she testified, "and I can't stay in a hostel with a child and I've got the furniture. I need a home for my child." But there was a hotel in a colored area called Bosmont, the prosecutor persisted. Why hadn't she moved there?

"I never tried," she said.

"So you didn't make the necessary enquiries?"

There was no response from the witness. "I'd like an answer, Miss Freeman," the prosecutor said.

"No," she replied lamely, "there are so many people looking for a place, I'm sure it would be full."

The prosecutor then got her to concede that she had applied for official permission to stay in the white area and had been refused. "So even after the reply you still stayed in the flat," he continued.

"Yes, I had no option."

"You had an option, Miss Freeman."

"I had no option."

"You had the hotel."

"I had the hotel," she acknowledged with a bitter laugh that sounded in the courtroom like a cry of pain.

That disposed of the argument of necessity. There was still the argument that she was obviously white. "Miss Freeman, as what do you classify yourself?" the prosecutor began.

"As far as I go around, I have always been accepted as white."

"I'm talking about yourself as a person. As what do you classify yourself?" Obviously the thought that a South African woman might not choose to classify herself had never occurred to the state's lawyer. Perhaps it had never occurred, either, to Cynthia Freeman who replied, "I classify myself as white, although I have been classified as colored officially."

"You classify yourself as white?"

"Yes, even my little boy."

But she had acknowledged, the prosecutor noted, that coloreds and Indians had moved into her apartment building in the white area. Why, he asked, projecting his own racial feelings, would she allow her little boy to live in a building inhabited by coloreds and Indians if she really regarded him as white? "I have nowhere else to go," she answered. But if she were really white, the prosecutor insisted, she could do what other whites do and move into a building occupied by whites only.

"I haven't got the money to move regularly," she said.

"And if you had the money?"

"Then maybe I would."

But then why did she have colored friends? Surely by her choice of associates, the prosecutor implied, she was betraying her genes in one sense or another. Real whites, he seemed to be saying, associated only with whites.

"I am a Christian."

"I'm not talking about your Christianity now."

"I went because I am a Christian, and as far as Christianity is concerned, everybody is alike. So whoever I visited is immaterial to me."

"Are you aware of the laws of this country?" the prosecutor asked, rhetorically throwing a roundhouse swing that seemed to catch himself on the jaw.

Finally the case turned on the flatness of Miss Freeman's nose, the position of her cheekbones, and whether her hair was really blond. The defendant said her nose had been injured in an accident and had required stitches.

"Just stitches?"

"Yes."

"That's all?"

A professor from Witwatersrand University testified that he could find no reference in the "anthropological literature" to high cheekbones as "a diagnostic criterion to indicate race" and that anyway, Cynthia Freeman's didn't strike him as particularly high. The prosecutor got him to acknowledge that the Race Classification Board had never sought his opinion. So therefore, he implied, the professor's credentials as an expert were in doubt.

Cynthia Freeman testified that her hair was naturally blond. Then why didn't she go to white hairdressers? the prosecutor wanted to know. Wasn't it really that she was afraid that they would recognize her as a colored and refuse to serve her?

Weighing up all these delicate points in a twelve-page opinion, the magistrate concluded that while the defendant's hair was probably natural, her nose was definitely flat and her cheekbones were high. "From the Court's observations," he declared, "it was obvious from the Accused's features that she was not obviously white." That is such a many-faceted gem of jurisprudence that it commands magnification: *obviously not obviously white!* "She could pass for white," this oracle declared, "but she was not obviously white." Moreover, she had not appealed to the Race Classification Board to be reclassified as white. She was therefore guilty as charged and given a sentence of fifty days in jail, to be suspended on condition that she move out of her apartment and out of the white area.

Cynthia Freeman's judicial humiliation was one of apartheid's lesser atrocities, one of the gross titillations that are a recurring feature of South African life. Edward Crankshaw had a similar sort of excess in mind when he wrote that the "sheer frivolities" of the bureaucratic system in Russia contributed more ultimately to the undoing of the czar's autocracy than did its brutalities. Perhaps the same will one day be said of the apartheid regime, which repeatedly brings itself into disrepute with potential allies by arbitrarily victimizing individuals it might just as well have left alone. But Cynthia Freeman still had her livelihood and might even acquire a vote, if she thought it would do her any good. She remained in the second tier of the racial hierarchy, more privileged than any black.

The fairest way to view the streamlined apartheid system, to understand the meaning and limitations of the claims made for "reform," is to consider the circumstances and attitudes of its black beneficiaries, the industrial elite of a disenfranchised mass. This elite has not been freed from the racial caste system but promoted within it. Its members are able, finally, to join trade unions that have the same legal standing as the ones whites join. The law makes collective bargaining with black trade unions optional for employers, and more than 80 percent, perhaps 90 percent, of black industrial workers are without representation. Still, the system has allowed an identifiable black power base to come into existence and left it room to grow. Blacks are no longer barred by law from the best industrial jobs. And they can even purchase a leasehold on houses and land in their segregated townships, those among them, at least, who are regarded as permanent urban residents. The difference between leasehold and freehold is usually said —by white would-be reformers, that is—to be merely symbolic in that it is of little practical difference to the black homeowner who is finally being permitted to develop an equity where he was once said to be a "temporary sojourner." But what it symbolizes is not trivial. The reason he cannot own land in what is deemed to be South Africa the way whites and browns can is that South Africa is not deemed to be his country.

Nevertheless, the not inconsiderable adjustments that have been made enable the major South African industrial groups, such as Anglo American and Barlow Rand, to emulate the American and European multinationals that have sought to sanitize their investments by adopting employment codes. Like the multinationals, the major South African companies boast that they are "equal opportunity employers." It's an odd boast because all of them, the South African companies and the multinationals, can appear to avoid discrimination on the basis of race only by practicing the most rigorous discrimination on the basis of racial caste. It is impossible to provide even the appearance of "equal opportunities" to the mass of migrants and "commuters," who are barred from taking advantage of the new housing opportunities. Hiring migrants would mar a carefully cultivated image. Therefore, the most progressive employers refuse to employ migrants. Raising that barrier in the interest of their own public relations, however, means tacitly accepting the official theory that the homeland blacks are fundamentally different, fundamentally foreign. By saying they don't discriminate, these companies mean simply that they try not to discriminate inside the factory gates among the workers they do hire. So toilets are now segregated on the basis of job status rather than race. Usually that amounts to the same thing, but, you are told, it's the thin edge of the wedge.

From the perspective of white managers, the rate of social reform in industry is breathtaking. From the perspective of Timothy Zimu, a black whose life has seemingly been transformed by the new opportunities, it is still the weight of apartheid that takes his breath away and leaves him almost speechless with anger. Only twenty-six when I met him, he had seen his wages triple in five years. His employer, the West German electrical giant Siemens, had given him special training and installed him in a supervisory position. The company hired no migrants, but Timothy Zimu's opportunities for advancement were far from exhausted. He had a color TV, a refrigerator, a stereo system, and a house full of new furniture, which is hardly what the world imagines when it thinks of an oppressed South African black'. He was planning to buy the house and a new car. If he compared his lot to other South African blacks', he was near the pinnacle of the pyramid. But he did not compare himself to other blacks or see himself as a privileged "third world" worker. He compared himself to white industrial workers at Siemens, who always seemed to be a rung or two above him. Most of those whites lived in a Pretoria suburb called East Lynne, which was built years ago on the site of a black township that was razed by bulldozers after it had been officially declared to be "badly situated." Timothy Zimu had spent part of his childhood in that township. He had seen what its destruction had done to his family, which had then been deposited by the state in Mamelodi, the segregated township that was now his home but also, as he experienced it, his prison. This old wound was rubbed daily, for the bus he took from Mamelodi to the Siemens plant and back again passed through East Lynne, where his supposed white peers lived in little ranch houses of a vaguely Southern California style that far outclassed his little brick township house. "If I want to live in East Lynne, I must live in East Lynne," Timothy Zimu said with sudden passion. "And I must get the same wages the people in East Lynne get."

It is not always failure of imagination that keeps most whites from trying to picture the world as it must look to Timothy Zimu. For those who understand that blacks are capable of the same emotions they would have, it is an exercise of will. Others seem to assume that blacks are too simple to see and register the affluence and security in which whites live. The white madam who thinks she is being generous because she pays her maid maybe $20 for a sixty-hour workweek never credits her "girl" with the ability to calculate that she pays her less in a month than she spends on a single trip to the supermarket. Madam never figures that her "girl" tells her brother or her husband or lover how well the whites live, that the level of white privilege is the worst-kept secret in South Africa, a constant source of resentment.

Frank Bartos, an American who came to Johannesburg from Peoria, Illinois, as a representative of the Caterpillar Tractor Company and stayed to manage a major Barlow Rand subsidiary called Wrightech, had the sensitivity to project himself into the circumstances of his most valued black workers. He realized that they might feel frustration even though they were now relatively well paid. He next did something few South African managers ever do: actually went to see how his workers lived in a township called Daveyton, which is in an industrial area known as the East Rand that is to Johannesburg what Hammond, Indiana, is to Chicago. He thought the conditions "horrible," although on the scale of what is normally available to black South Africans, Daveyton was much nearer the best than the worst. Being a doer, Bartos set out to make Wrightech's employees the best-housed black workers in the country. It wasn't only altruism or a recrudescence of Peoria values; he was trying to secure for his company a stable force of skilled black workers. So he put Wrightech solidly behind a development of 108 houses at the edge of Daveyton. The price the workers would have to pay was steep, but these were to be nothing like the tiny township houses they deride as "matchboxes." Bartos assured me, "You'd be happy to live in the houses we're building."

All 108 houses were occupied when I went to visit them a couple of years later. To tell the truth, I would not have been happy to live in them. From the standpoint of design and orientation within the larger community, it should have been possible, I imagined, to have done much better for the same money. But the little ranch houses were certainly decent; in South Africa as well as the United States it would not have been difficult to find white industrial workers in less appealing houses. The coloreds and Indians who were the targets of the racial inquisition in Hillbrow and other white fringe areas would certainly have envied these homes. And by comparison to the rest of Daveyton, with its rows of mass-produced township housing, these were palaces.

Wrightech had gotten a showpiece, and its workers had gotten a little piece of the American dream as it used to be dreamed in Peoria.

But there was a problem that went deeper than design: Wrightech, another company that hires no migrants, had inadvertently invented a new kind of apartheid within apartheid. Its workers now lived together and apart at the edge of the township in a tiny Levittown all their own that was arrayed around two horseshoe-shaped streets, each named after a white corporate official. There was Frank Bartos Crescent and, honoring the company's industrial relations manager, Andre Oosthuizen Crescent. "Tycoons Village," one of the Wrightech householders told me, was the sobriquet with which the development had been tagged in Daveyton's shebeens. The Wrightech workers knew they had made a worthwhile investment, they wanted to believe they had done something important for their families, but they were also apologetic because they knew that their old neighbors were now uncomfortable with them. The feeling, as they sensed it, was that they had been bought, that by moving into Frank Bartos Crescent, they had somehow broken ranks and aligned themselves with white privilege. It was a feeling they could admit to sharing sometimes.

"The people here think of you as somebody pompous," one of the householders said in a voice that was more sorrowful than resentful. "You're identified with whites. You're identified as not pulling your weight. If you're here, you're confined here. All your friends are here. And it's true, you're less likely to take risks." Other Wrightech workers who hadn't gone in on the housing scheme now had enough money to buy cars, furniture, and appliances on credit. The householders were too heavily mortgaged themselves, so they were less mobile than their peers and thus more isolated in their Tycoons Village. The reserve they felt in conversation with other blacks was like the reserve they felt in conversations with coloreds and Indians who worked at Wrightech. Layer on layer, apartheid imposes its own stiff etiquette; while some barriers come down, others go up.

A black doesn't know how to talk to a colored anymore, one of the householders said, unless he knows how the man feels about the new racial franchise he is being offered. If he is planning to use that vote, he has to be regarded as siding with the whites against blacks. "We don't ask and they don't tell," the householder said. Cut off from coloreds, cut off from other blacks, he seemed to feel, in this conversational moment, as if his whole life had shrunk to Wrightech. I asked if he thought he would ever leave Frank Bartos Crescent. He replied by talking about the revolution without using the word. "If something drastic and tragic happens," he said dreamily, "I'd move to Natal. I'm not a Zulu, I'm a Tswana, but I like it there." His remarkable euphemism caught the ambivalence he had been conditioned to feel; he was saying, after all, that if "something drastic and tragic" happened, he would be free to choose where he lived.

Doubly segregated and still disenfranchised, the Wrightech householders represented perhaps the tiniest of the proliferating subcastes. They were the elite of the black industrial elite, and on balance, it seemed, their experience confirmed the calculation that inspires South African businessmen and some Western investors: the possibility that black acquiescence in the status quo, if not active loyalty, may be bought or at least rented on a medium-term lease.

If you know the way, it is less than a half-hour drive from Daveyton to Vosloorus, another of these little apartheid islands that can be found beyond the mine dumps and railway yards in a seemingly illimitable sea of white suburbs. The men's hostel for black industrial workers there offers an instructive contrast with the tiny enclave on Frank Bartos Crescent. The point of the contrast is not in the physical conditions of the hostel, a maze of dilapidated one-story barracks buildings that looks, not inappropriately, like a camp for displaced persons. It may be a squalid, menacing place when judged by third world standards, let alone the affluent standards of white South Africa, but I know places as squalid and certainly more menacing in New York City. The real point is in the human contrast between the black householders and the black hostel dwellers who live with twenty or more men in grubby little cubicles, where the walls are coated with grease from the kerosene stoves the men use to cook their meals and some have to sleep on the floor because there are never enough beds. And the real point of this human contrast is that there is none. The men at Vosloorus and the men in the Daveyton enclave have essentially the same life histories: poor educations interrupted early, menial work in an industrial area for wages that only recently had become more than negligible. Despite all the theories about multiethnic societies that South Africa underwrites or plagiarizes, then pumps out into the world as a smoke screen for a system of racial dominance, they could not be distinguished on an ethnic basis. There were Sothos, Tswanas, and Zulus mixed together in Frank Bartos Crescent; ditto in the Vosloorus hostel. But they had different stamps in their reference books, certifying that they belonged to different legal subcastes. The mechanism of apartheid, designed to limit the number of urban blacks, makes the Daveyton men insiders and the Vosloorus men permanent outsiders.

Though they live their whole working lives in the same East Rand area, working at factories virtually next door to Wrightech or Siemens, the odds are overwhelming that they will never be hired by such supposedly progressive employers, never invited to take part in literacy or training programs, let alone fancy housing schemes. Yet they, too, are near the top of the pyramid of working blacks, beneficiaries despite the suffocating circumstances of their lives of the vaunted "new dispensation" for black labor. They have jobs in the white area, after all, are eligible to join unions, and their wages have risen dramatically. After ten or fifteen years, under the most recent interpretation of the law, they might even earn enough status in the urban area to go out in the job market and try to find better employment, without opening themselves to automatic expulsion to their homelands: a reward beyond the reach of any migrant laborer on the mines or sugar plantations and almost beyond the comprehension of unemployed black youths in rural areas. Yet the Vosloorus blacks don't see themselves as labor aristocrats. They are short, somehow, on gratitude. "We are still living on hungry stomachs," said a member of the black Metal and Allied Workers Union named Robert Mashile whose wages had doubled in three years. He had a little more cash in his pocket, he admitted, but prices had risen steeply; his wife and five children were still in a homeland called Lebowa, and he himself was now in his sixteenth year in the Vosloorus men's hostel. That was his life, and he didn't have a prayer of wresting even a lodger's permit from the apartheid bureaucracy so that he could crowd in with someone else's family in the township. Basically nothing would change.

Yet it was always possible for me to skitter around the base of the pyramid—whenever I thought I had reached the bottom, I came to the brink of a lower depth—and meet intelligent young men who felt for those in Robert Mashile's position the same envy, the same sense that they were standing on the far side of a social abyss, that he would feel for the Wrightech householders; that the householders, in this ever-receding process of alienation that the legally imposed caste system constantly nurtures, feel for the colored and Indian workers who don't have to carry reference books; that the coloreds and Indians are bound to feel for whites. In one of the poorest areas of one of the poorest homelands, a region called eastern Pondoland in Transkei, where there has been less development than there has been in many parts of Bangladesh, I encountered a former mineworker named Jalisi Mjoki walking along a rutted rural road in patched cord jeans and what was once the jacket of a track suit. He was twenty-nine and had lost his job at an Orange Free State gold mine because he had briefly gone AWOL to attend a family funeral. With that blemish on his record, he found it hard to break into the migrant labor system again through the authorized channels. So he went to Durban, the nearest industrial center, where he was now technically a foreigner as a result of Transkei's internationally scorned sovereignty. Of course, he had no authorization to be there, let alone work there.

For five or six weeks he managed to survive, getting work illegally for a day or two a week on building sites. But his employers, mostly Indian businessmen, chased him away whenever the police were in the vicinity, and most of the time he had neither money nor a place to stay. Finally, out of fear and exhaustion, he returned home. An able-bodied, well-spoken young man looking for work in a rich land, he felt hunted. "I'm not used to running away," he said.

I asked if he ever thought about the reasons for his joblessness. "I've thought about this," he replied gravely, "and I think it's because whenever a person leaves a job, there are five or six waiting. I don't know how to solve it, but I think the problem lies with the people who are permanently employed. They should be made to give others a chance." In other words, he was blaming blacks, labor aristocrats like Robert Mashile and Timothy Zimu, rather than the whites who decreed his status in a lower subcaste. This was a tremendous plus for the system, I thought, one of the secrets of its remarkable durability. I don't regard myself as leftist or radical—that is, I generally deplore the consequences of revolutionary fervor as much as I do its causes. I understand, too, that opportunities for employment can diminish very rapidly if there is a sudden collapse of an economic system, that the pie can be reduced to everyone's detriment while it is being divided equitably. In other words, I don't despise the standard arguments for peaceful evolution in South Africa or elsewhere because they are standard. But at that instant I fervently wished that there existed an underground that really knew how to find young men like Jalisi Mjoki and raise their revolutionary consciousness. That night, when I drove out of eastern Pondoland, the sight of a fire burning across a ridge of dry winter grass made me think of the young Mao Zedong in Hunan, who wrote, "A single spark can start a prairie fire." I quoted that fragment of revolutionary history to the young black from Durban who had come along with me as an interpreter, then wisecracked, "It's a shame a single prairie fire can't start a spark."

If Jalisi Mjoki had been "authorized to seek work" in a white area, he would have been expected to confine his seeking to an official labor bureau, a kind of commodity exchange where black labor is traded on the basis of supply and demand. A prospective white employer is expected to fill in a form headed "Registration of Vacancy/Application for Labor." He can even phone in the request, offering work of any duration, at any pay. Given the inexhaustible supply, there are bound to be takers. On a summer day at Park Rynie, a quiet retirement community on the Indian Ocean, I was permitted to leaf through the latest batch of these forms in an office that looked out through a protective wire screen on an open enclosure where the "work seekers" waited. This is what I found: the Sugarlands Butchery offering $15.75 a week for a black who was "clean and bright"; a suburban homeowner bidding $42 a month for a "house boy" who "must be clean and not fat"; the Summer Sands Hotel looking for a cleaning man who "must be prepared to work very hard on the night shift" for $97 a month. The words "very hard" had been heavily underscored. The Post Office in Durban had phoned in its request for sixty men to dig trenches for telephone cables, a job that would last for six weeks and pay $3.60 a day. Another resort hotel, seeking a "bedroom boy" at $96 a month, required not only that he have "a little English" but that he "must be well-built." A liquor store needed a "boy" of "sober habits"; a laundry, a "boy" who "must not be young." A factory was ready to pay $150 a month for a security guard able to speak English and Afrikaans.

"We are doing a lot of good," a white administrator named Hennie Venter said that day. He was wearing the summer uniform of his caste, a leisure suit with a short-sleeved tunic, in his case, pea green with little black checks. It was time for a little popular ethnology, the inevitable destination of conversations between men in his line of work, I found, and a foreigner who could not be expected to have a handle on racial subtleties. "The black is economical subsistence-oriented," he said. "Western man looks to the future; the black lives for the day." The reporter mildly remarked that this stereotype seemed in South Africa to have the force of law, that it was not only what the system expected of most blacks but what it required. "If a system is working," Hennie Venter said cheerfully, "why not let it work?"

It was put as a reasonable man's question, in a reasonable man's voice. The office in which we were sitting would have looked much the same if it were in a welfare center in New York or a vocational training center there or a narcotics rehabilitation program: all efforts at containment, a shrewd South African visitor might conclude. There Hennie Venter's co-workers would not have been invariably white, nor his clients invariably black, but the civil servant's sense of being unappreciated, beleaguered, engaged in work that was possibly worthwhile and at least necessary or unavoidable would have set much the same tone of bland self-justification. In New York, however, Hannah Arendt's resonant phrase "the banality of evil" would probably not have floated into a visitor's mind. In Durban it seemed exactly right, more clearly apposite in this setting than it was when she applied it to Adolf Eichmann in Jerusalem.

The afternoon wound up in a large labor bureau called Prospecton, which is just down the road from the Toyota assembly plant in an industrial area south of Durban. There the pen where the "work seekers" waited was big enough to be turned into a skating rink. It was late afternoon, just before the close of business, and trading on the floor of the exchange had gone slack, but there were still 120 or 150 men sitting on benches, in case some work turned up. Normally, I was told, it was a black functionary who appeared at the window with the wire screen to select the candidate for a job. Supposedly workers were chosen on the basis of their qualifications, on which they had already been graded, and how long they had been waiting. I asked a white official whether there wasn't an inevitable temptation of bribery in such circumstances. The question did not make him defensive. "It happens in every line of work," he said unconcernedly. "You wouldn't understand, but it's part of their culture. When you go to see your chief to get a ruling, you must give him a lamb or a goat. They say, 'You must open the chief's mouth.' " If the black functionary who picked the candidates for a job had his eyes opened in this manner with cash, I wondered, was he expected to give a cut to white officials out of respect for their grasp of his traditions? Could that be part of *their* tradition? I would have been stretching my luck to ask that question. I could not have expected a candid answer, but I thought I knew what it might be.

What turned up on this afternoon behind the wire screen was my white face when I peered out from the inner office to take in the scene. Immediately there was a commotion among the "work seekers," men on their feet, arms waving, shouts of "Boss, please, boss." The white officials to whom I had just been introduced found comic relief, indeed hilarity, in the scene. "They all think you're an employer," shouted my escort, a good-natured old fellow on the verge of retirement after four decades in the apparatus of racial administration. "Tell them it's OK, you want someone to work in New York for you! Tell them it's OK!" I slunk away. Suddenly I needed to be by myself, as if I wouldn't be able to trust my breathing until I was out of the place.

On the other side of the subcontinent, near the Daniel F. Malan International Airport in Cape Town, the authorities in their gnomic and inscrutable deliberations have created an astonishing exposition of the racial caste system in operation. Of course, this was not really arranged for the convenience of foreign voyeurs on tight schedules, but it is now possible to fly in and absorb the whole bitter lesson in a couple of hours. There in a space of about five square miles roughly 200,000 browns and blacks have been distributed on a checkerboard of officially demarcated racial enclaves, each with the standards and regulations appropriate to the caste or subcaste licensed to inhabit it. Cape Town is the only metropolitan area in the country where blacks are in a minority. The largest population group there is not white but colored, yet it is a fundamental white aim to ensure that blacks will forever remain outnumbered in the western part of the Cape, the cradle of white "civilization" in Africa, whatever happens in the rest of the country. The reason is never stated, but it seems plain enough: Those who cannot abide the idea of black government can always imagine that they will be able to hold their original beachhead on the continent, if it ever becomes necessary to run the Great Trek in reverse. Because of the numerical predominance of the coloreds, Cape Town is more flexible on issues relating to the color bar than the rest of the country. But because of the official antipathy to black settlement there, it is also where the system of racial exclusion known as influx control is practiced most ruthlessly. The whites of Cape Town and even the Afrikaners of the *Boland,* the city's hinterland of orchards and vineyards, look down on the whites of the Transvaal as bloody-minded political primitives, but until 1984, when its special status was made less blatant in law, Cape Town was the only city where blacks couldn't even purchase the leaseholds on their homes. Half the blacks in Cape Town are deemed to be "illegals" under the draconian administration of influx laws aimed at restricting the permanent black population to 20,000 families.

The result is an unending war of attrition between the authorities and the "illegals," the overwhelming majority of whom have origins in Transkei and are thus held to be foreigners even if they have lived and worked in Cape Town for years, married, and brought up children there. Usually it is the wives and children that the law seeks to expel in order to preserve the hierarchy of castes in the western part of Cape Province, which was officially proclaimed a "colored labor preference area," meaning that no black could have a job until white officials had certified that no colored was available to take it. Thus the same racial system that hunts coloreds like Cynthia Freeman on the fringes of the white areas in Johannesburg manages to claim solicitude for coloreds as its excuse for hunting blacks in Cape Town. This is not a procedural hunt with writs, affidavits, and other pieces of paper as the state's weapons; it is a hunt with riot police, dogs, and tear gas, usually in the middle of the night. With each major raid to flush the "illegals" out of the black townships, a squatter camp arises in scrubby bush on the sand flats near the airport. Pathetic little shelters, makeshift yurts, are created out of twigs, cardboard, and the sort of plastic sheeting that is used to make garbage bags. These become the targets of the police, who tear them down and set them aflame. Usually then there is an outcry, and sometimes—when enough families have been broken up, enough jobs lost, enough children hospitalized with pneumonia, and, crucially, enough TV footage broadcast in Europe and America—the authorities call a temporary cessation of hostilities. With each such truce a tiny new subcaste is created with something less than a right to remain but at least an ambiguous commitment that the dogs and police won't be set on it again for a period of uncertain duration while the authorities review its status. Hence the checkerboard.

You can start at the privileged end by driving to Mitchell's Plain, a segregated township for coloreds that was built as an apartheid show-case, mainly for coloreds who were bulldozed out of District Six, their old neighborhood in the heart of what they ought to be able to regard as their city. Tidy little town houses, landscaping, and floral beds near the main thoroughfares and shopping centers that look as if they belong in the suburbs of San Diego are supposed to help them forget what they lost. Then you can drive on to Nyanga, an established black township with unimproved matchbox houses and minimal facilities. Next to Nyanga is New Crossroads, a newer and much smaller subdivision for blacks that was meant to be a showcase but became frozen at an early stage of development when the authorities hatched a master plan for the 1990's that would involve rounding up all of Cape Town's blacks and depositing them in a new township called Khayalitsha ("new home") next to Mitchell's Plain. Meantime, there is still old Crossroads, a crowded warren of metal shanties that looks like a social disaster but is actually a triumph of black assertion, for it came into being without authorization and has been allowed to remain. Only half its population of about 40,000 can prove they were there when the authorities, under international pressure, called off the bulldozers that were about to raze this encampment and relented in their plan to force its inhabitants back to Transkei; those who came to Crossroads later, in the hope of gaining legal status in Cape Town, are still deemed to be "illegals," but their cases are said to be under review.

Next to Crossroads, but separated from it by a sandy no-man's-land of less than 100 yards, are the remnants of later struggles with the police, divided and subdivided into further tiny enclaves. Some have official permission to build shanties; others are required to live in tents. The distinctions among the groups are arbitrary, governed only by the terms granted them for temporary relief from police dogs and mass arrests. Like rings on a tree or archaeological strata, these encampments chronicle a struggle for existence, and every eight months or so, when the authorities launch a new offensive against black "illegals" in Cape Town, another stratum is formed.

Everyone understands that the tidal movement of black population has its origins in the absolute poverty that exists in black rural areas. In their effort to resist it, the white officials are like the Irish king Cuchulain fighting the waves ("the invulnerable tide," wrote Yeats) or perhaps Dutchmen building dikes. Heartlessness and stubbornness are prime ingredients of their struggle, but they are matched by the obstinate courage of the hunted people who stand their ground out of desperation and a fundamental refusal to be designated as "illegals" in their land. That courage can be very moving, suggesting words like "indomitable," but the truth is that heartlessness prevails. The people in Mitchell's Plain do not make common cause with the people in Nyanga. The people in Nyanga and New Crossroads do not help the people in old Crossroads, where some of them first gained a foothold.

The people in the Crossroads camp are divided between those who are certified to be there and those who are seeking certification. And neither faction normally gives support to the people in the adjacent encampments on the sand flats, who give little or no help to each other. The system builds its dikes. It designates all blacks in Cape Town as foreigners, even those it accepts as "legals"; then it compartmentalizes the "illegals" into as many small, vulnerable groups as possible. Sometimes it retreats, but always it dominates.

It dominates, and yet the word "indomitable" still must be applied to its victims. If I mention several of the individual "squatters" and "illegals" I met over two years in the area near the airport in Cape Town, you will understand why.

Goodwill Zisiwe was trying to get warmth from a stinking, smoldering tire that had been thrown onto the dying embers of a fire at a bush camp near Nyanga when I encountered him on a cold, damp Saturday morning. He was a handsome young man of twenty-two, short and wiry, with a mild expression that reflected none of the tension and defiance that were inherent in his situation. The defiance was in his very presence at the bush camp, for he had been arrested at the same spot a couple of weeks earlier and thrown into Pollsmoor Prison, where he shared with twenty-one others a cell from which he had just emerged. The tension came from not only his general homelessness but his anxieties about his wife, Nofine. She had been in the final stages of pregnancy when she had been taken into custody. Some women who had been with her in the women's section of the prison told him that she had later been transferred to the prison hospital to give birth, but he had been unable to get information on her condition, the delivery, or the sex of his child. In the meantime, he had lost his job at a lumberyard. His white boss had been apologetic when he said he could no longer run the risk of employing a black whose papers were not in order.

I met Goodwill Zisiwe again nearly two weeks later, when I visited the bush camp at midnight. Nofine and their healthy new son were out of prison, he told me proudly, staying for the night in a church basement. There were roughly 600 persons in the camp that night, and the garbage-bag yurts had once more been erected. Small fires inside illuminated these flimsy shelters like Chinese lanterns, with long shadows flickering on their inflammable plastic surfaces as the huddled groups around the fires shifted positions.

"Dear little round house," a white woman who was there on a

philanthropic errand cooed. "We very sorry," she said, speaking pidgin, or rather baby talk, to a self-possessed young black man, who sized her up with a long, cool stare.

"Why?" he asked.

"We sorry you not have house, permit, warm clothes like us. We *very* sorry."

It was an excruciating moment. The good woman had not really noticed anything about the man except his status as victim. For an instant it seemed to be touch-and-go whether he would respond to the decency of her sentiment or the condescension of her tone. He took a long drag on a cigarette, then split the difference, offering a neutral monosyllable. "Oh," he said mildly, a little dismissively but without apparent hostility. The white woman had now become the object of condescension, but she didn't seem to realize that either.

Another man went by, carrying a roll of plastic sheeting. "One man, one room," he quipped. A group around a fire that included Goodwill Zisiwe broke into laughter.

There were inspirational speeches and hymns in Xhosa for those who stayed up, and Goodwill Zisiwe was one of the speakers, holding forth in a manner that commanded respect. Then the group sang a hymn. I asked what it meant. "God's spirit is with me like a bird," I was told.

They were as dispossessed a group as I had ever seen, worse off in some obvious ways than the sidewalk dwellers of Calcutta, and yet they were singing about divine providence. I was inclined to the proposition that God's spirit had flown away, but I found myself powerfully moved. About six hours later, just at dawn, the police stormed into the camp and burned it down again. I had no way of knowing whether Goodwill Zisiwe had been re-arrested, but it was bound to happen. If the police missed him in that sweep, they would get him in another. And still, it was clear, he would return.

Several months later I met Elsie Nyobole and Cynthia Balinyanga. Both had been deported as aliens to Transkei, a distance of 800 miles, and both had returned. In the process Elsie Nyobole had lost her husband and Cynthia Balinyanga had lost her child. At the risk of stridency, I would like to repeat that: Mrs. Nyobole had lost her husband; Mrs. Balinyanga her child.

Elsie Nyobole had last seen her husband, Menge, two months earlier at Pollsmoor Prison, where they were put on separate buses for expulsion to Transkei. When she got to Umtata, the territory's capital, he was nowhere to be found. After waiting for a few days in a church, she wrapped her baby in a blanket and took a bus 120 miles to the town of Lady Frere, where Menge's sister lived. Failing to find him, she returned to Umtata, then resolved to seek him in Cape Town. This entailed taking a bus to Graaff Reinet, where it ran into a police roadblock set up to intercept "illegals." She got off the bus and walked through the bush from midnight till dawn with her baby on her back and her possessions in a shopping bag. Arriving at a hamlet called Aberdeen, she boarded another bus that got by one roadblock at Beaufort West, then met another at Worcester, where, to avoid the police, she took a train to Paarl; where she caught a bus to Franschhoek; where she was able to get a place in an overcrowded taxi back to Nyanga, the place where she had been arrested originally. By then she had the equivalent of $1.10 left, and there was still no trace of Menge. So she moved with her baby into a two-room Crossroads shanty that already housed seven people. I met her the following week. When I asked if she was weary, she said she was weary. When I asked if she was sad, she said she was sad. Otherwise she did not display her emotions.

Cynthia Balinyanga's odyssey was nearly identical, except for a grotesque twist worthy of some story of disruption in the Thirty Years' War or a picaresque novel of the seventeenth or eighteenth century in which highwaymen set upon innocent travelers. When her bus from Umtata hit a roadblock, the passengers scattered into the bush in the middle of the night. In the confusion and darkness, a woman kindly offered to carry Mrs. Balinyanga's four-month-old son. The two women then got separated on the other side of the roadblock and, in the darkness, boarded different buses. Mrs. Balinyanga knew only the woman's first name, Nonceba. She had searched high and low in Cape Town's townships but really didn't know where to look and therefore still didn't know when I met her whether Nonceba had ever made it to Cape Town or had been re-arrested and sent back with the baby on the via dolorosa to Umtata.

There seemed to be no limit to the number of such stories that could be gathered in Cape Town with hardly any effort, but there was a limit to the number of times they could be presented as news. On later visits to Cape Town, I must admit, I made a conscious effort to steer myself away from them. So it was nearly two years later that I met Jerry Tutu, the leader of a remnant group of "illegals" that had escaped arrest in yet another raid on yet another camp of "squatters" in the bush. It had been twenty years since he had come to Cape Town, he said. At that time there was no question that Transkei was part of South Africa. He had six children, and each of them had been born in Cape Town, but like tens of thousands of others, he had never been able to get official authorization. So his family had lodged illegally all over the city. Asked where he was from, he didn't mention Transkei but reeled off a list of Cape Town neighborhoods and townships: "I come from Kensington; I come from Guguletu; I come from Elsie's River. I come from all these places." But now, although he still had his job on the night shift at a plastics factory, the Tutus were displaced persons, sleeping in a church hall that was used as a nursery school during the day, when he was not working, so he had to try to cadge his sleep outdoors on a veranda.

Jerry Tutu was distraught. He had been black in South Africa all his life, but he could not believe what was happening to him. He seemed to be at a dead end. He had no land, no extended family, no place to go back to in Transkei. His own family had dispersed all over South Africa. "My heart is not feeling nicely," he said. "I'm the same like dead. I think of these things, the government and all, and sometimes I cry."

It may be said that these cases are exceptional. What is exceptional is the resistance these individuals muster to the almost irresistible pressure the law puts on black families to resign themselves to conditions of separation and fragmentation that are normally synonymous with a system of enforced migrant labor. The expectation that families can be held together is one that many, perhaps most rural blacks are conditioned early on to give up. Some who go on annual labor contracts start second families where they find themselves. Then they do or don't send money home to the families they left behind. Others squander their wages on prostitutes and drink. Many others just drink. In the mine compounds, where there is usually no easy access to female company, there is a homosexual subculture, as there is universally in prisons and other maximum-security institutions. In the mines, in the township hostels, in any group of contract laborers, there are always some who fill the void in their lives with religion and a few who walk a narrow path of abstemiousness and frugality in order to overcome the odds and realize some dream, perhaps by winning an athletic trophy, starting a business in the homeland, buying a car, educating children. It is hard to generalize, for there are more than 800,000 black migrant laborers in South Africa, at least 250,000 of them in the industrial belt that has Johannesburg as its center—a foreign legion on its own soil.

I had seen where they worked. I had seen where they lived. I had seen how they meandered on Sunday afternoons, the most poignant time of the Johannesburg week, through downtown streets or suburban shopping malls, gathering on curbs or parking lots or construction sites, in the little interstices of white private property, in areas where there were not even segregated facilities for blacks. A barbershop was where a man with a razor and pair of scissors stationed himself under a tree; a shebeen, the far side of a hedge or wall where the drinkers would be sufficiently unobtrusive and inoffensive to white property holders to be ignored by the police. I had also seen the rural areas they left behind. What I had never done was travel with a migrant worker between his two worlds to see how he made the bridge, whether he was, in the words of a South African academic, not a man of two worlds but "a man of no worlds." So I asked two blacks whom I saw nearly every day in Johannesburg whether I could visit their homes, preferably in their company.

Napthali Ngcobo was the uniformed watchman and factotum in the lobby of the building where I installed my office. A chubby man with eyes that participated in his ready laughter, he had the presence and instincts of a natural politician. Most whites brushed by without noticing, but on his corner in downtown Johannesburg he was a figure of some celebrity among blacks, chaffing the messengers, drivers, and cleaning women as they came and went, like a candidate getting down with the folks at a factory gate. He was in his mid-forties like me, but the Afrikaner caretaker who bossed him around, a man at least ten years older, called him with grudging respect *madala* ("old man," rather than the usual "boy"). I got the impression that he was a person of enterprise and convictions. Sometimes I saw him with a Bible; sometimes, a racing form. Various young women seemed to sit in his cubicle under the stairway as if it were a confessional. One evening on my way to the movies on the other side of town, I found him supervising the parking lot into which I had driven. When finally I got him to tell me the story of his life, my sense of him was confirmed. Napthali, it emerged, was a fully fledged faith healer, a Zulu Oral Roberts, whose powers had been revealed in a series of remarkable dreams in which he was instructed by a tall and imposing Zulu in a white coat.

He was then living with his family in Zululand, having been laid off when the dairy company for which he had worked in Durban closed. During the one month a year he now spent with his family at home, his reputation for miracle cures still drew crowds. The rest of the year he could often be found preaching on Sunday mornings in Soweto at an independent black church called the New Swaziland Church in Zion. There he met a thirty-five-year-old cleaning woman at a downtown bank called Winna, who now shared his bed in the cramped rooftop quarters where he lived with only a curtain to screen the couple from a young cousin who shared the same room. It was the same rooftop, as chance or fate would have it, that I had been watching on my first weekend back in South Africa when the police assaulted the inhabitants. Napthali would have been one of them had he not been in church.

Winna had twice traveled down to Zululand to stay with his wife. The New Swaziland Church in Zion did not object to this arrangement, which could be regarded as an adaptation of Zulu tradition to the circumstances decreed by apartheid. He was earning about $235 a month, and most of it still went home: $60 to keep an eighteen-year-old son, his hope for the future, in a boarding school; another $110 or so for his wife, who ran a household that still contained five of their eight children, plus his father, who wasn't sure of his age but recalled that he was supposed to be eleven in 1908. Another son had left a wife behind to come to Johannesburg, where he grilled hamburgers at a Wimpy fast-food joint in an Afrikaner neighborhood. Napthali, it seemed, had successfully fitted the disparate pieces of his life together and achieved a measure of contentment, but in his own mind, in reality, too, this had been done in spite of the system, not thanks to it. "The whites don't care at all," he said. "They are the ones who make it impossible to live with your family. Even if you have money, they won't allow it."

Zalaowakho Mhlongo, known as Drum, relied more on the products of South African Breweries than religion, enterprise, or personality to ease his adjustment to Johannesburg. My wife and I had been determined to keep our domestic arrangements in Johannesburg as close as possible to what they were in New York. That meant we would not live in a house with a big garden, swimming pool, and tennis court, and we would not have servants. But apartments in Johannesburg all come with "flat cleaners" to do light housekeeping. Drum was an ambulatory appurtenance, a fixture, attached to the apartment we took. We were not expected to pay him, but when we discovered that he had a wife and children in Zululand and that the building gave him a rock-bottom wage amounting to less than $110 a month, we felt compelled to add to it on a fixed weekly basis with both cash and food. Drum understood some English and seemed to be under the impression himself that he spoke it, but the pleasant sounds that bubbled from him in response to our greetings were always unintelligible. Thus, although he spent an hour a day in our apartment over a period of many months, we never found out much about him beyond what we could plainly see: that he was terribly poor and usually hung over after the weekends. He shuffled, mumbled, and smiled, and we learned to take him for granted.

Gradually the absurdity of this arrangement—or, more precisely, its creepiness—got to us, and I finally asked a black journalist and friend named Chris More to come over on a Saturday to help us get to know Drum by explaining us to him and interpreting what he said. The scene was not without comedy—the goody-goody foreigners asking the black servant to sit down for the first time in a living room he had been vacuuming daily, especially since Chris was late and we were finding it impossible to get across the message to Drum that we weren't detaining him because he had done something wrong. The poor man looked miserable and tense until Chris showed up, but then a very pleasant transformation ensued. Invited to stay for lunch, he eased himself into the situation and gradually relaxed. Given the opportunity, he was not at all inarticulate. "If you go around showing what you're feeling inside," he said, explaining the obvious, "you'll be out of a job." Soon he was responding to our questions about his life—his wife and seven children lived near Durban, where he was not, however, author-ized to work—with questions about ours. "What are you doing in this place?" was the first. "Do you treat blacks in your country as badly as we're treated here?" was the second.

As it happened, Napthali and Drum got their annual leaves in different months, so it was arranged that Chris and I would drive to Zululand with Drum and then try to follow the directions Napthali gave us to his kraal, or homestead, on the Tugela River, where we would introduce ourselves to his family. Funumuthi Mhlongo, known as Philemon, a nephew of Drum's who also worked as a flat cleaner in our building, was going on his first leave in fourteen months, so he came, too. Philemon was a striking young man, lithe and handsome, a jogger who was articulate in remarkably good English. Early in the morning

I would see him arriving at our building in smart running outfits. If it were not Johannesburg, it might have been possible to imagine him as a young executive who then changed into a three-piece suit. Instead, he changed into blue coveralls. Sometimes, when I went out jogging, I would find him in the elevator on his knees giving the brasswork its daily polishing, as if we were on the first-class deck of a cruise ship. It was hard to say who was more embarrassed by these encounters. In the fifteen seconds it took the elevator to reach the ground floor, Philemon would stop his polishing and freeze in a kind of crouch as we exchanged awkward greetings.

But now riding in my Peugeot on the national road to Durban, he was a smooth and easy conversationalist. I had to ask only once for him to fall into the habit of calling me Joe instead of sir. He had never used the egregious "master," which remains the common coinage in Jo'burg for exchanges between flat "boys" and flat occupants. His daily runs in Johannesburg, about four miles each way, took him to another white suburb, where he apparently had a girl friend who lived in the backyard of a family she served as a maid. Now, returning to his three children and twenty-four-year-old wife, to whom he had written only once in fourteen months, he was wearing a track suit and carrying an Alitalia flight bag that contained a diploma testifying that he had finished 173d in the 1983 running of Johannesburg's major marathon, up from 307th in 1982.

If I had lived by any maxim as a reporter, it was that every person is an expert on the circumstances of his life. Black migrant laborers, it seemed to me, were the ultimate experts on black migrant labor. So the drive down to Durban turned into a rolling seminar, with me as student, on living and working conditions in the building where I had made my home for two and one-half years. Our building was what is known in America as a co-op; as renters we were not privy to the deliberations of our owner-neighbors, whose standard of living was indicated by a census I took in the garage, where I counted: two Rolls-Royces (belonging to a husband and wife), seven Jaguars, eight Mercedeses, one Porsche, one BMW, and one Lancia, plus run-of-the-mill Cressidas and Rovers. The price of one of these vehicles, I calculated, was roughly equivalent to the total earnings over twenty years of the men who were paid to wash and polish them. The building, I now learned, was the only one in the neighborhood that didn't give vacation pay to its staff. Drum and Philemon had drawn Christmas bonuses of less than $30 each for their trip home. Until the previous year, when they had been given meager raises, their wages had been frozen over several years of steep inflation.

Philemon was one of the hustlers in the building who earned a little more by washing cars on a piecework basis. I asked how much. Those of my neighbors who had their cars washed six out of every seven days paid what came to a little more than $5.50 a month, less than a quarter a wash; those who were satisfied to have theirs washed every other day paid a little less than $4.50 a month, not quite 30 cents a wash. What they paid in a month to these migrants—who had no opportunity because of their legal status to sell their labor in a modern metropolis at a higher price—was only slightly more than what I had been paying for a single car wash at the garage where I parked downtown. One of the flat cleaners, an incipient capitalist, stayed up most of the night to wash fifteen cars, thereby doubling his earnings for the month. These few figures, for a neighborhood of English-speaking whites who vote overwhelmingly for the liberal opponents of the government's racial policies, pointed to meanness and the will to exploit as ingrained cultural reflexes, comparable to what would be found in the most caste-ridden Indian village. Of course, I was the only person in the car who found this surprising.

We reached Durban late in the afternoon and then drove up the Indian Ocean coast past the large sugar estates to an Indian community called Stanger, where we turned inland again, doubling back on ourselves. I had been taking directions from Drum and Philemon without looking at a map. Now I discovered they had only the vaguest idea of the actual geography between their homes and Johannesburg, that we had been following the routes of the buses they normally took: an express to Durban, then the local milk run into Zululand. By the most direct run the drive would have been 360 miles. We had gone 475 by the time they showed me where to park, near a trading store at the foot of a hill, about 10 miles from an obscure hamlet called Mapumulo.

The light was failing as we started up a steep, narrow trail that must become a mud slide, I thought, when it rains. The generator used by a white family named Bignoux who had been running the trading store for forty years—the only whites within twenty-five miles in an area inhabited by tens of thousands of Zulus—made the only sound that competed with the raucousness of the crickets. There were Zulu kraals made predominantly of round thatched beehive huts up and down the slopes that rose from the narrow valley. Yet the only visible light was the one shining from the trader's house. Before we had gone far, we came upon a group of young men, relatives of the two Mhlongos, who softly and deferentially greeted their elders, shouldering the bags without any requests having been made, a service that Drum and Philemon accepted naturally as their due. When we reached the farthest ridge, Philemon quietly informed me that we were now approaching Drum's kraal. A group of women was descending the trail. Again there was a soft exchange of murmured greetings. Their import came as a shock to Philemon, but this was not immediately apparent. The women had informed him, he told me after some moments, that he would not find his wife and children in his father's kraal because they had gone to Newcastle, 175 miles away, to visit her mother.

By this time we were standing in the gathering dusk on a flattened bare clearing in front of three huts. A few goats were tethered nearby in a pen made up of brambly branches. A couple of scrawny chickens darted along the edge of a small patch of sickly corn. This was Drum's domain, and now, snapping out of the hung-over haze in which he had seemed to be plunged during most of the drive, he squared his shoulders and took a lordly stance on the slope with one foot advanced in front of the other like a grandee posing in his armor. Actually he was wearing a windbreaker in an electric shade of blue with matching trousers. A purposeful, thickset woman bustled out of one of the huts, shot across the clearing, and disappeared into another, passing within two yards of Drum, who, his chin now thrusting at the heavens, hardly seemed to notice her. This was his wife, Thandekile, whom he had not seen in a year, on her way to inform his elderly mother that their Odysseus had returned. She zoomed back again to the first hut, apparently to ensure that it was in suitable order, then re-emerged to invite her husband to come inside and rest. The greetings between husband and wife and between Drum and his children were all in the eyes and murmured, brief civilities; there was no touching. This was the customary way in which a warrior returned to his kraal, I imagined, but I could not help thinking that it was also appropriate as a welcome to a husband and father who was a strange figure, if not a stranger, having spent no more than fourteen months at home over the previous fourteen years.

Inside, Drum sat against the wall on a straw mat that had been spread for his comfort. There were only four pieces of furniture: a table covered with oilcloth, two chairs that were reserved for Chris and me, and an armoire for clothes, which was supplemented by a cord fixed to the wall and weighed down with garments. The children were mostly shoeless; one, an undersized girl of eight who would have been considered small for five, was visibly ailing and malnourished. With their mother they sat against the wall opposite Drum. A candle, probably saved for just such a special occasion, flickered in between from a long-emptied brandy bottle that served as candlestick.

Drum ended the formal audience by going into the next hut with his wife. After what I hoped was a decent interval, we trailed along. Then Philemon took Chris and me over the ridge to his father's kraal and the tidy, rectangular and therefore modern bungalow he had erected there for his family. On the wall the diploma from last year's marathon hung alongside a color snapshot of him at the finish line. He had met his wife, Sonto, also known by her Christian name, Theresa, in Durban, he told me, after he had already started as a migrant laborer. She had grown up in the Newcastle township and was only sixteen when they were wed. They had never spent more than a month together in nearly nine years of marriage. Sonto and the three children were supported by money he sent his parents; it was not sent directly to her.

I tried to imagine what it was like for a young woman from a township to live on this hillside, in a kraal, far from her relatives and friends, waiting for her dashing husband to return from *Egoli* ("the city of gold") in his track suit with another diploma. Waiting fourteen months. He had not written to say when he was coming, Philemon said, formally excusing her for her absence and, at the same time, covering his hurt and embarrassment. The obvious thought that Sonto's absence might be more than temporary crossed my mind; I could not tell whether it had crossed Philemon's. I told him that it would be possible for me to drive him most of the way to Newcastle a couple of days later. "Oh, that won't be necessary, Joe," he said. A slight tightness in his voice seemed to carry a hint that he felt it would be inappropriate for a Zulu husband to go chasing after his wife. He would pass his month at home keeping in shape by running along the dirt road that wound through the valley beside a small stream called the Dlakhati and waiting for Sonto to return.

Back in Drum's kraal, we went into the third hut, the cookhouse, to be introduced to his mother, who extended a leathery hand to shake mine and accepted without question her son's explanation that I had come from America to see how they lived. I had now been inside all three huts, and I had seen no radio, no lantern, no stove. Not much of the modest extra income Drum had gotten from us had filtered home, it seemed. The only gift that he had brought this evening was a hamperful of food that I had purchased at a supermarket in Ladysmith on the way from Johannesburg. This was bare subsistence. There was no country in the world where these people would not have been considered poor. Finishing with me, the old woman examined Chris closely, quickly establishing that he was not a Zulu. Once she had fixed his place in the tribal firmament as a Tswana, she let him know in a dignified and courteous manner that he was welcome.

Except for a few stars and an occasional faint flash of headlights from a car or bus five or ten miles away, it was pitch-dark as we descended the hill. One of Drum's daughters clutched my hand all the way down. Drum led the way with a flashlight that he said we had given him. Several times in South Africa I had been told quite seriously by whites that blacks saw everything in two dimensions, that their brains conveyed no impression or concept of depth. Now, in the same conviction that skin color has everything to do with the way the world appears, one of the children asked a question in Zulu that made Chris laugh out loud. In a whisper he translated for my benefit. "How does the white man see in the dark?" the youngster wanted to know.

A couple of days later, along another dirt road through the Zulu hills, about eighty miles away, Chris and I found Napthali Ngcobo's wife. Our sudden appearance, she later told us, had given her a fright, for she assumed us to be police bearing bad news. "I had only time to pray," she said. "I thought, 'Has my husband passed away? Has my son died? Only you can help me, Lord.'"

Napthali's kraal, set on a hillside above the river in closely settled country where there had been minimal development, was something of an estate compared to Drum's. Pawpaw trees grew in the yard. The main house was made of the traditional mud and thatch, but it was handsomely trimmed in blue paint, and there were windows with real glass and curtains blowing gently in the breeze. It was adequately, though modestly, furnished. On his annual trips home, Napthali had brought kerosene lamps, a clock, a kerosene stove, a radio; and his wife, Martha, a large, capable woman who had been working in her garden when we arrived, had tea to serve us, which Drum's wife had conspicuously lacked. With it came slabs of steamed bread, hot from the stove. "If he had been with you," she said after Chris had mentioned our original plan, "I would have taken a goat and . . ." She drew her finger across her throat and laughed heartily.

On a shelf near the table at which we were entertained, there was a framed color photo of Napthali in a guise in which I had never seen him. Instead of the brass-buttoned watchman's uniform he wore in the lobby, he was shown in a navy suit, a clerical collar, and a tunic of episcopal purple. One hand held a Bible; the other was gesturing, showing the way. Someone, possibly Napthali himself, had stuck little red, green, and blue stars, the sort schoolchildren paste into notebooks, in a kind of arch or nimbus around him. What was riveting about this apotheosis for me was its setting, for I recognized the rooftop where he lives. The sainted Napthali was shown standing by the parapet where the cops had pummeled the blacks on the first Sunday after my return to South Africa, now more than three years in the past. Something moved me, or maybe more than one thing: the endearing half-comic image of the self-created holy man living a dream that whites could not batter, but also the notion that I had finally come full circle in South Africa. Whatever went into it, it was a feeling that could be enjoyed without heavy thought.

"Say hello to my husband," Mrs. Ngcobo said sweetly. "Please say hello to my husband."

CHAPTER 5

—

FORCED BUSING

Albino Carleo is also the son of a migrant laborer. He was still being carried in his mother's womb when his father, Gaetano, suddenly closed up his small butcher's shop in Cava de' Tirreni, outside Salerno, said *arrivederci* to his wife and the three young Carleos already on hand, and sailed for Durban. Gaetano Carleo, being white, determined, and hardworking, was ultimately to prove that South Africa can be a land of opportunity, but it didn't happen all at once. In his first five years there, he drifted from job to job in the mines and on the railroad, overseeing black construction workers and learning Fanagalo, a mainly Zulu pidgin developed by the whites as a language of command, before he learned English. When Albino first glimpsed his father at the age of five, it was the height of the Depression, and Gaetano had little to show for his efforts. But his life had become a quest, and he was not about to call a halt, so after only a week back in Cava de' Tirreni, he headed for New York and opened a grocery in Brooklyn with his savings from Johannesburg. The South African climate had spoiled him for North America, however, and three years later he was on the rebound again with a brand-new American automobile as trophy and venture capital. Back in Johannesburg in 1936, he bought a secondhand Ford bus with the proceeds from the car and staked out a route from a black township called Alexandra to the center of town. It was a shoestring operation, with the owner serving as driver and mechanic and actually living with his bus in the black township, but he called it the Rapido Bus Company.

Albino's mother died without ever seeing South Africa, and he then lived through World War II without any possibility of contact with his father, who was briefly interned as an enemy alien in the Orange Free

State. The son was thus already a young man when he followed his father's footsteps as a migrant and, surviving an air crash in the Belgian Congo en route to Johannesburg, finally learned to know Gaetano by learning the bus business. Now in his eighties, Gaetano Carleo spends most of the year in his homeland at Cava de' Tirreni, while Albino oversees a corporate group with about 9,000 employees, twenty subsidiary companies, and a fleet of 3,500 buses from a headquarters of vaguely Neapolitan design in a quiet white suburb of Johannesburg.

The Rapido Bus Company changed its name to Rapid early on and then was absorbed into another small bus company, which gradually branched out under various names and corporate identities into black "locations," the inhabitants of which found work in the white industrial belt, until finally the major private bus company, known as Putco, found it expedient to deal with the competition presented by the Carleos by buying up all their operations. Looking for something to do with the proceeds and realizing that buses were what they knew, the Carleos then turned around and purchased a controlling interest in Putco. Ownership of this franchise immediately threw them into a delicate relationship with the official managers of the apartheid system, the social engineers who were busy shunting blacks and drawing boundaries in order to create what they hoped would be a stable racial order. It was a relationship of mutual dependence. As the apartheid era progressed, the social engineers looked for ways to limit the number of blacks who stayed overnight in the urban areas, either as residents with their families in township houses or as migrants in single-sex hostels. Their aim was to build up a class of "commuters," blacks who could be allowed to work in South Africa so long as they shuttled back to their "homeland" every night across a presumptive national boundary. In its most elaborate and mature form, apartheid required buses, more buses every year as more blacks were flushed out of the white areas into officially designated resettlement sites known as "closer settlements," vast rural slums with urban population densities but no urban amenities beyond the buses that represented their slender lifelines to the cities.

Before there was a clinic or an assured supply of safe water in these settlements, there had to be a bus stop. Putco thus grew with the elaboration of the system, but as its routes extended over longer distances, the fares it had to charge to meet its costs and show a profit soared far beyond the means of the menial laborers it carried. Therefore, a key element in its business, more important finally than the maintenance and life expectancy of the buses that rattled into the bush over rutted dirt roads or the cost of gasoline, became the negotiation of the subsidies the apartheid government was willing to pay to make the system work. The authorities could have run their own bus companies, but the costs would have been enormous, and so would the risks. The tactic of the bus boycott was used by blacks in South Africa before it was tried by Martin Luther King, Jr., in Montgomery, Alabama, and later, when resistance ceased to be nonviolent, buses were usually among the first targets to be attacked in the townships. It was a matter of realpolitik to distance the bus companies that served black areas from the state.

It had been enough for Gaetano Carleo to know buses. The maintenance manual Albino Carleo needed to study was written by Machiavelli, for he had to present an amiable face not only to his exclusively black public and the apartheid bureaucrats but also, as the system began to realize its aims, to the assorted tribal chieftains, headmen, flunkies, sellouts, and politicians who emerged as ministers in the new homeland states. Today Putco promotes itself as an "equal opportunity employer" and maintains a Putco Foundation to support black community charities, while also giving seats on its board to former high officials of the Department of Cooperation and Development and cultivating homeland leaders. When I met him for coffee in a paneled office with arched windows that looked as if it might have been inspired by the abbot's study in some unusually prosperous monastery, Albino Carleo was surprisingly ready to expound on various subjects of social concern, including the "quality of life" in urban areas and the responsibilities of corporations. He also talked about getting along. "If there was a black government," he said, "I would talk to them with the same sincerity of purpose that I have when I talk to the white government. But that's a thing of the future. If a small minority has de facto power, it is stupid to challenge them. What you can't get by force, you get by persuasion. People who accuse me of being a stooge don't know what they're talking about. I must have good relations with the government in order to give good service to the black community."

A short man, slightly proboscidean, with eyes that acknowledged the amusement he got from his own discourse, he spoke rapidly in a high-pitched voice, occasionally pacing the tiled floor. He was being generous rather than defensive, setting out a practical philosophy that had been learned in a hard school. "People like to feel important, and if you display a sense of knowing they're important, they like you," he said. "They like you and trust you because you represent a measure of their greatness." It was a philosophy he applied to whites and blacks impartially. He had just given a dinner in Pretoria, he said, offering an example, for the chief minister of a soon-to-be-independent homeland called KwaNdebele, a former truck driver named Simon Skhosana who was accompanied by the third of his five wives. KwaNdebele had been Putco's most important growth area for five years. In that time the population of this obscure tribal enclave had nearly doubled to 465,000. Or so the chief minister had boasted. Others say it is 300,000. Possibly no one knows. The last accurate count had been taken at the time of the 1970 census, before there was a KwaNdebele, and then only 32,000 people had lived in the area. "He was very proud," said Albino Carleo, allowing himself a touch of condescension in order to display his social conscience. "It is difficult to make people understand that the population explosion can destroy the world."

But the population explosion in KwaNdebele, unlike the wider world, has little to do with breeding and practically everything to do with apartheid. In a period in which South Africa is alleged to be changing and phasing out apartheid, the expansion of Putco into the *bundu,* or bush, of the homeland provides as accurate a measure as can be found of the real thrust of change. The bus company had to draw its own maps, for its new routes were on roads that had just been cut; its buses came in right behind the bulldozers. In 1979 Putco started to run two buses a day from Pretoria to the resettlement camps of KwaNdebele. By 1980 there were 66 a day, which jumped to 105 in 1981; to 148 a day in 1981; then 220 a day in 1983 and 263 a day in 1984, when the government was expected to pay Putco a subsidy of $26.5 million to keep its buses rolling to the homeland. That worked out to about $25 a head a week, more than $1,000 for each "commuter" a year: a negative social investment that went up in gas fumes when it might just as easily have gone into new housing for the same black workers nearer the industrial centers if that had not violated the apartheid design. It was the price the white government was willing to pay—and go on paying, year after year—to halt the normal process of urbanization. The KwaNdebele bus subsidy—the government's largest single expense in the development of this homeland—was higher than the KwaNdebele gross domestic product. This is basic apartheid economics. It had to be so high because KwaNdebele, a state supposedly on the way to independence, was utterly devoid of a productive economy or resources. The racial doctrine sets the priorities: First you invent the country; then, if you can, an economy. In the meantime, there are the buses to carry the homeland's citizens to jobs in the nearest industrial center. In KwaNdebele's case that meant Pretoria, which is fifty-five miles distant at the homeland's nearest point.

The first time I saw KwaNdebele, two years earlier, it was a rash of "closer settlements" spotted over open veld that had previously provided grazing for some thirty white farmers. At a place called Kwaggafontein, I came upon the Nduli family, who had just been evicted from their kraal on a white farm near Middelburg, about fifty miles away. I found them with their paltry belongings on a plot white officials had staked out on a grassy hillside, which was fast being blighted by squalid shanties. Rose Nduli was literally sitting on the veld while her son, Kleinbooi, wearing a brown shoe on his right foot and on his left a black boot laced with copper wire, chipped away with a shovel at the dry stuccolike earth in order to prepare the ground for a shelter. Kleinbooi said they knew none of their neighbors. He knew that he had landed at a place called Kwaggafontein, but he hadn't been told that KwaNdebele was supposed to have deep significance for him as his homeland. When I asked who brought him there, he replied simply, "GG." The initials are the first two letters of the official license plates on the government trucks used to move blacks out of white areas. Throughout the rural Transvaal and Natal, it has become the universal shorthand among blacks for the white government, its pervasive authority, and its arbitrary ways, which seem to be beyond ordinary comprehension. GG is as predictable as natural calamity. GG scoops you up when you least expect it and drops you somewhere you have never seen, leaving it to you to patch together the torn and ragged pattern of a life. And like natural calamity, it evokes depression and resignation, rather than resentment. "The law is the law," Rose Nduli said, "and we have nothing to say about it."

I heard only one angry voice at Kwaggafontein on that visit. It belonged to a man named Jim Masetlana, who started his working life as a tenant on a white farm and then was moved three times by GG in nineteen years. Without meaning to do so, I had uncapped his resentment by offering the cold comfort that he probably would not be harried anymore now that he was in a homeland. "This is no

homeland," he said, waving his hand at the dreary refugee camp growing up around him. "It's just a township. Where I grew up was really
a homeland. I had land. I could plow. Even the white farmers give you
land to plow. This type of homeland I have never seen. They have no
business taking us from the place of our birth."

Kwaggafontein made as little sense to me as it did to the people who
had been dumped there. But I saw a lot more of resettlement in South
Africa and its effects. By the time I went back to Kwaggafontein, I
could make a dubious boast that, to offer a wild guess, probably fewer
than 100 South Africans could match: I had been to each of the ten
homelands, and I had seen most of the major "closer settlements." I
did not expect to be surprised again. I thought I understood that this
process—known euphemistically as resettlement, bluntly as removal,
and cynically as repatriation—represented a final stage in a campaign
to alienate blacks from their land that had already gone on in the
Transvaal for 140 years. For 70 years it had actually been illegal for
blacks to purchase land in more than 86 percent of the territory the
world still knows as South Africa. For 35 years they had been forced,
cajoled, and squeezed off "black spots," land to which they had secured
proper title according to the white man's law, prior to the passage of
the Native Lands Act in 1913. I knew that resettlement was central
to the government's audacious plan to redefine the bulk of the black
population, if not all of it, as foreign. At first I had thought this was
just an ideological word game, not to be taken seriously. But the misery
and endemic malnutrition I had seen in out-of-the-way resettlement
camps from Thornhill in supposedly sovereign Ciskei in the southeast
to Rooigrond in supposedly sovereign Bophuthatswana in the north-
west had long since cured me of the easy notion that this program of
exclusion and partition existed only on paper.

I also understood its dimensions. I had studied the conclusions drawn
by a dedicated group of white South African academics called the
Surplus People Project from its encyclopedic five-volume study of
forced removals: that apartheid had moved more than 3.5 million
people in 20 years, more than 2 million of them, it seemed clear, into
"closer settlements" in the homelands. Mostly rural people who had
lived as sharecroppers and labor tenants on white farms, they lost in
these removals even the possibility of subsistence farming, for what
made a closer settlement "closer" was the absence of grazing land and
the restriction of cultivation to tiny garden patches. Charles Simkins

of the University of Cape Town, who had done the most careful analysis of the process, estimated that 3.7 million South African blacks were living in these squalid encampments by 1980. He called the process "displaced urbanization" and showed how the government's strenuous efforts to impose the apartheid design were paying off: In 1960, 39.8 percent of the total black population was crammed into the former tribal reserves; by 1980 resettlement and gerrymandering had raised the proportion to 53.1 percent. In absolute terms the number of blacks on the same 13 percent of the land had more than doubled in those 20 years, from 4.4 million to 11 million. And nearly half of these had already been stripped of their South African citizenship.

I thought I understood all that, but I was not prepared for the visual shock of what Kwaggafontein had become in two and a half years. It was no longer just a spot in a rash of "closer settlements." Now it was a part of a nearly continuous resettlement belt. You drove through the Pretoria suburbs and then through more than forty miles of rich farm country before you hit it; then you could drive another forty miles, and it was seldom out of sight: a serpentine stream of metal shanties and mud houses the metal roofs of which were typically weighted down by small boulders to keep them from blowing off in the Transvaal's violent hailstorms. Such sights can be seen in other countries, usually as a result of famines or wars. I don't know where else they have been achieved as a result of planning. The hillside where the Ndulis had been dropped was now as densely settled as Soweto. It no longer looked like a hillside. What it had become was a slight swell in a sea of shanties. I turned off the highway there and followed a dirt road for five miles to see how far into the *bundu* the settlement now extended. This brought me to a place called Frisegewacht that seemed to be near the homeland's outer edge, for when I looked past the last shanty to the next rise, all I could see was open, unspoiled, empty grassland belonging to a white cattle farmer.

At Frisegewacht I met a man who had to get to work at a munitions factory in Brits by seven in the morning. The man was not an Ndebele by ethnic origins but a Swazi, and he had not been put here by GG. He had come after being expelled from a white farming area because the Swazi homeland was too remote from any possibility of employment. Here at least he could live with his family. He was earning $85 a week, an unusually high wage for a black industrial worker, but he had a desperate problem. He was regularly late to work in Brits, which was on the other side of Pretoria, a distance of nearly 100 miles by road from where he lived, because the first Putco bus often didn't reach Frisegewacht until four-fifteen in the morning. His white supervisor— who lived, of course, in Brits—was not interested in excuses, so his job was in jeopardy. To be on the safe side, what he really needed, he said, was a bus that would come at three-thirty. As we chatted, a blue Putco bus came around the bend on a dirt track. Here we were, out in the veld, about 75 miles from Pretoria, more than 5 miles from the nearest highway. It would not have seemed much more incongruous to find a red London Transport double-decker there.

I asked the man who worked in Brits what time he got home. That depended, he said, on whether the Putco driver was willing to go to the last stop at Frisegewacht. Sometimes the driver turned around a couple of miles away, obliging his passengers to walk. On those nights, he said, he seldom got home before ten. On a good day this "commuter" left at four in the morning and returned, seventeen hours later, at nine at night. Then, if he ate quickly and went straight to bed, he got five hours' sleep. The vista across the veld from Frisegewacht, when you faced in the direction of the white farmer's grazing land, was fine. The climate was undoubtedly salubrious. The man could live with his family, and he was not badly paid. But Frisegewacht had to be mentioned, along with the mine compounds and single-sex hostels, as part of the South African gulag. It was frightening in a different way from the more remote "closer settlements" I had visited where migrancy was the only possible answer to unemployment. The harsh conditions and barrenness of such places, the absence of any visible economy, seemed to portend a breakdown in the system. Or so a visitor could imagine. But Kwaggafontein and Frisegewacht were actually taking root. Their black inhabitants, by their capacity for sheer endurance, were rescuing a seemingly harebrained scheme concocted by white ideologues and making it durable. There were little signs of commerce that I noticed as I drove back to the highway: shops selling groceries, meat, and even building materials, all trucked in from the white areas. Some of the shanties, hovels no longer, had been handsomely improved. For blacks in more remote areas, Kwaggafontein could represent a thin ray of economic possibility, a way out of the maze created by government regulations. GG no longer had to dump them here. Responding to heavy pressures and tiny incentives, they were coming on their own.

Wage earners, after all, lived here. They had cash in their pockets, and they were capable of turning a "closer settlement" whose reasons for being were strictly abstract into something like a community. In Pretoria, I was told, KwaNdebele was viewed with pride as a tremendous success for the racial planners: an answer to the problem of migrant labor, developed from nothing in little more than a decade. Blacks didn't want to live in towns, a high official told a friend of mine. They were much happier with their own kind out in the bush. The Afrikaans term he used was *doodgelukkig* ("dead happy"). That seemed singularly apt for emergent KwaNdebele, a nation of sleepwalkers.

To catch the first Putco bus from the Wolverkraal depot in Kwa-Ndebele, the photographer David Goldblatt and I calculated, we would have to leave the Bundu Inn (a white hostelry that went "international" after finding itself in a homeland) no later than one-thirty in the morning. It is then that KwaNdebele's first "commuters" start to stir. Wolverkraal was even farther from Pretoria than Kwaggafontein or Frisegewacht. The black settlers of the new state who boarded the bus near there had to ride about 95 miles before transferring to local buses that would take them to factories where they worked, in areas where they were forbidden to live. That meant a minimum of 190 miles every working day in buses designed with hard seats for short hauls on city streets. They were fortunate in a sense—they did have work—but they were spending up to eight hours a day on buses. The distance they traveled annually, I calculated, came to more than a circumnavigation of the globe.

The Putco depot was just a fenced-off clearing in the bush with a tiny shack for the dispatcher and nothing else: no floodlights, no time clocks, no coffee machines, no grease pits. Rain during the night had cleansed the air and drained a layer of clouds that had glowered over the veld at sundown, leaving a light breeze and a full moon to limn the hulks of the ranked buses. I counted fifty-two of them. Two others, I was told, had left the yard at one in the morning to round up the drivers who stayed in nearby "closer settlements." One of these staff buses had then got stuck in the mud, so Putco was going to be a little behind schedule this morning in KwaNdebele. The engine of the other staff bus, which had rescued the stranded drivers, was the first night sound I heard.

It was about twenty past two when the lights inside the buses at the depot started to blink on one by one. Number 4174, which we boarded after being told that it would be the first out of the yard, had one bulb glowing dimly inside a red globe, another in a green globe, casting together an eerie light into a gloom made stygian, despite the clear night outside, by the coating of caked mud on the bus's windows. A sign near the cage in which the driver was encased declared that number 4174 was certified to carry 62 sitting passengers and 29 standing. I did another quick calculation: The fifty-two buses represented roughly one-fifth of the homeland's daily convoys to the white areas; the number of "commuters" who were thus being subsidized by South Africa to live beyond the pale—the pun was inadvertent but hard to erase—came to roughly 23,000 on the KwaNdebele run.

At two-forty in the morning, number 4174 left the depot and headed north and east, *away* from Pretoria, to pick up its first passengers at a place called Kameelrivier. In the Ndebele homeland, it seemed, all place-names were still in Afrikaans—the names, mostly, of the white farms the state had bought up in order to ghettoize the bush. The headlights showed six men and four women waiting patiently beside the dirt road, in what appeared to be the middle of nowhere, when the bus made its first stop, ten minutes late, at two-fifty. At that place and that hour, the sight of a couple of whites on the bus was as much to be expected as that of a couple of commuting walruses. Momentarily it startled the passengers out of their drowsiness. Once our presence was explained, it became possible to ask a few questions as the bus rattled to its next stop.

John Masango, the first man to board, said he worked six days a week at a construction site near Benoni, an industrial town forty miles on the far side of Pretoria, taking three buses each way. Even at the concessional rates arranged by the authorities for KwaNdebele, the total bus fares he paid out in a week gobbled up one-quarter of his wages. He was fifty-three years old, and on days when he was not required to work overtime, he could get back to Kameelrivier by eight-thirty at night. Only on Sundays did he ever see his home or his family in the light of day. Most nights, after washing, eating, and, as he put it, "taking care of family matters," he was able to get to sleep by ten or ten-fifteen. With four hours' sleep at home and a couple of hours' sleep on the bus, he managed to stay awake at work. It was important not to be caught napping; you could lose your job. While I was still thanking him for his patience, John Masango reached into a bag he was carrying and extracted a little rectangle of foam rubber about the size of a paperback book. He then pulled his blue knitted cap over his eyes and, leaning forward, pressed the foam rubber to the back of the seat in front of him; in the final step in this procedure, he rested his forehead against the foam rubber and dropped his hands to his lap. As far as I could tell, he was out like a light.

Emma Mokwena was on her way to a part-time job as a cleaning woman for an Afrikaner family called the Van der Walts who lived in one of the new suburban developments burgeoning on the veld between Pretoria and Johannesburg. She was expected at work by seven in the morning, in time to prepare breakfast for her employers, who rose to face the new day four and a half or five hours after she had to get up in KwaNdebele. She did not, however, have to serve the Van der Walts tea in bed, as live-in servants are often still expected to do in South Africa. She worked for them two days a week, for other families in the same suburb on other days. Usually she worked for seven hours, leaving at about two in the afternoon, in time to return to Kameelrivier to prepare dinner for her five children aged fourteen down to two and a half. In a month she earned about $120, of which a little more than $30 went in bus fares. It could have been worse, but fortunately her employers underwrote the $1.20 she spent each day getting from Pretoria to their homes and back. When she saw I was finished with my questions, Emma Mokwena pulled her blanket snug over her shoulders and unfolded the collar of her turtleneck sweater so it covered her face. She then leaned back in her seat, half-slumped against the woman with whom she had boarded, now similarly mummified.

By this time it was only three-twenty, and number 4174 had yet to reach the narrow ribbon of asphalt that connects KwaNdebele to Pretoria. But it had stopped by enough "closer settlements" to fill all its seats; anyone getting on beyond this point was bound to stand, not just this morning but every morning in the week. There were still nearly two and a half hours to go to Pretoria. Thus some people *stood* on the bus nearly twelve hours a week. These calculations were beginning to make me more tired than the ride, which was grim enough, especially since I had lost my seat and was now standing, too, squeezed in next to a man who was managing to doze on his feet.

Another "commuter," a construction worker whose job was at a site in a section of Pretoria called Sunnyside, stood long enough to tell me that he had received several reprimands, each formally inscribed on his work record, for falling asleep on the job. This man represented a particularly telling example of the dramatic changes that have occurred in the lives of some South African blacks, for his family had been landowners in a "black spot" called Doornkop, from which they were expelled along with 12,000 others in 1969. The compensation his family got from a government that never ceases to profess its devotion to principles of private enterprise came to less than $300. The man smiled bitterly as he mentioned the figure. Then, excusing himself, he removed a folded piece of newspaper he had been carrying under his jacket and spread it neatly on the floor between his feet. Next, with the suppleness of a yogi, he collapsed himself into a seated position on the paper with his knees drawn up to his chin and dropped his head.

I looked around. Aside from the driver and one man who was smoking about four rows from the rear of the bus, David and I and a black Putco official who had graciously come along to run interference for us appeared to be the only persons out of more than ninety who had not now dozed off. The center aisle was packed with bodies wound around themselves like anchovies in a can. The motion of the bus threw some happenstance couples, men and women who got on at different stops, into intimate contact. A young woman's head slumped on the shoulder of the man seated next to her, who was too far gone to recognize his good fortune. Nearer the front a young man clutched restlessly in his sleep at the sleeping woman next to him. Some of the heads lolled backward, but most of the forms were bent forward like that of the man who carried the foam rubber. By three forty-five the bus had reached the highway, and the ride was now smoother. Their heads covered, blankets over their shoulders, the passengers swayed like Orthodox Jews in prayer. Or, in the eerie light of the two overhead bulbs, they could be seen as a congregation of specters, souls in purgatory.

Twice they were jostled into consciousness: once when number 4174 pulled off the highway onto the rough shoulder for a routine Putco checkoff; another time when the driver slammed on his brakes, barely missing a truck that had stopped by the side of the road as if to let him pass, then eased its way forward directly into our path. Shaken, our black driver got down to yell at the black driver of the truck. A small crowd gathered in the dark patch between the two sets of headlights. The truck driver expressed remorse. He had been giving a lift to three women, who were crowded into the cab of his truck with him, wrapped in blankets like the women on the bus, and asked the one who was nearest the window to tell him whether the coast was clear. Apparently without looking, she had mumbled something that he took to mean "go."

The first streaks of dawn showed on the outskirts of Pretoria. We saw plenty of blacks heading for work but no sign of white life as number 4174 proceeded through the first of several white neighborhoods until we came upon a jogger, a hyperventilating gray-haired man in his fifties wearing a T-shirt that had, stenciled on his chest in red as a greeting to all comers, including the passengers on a Putco bus, a blank "happy face" with a turned-up smile. Posters strung up on lampposts and trees by extremist white parties resisting the new constitutional proposals also seemed to mock the "commuters," who were excluded, in any case, from the supposed "new dispensation."

"Protect Our Future," the posters exhorted. "Remember Rhodesia."

It was October, and Pretoria's splendid jacarandas were in full blossom but seen from the vantage point of a black commuter bus, the sight left me indifferent. It was like looking at Bali or the Himalyas in tourist posters for holidays you would never take. It was only a few moments now until we turned into Marabastad, once a teeming black residential neighborhood at the very edge of Pretoria's downtown, at present a stretch of razed, overgrown real estate lying as a no-man's-land between the capital's commercial center and a tiny enclave of Indian-owned shops adjacent to the terminus where the buses from KwaNdebele disgorge their black passengers. Number 4174 ended its ride there at five-forty, exactly three hours after it had begun in the *bundu* at the Wolverkraal depot.

This left us leeward of a lavish new temple of apartheid: a combination rail and bus terminus called the Belle Ombre station, which will function one day, according to the dreams of the social engineers who do South Africa's long-range planning, as the hub for a series of bullet trains to the homelands. The first of these, a high-speed rail line into the nearest section of Bophuthatswana, had just begun operation, bringing back to Marabastad on a daily basis many of its old residents, or their descendants, in the status of aliens. At a quarter of six in the morning, there was piped music at the Belle Ombre station to cheer the homeland blacks on their way. A high-pitched pavilion with airy esplanades and structural piping painted in bright primary colors, the station seemed to exert a gravitational pull that sucked the groggy KwaNdebele "commuters" down its ramps to waiting Putco buses that would carry them on the next stage of their journeys to work.

Since they spend more of their working week on buses than they do in their "closer settlements," the KwaNdebele "commuters" have little energy to spare for the study of the history of their nation-to-be. It rewards a little contemplation, nevertheless, for it exposes the dubiousness of the ethnic theorizing in which the best apartheid brains indulged themselves to justify, more than a half century after the fact, the grossly unequal territorial division that was written into the Native Lands Act. The basic theory is that the black people share no single identity or set of values, unlike the whites, whose skin color can be taken as a badge of "civilization," that history has ordained a process of spontaneous fission of what appears to be a black majority into ten distinct nations, each with its own language, culture, and identity. What the Afrikaners have done, of course, is to project their own dream of nationhood onto their neighbors. "We did unto others what we would have others do unto us," the former prime minister Balthazar Johannes Vorster observed in a growl that carried no dulcet overtones of loving anyone's neighbor when I visited him in Port Elizabeth before his death.

That is convenient and even appealing as rationalization, but it doesn't bear much thought. Would the Afrikaners, for instance, have been satisfied by the land settlement that has been foisted on the Zulus, whose sense of nationhood is slightly older than their own and whose numbers now outrun theirs by three to one? It can be answered that it was the English who did unto the Zulus. The Afrikaners, building on that model, tried their best to do unto all the others on the basis of their own theories of nationality, which turned out to be bad history and worse anthropology when applied to the ethnic strains, lineages, and clan groupings that have been woven into the subtly variegated tapestry of black South Africa. It was the bureaucrats in Pretoria, finally, who determined that there were ten black nations. They could just as easily have counted two, three, or twenty. Black nationalists, of course, count one.

Two or three would have meant the surrender of large amounts of white land and the creation of black power bases, plausible states, from which a successful challenge to white dominance might have been mounted. Twenty would have been unmanageable. Ten was an arbitrary compromise, a way of diffusing the demand for black political rights without being any more ridiculous than necessary. Originally the bureaucrats counted nine. Then they counted again and came up with KwaNdebele. In fact, scholars generally divide the black peoples of South Africa into two broad linguistic groupings, the Sotho and Nguni, which overlapped territorially and sometimes fused as political orders rose and fell in an elusive history that plainly predates the arrival of the whites. Powerful chiefs did not practice apartheid. They conquered neighbors and absorbed them. When a tribal grouping was on the rise, others fled, colliding with and dislodging groups that lay in their path. Often these collisions resulted in the formation of new groups; like chemical allotropes, the difference was in their form and appearance rather than their basic nature. The dialects they spoke were mutually intelligible; their values and customs, broadly similar. There was no more in the way of ethnic differences in the nineteenth century between the people who came to be called Zulus and the people who came to be called Ndebeles than there was between the followers of rival Afrikaner leaders in the period of the Trek, such as Andries Pretorius and Andries Potgieter. All Afrikaners spoke the same language, but they ended up in two frontier republics, from which tiny tribal groups continued to splinter off in search of their own place in Africa.

The Zulus and Ndebeles also spoke the same language, but when the great Zulu warrior Shaka was establishing his kingdom, rivals and rebellious vassals fled in waves from what became Natal to the Transvaal, where they ruthlessly attacked and plundered the resident Sotho clans. One of the rebels was a chief called Mzilikazi, who appears to have defied Shaka in 1823 by refusing to hand over as tribute some cattle he had captured in battle. When they reached the Transvaal, Mzilikazi and his warriors were few in number, but they expanded rapidly, absorbing defeated enemies. The new political compound was the start of the Ndebele nation. It had been going for fewer than fifteen years when it clashed fatefully with the first Afrikaners to reach the Transvaal. That battle, in 1836, was seen by some Afrikaners as the basis of their claim to the whole territory. The Ndebeles may have been interlopers, but, the whites reasoned, they had achieved suzerainty over all the other tribes; therefore, suzerainty was deemed to have passed to the handful of white pioneers who overcame them with firepower. The whites devoted the next half century to making a reality of this theory, which no blacks ever accepted.

Meanwhile, Mzilikazi fled with his warriors across the Limpopo

River into what became Rhodesia and now is Zimbabwe. Several distinct remnants calling themselves Ndebeles remained in what became South Africa. As peace returned to the Transvaal, these groups were partly re-absorbed by the various tribal groups Mzilikazi had crushed. There were thus Sothos who went across the Limpopo whose descendants are known as Ndebeles, and there were Ndebeles who remained behind whose descendants today speak the language of the Sothos, Sesotho. Some of these Sesotho speakers continue to call themselves Ndebeles; others do not. Still other clan groups that thought of themselves as Ndebele continued to speak the Nguni dialects now known as Sindebele, which are so similar to Zulu, still, that Zulu texts are often used to teach Sindebele.

Ndebeles married Sothos. They married Tswanas. They married Zulus. They lived side by side with Pedis, Tsongas, and Swazis. When they moved to the cities, all these various kinds of blacks tended to forget what they were. "A man sounded ridiculous," observed Can Themba, a black South African writer whose stories and early alcohol-induced death were reminiscent of Ring Lardner, "for boasting he was a Mopedi or a Mosuto or a Xhosa or a Zulu—nobody seemed to care. You were an African *here,* and somewhere *there* was a white man: two different kinds of humans that impinged now and then—indeed often —and painfully."

Then, in their will to create a fixed and stable order that had never existed, the white authorities started to draw the boundaries of ethnic "homelands," which closely approximated those of the old tribal reserves. They even dreamed of retribalizing urban blacks, to whom the homelands seemed a huge irrelevance, even an insult. Ethnic identities that had tended to blur and decline in importance suddenly had everything to do with what kind of third-class citizen a black was going to be. Some who regarded themselves as Ndebeles discovered they were living in a country called Bophuthatswana that was established for Tswanas. Now not only were they to be worse off than whites, coloreds, and Indians, but they were also to be worse off than Tswanas. Others discovered they were living in a state called Lebowa where Sothos and Pedis were supposed to have the upper hand. Apartheid revived old enmities among blacks and created new ones. This obviously did no harm to the actuarial prospects of the white regime, but once started, the process of division and alienation was hard to stop. It was the white authorities who drew the boundaries and decided, essentially for their own convenience, that there would have to be two Xhosa states, rather than one, but no Mpondo, Mfengu, or Ndebele states; that the Zulu homeland would be scattered in forty-one fragments across a single South African province, while the Tswana homeland would crop up in three provinces in six or seven pieces; or that, finally, the dream or delusion that any of these states could develop a degree of economic self-sufficiency had to be abandoned. But when a motley assortment of Ndebele chiefs resisted and asked for a homeland of their own where they could have the fancy houses and cars that the Tswana chiefs were now getting, the white bureaucrats were put in a ticklish position. Apartheid was their idea, one Ndebele chief said, so it was up to them to "unscramble the egg" of black South Africa.

The white officials closest to the scene knew the impossibility of compartmentalizing blacks on an ethnic basis in the Transvaal; the truth was they were scattered and interspersed, had been for more than a century. Thus the homelands could only approximate the ideal of distinct ethnic enclaves that they were supposed to represent. But the theory of separate nationalities had to be pursued, so when they laid out the "closer settlements" of the eastern Transvaal, they tried to group the Pedis on the south side of the highway that ran into the reserves and the Shangaans to the north, then declared the road to be a boundary between Lebowa and Gazankulu. Of course, it remained just a backcountry road; there and elsewhere the boundaries were porous. At least one-third of the population of the Tswana homeland was non-Tswana, and more Tswanas lived outside the homeland than in. It was one thing to finance resettlement programs to get blacks out of white areas, but the white regime's devotion to theoretical consistency was not so great that it wanted to start financing resettlement to get blacks out of black areas where they were judged to be ethnic misfits. Apartheid could no more create a pure Ndebele state than it could a pure Afrikaner state; it could only replicate itself, creating a tribal satrapy in which power was unequally distributed on an ethnic basis. The apartheid ideologues knew all this but were flattered by the Ndebele demand, which they embraced as an expression of Ndebele nationalism and therefore as proof that their theoretical ditherings had some validity. Oppression of Ndebeles by Tswanas vindicated their own oppressive policies, demonstrating what chaos there could be in South Africa if they weren't there to draw boundaries. So they compromised: There could be a homeland for southern Ndebeles but not for northern Ndebeles, who would continue to live in Lebowa. As soon as the boundaries of the new state were declared, a group of Pedis demanded they be redrawn, for it included their traditional holdings.

What makes this twisted chronicle worth recounting is the result. Tiny, obscure KwaNdebele burst into existence in all its squalor as blacks came by the tens of thousands to put up shanties in new "closer settlements." Putco subsidies were negotiated, and the buses started to roll. Then it was realized that many in the soaring population were not Ndebeles at all. Some say 40 percent, some say half, belong to other black ethnic groups. The tribal state not only lacked infrastructure, an economy, and a significant history on the land it had suddenly come to occupy but wasn't even tribal, except as a corrupt patronage machine that could be relied on to discriminate against non-Ndebeles, who would still come to this most pathetic of homelands because it was the place nearest the industrial areas where they worked in which they could legally settle with their families. They come, these Zulus and Shangaans and Swazis, because it makes more sense to ride the buses than to wait in more remote homelands for jobs to come to them.

Buses. You always come back to buses. A survey by the Human Sciences Research Council in Pretoria found that only 22.6 percent of the 534,000 black "commuters" had to travel three hours or more to work, but 71.3 percent had to travel more than two hours, and more than half were away from their homes at least fifteen hours of every working day. These figures can be interpreted to mean that blacks are voting with their feet for apartheid, yet it isn't tribal chauvinism but crude need, amounting to desperation, that propels them through the man-made labyrinth of unfathomable regulations. Whatever the figures say about black motivation, they are unambiguous on the built-in inefficiencies of a system that insists on moving people on the basis of race and only then worries about the basic economics of keeping them alive. At dusk, in different seasons and years, I followed the bus convoys that run between a tiny black state called Qwaqwa and Harrismith, a small commercial center; then between nearby Ladysmith and the three resettlement sites of Ezakheni, Ekuvukeni, and Limehill that white officials had strung out along a dirt road into a desolate, undeveloped patch of the Zulu national state. I followed the convoys between Vryheid—that's "freedom" in Afrikaans—and Nondweni, another of at least twenty-four "closer settlements" in Natal, along a dirt road that offers vistas of endless white grazing land and, adding insult to injury, a monumental laager, or circle, of sixty-six covered wagons cast in bronze, now slowly rusting and oxidizing in the wind, that Afrikaner patriots erected on the veld at Blood River, the Sinai where their forefathers made their covenant with the Lord, which enabled them to vanquish Dingane's hordes and consign the descendants of those Zulu warriors to buses. And always there was the reflection that the people on those buses, who theoretically come to South Africa only to work and then leave it nightly, are the lucky ones with jobs.

The Harrismiths, Ladysmiths, and Vryheids are supposed to be industrial "growth points," but they don't begin to supply the jobs needed to sustain the rapidly growing number of potential "commuters" in the "closer settlements" at the end of the bus routes. And there is still a whole other category of these resettlement camps—forgotten, forsaken places like Qudeni, another sixty miles down the dirt road from Nondweni—that are impossibly remote, beyond any social engineer's dream of a commuter route, where the only income is what migrants send home. All these came into existence as a result of the relentless pressure of the government while it was simultaneously seeking—and sometimes receiving—kudos at home and abroad for changing direction.

The contradiction has to be handled with some delicacy. Wherever possible, blacks have to be coaxed, wheedled, and conditioned to move "voluntarily." Persuasion is most effective when care is taken to ensure that they have no alternatives. Instead of harassing black farm tenants and laborers to vacate their homesteads in white rural areas, the authorities concentrate on bringing white farmers around to the view that it is in their interest and a matter of patriotic duty as well to expel surplus blacks. When they decide to force the issue, the authorities try to avoid mass resistance by plucking up small numbers at a time, with maximum stealth and speed. Care is taken to ensure that the blacks who man the GG trucks in these removals are never from the region, never of the same ethnic group that is being moved. On the dirt road that runs to the resettlement sites outside Ladysmith, there is a small encampment of migrant workers from far-off Venda who are employed to move Zulus. At Seymour, a remote rural hamlet in the eastern part of the Cape that was about to be handed over to supposedly sovereign Ciskei, I watched one afternoon as Zulu workers erected rows of temporary metal shelters for Xhosa families that were about to be moved out of a white area fifty miles away. Some white official had selected the only soccer field in Seymour's black township as a convenient site for the coming resettlement. By midafternoon there was no soccer field left.

The land set aside for human habitation in mountainous Qwaqwa, scarcely twenty-five square miles, filled up with nearly a quarter of a million people in a decade of resettlement. Supposedly the homeland for 2 million southern Sothos—the dominant black group in the Orange Free State, where blacks still outnumber whites by more than three to one and where they haven't been permitted to own land for more than a century—Qwaqwa then had something like 88 percent of its nominal population living outside its borders. Even so, its overpopulation seemed so conspicuous and unnatural when I came upon this apparition of shanties and hovels for the first time—after driving for several hours through scenic national parks and open grazing land in an adjacent white area that looked like Idaho or Montana—that I found myself groping for Oriental comparisons. Did it remind me of Peshawar? Could Yemen look something like this? With level land fast running out near Phuthaditjhaba, the government center and capital of this vest-pocket state, newcomers were finding it necessary to hack their building sites out of steep slopes. For an hour or so, I experimented with taking pictures of these hillside settlements, hoping to get an image that conveyed the hivelike density of the place, but gave up in frustration. One picture of mud houses squeezed together in a barren landscape looked more or less like another. It wasn't the houses themselves that accounted for the overwhelming sense of abandonment and claustrophobia that you might expect to find in a refugee camp; it was the accumulation, the totality of them, with little in the way of a visible, supporting economy. It required a panoramic shot with a precise depth-of-field calculation, which was beyond my competence. And it required the immediate contrast of white South Africa, in all its plenitude and spaciousness, next door. How else could you make an image of exclusion?

I was still trying to put my finger on what it was that made this encampment masquerading as a nation seem so apparitional when I found in the waiting room of the chief minister in Phuthaditjhaba a bound volume of learned papers entitled *Ontwikkeling in Qwaqwa* ("Development in Qwaqwa"). The papers had been delivered at an "interdisciplinary," not to mention interracial, conference that had been held for black and white officials in the new homeland capital under the auspices of the University of the Orange Free State. Achieving a level of self-parody, it was a sublime example of the ability of white South Africans to blind themselves to the visible consequences of the policies they support, a kind of political double bookkeeping in which the tax evader seeks to make sure that the taxpayer's money is not wasted. Here was a group of Afrikaner academics worrying about the problems of "nation building" in a minuscule country that had no existence at all before 1974, except as a remote reserve for two obscure tribal clans. Now, as a result of the white government's resettlement efforts, it had blossomed before their eyes as a full-fledged "LDC" (less developed country). They had grown it themselves in their own social hothouse, and now whatever the World Bank had to say about Bangladesh or Gunnar Myrdal once said about India could be said by them about Qwaqwa. So I found a certain S. F. Coetzee pointing to the danger of "the high population growth rate in the LDCs" and "the high unemployment rate in the LDCs," as if these provided an explanatory context for "a developing country such as Qwaqwa." Unemployment, he tells us gravely, "is causal to a new phenomenon, to wit the so-called 'marginal men' or people who, due to their situation of unemployment, are not concerned with the community at large and therefore also not with development." P. H. du Preez painstakingly diagrams a community development program to bridge this gap. Qwaqwa, it appears, requires "initiators" to form "nuclear groups" that will then be responsible for the "activation" of "normative transformation in a non-directive manner." P. H. du Preez, identified as an employee of the Department of Cooperation and Development in Pretoria, which runs the resettlement programs, extracts a potentially subversive thought from the American sociology texts he is plagiarizing. "Responsible freedom," he says, "can only be realized in a democratic community."

There are a few paradoxes here, obviously, that he has to steer around. Most of Qwaqwa's nominal population lives outside its borders, where black "initiators" who encourage "activation" usually get into trouble. For reasons he does not mention, "responsible freedom" appears to be available only in an indigent community formed by uprooted people living on the earnings of absentee relatives, and these absentees remain "marginal men" even when employed because they are legally barred from citizenship where they work. If P. H. du Preez dissociated like this in private life, he would be judged severely neurotic. But in South Africa it is possible for a white to earn a respectable living lecturing on community development and participatory democracy to black refugees from communities that have been destroyed by arbitrary laws enacted by whites, without blacks having had the slightest say.

The chief minister, a former school inspector named Kenneth Mopeli who had a photograph of South Africa's white president hanging over his desk, was also dissociating a bit. His distress became evident when, interrupting his account of the efforts his white advisers made to coax him to seek independence for Qwaqwa, a black aide entered the room and handed him a folded note with a look of great urgency. The chief minister read the note and scowled.

"I am very shocked," he said reprovingly. "I can see you are one of those foreign journalists who come to South Africa with preconceived ideas to write one-sided articles. It says here that you were taking pictures of poor houses and shanties."

I said there were certainly lots of shanties in Qwaqwa but I hadn't been focusing on the worst of them, only trying to take pictures that showed the density of population in his state. Some of the mud houses, I added, venturing to placate him, seemed to have been lovingly improved. Yes, there was poverty, the chief minister now acknowledged, but there were also some "points of light." He said the phrase first in Afrikaans, then translated. For instance, there were the eight houses the South African government had built for himself and members of his Cabinet at a cost of more than $1 million. When I said I would be happy to visit and photograph them, the chief minister became less tense. "Leaders should live in houses their people can be proud of," he said. There was now an uneasy, defensive note in his voice. Giving him the benefit of the doubt, I guessed that he was repeating a rationalization he could not entirely accept.

Phuthaditjhaba's ministerial mansions were on top of a hill, with a commanding view of resettlement blight and nearby mountains, including the flat-topped mesa, a near replica of Cape Town's Table Mountain, which gives Qwaqwa its name and stands as a symbolic barrier to white South Africa. There was a gate and a guardhouse at the only gap in the chain-metal fence surrounding the compound. Each residence came with a high alpine gable and a three-car garage. A swimming pool and a tennis court were under construction. Across a ravine that was filled with shanties there was another compound, visible through the fence, with a fence of its own and houses that were noticeably less opulent. This was the segregated enclave for the white officials who advised the Qwaqwa Cabinet. I was encouraged to wander through the chief minister's residence; then, preoccupied by two questions, I stood for a time on a rear patio where empty pint-size whiskey and brandy bottles were accumulating in a small pile. One question was what would happen to Qwaqwa and, specifically, these absurd mansions if the South African system ever collapsed. A decent successor regime, I speculated, could turn them into an old-age home, a mental institution, or a center for rural development; a nasty regime would take them over for local party and military leaders, in which case their purpose would not have greatly changed. The other question was more difficult. I couldn't decide whether I was right in my initial instinct to impute cynical motives to the white advisers who offered mansions and Mercedes cars to black homeland leaders they had cultivated and advanced. Perhaps it wasn't cynicism but zany, self-exposing idealism, really doing unto others what they would have others do unto them. Perhaps they needed to believe that this was what "nation building" was all about or that since people expect their leaders to live in big houses, the reverse can also hold true: that they'll accept as their leaders whoever is put in the only big houses they can see. Perhaps, I thought gloomily, they weren't entirely wrong.

The next time I visited Qwaqwa I was in the company of two blacks from Soweto, neither of whom was likely to accept this line of reasoning. A new shopping center had been located, logically enough, next to a new bus depot. In the foreground was a Kentucky Fried Chicken outlet; as far as I knew, Colonel Sanders's first entry in South Africa's black homelands. *Nou Oop* ("Now Open") said the Afrikaans sign in the window. The shopping center was about to be dedicated by Chief Minister Mopeli, a band, and a corps of drum majorettes. Surveys have indicated that the average Qwaqwa household scrapes by on less than $500 a year for food, but the shops featured luxury items—Bally shoes, Italian "casuals," Japanese cameras. Barclays, Standard, and Volkskas banks were also represented. Presumably these catered to the civil servants and teachers who occupied the cement-block township houses that had been built nearby. A small consortium of physicians had opened an office above a drugstore run by an Afrikaner pharmacist. Drs. Berke, Burger, Le Roux, and Van Zyl, all graduates of the University of Pretoria, were its principals. "L. E. Du Toit," said a sign over the liquor store, was "licensed to sell wines and spiritous liquors."

"Weird," one of my Soweto friends said, looking around, as we waited for an acquaintance of his, a black lawyer who was the sole representative in Phuthaditjhaba of a law firm called Du Plessis & Du Plessis from a nearby Free State town. The office the man ran netted for Du Plessis & Du Plessis more than $5,000 a month, of which he was paid only $425, although he qualified as an attorney in the Free State. So for the third time he was handing in his notice, he said, and this time he was going to make it stick. He had already agreed to join a black firm in Nelspruit in the eastern Transvaal, which meant he would probably end up living in the Swazi homeland of KaNgwane. It didn't matter, he said. He wasn't Swazi, but he wasn't southern Sotho either.

I asked one of my companions how he was typed ethnically. "My family language is Xhosa," the Soweto man replied. "My citizenship is black." Later that evening he showed me a broadside for a "Black Solidarity Rally" that had just been banned by police order in Soweto. THE TRUTH the paper announced. NO PEOPLE CAN BE OPPRESSED FOREVER. This welcome news had been deduced, with dubious logic, from the proved mortality of Balthazar Johannes Vorster, the former prime minister, who had just died in Cape Town. Whatever else had happened, the broadside seemed to be saying, the movement had outlived at least one of its oppressors. It then offered what it termed a "political definition" of blacks: "those people who are, by law or tradition, socially discriminated against, economically exploited and politically oppressed by the South African way of life." But the fact remained that there would be no solidarity rally in Soweto; there would be drum majorettes at the new Setsing Shopping Center in Phuthaditjhaba instead. And that was the new South Africa.

Qwaqwa still struck me as a man-made calamity, but here, as in KwaNdebele, a return visit left me with the eerie feeling that the grand design of the apartheid planners looked a little more durable, if not less absurd, than it had on first impression. The social engineers, I thought that night, were gradually gaining ground. The next morning at the Hotel Qwaqwa I was awakened at four-thirty by the first buses leaving for Harrismith. After KwaNdebele, I was able to roll over with the thought that four-thirty wasn't so bad.

My friends from Soweto, I should add, were less easily impressed by white power, less easily dismayed. As we drove out of Qwaqwa to continue our tour of resettlement sites, one of them refortified himself by reaching into a seemingly unlimited repertoire of memorized poems with revolutionary themes and sonorously recited a translation of the Portuguese verse of Agostinho Neto, the deceased Angolan president:

> Come with me, Africa in fancy trousers
> let us go down into the street
> and dance the tiring dance of men . . .
> let us look clearly at the bowed shoulders
> of people going down the alleyway
> black black of misery black of frustration
> black of anxiety
> and let us give them our hearts

There was no Kentucky Fried Chicken, hotel, or other homeland razzle-dazzle at Ekuvukeni, where we spent the next night. This was a resettlement site, unadorned, out in the bush, black black of misery and frustration. "Here there's nothing, nothing, nothing," said a widow who had been there for three years. We were now on one of the many islands of the Zulu national state, the landlocked archipelago called KwaZulu. At dusk we ventured into a neighboring country called South Africa to visit Matiwaneskop, a "black spot" in which the authorities had signaled their intention to buy out and raze the community by painting numbers on every house and shanty they planned to take over by inexorable eminent domain. Matiwaneskop's land, in fact, had already been formally expropriated.

On the way there we passed the ruins of a community called Steincoalspruit, where more than 11,000 blacks had lived on land first purchased by blacks in 1877. One hundred and one years later, nearly the entire community, all but a tiny number of landowners who got a temporary reprieve by going along with the eviction of their tenants, was moved twenty miles, across the homeland border to Ekuvukeni, by GG. Since my last drive down this road, I noticed, a subsidiary of Anglo Vaal, one of the South African mining houses, had started open-pit mining on the land of the displaced community. In Natal the "black spots" with coal usually seem to be expropriated first. The white officials responsible for these moves could tell themselves that it would make no difference after a few years or a generation to the "black spot" blacks that they lived in Ekuvukeni rather than Steincoalspruit. But

Matiwaneskop—one of 195 remaining "black spots" due to be rubbed out in Natal—was resisting. And that resistance was a measure of the difference, for Ekuvukeni had no will left for resistance and nothing to defend.

In the eyes of a white official who goes home to a California-style suburb every evening, what Matiwaneskop had to defend may have looked paltry, but virtually everything it had, including a new secondary school, it had built itself without support from a government intent on knocking it down. The people here—there were about 12,000—needed no lectures on community development or traditional values. In a letter their elders sent to the government to protest the threatened removal, they included on their list of "tribal achievements" the building of ten churches, sixteen schools, a library, and a mechanical workshop. They still had land for cultivation and grazing, they said, and had never known drought (unlike Ekuvukeni, where the water supply had dried up and water was then being trucked in). Yet they were only fifteen miles from Ladysmith, where many of them worked. And most important, the elders noted, "The graves of our forefathers, the traditional burial places of our chiefs, are the bonds that tie us inseparably with this place." The bureaucracy, which is tenderhearted about tribal traditions that serve its purposes, doesn't tolerate any heathen mumbo jumbo about forefathers' graves when a long-planned removal is in view. But the elders had become skilled diplomats in fending off white officials who came to lecture them about their duty to obey the laws, under which their valid title deeds had been annulled. The last official visitor, it seemed, had nearly been undone by their generosity, reverence, and Christian compassion.

The scene, as it was described to us, was one I would have dearly loved to witness. An honor guard of young blacks formed a gauntlet outside the community hall that the commissioner from Ladysmith had to walk when he arrived to address a meeting he had requested. About 1,000 members of the community were waiting inside. Many white officials still like to be called "father" and "lord" in the old colonial style, and this commissioner, it seems, got the full treatment, including the gift of a sheep. Percy Hlope, the principal of the secondary school, explained why the community had decided to present a sheep rather than slaughter an ox. "I told him," Mr. Hlope said, smiling through a distinguished gray beard, "that he had chosen to work with black people, poor people, the most despised people in the land, and that therefore, he had identified himself with Jesus Christ. In seeing him before us, I said, we saw our Redeemer and therefore we thought it fitting to give him the only creature that can be identified with Jesus Christ."

The "Redeemer" was visibly moved, as well he might have been, by the moral superiority of the people who were supposed to be his wards. And when the time came for him to respond, he never got around to delivering the message that was presumably the point of the meeting: that Matiwaneskop's time was running out. Instead, Mr. Hlope said, he promised to report the community's sentiments to higher authority. The attitude of higher authority was indicated by a deputy minister with an unctuousness that was unusually sickening, even for a South African deputy minister. "Everyone of us," he wrote to a "black spot" community that was similarly threatened, "has to make sacrifices in some way or other to further peace and prosperity in this beautiful country of ours."

There were few signs of prosperity in Ekuvukeni and not so much peace either. The elderly catechist's widow with whom we stayed complained of the drunken hooliganism of the unemployed youths who found no jobs at the official labor bureau. I could believe her. At nine in the morning a crowd had already gathered outside the local beer hall, waiting for it to open. Elsewhere women gathered with plastic buckets to wait for the water trucks.

In Zulu, Ekuvukeni means "the place of awakening." Apartheid bureaucrats love such names. In Ciskei they named an equally dismal resettlement camp Zweledinga, "the promised land." The place of awakening this morning was deathly still except for the singsong chanting of ninety children, aged three to seven, who were crowded into a windowless metal shed that served as their nursery school, and the hymns of some church ladies, who were praying and making a collection for one of their neighbors whose husband was seriously ill. Because of labor migrancy, women typically outnumber men by three to two in places like this. These were wearing the prim Pilgrim uniforms that many of the black churches in South Africa favor, the combination of colors defining the creed and confession in each case. Some wore broad white collars on red tunics, others on blue and black; still others had black or blue collars on white tunics. "Hello, Umfundizi," they said to me, assuming me to be a priest. "How is Father?"

In one shanty we visited I saw a leper in a condition more shocking than what I had been accustomed to witnessing in Benares, Calcutta, or Rangoon. The man, who seemed half-demented, had never received treatment; his sores were unbandaged. The clinic had told him, he said, that he had "kaffir poison," that he was the victim of black magic, and he therefore believed his condition to be hopeless. Such interpretations came easily in Ekuvukeni. Among the few signs of prosperity in the place was the new house being built for the local muti man, the witchcraft specialist who prefers to be described as a traditional healer. The muti man was only thirty-four. If Ekuvukeni had a Jaycees Club, he would probably have won its citation as the "most successful young man" in the settlement. When we encountered him, he was wearing designer jeans and listening to Aretha Franklin on his cassette deck. The muti man readily showed me some of his powders and herbs and told me what compounds and unguents were good for what needs: The fats from male and female puff adders and doves were useful in love potions; "employment medicine," enabling anyone suffering from fear and anxiety to face an intimidating white boss, involved extracts from snakes, monkeys, giraffes, and a particular kind of small cat that runs wild in the bush. He had to learn his nostrums, he said, but prophecy was a gift with which he had been born. I asked if he had anything to prescribe for liberation. "Ah, *inkululeko,*" he responded in a soft, deep voice, using the Zulu word. The problem of *inkululeko,* he said with some incisiveness, was the problem of disunity among blacks. There were highly complex medicines that could overcome this, but for the treatment to work, he said, he would have to take the initiative of gathering the various groups together, and he would have to give his potions away free. "It would be bad for my living," he said. Besides, no one had asked.

There were times when South Africa left me completely nonplussed, and this was one of them. I didn't know whether to be appalled or moved by the ability of people to endure in a place like Ekuvukeni. The mood was short-lived, as a result of a call of nature. For three years I had seen and counted the outhouses of corrugated metal that the white authorities erect on each little plot when they are laying out a "closer settlement." In my mind these privies, looking like sentry boxes and lined up in military formation, were a visible index and symbol of the resettlement effort, like the buses. Now I had to enter one.

It proved to contain a crude bucket contraption secured on a metal base, as marginal a sanitary facility as could be imagined for a dense settlement of more than 20,000 people built with neither drainage nor sewage systems. The most unpleasant discovery came when I was ready to leave. Somehow the door had locked behind me, and I couldn't get out. I stood on the seat, which was a balancing act, for it tipped with my weight. Once I got it steady, I could look out into the settlement through a gap of eight or ten inches between the outhouse roof and the top of the door. Having no idea how to shout for help in Zulu, I hollered hello. There were children playing on the other side of the road, maybe fifty yards away, but they took no notice. Next, I clambered down and tried to kick the door open; the latch held. Then I tried and failed to lift or push the outhouse off its base. Finally, I was up on the seat again, waving my arms, which I could squeeze through the gap up to the elbows, and baying my hellos. First I was amused, then agitated, then agitated and amused together; mostly agitated, I admit, but I couldn't help picturing the spectacle I was going to present to whoever found me: hung up in the latrine, my white hands gesturing spastically; my reddening, exasperated face mostly hidden by the door and Italian aviator-style sunglasses that I had to keep on so as not to lose a potential rescuer in a myopic blur. It was no solace to think that probably no journalist had carried his investigations of resettlement in South Africa further. Finally, my shouts drew the attention of an old man in rags with a wizened face and a wispy white beard who viewed me with some astonishment for a long moment, then smilingly lifted the outside latch I couldn't reach and freed me. It had taken no more than fifteen minutes, but Ekuvukeni now looked slightly better to me and a lot more welcoming. I hadn't crawled out of my white skin for even an instant, but my exaggerated freedom of movement—an essential part of my identity, certified by a walletful of embossed plastic that entitled me to fly anywhere in the world at short notice—had been briefly compromised. After that there didn't seem to be much point in wondering about which of several precious attitudes to adopt to the fact that people endure after they are corralled in a place like Ekuvukeni. What else are they to do?

It was in Nondweni, where I drove the next day, that I first started counting latrines. Now, three years later, I found a little depot there where the prefabricated components of outhouses and temporary metal shelters were piled behind a wire fence, ready for use as new refugees from the white areas trickled in. GG beneficently allows newcomers to keep the sheds for a few months until they put up their own houses of sun-dried mud blocks. Sometimes it hands out green tents. The country was studded with remote, windswept hillsides on which these had suddenly appeared, places the names of which were less known in the smarter white quarters than the names of Aegean islands or Adriatic ports. And yet for those who have seen them, there is a compulsion to go on naming these places. I had counted tents and latrines at a place called Kammaskraal in Ciskei, a "closer settlement" so isolated that even the authorities who brought it into existence had to wonder how it could survive. Eventually they put its inhabitants back on trucks and carted them off to a forsaken, deteriorating homeland town called Peddie, where they were installed in mass-produced two-room wooden houses in yet another "closer settlement." At Peddie I counted latrines on uninhabited plots that had been laid out around the edge of the place. These latrines, usually the only public indication the secretive bureaucracy gave of future removals, showed that resettlement in Peddie wasn't finished. It never was, as far as I could tell. At Qudeni the outhouses were set out at regular intervals on the hillside beyond the last row of inhabited plots. The latrines, it was rumored, had already been set up for the Matiwaneskop people at a site not far from Ekuvukeni, at the end of a road that bristled with official "no trespassing" signs in Zulu, Afrikaans, and English. At Compensation, the ironic name given to another KwaZulu site that was the destination for a relatively self-sufficient "black spot" community called Kwapitela, the rows of numbered latrines on vacant lots meant that the official net was tightening around still another black community, where houses would already have been numbered and landlords promised a fat payoff for their property if only they made it easy for the authorities by evicting their tenants.

At each of these places, I met blacks who had been separated from respectable livelihoods they had been enterprising enough to organize for themselves despite the difficulties South African law and custom put in their way. There was Judeah Nido, a displaced person from Kwapitela, ten miles from the border of the internationally recognized black state of Lesotho. Judeah Nido owned his own Ford pickup truck and used it to run a taxi and transport service from Lesotho to Pietermaritzburg. Moved forty-five miles inland to Compensation, he was too far from the border to keep up the old route, and there was not enough money or demand where he had been deposited to start a new one.

Having been self-employed, he now faced the prospect of becoming a migrant laborer. "I'm still trying to think of something else," he said. Ephraim Koheswa, also from Kwapitela, had just purchased an old tractor from a white farmer with the idea of renting out his services to black tenant farmers. At Compensation there was no provision for farming and thus no need for his tractor. That is what happened to Ephraim Mdlulu, a black tractor owner who was moved to Qudeni. And to Simon Mkodi at Rooigrond and Sam Pita at Thornhill, both of whose tractors ended up as rusted hulks on a resettlement plot. Maybe they were not typical, but I kept running into sturdy black yeomen whom the system had turned into outcasts, telling them, in effect, that they had overreached. "We are people who work with our hands," Sam Pita said, holding his own strong hands in front of his face for my inspection. "To stay just doing nothing is terrible."

Liberal and religious opponents of removals tend to react to each one as if it were an isolated outrage, a throwback, an aberration that can be stopped or delayed if the outcry is loud enough. They fight the evil on a case-by-case basis because they know from experience that the sense of injustice among whites is a shallow pool that will dry up as soon as they seem to be attacking the system. But they also know, of course, that removals are not aberrations, that they are part of a coordinated campaign. Somewhere in Pretoria, I imagined, there had to be a situations room with secret charts and maps detailing the next phase. The authorities don't want too much controversy at any given time, but if attention is focused on a threatened community in the Transvaal, it may make tactical sense to hold off there and concentrate on another flank in the Cape or Natal where resistance seems to be softening. Some mastermind at a central point, it seemed to me, had to make such decisions. The great edifice of apartheid is far from completion. Six of ten homelands have yet to embrace the ambiguous sovereignty South Africa dangles before them. More than 1.5 million blacks are still due for resettlement across their borders. It is not the work of a single generation, but it will never be done at all if there is any letup. The apparatus must go on, fighting on all fronts at once, because it is up against the human instinct for survival and the imperatives of black rural development in South Africa, all of which point to an antithetical program: moving people out of the reserves, not in, and land reform in the presently sacrosanct white areas.

Each latrine that I counted seemed to me a marker, a tangible expression of the determination, skill, and sense of mission that a tiny and secretive white elite brings to the task of making the real South Africa, with all its energy and contradictions, conform to its own dream of order. It is a bizarre dream, but it is becoming the miserable reality all over the country in these unknown, hopelessly out-of-the-way places. Finally one day I reached a place where there were more markers than I could take in at a glance. The familiar formation of metal latrines stretched across undulating land, row on row gleaming in the morning sun. I would have had to hover in a helicopter or walk the hillsides for a couple of hours to count them all. I guessed there were about 1,500. A network of roads and plots had been laid out. There was even a school and a clinic. All that was lacking was human habitation. A "closer settlement" waiting to happen, the place had the fearful symmetry of a war cemetery and depressed me more than any of the squalid encampments I had seen because, I think, it represented in pure form what was most disturbing about the whole resettlement effort—the overweening white willfulness that was its only reason for being.

The place had been named Frankfort by German mercenaries, veterans of British units in the Crimean War, who were offered land on which to settle in the eastern Cape, known at the time as British Kaffraria. Simultaneously a Scotch Presbyterian mission was founded about thirty miles away at a place called Mgwali for Xhosa-speaking blacks by the first black missionary the church had trained. The black missionary, Tiyo Soga, had returned from Scotland with a Scottish wife. They had four sons before he died in 1871 at the age of forty-two, and one of those sons, Allan Soga, was present at the founding meeting of the African National Congress in 1912. In 1983, 23 years after the ANC was banned and forced underground, the black community at Mgwali was being led by a former political prisoner named Wilson Fanti, who had spent 10 years in jail for activities in support of the illegal organization. That, it might be said, is a tradition on which a "nation builder" might build. But the South African authorities had determined that Mgwali was a "black spot" and that Frankfort fell within the borders of supposedly independent Ciskei. So they bought out the descendants of the German settlers after nearly 125 years and built the resettlement site for the Mgwali blacks who were now aliens in the Republic of South Africa. They could not be allowed to remain. Later, when I wrote about Frankfort, I was reminded of a refrain from

Yeats: "Fifteen apparitions have I seen;/ The worst a coat upon a coat hanger." Fifteen hundred privies, I decided, was my worst.

The South African official's wife put together a couple of bits of information and came up with a strange result that left her incredulous. "Is it true," she asked with friendly curiosity, "that you are actually writing a book on KwaNdebele?"

My wisecracking reply, delivered at a diplomatic party in Pretoria, struck me—but only me—as very funny. Its references were cross-cultural, yielding blinks, squints, and blank stares. "Yes," I said, "I'm calling it *The Boys on the Bus.*"

"Well, maybe you should see the other side," she said.

The other side proved to be a cattle ranch of more than 14,000 acres that two friends from her university days had been developing for twenty-four years. They had a herd of about 2,000 head plus three dozen or so prize studs for breeding. The reward for their life's work was a decision by their government to expropriate the land as the site of the new capital for KwaNdebele. An independence ceremony, after all, cannot be held in the middle of a refugee camp. The show desperately needed a set and the show, of course, must go on. Dirk van Deventer and his wife, Paula, had been informed that it was their patriotic duty to negotiate a good price for their holding and move on.

Tall and lean with craggy good looks and an uproarious, humorous manner that was nothing if not forthright, Dirk van Deventer was the South African Boer at his most appealing. His wife, who had earned an agriculture degree and held some of the cattle and land in her own name, seemed tentative in his long shadow. She had not pampered herself like the Pretoria wives—too much time outdoors on the veld had weathered her skin—but the mixed suggestions of vulnerability and strength in her look made her seem real, interesting, and appealing, too, in a way they could never be. The husband, whose right wrist was in a cast, made the *braai,* or barbecue, on a large boulder under an *enkeldoring* ("single thorn") tree, a kind of acacia that was prevalent enough on his land to have given its name to his farm. An ostrich, kept as a pet for nine-year-old Edward van Deventer, lumbered and scavenged nearby. It had recently swallowed his car keys, our host complained, mixing imprecations with a zestful laugh. As the steaks, chops, and *boerewors* (sausage) sizzled over the embers, he held forth in the same fashion on the injustice and lunacy of the pending expropriation, on the blight, erosion, and cattle thieving that had risen in the area with the rise of KwaNdebele. The nearest "closer settlement" was only four miles down the road, and some nights, Dirk said, he sat with his rifle in a drainage pipe near his fence, hoping to sight a poacher. "I'd kill him, too," he said, in a tone of boyish braggadocio rather than menace, "black or white."

Most of his neighbors had decided to be "realistic" and sell for the sake of South Africa and its future, not to mention the prices that were being offered and the opportunity to put some distance between themselves and the black homeland. "You voted for it, you do it," he said he told them. This was no closet liberal speaking. Dirk was what is known as a *bloedsap* (which is a political anagram describing a vanishing breed among Afrikaners, ultraconservatives reared in the South African party of Jan Christiaan Smuts and, "SAP" by "blood," still hostile to the governing Nationalists). It would never have occurred to him that there could be such a thing as a sensible black government in Pretoria or that if such a thing existed, its desire to keep its population fed might very well impel it to preserve him on his land. In a roundabout way I uttered this unthinkable thought by repeating what a black agricultural official in Ciskei had said to me about a planned expropriation of white farms on its borders. "If I were the Mugabe of this place," the man said as we drove by prosperous holdings that were likely to be turned into "closer settlements," "I'd do anything to keep these farmers here." In fact, that was still Robert Mugabe's policy in Zimbabwe. But although it was the white government that now wanted to move the Van Deventers, he saw it as a surrender to "Africa" and "communism" and, synonymous in his mind with both those terms, which were synonymous with each other, as a surrender to ignorant and wasteful husbandry.

After lunch we drove into the veld to inspect the site of the new capital, or rather towheaded Edward did the driving, holding his head to the right of the steering wheel of the *bakkie* (pickup truck) since he was too short to see over it, while his father shouted directions from the back in Afrikaans. "Drives a tractor as well as anyone on this farm," the father said in English. "Works all day." At the age of six, the boy had to have his rifle taken away for a whole year, his mother interjected, because he had lied about killing some doves. "He said they flew between him and some wild birds at which he was aiming *after* he pulled the trigger." So for a year he fished. Now he shot, fished, drove, and, it was presumed, always spoke the truth to his parents.

As the little boy drove up an incline, his father pointed to a patch of red earth next to a stream at the bottom of the hill. "There's the independence stadium," he said with a sharp-edged laugh. "The secretariat buildings are up there," he said, pointing up the hill. "The civil servants live over there, I think." *Enkeldorings* were living there now; his cattle grazed among them.

I asked about the casino, the inevitable homeland casino that was usually the first fruit of independence, the fruit being in the windows of the one-armed bandits. Only fifty miles from Pretoria, it was to have been built by Holiday Inns in the hope of taking the traffic away from Sun City. But now the Dutch Reformed churches of Pretoria were up in arms about this threat to the moral fiber of the community, and even more important, the holding company that owned Sun City had just taken over the casino operations of Holiday Inns. Maybe the casino was not inevitable, after all, meaning the new state would have no industry.

But on an early-summer afternoon, such fantasies quickly ceased to be diverting. Dirk hollered to Edward to stop the *bakkie*. He wanted to show us the veld, which had greened after long-delayed rains. After jumping down, he bent over to pick up some leaves, then asked us to smell. They had a delicate, lemony fragrance. Then he pointed to a tree with bright yellow blossoms, which he identified as the *huilboom* ("cry tree"). Off in the distance a single cow stood transfixed on a ridge. Sensing a sadness in her stance, Dirk had Edward drive in that direction. His tender husbandman's intuition was borne out; a dead calf lay rigid nearby.

We drove on past an old abandoned tin mine and the houses of some of his twenty-seven laborers. It was there that our host explained the cast on his wrist, which had fractured when his fist collided with the head of one of the twenty-seven. The story was told with a mixture of outrage and bravado. The man had begged off from work, saying he had to take his daughter to a doctor. Instead, he went off on a spree and got drunk, returning to drive an expensive John Deere tractor in that condition. What was worse, the daughter really was in need of seeing the doctor, desperately so. When she had to be rushed to his office, Mrs. van Deventer discovered the father's neglect. But now she was afraid that her husband's manner of recounting the incident was leaving his American guests with a misleading impression. "You're not the kind that just beats them," she interrupted. "You hit them. Then you talk to them. Then you hit them again."

Now the *bakkie* was at the edge of the highway, and although it was only a matter of driving across the road to the other side, Paula wanted her husband to take over the wheel. The boy did not have a license; he should not be driving on a public road. Dirk was adamant; the boy must drive on, must take us all the way back to the house. "I'll do nothing to discourage him, nothing to dampen his enthusiasm," he said. I had often heard Afrikaner farmers say that they treated their black laborers the way they treated their children. This wonderful father helped me see that as another piece of sentimentality and folk myth. He would never have imagined his laborers capable of the sturdy independence he was so passionately nurturing in his son.

If he had to move, Dirk van Deventer said as we left, he might try ranching in northern Cape Province. But he was a Transvaaler at heart. He would miss the trees. His brother-in-law thought he should move to America, a suggestion that comes up increasingly as a tease in Afrikaner conversation. I meant it as a tribute when I said he would fit in well in Texas.

The day at Enkeldoring farm was supposed to show me the "other side." Other side of what? I wondered. It seemed to me to be the same side as Frankfort, a victory for the demented visions of the social engineers in Pretoria and maybe a handful of homeland ministers, for whom South Africa would now erect pretentious mansions on the Van Deventer farm, and a defeat for everyone else. But the failure of the homelands—the blight, erosion and thieving, the resettlement, and buses roaring by the farm at four in the morning—served a deeper need than mere social order. Or so I was coming to suspect. These black states or parodies of black states are bound to fail, bound to turn to the white government that created them. In their failure, they nicely confirm the white man's fixed idea of "Africa" and teach blacks a lesson about their fundamental irresponsibility and dependence; the turning back confirms the white's fixed idea of himself.

"You can live," an Afrikaner tycoon said to me once, "by having the feeling that at least you're indispensable."

CHAPTER 6

∎

GENERALISSIMO

"Some words," the novelist Jean Rhys wrote, "have a long thin neck that you would like to strangle." For any outsider who returns to South Africa after an absence of months or years, the word "change" is likeliest to provoke spasms of what might be called lexicide. The challenge implied in "change" usually comes in a question, put in such a way as to flatter the outsider with the idea that his judgment will have special weight and value because he is in a position to be objective. But an objective and balanced answer is seldom wanted; the outsider becomes attuned to nuances in phrasing that signal the required response. "Do you see the changes?" was usually not a question, I discovered, but an assertion that they were all around, that they were dramatic, and that if you didn't acknowledge them fast, your political and intellectual credentials would be open to question. "Do you see *any* changes?" was an arch way of asking whether you were simple enough to be taken in by the country's official, quasi-official, or corporate image makers. A question could also be a question in rare cases, but after detonating a couple of nasty arguments with aggressive South African whites by being too unguarded, I learned to test the conversational ground before assuming that anything was expected from me beyond polite confirmation of what was already held to be self-evident. "You had better learn," exploded an English-speaking lawyer whom I had unintentionally provoked, "that there is such a thing as barbarism!" There is such a thing as apoplexy, and he seemed to be on the verge of it.

So I got a little evasive. "Yes, it has changed," I would sometimes say, drawing the expected comparison to my first incarnation in the country, "but not as much as New York in the same period." That

155

response was mildly provocative, interesting, and probably true without being open to challenge as a political declaration. On other occasions, veering dangerously toward earnestness, I would remark that there remained an apparent political conflict in South Africa that did not seem to have been resolved. If that was said blandly enough, no one was disposed to argue. Finally, after I had been back in the country for nearly a year and thought that I had my responses down pat, I was surprised to hear myself blurting out an answer I had never before tried. "Do you see the changes?" asked an Afrikaner businessman next to whom I was seated at a Cape Town lunch. The warning bells sounded faintly in my head, but I thought I was being flippant when I replied, "Yes, I never imagined they would be able to carry apartheid so far." Only when the words were out of my mouth did I realize that this was the answer that had gradually been taking shape in my mind all those months; to me, at least, they had the ring of cold truth.

Who could have imagined KwaNdebele or Qwaqwa? Or a resettlement program extending into the 1980's and beyond? Or black TV, where Zulu gangsters and Zulu detectives could fight it out in a Zulu city where Zulus owned bars and hotels and drove fancy cars and a white face was seldom seen? Or the four independent homelands that were supposed to be striving, in sad isolation from South Africa and the world, to fit themselves to that paradigm? It was only necessary to run your finger down the column of black population estimates published by the Central Statistical Services in Pretoria to see how far apartheid had gone. Despite a high birthrate, the number of blacks in South Africa regularly showed a decline, according to the official estimates. In 1976 there were 18.5 million blacks; by 1977, the official statistics claimed, there were only 15.7 million. Between 1973 and 1982, if you could believe what you read, there had been virtually no rise at all. Apartheid double bookkeeping, subtracting blacks every time there was an independence ceremony in a homeland, made this miracle possible. Who could have imagined that?

Not only people but places disappeared as a result of this white magic. In 1981, if you wanted to look up a telephone number for one of the major black townships in the region known as the eastern Cape, such as the township of Mdantsane outside the Indian Ocean port of East London, you looked in the directory for the region where the numbers for East London and Mdantsane both were listed. Mdantsane didn't have many phones, but with a population of more than 300,000, it had four times as many inhabitants as East London, to which it was attached as an annex. It was, in fact, the major human settlement in the region, but then it started to fade. In 1982, if you looked up Mdantsane in the phone directory, the listings were gone, and a small note in boldface type advised, "See Ciskei phone directory." The homeland of that name, the borders of which remained a matter of guesswork, impossible to locate on the ground, had just achieved its putative sovereignty. In 1983 the phone directory for the region made no mention of Mdantsane whatsoever or a dozen other places from Alice to Zwelitsha that used to exist in the eastern Cape. The only mention of Ciskei was on the list of foreign states that could be reached from East London by direct dialing. It was there in its alphabetical place, between China (meaning Taiwan) and Cyprus. Mdantsane, it could be deduced, was now afloat somewhere between Nicosia and Taipei. Now who could have imagined that?

Who could have imagined Phuthaditjhaba or Lebowagoma or Giyani or Bisho, the new homeland capitals dispersed and hidden away in the bush—the names of which, let alone locations, were unknown to most whites—with their ministerial mansions, lavish government centers, courts, prisons, teachers colleges, and supposed universities or their tiny suburbs with ranch houses fitted with attached carports? Apartheid had a limited number of beneficiaries, but for some it had become an enormous pork barrel: the big construction companies that built these grandiose and otiose centers at huge cost to the mainly white taxpayers, the white civil servants who could reach grades and pull in salaries in the black states that would be beyond them in Pretoria, and the tribal cabals of black legislators and bureaucrats whose salaries and cars became a tangible stake in the whole unwieldy structure, its ultimate reason for being. "The new policy of native self-government," Jan Christiaan Smuts promised his Oxford audience back in 1929, "will provide the natives with plenty of bones to chew and plenty of matters to wrangle over—and they do love to talk and dispute *ad infinitum*— and in that way will help to fill their otherwise empty lives with interest." Even Smuts, who cultivated the role of a visionary, could have foreseen only dimly that the calculation he was voicing with such benign contempt would remain, after more than a half a century, the central thesis of South African statecraft.

And who, I would ask myself, could have imagined a figure like Lieutenant General Xhanti Charles Sebe? Director of state security in "independent" Ciskei, a flamboyant black cop who sometimes wore a black Stetson with his smoked glasses and Christian Dior suits, this black generalissimo not only went along with the system that produced him but was as dedicated as any white to the task of rooting out its enemies. Apartheid filled his life with interest. It sent him to courses on intelligence gathering and bush warfare, put white colonels under his nominal command, and gave him a wedge of territory to secure in the many-sided struggle against "terrorism." It put a helicopter and a couple of planes at his disposal and also a fat-cat BMW sedan with frosted glass so that the assassins who were presumed to be lurking in wait for him could never know whether he was inside or where he was sitting. It gave him an armory of fancy weapons and listening devices; four small military bases, including one where black paratroopers and commandos were undergoing training in a supposedly secret program; a prison system all his own; a chestful of medals and a real security problem in an area that had long been the crucible of black resistance to white dominance. And so for three brief years he wielded more power and accrued more notoriety within the South African system than any black man had before him. He was exactly what the system needed to generate for its own survival, a dependable black ally who believed, more or less, in its purposes. His power, which was turned effectively against his own people, was real, not symbolic, and this was how the system answered the demand for black power that had been inspired in the region only a few years earlier by Steve Biko, whom Charles Sebe, then a lowly sergeant in the South African security police, had been assigned to shadow.

When the black general fell, his white handlers in the South African security apparatus did everything they could, short of bringing down the Tinkertoy government in the homeland they themselves had created, to get him back. Later, I imagined, they must have felt like the early space scientists after an accident with a rocket, telling themselves that since they had got one into orbit, they could do it again.

Charles Sebe could be viewed from a standpoint of liberal piety as a victim, too, of course, but I viewed him as a walking, breathing allegory of the whole racial conflict. If you considered what Ciskei really was—a sinkhole of despair and social misery into which the white authorities continued to pour surplus blacks from adjacent white areas —his enthusiasm for his mission had frightening implications. Of course, the white state had the capacity to put blacks on its payroll and set up homeland leaders in conditions of vassalage, but getting blacks actively engaged in the defense of this setup was something else. Yet it wasn't only Charles Sebe's enthusiasm for the conflict that set him apart. Even more, it was how easy it always seemed to imagine the small twist of fate that might have landed him on the other side, where he would have had the same appetite for half-baked doctrines of guerrilla warfare that he now had for half-baked doctrines of counterinsurgency. He had sold out, it was true, but that was long before he could have imagined the rewards and power that would later be placed within his grasp. He had sold out because he wanted to be on the side of power and authority. Every culture, every society, produces such men. The ability of the South African racial system to perpetuate itself turned in part, it seemed to me, on its ability to recruit and reward blacks like Charles Sebe. That he could exist at all—even though it was in the context of a homeland that was a grotesque social deformity—suggested to me that the racial system might be more durable than I had imagined.

So I made a point of getting to know him and found, before long, my thesis adumbrated in a really scary way in the discovery that this black militarist's dedication, energy, and power were being transmitted to a coterie of seemingly capable black aides, well-spoken, well-armed young men in expensive suits and cars who had found that they didn't have to join the underground to be where the action was in Ciskei. Created in his image, they showed Charles Sebe to be a leader. "My boys," he would purr, suddenly tender and avuncular, "I motivate my boys." Within a few months after I encountered them, they all were in one of General Sebe's jails, along with General Sebe. That surprising denouement put an ambiguous ending on my allegory, but there would be others to take their places.

I don't think Charles Sebe ever learned my name. When I phoned from Johannesburg and identified myself, there would be a pause on the other end, a palpable moment of uncertainty; then he would ask in a gravelly half whisper, "Is that my friend?"

"Yes," I ventured with considerable uncertainty myself the first time we had this exchange, figuring that anything less might cut it short.

All our subsequent phone conversations went the same way. "Oh, hello, my friend!" he would reply.

The truth was I liked him. I could not respect him for his commitment the way I respected the black trade union leaders in East London who were constantly on the receiving end of a campaign of harassment that he organized in close liaison with his mentors in the South African security police. But he never went in for the strained apologetics and cynical calculations of the other homeland potentates who would tell you how they were using apartheid to fight apartheid from the inside or how they still supported the aims of the black nationalist movements even when they felt constrained to lock up their adherents. In Umtata, the capital of the nearby Transkei homeland, I met Tsepo Letlaka, who had jumped in several stages from being a leader in exile of the Pan-Africanist Congress, one of the banned nationalist movements, to being minister of justice in a black state that emulated South Africa by outlawing the movement in which he had once been active. He insisted that he had "grown up in the liberation movement" and his commitment was "completely unchanged." Transkei, he argued, was a fulfillment of Pan-Africanist principles, being black and independent. It was only the failure of the nationalist movements to recognize this that forced the homeland to act against them. There was a more obvious explanation. Tsepo Letlaka had found a job and come home; whether he was a genuine nationalist or an agent in his exile phase, or a little of both, he was in from the cold.

Charles Sebe never had to backtrack or squirm. A romantic who found it possible and necessary in every moment of his waking life, even in idle conversation, to cast himself in a heroic role in a drama, he had been groomed by the security police for the part of a black anti-Communist crusader, and though he must occasionally have realized that he was acting in a theater of the absurd, he lived it. Even his victims found it hard sometimes not to share in the pleasure he derived from his role. The East London trade unionists all could do wonderful imitations of his slow, self-dramatizing, staccato pattern of speech, in which each syllable was milked for maximum effect. Constantly inventing his own recitative, Charles Sebe invented himself. "I think he belongs to the film stars," Thozamile Gqweta, the president of the black South African Allied Workers Union and an authentic mass leader in the region, said to me once, fastening on the general's capacity for role playing. "He would make a very good movie. He's a bogus chap, but he's very good at what he does." By that time Thozamile Gqweta had lost count of how many times he had been in General Sebe's jails.

The first time I saw him he was standing at attention behind dark aviator glasses, a lean, almost feline figure, at the elbow of Ciskei's president, his own elder brother, Lennox L. Sebe. The brothers could scarcely have looked less alike. The president, a former school inspector and country preacher, was darker and heavier, ponderous in manner as well as physique. Charles Sebe was all coiled energy; whatever effect he was seeking that day, he made me think of a sinister Tonton Macoute from Haiti. The president did all the talking, seeming almost to choke on some undetermined or unnamed resentment as he laboriously explained to an invited group of foreign journalists why he had decided to accept the dubious gift of sovereignty on South Africa's terms. The occasion was a preindependence referendum on that decision, in which all the levers of tribal loyalty and patronage had been used to turn out in his one-party backwater a popular response that could be held up as an endorsement. Gqweta and the other trade unionists who could have led an effective opposition were locked up for the duration of the campaign, and no opposition views were aired, but a panel of supposedly impartial foreign observers was flown from Pretoria to supervise the proceedings. They included John Sears, a Washington lawyer who had been sacked as Ronald Reagan's campaign manager earlier that year and now, when he might have been on his way to a top job in the White House, found himself on the sidelines in this improbable and pitifully destitute black Zion, having just negotiated a contract to represent South Africa as a lobbyist that was said to be worth half a million dollars a year to his law firm.

Charles Sebe was a brigadier that day, having just been promoted from colonel. He was a major general when, a year later, I had my first conversation with him. On a Sunday, proclaimed a sabbath of thanksgiving because it was only a few days before Ciskei's independence ceremonies, I spent an afternoon with him in the heavily guarded compound where he made his home, surrounded by the homes of his most reliable lieutenants. The place was on a ridge at the end of a dirt road, only a couple of miles outside King William's Town, a small white trading center that had been promised to the homeland as its capital, then retained as a part of South Africa at the last moment. The new blue-and-white Ciskeian flag was already flapping from a dozen flagstaffs at the prefabricated independence stadium that South Africa had hastily thrown up at what was to be the site of the new substitute capital, a $50 million showpiece named Bisho that was, otherwise, still on the drawing boards. But just as conspicuous that weekend were the banners of a competing black nationalism that had been on view at a mass funeral for a black lawyer who had represented Gqweta's union. His name was Griffiths Mxenge, and he had been brutally murdered in mysterious circumstances in Durban. Fifteen thousand supposed Ciskeians had turned out at his funeral to express their belief that his death was the work of the South African security police. It was the biggest funeral the region had seen since the one four years earlier that had been held for the martyred Biko, whose grave, in a black cemetery between the railway tracks and a gravel pit on the outskirts of King William's Town, was marked by a granite headstone that raised its own muted protest against the ceremonies that were about to be enacted in the stadium. "One Azania one nation," the headstone proclaimed, using the name that some black nationalists would like to attach to a black-ruled South Africa.

The general did not seek to play down the significance of the previous day's funeral. "It was," he said, squeezing off each syllable like a retaliatory shot, *"the re-vi-val of the Af-ri-can Na-tion-al Con-gress."* Charles Sebe, it seemed to me, usually spoke in italics. The eastern Cape, South Africa's traditional cockpit, where blacks and whites first met and clashed, had a long lineage of black nationalist heroes stretching back decades before Biko and Gqweta. As early as 1930 a black trade union had briefly shut down East London with a general strike. What was a little new was a black general on the other side of the conflict, one whose sense of vocation could now be offended by the insinuation that his former colleagues in the security police might have had a hand in eliminating Mxenge, who had been repeatedly and sadistically stabbed.

"No professional policeman or security man would embark on a stupid exercise of that nature," he said. "You know yourself these kinds of assassinations are scientific. They are done in a very scientific manner. We have AK-47s. They could have been used to take him while he was leaving his office. Then you would have a ballistic examination that could not be disputed by anyone. It would say there were Russian-made bullets, Makarovs and Tokarevs—we do have them."

That, he was saying, was how "we" would have done it. By "we" he obviously still meant the South African security police, in which he had never made officer's rank.

"In South Africa, there is a ceiling for blacks, yes, there is a ceiling," he remarked in a later conversation in his office in Zwelitsha, ostensibly still a ramshackle black township at the edge of white King William's Town but, by then, the provisional seat of a supposedly sovereign government. Charles Sebe was now a lieutenant general and a world traveler. The office was decorated with souvenirs from Israel and Taiwan, a jumbled display of flags, certificates, plaques, and scrolls. There was also a shredder and a Chubb safe containing a portion of his personal arsenal. The general was supposed to have command of all of Ciskei's burgeoning security services, its prisons and police, its fledgling army and intelligence service, but interrogation and intimidation of suspected enemies of the homeland regime or South Africa remained a big part of his business. This gave a potentially sinister point to the otherwise quaint piety that was exhibited in a frame over his desk. "The most beautiful gift we can give each other is the truth," it proclaimed.

I was wondering how I might interpret that had I not come to his office on a voluntary basis as the general, slightly qualifying his loyalty to his previous employers, gently picked at what seemed to be the scab on an old wound. "Why is there no black man working in Pretoria as an officer of the security police?" he asked. "And why don't they sit around the table with blacks on a decision-making security matter in southern Africa?" In other words, if he was really a commander now in a sovereign state, as he was supposed to be, why didn't he deal directly with his opposite number in Pretoria? Why did he still have to go through the chain of command, reporting to the white general's underlings in East London and Port Elizabeth? I volunteered no answers.

"It's a naïve type of an exercise," he concluded.

That was the closest I heard him come to expressing resentment of his former bosses. On another occasion he insisted that he had never experienced any racial slights, never been made to perform menial tasks such as serving tea to white officers, in his twenty-five years in the South African police. Nor, he claimed, was he ever subjected to indoctrination about the virtues of the system. "I was lucky for the whites to accept me for what I was," he said. "I never had conflict with them because I was dedicated to my job." He was what they wanted him to be, eager to please, and soon proved his worth by joining the African National Congress under an assumed name in Cape Town. In 1962 in Port Elizabeth, two years after the organization had been banned, he participated in the arrest of one of its key leaders, a black Communist named Govan Mbeki; in the same period, he boasted, he was active in the mass roundup of suspected members of the Poqo movement, which spread from Cape Town to Ciskei and Transkei. Charles Sebe could remember having sympathy for the ANC "because," he said, "I was a black man and it was they who were for the upliftment of blacks." But more important were the drama of undercover work and the approval, the personal upliftment, that came his way as a result of his dedication. If he felt any twinges of conscience or sense of contradiction, they were submerged in the idea that the fight against black nationalism was also a fight against "communism." But still there was the problem of the ceiling on promotions for black cops. Ultimately, he said, he was paid more than a sergeant would normally get ("I carried my promotions in my pocket"), but he yearned for the recognition and opportunities that could come only with rank; as a black NCO he always had to satisfy his instinct for command vicariously. "When the day came for our independence," he said, "my vow was 'I will show the world I am a future officer to contend with.' "

One of his last tasks as a South African cop had been to tail black nationalists drawn to King William's Town by Biko, the most important black nationalist to have emerged since the suppression of the main black movements, who had been confined to his hometown by ministerial fiat in 1973. Biko's friends remember that they had only to look in their rearview mirrors to see Sergeant Sebe in his dark glasses, riding on their bumpers in an unmarked car. The general would always exercise his gift for dramatic narrative when he talked about those days. "Biko was nobody's fool," he said. "You know what Biko used to tell me? Biko used to say, 'Charles, look, one guy I like is yourself because you are very straight about your job. You don't compromise. And I am straight about my politics. I don't compromise. Now, if we overcome, I can never be ashamed to propose you as in charge of the security services.' "

The recollection made him laugh, shake his head, and jackknife forward in his seat. "Really! That is what he said to me," he went on. "Then it was a big joke."

Biko's friends remember that Charles Sebe was often the butt of such jokes. They all were younger and better educated than he was— Biko himself was twelve years younger—and thought that he was a character, this eager black cop. They were laughing at him as well as with him, and he, of course, always knew it. Underneath the carapace of his new authority and rank, their contempt must still have rankled, but like Mbeki, the ANC leader he had helped arrest, Biko was now his connection to the history of his times. Lennox Sebe, the president, went so far as to claim a family connection, telling me that Steve Biko's father had worked as a clerk in what was called the Native Affairs Court in King William's Town, where his father had worked as a Xhosa interpreter. "He had a feeling for the people," the president said of Biko, gingerly appropriating the memory of the martyred man who had dismissed the Sebes and their ilk as "puppets who work against our interests."

I pressed Charles Sebe for his feelings at the time of Biko's death in 1977. "I was very much involved in collecting intelligence about him, but he was a human being, *a hu-man be-ing.*" The general often repeated himself for emphasis. "He never had a gun to shoot at me, and I was on the other hand," he said. "If I was on the other hand, him having a gun to shoot at me, and then I shot first, I would be *very* pleased. But my answer is, he was a human being. I don't like scandal, my friend, I don't like *scan-dal.*"

I then asked him if he knew Pieter Goosen, the security police officer who oversaw Biko's interrogation and dispatched him in a comatose state in the back of a Land-Rover to Pretoria. "He's my friend!" Charles Sebe said. "I don't judge a person because that's not my work," he went on. "If he has got to answer to God, O.K., he'll answer to God. It's not my interest."

"They are haunted by Biko," one of the dead man's closest friends said to me of the Sebes. But it was much easier to claim a tie to him when he was safely out of the way than it would have been were he alive to refute them. "He was not a stranger," the president said, turning misty-eyed. "He was a son of the soil. The circumstances of his death made the whole nation bitter."

Now he was re-inventing history for my benefit. By the "whole nation," he did not mean Biko's Azania but his own Ciskei, for which he would, if only he could, claim Biko as a hero. Lennox Sebe was now officially "President for Life," exalted by an Assembly in which elected representatives are permanently outnumbered by tribal chiefs who have been, in effect, mobilized into a political patronage machine run from the top. He had recently acquired a ten-seat executive jet and a Daimler limousine. He was about to move into his new presidential mansion in Bisho. His bust in bronze sat on a pedestal in front of the new Legislative Assembly Building, and fastened on the pedestal was a bronze plaque with a panegyric in the form of a 120-word run-on sentence

extolling him for his "singular efforts of dedication and patriotism."
Yet this onetime school inspector and country preacher, who had
agreed to play politics by the white man's rules, was subject to fits of
depression lasting sometimes for weeks, during which no decisions on
matters of state could be taken in the homeland. What was haunting
him was not just Biko—the proud, self-liberated black who had to be
broken because he would not bend—but the unnerving suspicion that
he himself was really an impostor.

Or so I imagined, giving Lennox Sebe the benefit of the doubt. It
was possible at least to entertain the notion that he had not meant to
end up as he had, in a position of exalted impotence, that he had started
with some vague idea that he could lead at least some of his people out
of apartheid, scrape some promise from the residue of a proud Xhosa
tradition of resistance to white encroachment that expressed itself in
nine so-called kaffir wars in the eighteenth and nineteenth centuries,
and maybe make something of his sad little piece of hinterland. And
now that he was on his pedestal, he sometimes must have glimpsed the
reality that his good intentions were just so much verbosity, filling his
otherwise empty life with interest.

Biko's funeral had been followed within six months as a mass rite in
the nationalist cause by that of Robert Sobukwe, the founder of the
Pan-Africanist Congress, whose influence was still felt in the eastern
Cape. The following year, in a bid to legitimize his leadership, Lennox
Sebe staged countervailing obsequies, dedicating a national shrine by
reburying what a crippled sorceress had certified to be the bones of a
rebellious nineteenth-century chief named Maqoma who had been
imprisoned by the British colonial authorities on Robben Island in
Cape Town's Table Bay, where contemporary black rebels from the
eastern Cape, such as Nelson Mandela and Govan Mbeki, were then
being held. If black nationalists could wear the mantle of Biko and
Sobukwe, Lennox Sebe seemed to be saying, then he could wear the
mantle of Maqoma. Illustrating the point, he draped a leopard skin over
his three-piece suit for the occasion.

It was the kind of tribal obscurantism the white authorities are only
too pleased to encourage: The sorceress was given access to normally
unreachable Robben Island; the bones were transported in a yellow-
wood casket on a South African naval frigate back to East London,
where they were received with full military honors; an army band and
honor guard were then provided for their reinterment, which was
covered by the South African broadcasting monopoly with all the

solemnity due a major state funeral. By all means, the authorities must have reasoned, let the Ciskeians find their heroes in the resistance that took place on the nineteenth-century frontiers—that was more or less what the Afrikaners did when they built the Voortrekker Monument as their shrine—and let them see Sebe rather than Biko as Maqoma's heir. Every nation, the Afrikaners believe, needs to find its own myth. This could be the Xhosa Götterdämmerung.

In fact, by commemorating Maqoma, the homeland was commemorating in part an act of national self-immolation, the greatest tragedy in Xhosa history, which occurred in 1857, when the old chief, who had been a great warrior and later a great drunk according to contemporary narratives, lent his active support to a sorceress who promised that the revered chiefs of the past would return messianically and drive the whites into the sea if the people would only purify themselves by killing their cattle and letting their fields lie fallow. More than 150,000 cattle were slaughtered. Estimates range from 20,000 to 40,000 of the number of people who then perished in the resulting famine, in a period in which the area's total population was no more than 100,000.

The calamitous cattle killing can be represented as a blind and desperate act of resistance to white rule. So can the decision of a homeland leader like Lennox Sebe to seek independence for his little state. But of course, there are many differences. The chiefs who supported the cattle killing were called Believers. Their sacrifices proved their selflessness. The chiefs who supported Ciskeian independence were rewarded with expensive sedans and houses; the question of belief never arose. "Powerlessness breeds a race of beggars who smile at the enemy and swear at him in the sanctity of their toilets; who shout 'Baas' willingly during the day and call the White man a dog in their buses as they go home." Those words were written by Steve Biko before he was silenced permanently several months before his thirty-first birthday. They cannot legally be printed in South Africa today, but Lennox Sebe from the sanctity of his position as putative leader of a putatively sovereign state can say anything that pops into his head about the evils of apartheid—"the oppressive yoke of political serfdom," he calls it— for unlike Biko, he makes no claim to equal rights in an undivided South Africa, although more than two-thirds of his nominal Ciskeians who find any work at all spend most of their waking hours across the invisible border.

Meanwhile, it is South Africa that keeps his indigent state afloat, underwriting 80 percent of its budget, and it is South Africa that trains his army and police to face a common enemy, who are, as he himself said of Biko, sons of the soil.

"You can tell me about other things," Charles Sebe was saying, blissfully casting himself in the role of spymaster, "and I won't differ with you. But security, intelligence, military, it's my trade, and the strategy is in my bloodstream. I like it."

To see change and development in Ciskei, it was necessary only to peek into General Sebe's domain. One new prison had been opened; another was nearing completion. And then there were the four "bases," as the general described them. "You will see for yourself," he promised. "You will see."

With a plainclothes black police captain as my escort, I drove down to the Indian Ocean coast to visit a secret base called Sandile, the one of which the general was proudest, for there, he said, "We are running parachute boys. Yes!" As soon as we arrived, a white captain with a maroon beret and a red mustache came up to our car on the double. "Are you the gentleman from *The New York Times?*" he inquired. "I must ask you to leave the base immediately." I replied that I had been sent there by the commanding general and asked who could possibly be in a position to countermand his orders.

"I'm not at liberty to say," said the captain in an accent that was sufficiently far from South African norms to remind me that Ciskei, like the other sovereign homelands, now employed mercenaries, veterans mostly of elite commands in the old Rhodesian Army. Outside the perimeters of the base, a platoon of black trainees was practicing assault tactics under the supervision of an officer who was either French or Belgian. Later that day I met the South African army colonel who had barred me from Sandile. Together we watched the Presidential Guard drilling on a parade ground and a white South African bandmaster putting the new Ciskeian Army band through a series of Prussian marches. Pretoria was obviously fairly serious about the homeland's military buildup. Charles Sebe had started out with a detachment of 3 when he founded Ciskei's security services in 1979; four years later he had more than 3,000 soldiers and police under his command and a budget, doubling from year to year, that had reached $27 million. I wondered how many young blacks from the eastern Cape the underground had managed to recruit and train in the same period.

It was Charles Sebe's mission in life to keep Ciskei from becoming a seedbed of resistance. He was a little embarrassed that I had discovered, in being turned away from Sandile, that his authority had its limits. But he didn't mind speaking about his close liaison with the South African security police. "I work hand in hand with South Africa," he said. How closely was documented by a piece of paper that accidentally fell into my possession. One day after cooling my heels in the general's anteroom for several hours, my patience cracked, and I decided to leave him a note saying I was going back to my hotel. I then asked his secretary for a piece of paper. I had only written "Dear General Sebe" when he appeared and ushered me into his office. I then jammed the paper into my pocket and only later discovered that I had been writing on the blank side of a typed report headed "Debriefing of an Agent in Connection with . . . Terrorist Onslaught in the Neighboring States and Ciskei . . . By Lt. General XC Sebe." In it he passes on intelligence that appeared to be at least third or fourth hand about a bombing that took place in Port Elizabeth a year earlier. Sebe is identified in the memorandum as the "Handler." His agent "in a neighboring state," apparently Lesotho, is identified as the "Source." The agent's source is the "sub-Source." The "terrorists" are said to have been based in Transkei and Ciskei but to have escaped back to Lesotho.

From the outside the underground war in the eastern Cape might not have looked like much, but Charles Sebe was living a life of high drama on what he conceived to be the cutting edge of the conflict. Once, patrolling Mdantsane late at night with his officers, he had been in a shoot-out with "terrorists," and now he advertised himself as a marked man. "Oh, yes, the Communists can rejoice if I die," he said. "But I don't bluff myself. I'm aware, I'm fully aware, I don't take chances. Day and night, even when I'm asleep, I know where to touch should anything happen." He rolled over suddenly in his swivel chair and came up smiling with an imaginary gun. "It's in my bloodstream. I'm a professional, and I live as a professional."

He was a happy man, possibly the only truly happy man in the whole of Ciskei, for he was living his fantasy. He had given speeches on "terrorism" in southern Africa in Jerusalem and Taipei. Now he had confirmation of his status from a citadel of learning that was geographically much closer but, in the South African context, light-years and even eons away. Charles Sebe, a former black constable who had gotten his secondary school certificate in a correspondence course, had been invited to lecture on "The Communistic Guerrilla Onslaught" to Afrikaner students at the University of the Orange Free State. That meant more to Xhanti Charles Sebe than being invited to lecture at Cambridge or Oxford could have meant to Jan Christiaan Smuts. Before he was a Boer commando leader, Smuts was a Cambridge prodigy. Before he was a constable, Charles Sebe was a dropout from a mission school in the town of Alice that sent its best graduates to Fort Hare University, just next door. Many of the big names of African nationalism—Nelson Mandela, Oliver Tambo, Robert Sobukwe, Robert Mugabe—were associated with Fort Hare before it was taken over by the government and purged of liberal ideas or influences, reduced under Bantu Education to what blacks disparage as a bush college. Now Fort Hare was in Ciskei, and any sign of restiveness among its students invited intervention by General Sebe's men. He had personally commanded them once when they stormed into the dormitories to suppress a protest. "We're just beating your B.A.," Sebe's men taunted one youngster whom I later met, whipping him with a sjambok, a flexible truncheon made of animal hides. "We haven't even started to beat you yet." In some recess of the general's mind, I thought, fighting "communism" meant fighting Fort Hare. Being laughed at by Biko and his friends, I imagined, must have sharpened his resentment of blacks who thought their university training made them anyone's equal. Being invited to the University of the Orange Free State meant that he was finally their equal.

"I would like you to be there," he said, "because I have highlighted quite a number of things in this paper."

When he rose to speak after a benediction and introduction in Afrikaans, the general was still wearing his cap, with the full complement of ornamental braid due his rank. Solemnly he gave his undergraduate audience a rigid salute. The white, rosy-cheeked expressions turned up to him couldn't have been more earnest had they been in church. Few of these young Afrikaners would ever have had occasion before in their lives to sit and listen to a black man delivering a speech, so Charles Sebe's presence in their midst was nearly as surprising to them as it was to him. Then, as they got their first earful, it became even more surprising, practically stupefying at times. Some, who were unused to spoken English, may have imagined they were having a hard time following the speaker because of language. But the general's exaggerated articulation made every word comprehensible; it was the connections between the words and the sentences they formed that became bewildering. This was only partly because his prepared text was lacking in coherence. General Sebe frequently wearied of reading and recharged himself every few minutes by speaking extemporaneously so that his remarks flowed like a meandering river that regularly branches off into turbulent tributaries or droned like a high-altitude plane that unpredictably dives down for strafing runs, then sails up again into the blue yonder. When he was flying on his own, without the text over which he sometimes stumbled, the general's hands rose and fell, catching fistfuls of air, and his voice teased out sounds that pleased his ears, rolling *r*'s and long diphthongs to which he added an extra beat and inflection. The roller-coaster effect suited the evangelist's role he was now playing as he depicted a struggle between forces of darkness, black "terrorists" manipulated by the *"dra-gon of comm-u-nism,"* and the forces of light, represented by the allied republics of South Africa and Ciskei.

"The subject is quite a complexed one," he said in his hoarse, throaty way. "Some of you might have nightmares tonight because of the big threat that I will talk about."

From their earliest days these Afrikaner students had been force-fed on Manichaean interpretations of an impending struggle, but to hear a black man assert that he had come to "psychologically awaken" them must have disturbed the order of priorities and categories on which they had been reared. After all, if there was any awakening to be done, it was supposed to be by white missionaries who concerned themselves with blacks. What business could a black have meddling with white souls? Some of the students seemed uneasily aware that here was a black man who surpassed them in ideological commitment; from their point of view, he was almost too good to be true. What was hardest to understand or accept, as his discussion ranged spasmodically from Soviet espionage in the field of high technology to the Chinese Revolution, the menace of the United Nations, and the rise of the Bolsheviks, was his easy assumption of authority. "I read about communism, I am still reading about communism *the-o-ret-i-cal-ly,"* he boasted, trilling the last word, "but I am also working communism *prac-ti-cal-ly."*

And communism, of course, was everywhere. Lenin himself had designed its program for isolating and conquering America, General

Sebe said, proving his point with spurious quotations from one of the scriptures that emerged from the loonier recesses of the American radical right, the book *None Dare Call It Treason,* which was an underground best seller in the Sun Belt when the John Birch Society was establishing its cells. There is an international traffic in cast-off conspiracy theories as well as cast-off machinery and garments, and now, by a process of small ideological transactions over two decades and hemispheres, this black security man was carrying alarums from the Dallas of H. L. Hunt and Jack Ruby to Bloemfontein. One of Charles Sebe's white "handlers," I guessed, must have initiated him into the political occult and its mysteries. One nation's lunatic fringe is another nation's security police.

The enemy within was inside South Africa, too: in its churches, its student organizations, and, above all, its black political movements. Black theology and white liberalism were equally infected. "I don't know what that is," he said, taking off from his text, "but in my context a liberal is a Communist." I turned in my seat and looked around the hall to see if anyone had blinked at that; as far as I could make out, General Sebe was getting an increasingly respectful hearing. He made little mistakes—he was off by a factor of 100 when he said there were 3 million Cubans in Angola—but these were not the sorts of slips his audience was prepared to catch. Nearer to home, I wondered if anyone in the room besides me knew that it was in this same city of Bloemfontein that the African National Congress, which the general was now lambasting for its "atrocious activities" on behalf of the Kremlin, first came into existence. That was in 1912, when the czar was still in St. Petersburg, and Lenin in Zurich, and it started off with the unbelievably moderate aim of providing the white government of the two-year-old Union of South Africa with a "direct and independent channel of informing itself as to the things uppermost in the Natives' mind from time to time." It wanted then only to make known their grievances, not to share in power. Grievances? The general allowed that there was social injustice in South Africa "some time ago," but, he said, "The struggle in South Africa is not between a black struggle and a white. It is a communistic orientated ideology professed by the African National Congress for the Communists to take over in South Africa as it is stated in their blueprint."

"You all heard about Mandela," he said, running down the names of the imprisoned and exiled leaders of the banned movement. "You all heard about Moses Kotane, Alfred Nzo, Oliver Tambo, but because of *comm-u-nism,* where are they now with their brains, with their academic backgrounds?" In fact, the question of Communist penetration of the African National Congress is, as the general might have said, "complexed." But as far as he was concerned, there could be no such being as a non-Communist black nationalist. And where, his implied but unspoken question asked, was Charles Sebe now, the former constable who had started with so much less?

If the answer was that the system had rewarded him with more power than any black had ever before wielded under its umbrella, he was here dedicating that power to its defense. It was not only South Africa that could adopt a forward strategy, striking across international borders at "terrorists." If infiltration into Ciskei from Lesotho continued, he promised, his "elite garrison of men" would go to the source. "The Republic of Ciskei," he vowed, "will fight side by side with the Republic of South Africa."

Only two or three persons in the hall abstained from the enthusiastic applause that greeted that conclusion. Charles Sebe had earned it by offering himself as proof to these young Afrikaners that their system of partition and exclusion had black support. Now, as he fielded questions, the sense that he had been well received encouraged him to more daring flights of rhetoric and wit. Did he really mean to say, a skeptical questioner asked, that there was no social conflict in South Africa between blacks and whites, that all black demands were manipulated by Communists? "That is my case," he replied firmly, drawing a lurid picture of infiltrators creeping through the night to kill him and his listeners in their beds, for which he won hand-stinging claps.

Was Ciskei ready to send its troops to do "border duty" against the Communists in Namibia? the next questioner demanded. "That is in process," he promised, to even bigger claps. Finally he brought down the house with his answer to a young man who wanted to know how he could support "separate development" and denounce apartheid: What, after all, was the difference?

"I've got to educate you," he began. "It's a matter of ignorance. You are white; I am black. I'm having my own traditions; I'm having my own norms. I live the way I live." Blacks wanted to own what whites owned and live in cities. "But not," he went on, *"in-ter-mar-riage.* What will you get from *in-ter-mar-riage?* You get a colored." The word was pronounced with contempt. "You don't get a white person, you don't get a black person, but a frustrated child, which does not belong anywhere. You go to America, you ask the American *Ne-groes,* 'What tribe do you belong?' " And here, in mimicry of the likely response, the general produced a totally surprising, unintelligible nasal sound that broke down, more or less, into these syllables: *"Ah me, ma me, ma me ma,"* the sound, presumably, of a black American hemming and hawing. It was this that inspired laughter and cheers, rather than his description of the pitiful condition of American blacks without a language of their own, without "roots" or chiefs. None of which, incidentally, had anything to do with what he really thought. Charles Sebe, like many black South Africans, hero-worshiped a stereotype of the cool, self-sufficient American black who intimidates whites. He studied videocassettes of American TV programs and movies that conformed to that image and wanted nothing more than to visit America; in fact, it seemed to be his hope that if I wrote about him and made clear his standing as an anti-Communist crusader, he might finally be able to overcome the State Department's refusal to grant a visa to a homeland cop. But Charles Sebe had not spent half his life in white government offices without learning how to pander to white risibilities on the subject of race. He was talking in terms of black pride, but he was rolling his eyes and playing Rochester. And carried away with his success, he neglected to answer the question about what was wrong with apartheid.

Afterward in the social hall, where wine and cheese were served, General Sebe enthralled a large cluster of eager students with his narrative of his shoot-out with the "terrorists." The medals on his chest clanked as he gestured and reeled his way through the re-enactment. Then he warned them to be on the alert for "indirect communistic attacks" in literature and theater, saying that he had made himself an expert in spotting subversive themes in plays and now personally censored any drama that was proposed for staging in Ciskei. I accosted one young man with thinning blond hair and a little mustache and asked what he made of the visitor. The response was ethnological. "Sotho people are very different," he said. "We have Sotho people on our farm."

As far as I could make out, he was saying that Ciskei might be able to produce a Sebe but that was no reason to change the social order where he lived. What would he have thought, I wondered, if he'd ever heard the likes of Steve Biko?

———

And then one day Xhanti Charles Sebe vanished. Like a rank-and-file member of a black trade union, he had been thrown into one of his own jails on the orders of his brother. Another brother, the transport minister, was also jailed. "Sebe Runs Out of Brothers," cracked a headline in *City Press*, a newspaper in Johannesburg aimed at blacks.

Reports from Pretoria, relying on leaks from official sources there, hinted that President Sebe had quashed a coup d'état after a timely intelligence tip from South African sources. Anything was possible, for this was basically farce, but those accounts seemed doubly implausible to me. I couldn't find a motive for the general to plot a coup or for South Africa to unmask him. He had already consolidated whatever power there was to be had in Ciskei—nothing moved, no appointments were made without his approval—and he was playing the role he liked best. And if the South Africans had been forced to choose between the two Sebes, it seemed unlikely that they would have gone for the woozy and wobbly elder brother when they had found in the general an almost perfect instrument of control.

So I sought and got an audience with His Excellency the President for Life, who was reluctant to go into the origins of the family feud but eager to supply his own dramatic re-enactment of how he had outfoxed and outmaneuvered everyone: not only the strong man brother with his personal security apparatus, his own vice-president, and other disloyal officials, or a white former South African espionage agent who held the rank of major general in the Ciskeian forces, but also South Africa's foreign minister and top police officials who had tried to intercede for Charles Sebe.

The feud, I learned from South African officials who made it their business to know, had its origins in a rivalry between the respective eldest sons of Lennox and Charles, which may have had something to do with a woman. The general had made his nephew a major, but the indolent young man preferred to be treated like a prince. Sent to an elite training program near Johannesburg, he declined to wear a uniform or take orders. Meanwhile, Charles's son was actually earning his paratrooper's wings (unlike his father, I was told, who had failed the course but wore them anyhow). The sons went to their mothers, the mothers went to their husbands, and soon a family skeleton was rattling ominously. It had to do with the question of whether the president was actually the son of the late Mr. Sebe, the former court interpreter, who had married his mother. The two other sons thought that only they were legitimate. Since the lineage Lennox Sebe had traced to support his own dubious claims to chieftainship went through his mother's husband, someone might have suggested that Charles, the next eldest, was the real chief if anyone was. Made more paranoid by the family tensions, the president decided to strip his brother of all his positions of command, leaving him only the intelligence service as a fig leaf to conceal his disgrace.

It was at this point that the president took up the narrative, which was as absorbing and entertaining for him as it was for me. A long-necked crane, the symbol of Ciskeian nationhood, looking dusty, if not diseased, after its encounter with a taxidermist, perched on a ledge behind the president's swivel chair and peered over his shoulder as he stretched out his legs and studied the pustulated surface of his ostrich leather shoes. In this posture his chin rested on his chest, which compressed his jowls to something like a pudding. Often his choice of words recalled his days in the pulpit. "I could clearly see him leaving the light and going into the road of perpetual darkness," he intoned mournfully, describing Charles's reluctance to accept the "decision of the nation," by which he meant his own decision to put the general in his place. The president had only recently lauded his brother in the Legislative Assembly for "total sacrifice and commitment," but now he said he had been "rudely shocked" by the discovery of his usurpation of power and administrative shortcomings. When he revealed the "decision of the nation" to the chiefs and headmen who composed his party's caucus, the fears and resentments that had accumulated as the general built his miniature police state finally were voiced. "They dared to tell me things that hurt me," the president said. Now he was playing Lear, suffering lèse-majesté at the hands of his own.

These events had occurred as Lennox Sebe was to leave for Israel on what was a state visit only in his own eyes. A few Israelis, recent immigrants from Russia, had discovered they could do profitable business in Ciskei by feeding the president's illusions that he had foreign relations extending farther than Pretoria. First they had persuaded him to purchase his jet, which then couldn't be landed on the grass runway that was Ciskei's only excuse for an airport, and now they were promising to introduce him to members of the Israeli government. But before leaving, he said, he took the precaution of inducing one of his brother's aides to keep him informed by phone of the general's activities. The

plot thickened rapidly: The aide found Charles Sebe drafting a memorandum to General Johan Coetzee, the commissioner of police in
South Africa, on his brother's unpredictable conduct. Charles's white
adviser, a former spy for South Africa whose overseas assignments
included a stint in Nicaragua during the Somoza years, had accompanied the president to Israel. From there, without letting the president know, he phoned "a very high official in the South African government," in hopes that the breach between the brothers could be healed
before it became public and destroyed Charles Sebe's usefulness. Lennox Sebe got wind of the letter and resolved to fly home, sending the
white adviser to Austria, he explained, to have him out of the way.
South Africa's foreign minister went to the airport to try to put in a
word for General Sebe, but the president fended him off. On his return
to Zwelitsha, he discovered that his own foreign minister's residence
had been machine-gunned the night before, but he saw through the
ruse: The argument was to have been made that "terrorists" were on
the loose and, therefore, the general had to be restored to his positions
of command for the safety of a state under siege.

"I was in Israel, but I make bold to say," he now declaimed, re-
enacting for my benefit what he then said to the Cabinet, "that the
whole trick comes from the Department of State Security. I'm saying
it in front of the general, 'Forget about terrorism.' "

He then ordered his brother disarmed and started arresting the
general's aides one by one until finally he had the white adviser clamped
into leg irons on his return from Vienna. Charles Sebe pleaded his
innocence, maintaining as he had so often in my hearing that he was
a professional. "Well, well, well," the president said, chortling softly
and triumphantly as he contemplated the pitiable vanity of that boast.
"It didn't click to him that the game was up. A word to the wise is
sufficient, but an advice to fools makes them go quickly to their *self-
appointed snares.*" The president, who also spoke in italics, was saying
the general had to be locked up, too.

The pious intonations and self-satisfied gurglings that were coming
from the presidential chair by the end of this two-hour monologue
would have alarmed me considerably if I had been worried about the
future of the South African homeland system. I wasn't, and they didn't.
Solemnly I asked whether there was any chance for a reconciliation.
Only Sir Ralph Richardson, in a role like Sir Anthony Absolute in *The
Rivals,* might have soared to the level of sanctimonious hokum that the

"President for Life" now reached as he expressed his astonishment over his discovery, only after the arrest, of the personal luxuries on which the general had squandered state funds. A rural development project for 100 people, he exclaimed dolefully, could have been started with the money that went to furnishing his brother's farm. "How can you trust such a man to speak about the cancer of communism when in the same breath he is plowing the ground for it and cultivating it?" he asked.

It was then that he invited me to see for myself. So as not to spoil the guided tour that was instantly arranged on presidential command, I refrained from inquiring about the source of the investment that was being poured into his own farm or the cost of his new Daimler.

Zwelitsha, the temporary capital where this conversational fratricide occurred, lies on a ridge above a small basin. Bisho, the new capital of independent Ciskei, is on the other side of the basin on another ridge. King William's Town, the surviving enclave of white South Africa, sits in the basin. To the naked eye, an unreliable organ when it comes to viewing white South Africa as it wants to be viewed, these are not three places but one. But it was now a matter of solemn treaty that each time President Sebe or any of his tribal courtiers felt impelled to flit between Zwelitsha and Bisho, they crossed two international borders. This anomaly would be virtually eliminated by the completion of a three-mile highway, at a cost of $8 million, that would run entirely through Ciskeian territory, with the exception of a tiny band of South African highway that it would have to traverse. Ingeniously, that would be done by means of a flyover so the Ciskeians would pass in a split second through South African airspace, without touching South African soil.

It would be prohibitively expensive, costing fifty times as much, to make the entire road network of the eastern Cape respect Ciskei's theoretical sovereignty. The shortest distance between two points in the homeland is often through South Africa; once, in a day of driving around the little state, I found that I had crossed its borders at least eighteen times. The arrangements around King William's Town tend to be even more confusing because there is a small black township called Ginsberg, where Steve Biko actually lived, that had to be left *inside* South Africa when Ciskei achieved its nationhood because an even smaller colored neighborhood and some white businesses lay between it and Zwelitsha and no cartographer could find a way to excise black Ginsberg without excising these whites and browns, even though Ginsberg and Zwelitsha are barely a mile apart. Whether Ginsberg's blacks are now Ciskeians or Transkeians remains a matter of hot dispute. Although they live in South Africa, they cannot be South Africans under South African law. Most people don't know where they are or what they are most of the time, but if you drive out of Zwelitsha and turn left, you enter South Africa; turning right, you are in Ciskei.

The official from the Department of Public Works who was instructed by President Sebe to escort me and lay bare for me the corruption of the Sebe family told me to take a right turn and then a left. This brought us to a government warehouse where the furniture and appliances from General Sebe's farm had been stacked. These included the three items that had most scandalized the president: a bar, a lacquered bed that had been discovered in a mirrored bedroom, and an imported refrigerator with an ice-making attachment. The president had told me that his underlings had wanted to install the refrigerator on his farm, which had been handed over to Ciskei as a gift from South Africa. "I said, 'Never!'" he had declared in the tones of a righteous man who clearly saw the danger of moral contamination. "'I'll stay with my old fridge.'"

"What will happen to this refrigerator?" I now asked my escort.

"It will probably go to the president's farm," he said.

"Have you discussed that with the president?"

"Yes. He just said, 'We'll see.'"

The assembled effects of the cashiered lieutenant general and former constable made a depressing rather than a garish sight. The spectacle promised by the president of a sybarite's shocking booty was not in the eye of this beholder, at least; there was nothing remarkable here—the bed was, after all, just a bed, the bar just a bar—nothing that could not be found in the middle-class homes of the white bureaucrats on Lennox Sebe's own staff. No doubt it had been ill-gotten with public funds while some black children were starving in Ciskei's resettlement camps, but the ordinariness of the objects cast a pathetic light on the whole enterprise of nation building in the homelands. "I'm having my own norms. I live the way I live," Charles Sebe had proclaimed in Bloemfontein. The stacked furniture and appliances in the warehouse said just the opposite.

The next stop on the tour took us across the two borders to Bisho and the new ministerial compound then nearing completion, which was Qwaqwa writ large. In a territory where the per capita income was scarcely $400, South Africa had spent several million dollars to build and furnish eighteen official residences, including the president's mansion, for the tribal chiefs at the top of the Ciskeian patronage machine. Each came with its own servants' quarters and, except for the residence reserved for the white chief justice, with its own tiled abattoir for the ritual slaughter of cattle and goats that the tribesmen would be expected to present to their leaders. Charles Sebe, who was to have lived in the residence nearest the presidential mansion, now stood accused by his brother of having ordered furniture that was costlier than the uniform furnishings ordered for all the other houses.

Seventeen identical vanity tables were being stored in what was to have been the general's dining room. The white architect who designed this black Xanadu had been ordered to the site to unlock the doors on the houses for my benefit, but he didn't have the keys. Charles Sebe's furniture, the architect said as we peered through the windows of the house he would have occupied, was only more expensive because the items had not been ordered in lots. The architect, a born-again Christian, wanted me to know that he had regularly read the Bible with the black officials who worked with him on the project.

The last stop on the tour was the general's farm, which was on the road to the Frankfort resettlement site he and his brother had pledged themselves to absorb into Ciskei when they negotiated for the territory's independence. A bulldozer had apparently been used to knock down the gateposts, but although it was still afternoon, the high security lights he had installed were shining on the old farmhouse, which must have been built by descendants of the Crimean War veterans who were brought to the frontier as part of a colonial scheme to create a stable social order by settling whites among blacks, a policy that, after a century, had been systematically reversed. General Sebe had built a barracks for his security guards and refitted the kitchen. There were the mirrors in the bedroom, but otherwise there wasn't much left to see. Tactfully I tried to explore the question of who actually owned the farms the Sebe brothers had arrogated to themselves. Initially they belonged to the state, but now it seemed they belonged to the family. Was it basically a matter of being able to keep title as long as you kept office?

"Something like that," the man from Public Works mumbled, eager to get off the subject.

"I wonder who will be living here next year," I said. "Maybe it will be Charles Sebe."

"Maybe," the official said noncommittally. "Surprising things happen."

White officials had hoped to promote such a restoration, but when I mentioned to one of them that President Sebe had sent me to the warehouse after I asked about that possibility, the South African shook his head and sighed resignedly. "Then there's no hope," he said.*

The whites now blamed themselves for having made Charles Sebe vulnerable by concentrating too much authority in his hands. Of course, that aroused jealousy, it was said in hindsight. Of course, *they* would fight among themselves. *They* always do. It is in *their* culture. This was what outsiders could never be made to understand about *them*. It was a mistake to rush history, a mistake to expect too much in Africa. Here, too, Jan Christiaan Smuts had crystallized attitudes that still prevail when he told his Oxford audience in 1929, "The native system may not be as efficient and incorruptible as direct white rule would be, but a certain amount of inefficiency or even injustice, according to white ideas, is excusable." Excusable, he meant, if only blacks suffered; he was arguing, after all, for apartheid before the invention of the word. On a contemporary application of this dictum, any minor excesses by the Sebes could be tolerated, and so, finally, could the fall of the general, even though, as one of his closest white colleagues was eager to affirm, "Charles Sebe was a good friend of South Africa." Not a good South African, mind you, since he was black, but a good friend nonetheless.

Having based their homeland system on the most retrograde and obscurantist tendencies in African tribal life, the whites could derive their usual solace from the results: At least they knew they were indispensable. With the fall of Charles Sebe, whites could run the security services in Ciskei as they did in the other black states, but what did that say about the durability of the system? If the only black leaders whom whites could recognize as authentic were the ones who were

---

*In fact, not quite a year later, Charles Sebe was convicted and sentenced to twelve years in jail on a charge of incitement. The accusation was that he had tried to break into one of the jails he had administered in order to free his former deputy, who had been arrested on orders from the "President for Life." The conditions and location of Charles Sebe's imprisonment, I am informed, are not known.

bound to be inefficient and corruptible, then how could they withstand the challenge of the inauthentic leadership that promised to be something else? Could they ever find dependable black surrogates? "I used to think this was the only way," said a white who had worked closely with the Sebes. "Now I think we're creating a monster."

I would have given a lot to know what lessons Charles Sebe drew as he did push-ups and sit-ups in his cell in order to keep fit. Would he have expected the whites to intercede successfully on his behalf? Would their failure to do so make him re-examine his loyalties? Or would the fact that he had been jailed by blacks in a black state make him nostalgic for the days when he worked directly for whites? It was logical to think his experience might have taught him new respect for Biko, Gqweta, and the thousands of other blacks he had seen go to jail for their part in the resistance to white rule, but somehow I couldn't imagine a jailhouse conversion. If Charles Sebe was going to continue to esteem what he had been, he had to take Ciskeian sovereignty half-seriously, at least, and that left him in the same quandary as the South African officials who couldn't move against Lennox Sebe without undermining their own proposition that he was head of an independent nation. No one else might believe it, but they were stuck with it and Lennox, while Charles was stuck in his cell.

The month the general was cashiered, I met at an impoverished settlement in Transkei a handsome youth named Bayanda Majole, who bore, or so I imagined, a striking resemblance to the young Charles Sebe who had signed up to be a constable when many of his peers were giving themselves to the nationalist cause. Bayanda Majole, who was eighteen, wanted to join the police; not Transkei's homeland police, he specified, but the South African police. Pressed for reasons, he was not at all inarticulate. "I'm a strict person, and I believe in enforcing rules," he said. "I also want to be able to protect myself."

Growing up in Transkei, not illogically, had disillusioned him with the whole idea of black rule. When there were fights between rival factions in the area where he lived, the Transkei police never wanted to know about them. The only black government he knew was corrupt and predatory, so, speaking with the same sort of spirit and anger that can be found in the young men his age who espouse revolutionary principles, he said he was not interested in freedom and independence. It would be better for blacks, he felt sure, if whites ruled the whole of South Africa.

"The black man must be the most unfortunate creature in the world," Bayanda Majole said.

"Why?" I asked.

"He doesn't think; he doesn't use his brainpower."

"Is that true of you?"

"In varying degrees."

The hillside on which we were standing offered a startling visual example of the deprivation that the South African system seeks to legitimize, for it was at the northern edge of the homeland separated by only a sluggish stream called the Umthavuna from what was supposed to be South Africa. On the white side of the river, you could see a homestead and a few farm buildings, many trees, extensive pastures, and terraced cabbage plots, which were irrigated by water pumped from the river. On the black side there were several hundred houses, mostly round and thatched, some rectangular with metal roofs, hardly any trees, hardly any grass, erosion out of control, no water pumps, and not even a single tap. Bayanda Majole had this contrast impressed on his mind every day of his life, and it made him angry at his own people, rather than at the few on the other side of the Umthavuna.

I had come there after getting directions from one of his brothers, Mandla, whom I had met in a tiny room in a hostel for migrant laborers near the airport in Durban. Mandla worked as a security guard for a transport company in Durban and also despised the homeland government. I met some bitter men that night in the Durban hostel. One, who was drunk, denounced his fate in raw language that landed, without softening euphemism or fuzzy moralizing, on an issue most discussions of the migrant labor system tiptoe around. "You can't fuckin' fuck your wife," the man said, glowering. But Mandla, a handsome young man in a stylish shirt with epaulets, was mild and self-contained. He was lucky, he knew, to be where he was. Now that Transkei was independent, Mandla and Bayanda were both regarded as foreigners in Durban. Bayanda would have found it next to impossible to follow his brother there and become a migrant laborer, but that was no great loss in his view, for the idea of spending his life in a hostel for migrants as his brother was doing didn't appeal to him. He wasn't interested in ambiguous outcomes, in making the best of a bad situation. As he saw it, you sided with either the blacks or the whites, and life in independent Transkei had settled that question for him. He was proud, consciously hurt in his pride, but inoculated, it seemed, against slogans about "black pride." And so he would enlist in the South African police if the South African Defense Force wouldn't take him.

It was not my place to argue with this young man, and I didn't feel inclined to do so. Bayanda Majole had helped explain Lieutenant General Xhanti Charles Sebe to me. He seemed to be a logical person and a logical outcome of the homeland system, an example, therefore, of what could be described as its success. This outcome was what the homelands were all about, showing that, properly channeled, black anger could be turned against black anger.

CHAPTER 7

CONTROLLED STRENGTH

Black anger isn't a problem only for the authorities to divert into storage tanks—homelands, hostels, and jails—or subject to an alchemy that leaves the ashen residue of self-contempt. It's a problem as well for anyone who wonders why there isn't more of it, why it doesn't boil over, why, finally, the system survives. The ordinary white conditions himself not to think about this, the way Californians try not to think about earthquakes, but inevitably there comes a moment when he glimpses something that forces him to contemplate the phenomenon of black endurance. In the instant before he pulls his mental blinds down again, he confronts the question of why blacks with all their numbers endure what he would find unendurable. There are any number of stereotypes that can be swallowed at such moments as tranquilizers, the most common being the one about blacks as guileless children of nature, content to pass their lives without the comforts and security whites have and crave. But even whites who reject stereotypes, including those who still harbor the hope that "liberation" will usher in the millennium of a just society, regularly lapse into wondering what it is about blacks that explains the long wait for their anger to make itself felt. Often then they resort to pseudo-Marxist speculation about the conditions in which "prerevolutionary" societies rise and shed their qualifying prefixes or to convoluted cultural and sociological theories. One I heard had to do with messianic cults that mix African beliefs in spirits with the promise of Christianity, the argument being that messianism as a cultural reflex helped sublimate or contain black anger.

Such speculation made me uneasy, mainly because I regarded it as a distraction from my task of looking at the reality of South Africa as it is. Theorizing about the future, I thought, was often a device for evading or excusing the present. In any case, I was not licensed as a seer. Theorizing about why the revolution hadn't happened was only a breath away from theorizing about when it would. I hated it when merchant bankers from New York or barnstorming congressional aides dropped in to fish for forecasts; usually the bankers wanted to know whether South Africa would be "safe" for five years. Yet in the strangely muddled South African present, with all its contradictions and the sense of drift to inevitable confrontation, it sometimes seemed necessary to ask what mixture of black complicity, resignation, or hope kept the system working. So one afternoon I tried out the messianism theory on Buti Tlhagale when I stopped to see him at his Soweto church. Father Buti, a young Roman Catholic priest with training in Rome, a background in the Black Consciousness Movement, and a fine, speculative mind that could be ironic as well as ardent, usually picked up an argument as if it were an artifact, examining it from various angles before taking it apart. This one he just swept aside.

"That's not how it is," he objected. "The students you see here aren't waiting for any Messiah. They just get cut down so fast. A student leader lasts for three to six months. The police are on to them very fast. They go to jail, or they go to exile. Or they wear out—they come home and they just sit. There are forty families right here in this parish with kids who have gone across the border. The security police visit them all the time. You'd expect them to be angry and resentful, but you never hear anything out of them. It's not that they're waiting for the Messiah. It's the pressure. They've just had too much."

There was courage and resentment among blacks, Father Buti was saying, but it was no match yet for the fear the security apparatus could inspire. The obstacles were fear and exhaustion, not faith. The gentle young priest fully grasped the implications of his argument, both for himself as a preacher of the gospel and for his people.

"We must hate just a little bit more," he said.

The argument might have seemed an abstraction if I had heard it when I was still finding my feet in the country, just another South African point of view. But I had already lived through one of the short cycles of repression he was describing. Young blacks I met when I first came back to South Africa had been grabbed from their homes by the security police, subjected to months of solitary confinement, beaten and tortured and interrogated, then released under various forms of legal restriction and extralegal intimidation. I had then heard their accounts of what they had been through. The contrast between the optimistic, spirited young men I had met early on and the taut, somber veterans they had become after this initiation, provided one measure of the widening gulf between black and white. These transformations had been accomplished in only a year or a year and a half. It had been a crowded, even exhilarating period in my life, but sitting down with them again, I felt as if time had stood still for me. I had been wandering around southern Africa, a professional tourist, a taster at a buffet, while they were being humiliated and broken down and pushed to what they sometimes felt to be their limits or a little beyond. I had been collecting impressions of a conflict that only occasionally breaks into the open; they had been at the front.

"But you shall be free one day," promised a poster in the offices of the South African Allied Workers Union on my first visit to East London. Stuck on the wall near the poster, for all to see, was a copy of the Freedom Charter, a populist manifesto advanced as a platform by the African National Congress and its affiliates when they were legal organizations. A generation later blacks were still debating whether the charter had been drafted and adopted by the "people," as the underground's own chroniclers have piously insisted ever since, or by a rally attended by 2,884 partisans that was effectively manipulated and stage-managed by Communists; in the meantime, it had become holy writ for most blacks who knew of it. "South Africa belongs to all its people, black and white," the Freedom Charter promised. If anything, that was conspicuously less true in the real world than it had been in 1955, the year the document was drafted, but the promise—seldom seen in print, seldom repeated from public platforms—had not dimmed.

The union's offices were crowded that Saturday morning with black workers, young men and women, who seemed to be hearing it for the first time. Nearly all of them awoke every morning in Mdantsane township, meaning they were on their way to being declared Ciskeians. They worked at East London factories the managers of which were being warned by the security police that the new union was a Trojan horse for the underground. By joining it, they were asking for trouble. Many of them would be out of a job and blacklisted in East London long before the town, let alone the region or country, belonged to all its people. Thozamile Gqweta, the union's president, had been in one of General Sebe's new jails in the homeland at that point for two months, and there was no telling when he would be released. All the signs pointed to confrontation and conflict, yet 100 or so young workers were backed up into the corridors, patiently waiting to pay their dues and receive membership cards; in six months a handful of black organizers with no previous trade union experience had signed up 15,000 workers. The atmosphere was that of a revival: Hope could surmount any barrier; salvation was assured, if not exactly imminent. The leadership—the portion of it at least not detained with Gqweta—seemed to share this headiness. In this setting I met Frank Tongo.

I had been welcomed warmly at the union's office that morning, but then the reception chilled. The union's general secretary, a labor organizer from Durban named Sam Kikane who was full of kinetic energy, ego, and rhetoric in what seemed an unstable combination, was responsible for the change. Looking me over with ostentatious suspicion, he finally decreed that I could not interview individuals but had to meet the whole regional committee at once. There was a long wait for the committee to gather. When it did, it seemed that it had been summoned to serve as Sam's audience, for he did all the talking, snapping his fingers in sustained fusillades whenever he thought he scored a point. First he challenged me to prove I was not a CIA agent. I said that my paper would fire me if I turned out to be anything other than what I represented myself to be. This was certainly true, but it didn't rate as proof in East London. Then, on an inspiration, I pulled out my new Zimbabwe press card. Sam was unconvinced, but the committee members decided that if I was good enough for Robert Mugabe, I was good enough for them.

Having completed my certification, Sam commenced an oration on "the workers' total struggle," slowing down when I seemed to be falling behind in my note taking and halting abruptly when he noticed that I had put down my pen. "Write that!" he commanded.

I thought I recognized Sam. I had run into him in storefronts in a dozen American cities. He came in all colors and spoke on all issues, and he would leave you with a notebook full of useless, sodden slogans if you let him keep the conversational initiative. Looking at him but speaking really to the committee, I said I was a journalist, not a stenographer, that my paper wasn't going to print the text of his speech, and that if I were to do the writing, I would have to understand what I was writing about. I might even have to interrupt him with questions. Sam, who was built on the proportions of a fire hydrant, bounced up and down in his chair as he ruled me out of order and instructed me to resume the transcription of his remarks, but Eric Mntonga, the regional chairman, gently deflated him by saying the committee was ready to talk. Frank Tongo, the regional secretary, would keep a record for the union, it was decided. It then took about a minute and a half for conversation to warm up to natural spontaneity.

Frank Tongo had a shaved head and a goatee and a bright, slightly caustic manner. He had been working for eight years in a clerical position at the Hoover Company, the American appliances maker. He wore a necktie to work but had emerged as the union leader when SAAWU, the acronym by which the movement was known, burst on the scene. The company's local managers, all white South Africans, wanted to break the union, he was convinced, but the top man was under pressure from the American home office, which had subscribed to a set of principles for American multinationals working within the apartheid system that had been drafted by a Baptist minister from Philadelphia, the Reverend Leon Sullivan. One of the principles promised collective bargaining with freely chosen union representatives, and Frank Tongo was confident that the enthusiasm and steadfastness of the workers would be enough to drive home this wedge.

Eric Mntonga, who also wore a necktie to work, carried confidence nearly to euphoria. A laboratory assistant at the Wilson Rowntree candy factory, he had just led his first stoppage, winning a minor skirmish with management in an early test of strength. "We've been longing, we've been looking for a union," he said, "and now we have it. They begged us to come back, and already things are changing. The managing director said that if anything doesn't satisfy us, I don't have to go to the personnel director; I can speak directly to him."

Before I left the SAAWU office that afternoon, I was assured that the power of the new black unions would ultimately put an end to the pass laws, the migrant labor system, and the Group Areas Act. I flew on to Port Elizabeth, where I met the leaders of a new black union in the motor industry, the Motor Assembly and Component Workers Union of South Africa. Also white-collar workers who wore neckties on the job, they could be recognized in New Brighton, the Port Elizabeth township, by the new Fords they drove. And they too were ready to declare openly that the freedom they sought was not limited to their factories or township. This meant, they realized, that they were bound to clash with the authorities. It wasn't that they were naïve about the likely outcome of such a clash, but as a matter of honor rather than of calculation they operated on the strength of the hopes that welled up behind them.

Both East London and Port Elizabeth had seen recent examples of what could happen to black movements that insisted on fighting local battles in the idiom of the national struggle. It was only three years, after all, since Biko's death and the banning of the organizations he led. The new unions were green branches sprouting from a trunk that had regularly been pruned. The security forces in the eastern Cape, black now as well as white, operated on the straightforward assumption that black resistance would always be there to be trimmed. The process had been going on for decades, but as it came forward to make its own sacrifice, each new growth of leadership seemed to derive in the first instance a touching but basically dizzy sense of invincibility from this miracle of regeneration. "Whatever they try to suppress here will pop up over there," one of the Port Elizabeth leaders confidently predicted.

On subsequent trips to East London and Port Elizabeth, I saw how hope was systematically cut down to size, how the reality of white power in South Africa gradually made itself felt. Scarcely half a year after my first visit to East London, I found that 2,000 members of the new union had lost their jobs. They included Eric Mntonga and 470 others who had been fired at the chocolate factory. Mntonga had just spent eighty-one days in one of General Sebe's jails. The British-owned candy company insisted that the union had provoked a showdown. Its case was half-persuasive until a security police memorandum on union-busting was leaked to some sympathizers of the union; then it could be seen that the candy company had followed the instructions point by point. On that visit I finally met Gqweta, a former salesman with the lean good looks of a trained athlete. He had been arrested repeatedly in the year that he had been the union's president without ever facing a charge. A few hours after we talked in offices from which SAAWU was about to be evicted under police pressure, he was again detained, this time by the South Africans instead of Sebe's men.

It was the second time in ten days that I found my routine reporting taking me into areas of intense police surveillance. The week before, a black student leader named Wantu Zenzile was arrested shortly after I spoke to him in my Johannesburg office. I was personally at no risk, but the realization that individuals who had sat three or four feet away from me just a few days or even hours before were beyond any possibility of contact with friends, relatives, and lawyers, that their where-abouts were unknown, and that they were probably in solitary confine-ment or undergoing intensive interrogation sharpened my awareness of the conflict as an ongoing cyclical process.

Back in Port Elizabeth that same month, I found that one of the union leaders I had met there was in detention and the others were no longer wearing neckties. The Ford Motor Company had taken the stand, reasonable enough in normal labor relations, that a blue-collar union could not be led from desks in its front office; the leaders, given the choice of leaving the union or returning to production jobs, were back on the assembly line. The grease on their overalls wasn't the only sign of the changes they had experienced. The accumulated strains of those months had different origins—the watchfulness of the police, shop floor confrontations with white supervisors, disputes over tactics within the new black labor movement, formal negotiations with the company's skilled negotiators, the militant hopes still welling within the black community—and it was normally impossible to respond to one of these pressures without intensifying others. All this showed in their faces and their voices, which sometimes now turned sardonic and bitter. They weren't less committed, but they seemed less hopeful, as if they were playing out their parts, doing what they had to do, what-ever the consequences.

What they had to do the last evening I was in Port Elizabeth was call off a strike at Ford and General Motors that they had started to put pressure on a third company, Firestone, which had dismissed some black strikers. The sympathy strike tactic was not leading to a new order; it was simply bleeding the community and the union, which had dreamed of becoming in Port Elizabeth what Solidarity was then prov-ing to be in Gdansk. I went to a mass meeting at which the facts were faced. It was dusk and the light was failing as 2,500 black workers stood in orderly ranks in a hall in the township to consider the necessity for a tactical retreat. The somber light, the somber mood, made for a moving chiaroscuro study in blacks and browns. There was little or no dissension; the gathering felt its own righteousness and strength, yet it recognized that these were still far from enough.

Months had to pass before it became possible to ask about what it was that really happened to the black trade union men who started to disappear at that point. I heard Frank Tongo's story first. The security police had let me find out the day before I saw him again that they had been following me, so we drove around through deserted streets near the beach area and then stopped, when it seemed we were unobserved, in a parking lot adjacent to a segregated white beach. I had seen two Frank Tongos on my earlier visits: the cocky labor leader at the union office and once, when I was being shown out of the Hoover headquarters by the company's managing director, the diffident black clerk. This Frank Tongo wore neither mask. He had been through something harrowing, and he definitely did not want to go through it again. The police had told him they would kill him, he said, if he talked about what had happened to him in jail. He didn't really believe they meant it, but he had become an insomniac since his release, and the threat was with him every night.

Yet, even before agreeing to talk to me, he had defied them by filing a lawsuit against the minister of law and order, contending that he had sustained "serious bodily injuries" and injuries to his "dignity and self-esteem." A young black man from Port Elizabeth named Sipho Mtimkulu, who had filed a similar suit against the minister of law and order, alleging that he had been poisoned with thallium while in police custody, had recently vanished in suspicious circumstances and was presumed by his friends and relatives to have been murdered. It was not hard to imagine the thoughts that kept Frank Tongo awake.

The white officers who worked him over at Cambridge, as security police headquarters in East London is known, appeared to put in a normal working day. He was taken from his cell in an ordinary jail at about seven in the morning and transported to Cambridge. At half past four in the afternoon, he was cleaned up and sent back. The time in between he spent stripped to his underpants in handcuffs and leg irons, periodically contorted into a human doughnut with his wrists manacled to his ankles. This made it possible for his interrogators to dangle him by a chain from a heavy board they had rigged between two desks so that his body was just off the ground. He could then be spun on the chain and beaten with sticks, a procedure that was followed daily to persuade him to acknowledge that the leadership of his union was operating on instructions from the African National Congress. Repeatedly he was told he could be killed and urged to "save yourself" by confirming stories that the interrogators claimed to have pried out of Gqweta and others. "They had it that I was the fullest member of the ANC," he said. When he denied it, he went on, a soft rubber hood was placed over his head, expanding like a balloon when he breathed out but sticking to his face when he inhaled in a manner that made him feel he was suffocating.

The humiliation and helplessness were worse than anything he could have imagined. And yet it could have been much worse: He was neither interrogated around the clock nor subjected to electric shocks. Nevertheless, on the fifth day, a Saturday, he collapsed and couldn't for a time be wakened. By then he was bleeding from not only the nose and the mouth but the ears; also, he found that he could no longer urinate.

Gauging how much abuse a given human organism can sustain must not be an easy task for the interrogators. They had made a mistake with Biko and had been under heavy pressure from the politicians ever since not to make any more. At the same time they were under equally heavy pressure from the same politicians to get information that can be secured only by means that they were adjured not to use. Operating on a fine margin, they may have feared that they had gone too far with Frank Tongo. In any case someone bungled and took him to a doctor who had the courage and sense of professional ethics to determine how the injuries had been sustained and then to insist on hospitalizing his patient. So it happened that Frank Tongo became one of the rare examples of a political prisoner released from detention while the bruises from a police assault were still visible on his body and face.

Three months after his release, Frank Tongo was fired by Hoover, which still claimed to be upholding the Sullivan principles. The managing director, a South African named Ted Ashdown, whose open and straightforward manner I had found convincing on an earlier visit, acknowledged to me that he had taken advantage of a slowdown and general retrenchment at the plant to weaken the union by dismissing some of its organizers. But in Frank Tongo's case, he insisted, the dismissal was justified; he even offered to show me the file to prove his point. I asked whether he had happened to notice the bruises on Frank's face when he returned to work. "I noticed them, but I don't recall that they were too bad. If they had really been bad," he explained, "I know we'd have asked him to stay home a little longer— for the sake of the secretaries."

Frank Tongo said that he had been doing the same job for seven years and that he had been told he would be promoted if he gave up his position in the union. But what was really telling was his recollection of what happened when he went back to work. Neither Ted Ashdown nor any of the other white managers expressed curiosity about his experiences in custody or the marks that were still visible on his face. "They never said, 'How did you get those bruises? How do you feel? Which doctor have you seen?' " he said, in a tone that was more expressive of hurt and surprise than the one he used in recounting his treatment at the hands of the security police. With some part of his mind, this supposed revolutionary had still believed that there was or should be a relationship of mutual loyalty between himself and the Hoover Company.

"Listen, Mr. Lelyveld," Ted Ashdown said to me in a confidential tone as he shifted the conversational ground from the nasty particulars of his former employee's case to the general situation in South Africa, "you've been in this country long enough to understand how things are." We were now speaking man to man, white to white. What followed was a twenty-year-old horror story involving a black worker who had given a friend change for a pack of cigarettes on the understanding that he would get the money back on payday. Payday came, and the borrower played dumb, denying there was any debt, whereupon the lender picked up an iron bar and cracked him across the skull, doing permanent damage.

He had just been reminded of the story, Ashdown said, by an Englishman who had told it to him in the first place when, new to the country, the Englishman had not yet accustomed himself to the reality that blacks can become violently enraged for almost no reason. Ashdown had then told him, "You'll have to get used to it. You're going to see a lot more of it." The Englishman had been suitably aghast, as much at the seeming casualness of Ashdown's response as at the casualness of the violence. But after twenty years in the country, the same Englishman had acknowledged the other day that the Hoover manager's prediction had turned out to be the unvarnished truth.

The old story was offered as a parable. That, I suppose, was why Frank Tongo couldn't urinate after five days in the custody of the security police, why he had to be dangled almost naked from a chain, beaten with sticks, and made to feel he was being suffocated by a rubber hood. It was because blacks were so violent.

A few days later, when I reached Durban, I noticed a small item in the afternoon paper reporting that Sam Kikane had just been released after eight months in detention. When I recalled my first meeting with the leaders of the new black trade union in East London a year and a half earlier, I was reminded of the scene-setting early moments in a movie about war or murder, the prelude of sunny innocence before the plot takes its first sinister turn. I wondered what detention had done to the one-man tumult Sam Kikane had been.

He embraced me as an old friend when I found him in a tiny union office in the Indian district at the edge of the white commercial center and threw himself into a blow-by-blow account of his jail experiences. Weeks of assaults, he said, were followed by two days of electric shocks designed to force him to acknowledge ties to the underground that he denied. When he lost control of his bowels, he said, he was told that he would be made to consume his own excrement. Later, he went on, a blow to the head left him unable to hear for two weeks. Then Sam started to hear voices, which were put into his head, he was still convinced, by an electrical apparatus that made him think thoughts that could not have originated in his own mind. "They were talking to me like a radio," he said. "The voices shouted to me!" He was then taken to a doctor, who gave him a shot, and the voices subsided. The doctor was a psychiatrist. So it emerged months later, when he complained to the South African Medical and Dental Council that the security police had arbitrarily removed a patient from his care without any consultation about the possible medical consequences. The patient, identified as Sam Kikane, was said to have been suffering from a "reactive psychosis." Sam himself rejected the idea that he had been hallucinating. I did not think that he was hallucinating about the electric shocks.

In a third city I renewed my acquaintance with another black trade unionist who had just come out of detention. Stories about interrogation and torture soon achieve, for the listener at any rate, a numbing redundancy. But this was the first of several I was to hear from brave and committed men who had to acknowledge that they had cracked under pressure. It was especially appalling because, as the man told it, all the admissions he made to satisfy his interrogators were false. First he had been questioned in the security police offices in the Sanlam Building in Port Elizabeth, notorious as the site of the interrogations in which Biko sustained his fatal injuries. He said the men who questioned him not only made a point of specifying that he was in the same room in which Biko had been questioned but also threatened to subject him to the same treatment. One of the officers claimed to have been involved in the Biko interrogation. If that was true, he was working the same beat in the same manner. The union leader was made to stand in his Jockey shorts on two bricks for two days and two nights; during all that time, he said, he was denied toilet facilities. Periodically he was slugged from behind on the right ear, always the right ear; guns were waved in his face, and he was informed in generous detail of the various ways in which he could be killed so that a magistrate at an inquest could be persuaded that he had committed suicide or been shot trying to escape. Electric shocks followed, he said, and so did a visit from an official called the inspector of detainees, who is supposed to collect complaints about maltreatment; the complaints are then referred to the officers in whose custody the prisoner remains. Finally one night he was removed from his cell and taken, with a canvas bag over his head, to a location outside the city, an isolated farm, or so he surmised, where a man can scream all he wants into the terrifying emptiness of the African night without any hope that his screams will reach a sympathetic ear. Wantu Zenzile, the student leader arrested soon after I met him, had also been taken to such a place, I had heard.

There the union leader was handcuffed to a pole and made to stand in his bare feet on something that felt like a soggy rag. A wire was attached to a toe, and the shocks started again. "I felt like I was being dissected or dismantled," he said. "Everything inside me just felt loose. Once they take you there, you'll have to prepare many yeses."

Now his interrogators weren't asking him for details of his union activities, he said, or background on people he knew. They were telling him the answers he was going to give them and drilling him to make certain he had them right. Soon he found himself admitting, he said, that he had gone to Lesotho to take instructions on trade union tactics from representatives of the underground, that he had met secretly with Bishop Desmond Tutu, a black Anglican whose prestige the security police were then bent on damaging,* in order to advance the underground's subversive designs. "And I've never been to Lesotho. Never —ever, ever," the man insisted. "Before my detention I never, ever met Bishop Tutu. I only saw him in the papers and on TV. But I had to admit it. They have it in writing. Later I went to the bishop and apologized. He just laughed and said, 'You're not the first.' "

*In part, to keep this "cheeky" Anglican from winning the Nobel Peace Prize, for which he had already been nominated. The official campaign of calumny succeeded only with South African whites. Tutu became a laureate in 1984.

Having satisfied his interrogators, the man was returned to his cell. There he was visited by a magistrate, who asked if he had any complaints. This time he summoned his courage and made a statement. The security police promptly came for him again. They had arrested his mother, they told him; she would be charged with the possession of subversive documents found in his house unless he withdrew the complaint. If he did withdraw it, they would let him see her and speak to her to confirm that she was no longer a prisoner. The complaint was withdrawn, so the story went, and the mother brought to see the son.

"Hello, Mamma," he remembered saying. "How are you?"

"Well, I'm OK," she said.

That was about as far as the conversation was allowed to get, he said. Only weeks later, when he was finally released, did he discover that his mother had been brought to the city on the promise that she would be allowed to see him. She had never been detained.

The Biko inquest found that no one was criminally liable for his death: Thozamile Gqweta was another who said that, four years later, he had that verdict flaunted in his face by white security policemen who wanted to convince him that he was entirely at their mercy. "They said that if I didn't speak the truth, I would go in the same manner that Steve went," he said. "They told me I must not be fooled by what was said in the press, that everyone knows exactly what happened to Steve."

The sense that Gqweta was Biko's natural successor was widespread in the eastern Cape. The police seemed to share it, although they must have known that the two men had never met and probably understood, also, that the movements they led were simply carried along by the same broad stream of black resistance, that they were episodes following one upon the other but otherwise unconnected. In one room in which the young union president was interrogated during an especially rough spell of detention, a poster showing Biko breaking his chains hung on the wall as a mocking reminder of what could happen. "We are going to assault you each and every day of your stay here," Gqweta said he was told at the start of what proved to be three months of detention in 1981. Over three years he was arrested eight times by South Africa and Ciskei without ever being brought to trial, but it was only in South Africa, he said, that he was assaulted or even questioned.

At each session, he said, he would be ordered to take off his clothes. "Up the wall!" his interrogators would then command when his answers failed to satisfy. This was the signal for him to stand on a trunk so that he could be handcuffed to the bars on a window, with his face to the wall. Then, he said, the trunk would be removed, leaving him dangling. In that position, he went on, he would be swung like a pendulum and beaten, not once "but approximately every day" for three months.

The next detention was more than twice as long and harder to bear, although he was never again assaulted. In the month before it began, there had been a succession of violent deaths involving persons close to him. His mother and the man she lived with died in a fire; at their funeral a girl friend was killed by a supposedly stray bullet fired by one of General Sebe's men; then Mxenge, the union's lawyer, was slain in Durban. In solitary confinement Thozamile Gqweta came close to a breakdown, suffering blinding migraines that continued to recur months after his release. At first, when he got out of jail, the sound of a human voice speaking at normal conversational levels caused him unbearable pain. Unlike Sam Kikane, Gqweta did not complain of hearing voices, but others speculated that he could have been deliberately assaulted in his cell by high-frequency sound waves that were beyond the range of human hearing.

Probably such speculation is an example of the paranoia, if that is the word, that the South African security system inspires in those it seeks to isolate as enemies. But the rationalization that South Africa is menaced by "terrorists"—who are only incidentally black South Africans, having revealed themselves to be "surrogates" of the Soviet Union—makes it possible for most whites to condone any form of counterterrorism, including torture, assassination, and bombings. It all can be denied and simultaneously defended; the price of liberty is high, the outsider is reminded. In the interrogation rooms the opposing sides in the conflict see each other without illusions, sometimes even with begrudged respect. The closer the interrogator comes to torture, the closer he comes to exposing himself and the system that employs him. To the degree the prisoner breaks down, he is exposed, too, in his human frailties. A relationship of intimacy and candor is thus established. "We are fighting for our cause," Thozamile Gqweta said he was told, in between beatings, "just as you are fighting for yours." Obviously this was both a wheedling compliment and a threat, an indication of how determined his interrogators felt themselves to be. Could it also have been a plea for absolution?

I have made a point of mentioning here the examples only of persons I met before as well as after the experiences they alleged of interrogation and torture. I don't claim to be a reader of minds, but this gave me some basis for believing or not believing that they could have been through the kinds of experiences they were recounting. None of them sought me out. None of them, except Sam Kikane, found it easy to dwell on the humiliating details. All of them were acutely aware that they were still subject to arbitrary arrest. It was not physical scars but a look in the eyes, an edge to a voice, and other intangibles of manner and demeanor that finally commanded belief. There were others whom I met only after their releases, still others whom I never met but only heard testifying in court, and others whose formal affidavits and statements about their prison experiences I was permitted to read. I estimate I was exposed to more than fifty detailed accounts of what can reasonably be described as torture by the South African police, all of which belonged to the period of my assignment in the country, enough to persuade me that these were not isolated incidents, that the violence was clearly countenanced and institutionalized.

The official explanation would be that all or most of these individuals were exploiting my gullibility, or my prejudice against the South African security apparatus, or the extreme self-restraint of the police; that those who appeared to be taking an enormous risk really knew, on account of the unfailing solicitude of the authorities, that they were taking no risk at all. The security system, like the racial system, is effective at putting a gloss on itself, obviously more for the sake of whites who don't want to know the harsh truth of what it takes to keep them secure than for blacks who cannot avoid it. A slick publication put out by the South African police talks about the problem of interrogation ("a nasty business," it acknowledges manfully, "whatever side of the table one is on") in a manner that is intended to sound urbane and detached:

> The interrogator has to get the facts as quickly and completely as possible and *without* the use of violence. At any moment he may uncover evidence which can be used to save the lives of innocent people. The detainee, on the other hand, has to do all he can to avoid answering questions. And he knows how to do a thorough job—from complaints of toothache, headache and earache, right up to self-inflicted injuries which have to be investigated. Once

facing the interrogator, the terrorist has been trained to antago-
nize the man by provoking speech and insulting behavior. The aim
is to incite the interrogator to violence. If the detainee succeeds,
he's a winner. There's an investigation, the media become involved, public sympathy is invoked—and the investigation grinds
to a halt.

The conclusion is that the security police have "no mean task" in
guarding the border against terrorists "and immobilizing dangerous
dissidents within."

Reasonable men in South Africa and beyond are asked to understand, in other words, that it is dirty but necessary work. They understand all too well and thus seldom dwell on the manipulation of facts
and ideas that is reflected in this gloss: in the fantasy of legions of black
"terrorists" trained to inflict injuries on themselves when they cannot
provoke their slow-to-anger but only human white interrogators to do
it for them; the casual interchange of the terms "detainee" and "terrorist" as if they were synonyms plucked from a thesaurus; or the further
blurring of any distinction between "terrorists," who may have information that will save innocent lives, and "dangerous dissidents," who
need to be immobilized.

The pressure the police feel to come out into the arena of public
relations and seek support in this way points to what is possibly the
strangest and most paradoxical feature of the South African system: the
constant interplay between arbitrary police power and traditional judicial forms. The security police are given effective carte blanche, then
regularly made to answer for their use of it in open court; this usually
requires lying on a colossal scale so the government and its supporters
can have clear consciences. So long as the political detainee is in the
custody of the police for interrogation under the security laws—a
period on which there is no real limit—he is absolutely beyond the
reach of the courts, which would be impotent to act even if a lawyer
could furnish proof that he was being tortured. But once he is charged,
released, brought into court as a witness or, as happens now and again,
taken from jail to a mortuary, his interrogators can be extensively and
even mercilessly cross-examined by one of the small fraternity of South
African lawyers that has continued the battle for civil liberties, usually
on the losing side. Obviously a political prisoner who has been in
solitary confinement will not find it easy to produce sympathetic witnesses, but if he has the means, courage, and stamina, he will be able

to sue and finally to tell his story in court. Chances are it will then be dismissed as uncorroborated, politically motivated, or even biased. (How, some South African magistrates have managed to ask, can a man who says he has been tortured claim to be giving objective testimony about the police?) But his story will get out.

This has happened so routinely that the white public and press have become inured to torture stories. The broad question of whether the system could survive without systematic use of torture is rarely raised. Instead, the issue has been narrowed to the legal contest in the courtroom, to whether torture can be shown on the basis of probabilities to have been used in a particular case. If so, the system can be seen to be denouncing torture; if not, it has been unjustly accused. Either way it is vindicated. Thus it was not front-page news and few persons were outraged when the following fragments of testimony—to offer a selection from a literature of sadistic practices that stretches by now to hundreds, possibly thousands of pages—became a matter of public record in South Africa:

> *He then suddenly struck me and I fell to the floor. He thereupon started kicking me in the stomach, in the groin and other parts of my body. He then proceeded to throw me around the room, grabbing my hair and generally manhandling me. At the end of the incident, his hands were covered with my hair. On one occasion he made me take off my shoes and lie flat on my back. He then stood on my shins and proceeded to hit me on my feet with a wooden block which was attached to a bunch of keys. . . .*

> *During the interrogation that night, they all drank brandy. Major Abrie asked me if I was ready to start talking. I repeated that my statement was complete. An ordinary canvas bag was placed over my head. It was a bit too small so Captain Visser had to tear it a bit in the corners to make it fit. Water was poured onto the bag. I was then given electric shocks. Electrodes were initially placed on my forearms and on my feet. Thereafter I was laid down on my stomach and the electrodes were placed on the back of my neck and on the small of my back. By this time I was lying in a pool of water. As the shock was administered each time, I would begin to scream and was then unable to breathe because the bag was wet. . . .*

> *When I arrived in the interrogation room, the three interrogators ordered me to strip, which I did. Des attached a pair of pliers to my penis. While I stood there, my interrogators laughed at me and Des told me that I was going to die that day. Des, with the assistance of Venter and the other interrogator, then blindfolded me.*

They then put cloth around my wrists. I was then handcuffed with the bracelets of the handcuffs placed on the cloth. My arms were forced over my knees and an object which felt like a metal bar was placed over my armpits and under my knees restricting me to a crouching position. The metal bar holding me in the crouched position was then balanced on two ironing boards so that I was suspended. During this time, they kept laughing and taunting me and saying I was going to die. They then started applying electric shocks to my knee. . . .

At one stage when the plastic bag had been removed from my head, the policeman who was handling the dog left it and the dog advanced towards me. The dog bit me. I was then taken back to the spot where the plastic bag was put over my face. Again I was made to sit down and my feet tightened. Then I was blindfolded. Some black cloth material was put over my eyes. My trousers as well as my underpants were lowered down to my knees. I was made to lie down and then I felt a terrible shock to the groin. . . .

He handcuffed me from the back. I then felt some electric wires which were being placed on my back and they were being cellotaped onto me. When he was questioning me, they then started shocking me with the electric wire. They were two, Van Wyk and Trollip. The one was busy shocking me, the other was saying, Praat, praat, praat ["Talk, talk, talk"]. They continued like that, asking me about certain people, until they decided to stop shocking me and then Trollip grabbed hold of my private parts and started shooking them and I, as a result of the pain, screamed again. . . .

Later a policeman called "Schalkie" came in with an elastic band and spent a long time shooting it at my private parts. They all laughed. . . .

None of this testimony, which happens to have come from three blacks, two Indians, and one white, was found to have been credible by the courts. On occasion it does happen that the former detainee is believed. Cedric Mayson, a onetime Methodist minister, testified in Pretoria that he had been kept standing naked for two days, during which he was mocked and assaulted. Thirteen security policemen corroborated one another's evidence that nothing of the sort ever happened. "If the accused's version of what happened in the first four days of his detention is correct," the prosecutor told the judge, using an argument that is usually decisive, "then thirteen policemen lied to the court." The judge accepted Mayson's evidence, but the thirteen returned to their assignments without anything's being said about disciplinary proceedings. Unavoidable embarrassment in court need not be fatal to the career of a dedicated member of the security branch of the South African police. Colonel Pieter Goosen, the officer responsible for the Biko interrogation, was later promoted to brigadier and reassigned from Port Elizabeth to Pretoria, where he was described by *Servamus*, the police magazine, as one of the closest associates of the head of the police, General Johan Coetzee, the man who oversees the battle against "terrorists" and "dangerous dissidents."

"I wish this were a police state," General Coetzee remarked to me with smooth good humor and affected modesty on the first of two occasions that he agreed to see me, before I regained my pariah status in the estimate of his organization. "Then I would have more influence." If he had that influence, he indicated, he would use it to bolster the defenses of the government and, specifically, its security forces in the psychological war that he felt was being waged against them. With an icy edge to his voice, the general referred to "the late Mr. Biko," whose death had been used as an occasion for heaping obloquy on his men and South Africa. The general was careful not to spell out his meaning, but I understood him to be saying that the Biko death was a regrettable incident in a war, in which regrettable incidents must inevitably occur. The fight against terrorism was a fight, in the first place, for the rule of law, he argued glibly, and, secondly, for the possibility that democratic processes can be developed in South Africa in an orderly manner; therefore, for democracy's sake, he said, "Let the experts fight it out with the terrorists in the shadows."

The shadows, presumably, meant the interrogation rooms. A judicial commission headed by an Afrikaner jurist who was later rewarded with the position of chief justice on the highest court in the land found that detention without trial, amounting to the suspension of all legal rights, was indispensable for the security of the state. "Information obtained from persons in detention is the most important and, *to a large extent, the only weapon of the police* for anticipating terroristic and *other* subversive activities [italics added]." The commission never looked at the question of how the information was obtained; it did not soil its judicial robes by acknowledging that threats, humiliation, beatings, and torture are an essential part of the process, a likely fate for anyone who becomes seriously involved in black nationalist politics. Fortuitously, two days after the commission's report was handed to the white Parliament, there was another death in detention, followed by another embarrassing inquest. The minister of law and order then found it necessary to publish explicit directions to the police to safeguard political detainees. "A detainee," his order declared, "shall at all times be treated in a humane manner with proper regard to the rules of decency and shall not in any way be assaulted or otherwise ill-treated or subjected to any form of torture or inhuman or degrading treatment."

Two things must be said about this order. The first is that there are few other authoritarian regimes that have sufficient conscience to formulate such a rule; the second, that few other authoritarian regimes are so hypocritical. The police were being told to do what the government had said they had been doing all along, but no court was given the power to enforce the directive. The interrogation rooms would be kept in the shadows. "If there is no torture," the redoubtable Helen Suzman asked in Parliament, posing the question that no one else cared to face, "why can they not just keep quiet?" Similar questions were asked in France during the Algerian War, so persistently that they sapped and ultimately undermined support for the whole idea of *l'Algérie française.* Alistair Horne's masterful study *A Savage War of Peace,* which is read as a manual on both sides of the South African struggle, acknowledges the possibility that General Jacques Massu's reliance on torture may have been the decisive factor in the French success in smashing the underground's networks during the Battle of Algiers but then approvingly quotes the judgment of a French official who resisted Massu on the issue of *la torture:* "All right, Massu won the Battle of Algiers; but that meant losing the war."

Is there really an analogy here for South Africa? Does each incident of torture, as Camus suggested, create "fifty new terrorists"? If it did, the "liberation" forces would be many times larger than they are. What institutionalized torture does create is the assumption, now widespread among blacks, that only violence can change the system: a clear echo of the white axiom that blacks understand only force. But the analogy to Algeria—which is tempting in many respects, in view of the ethnic proportions and social structure that were maintained there under the French—breaks down finally because there is no mother country, no De Gaulle waiting in the wings, and no way for the whites to wash their hands of the problem without relinquishing their privileges and power.

Helen Suzman has been pointing out the sinister effects of solitary confinement and torture for more than twenty years, and for almost as long, South African courts have been an arena for testimony on how interrogation actually works. And most whites would rather not hear about it. Tacitly they accept the expedient logic of yet another of the judicial commissions that are always ready to pour sophistry on troubled waters, which found the country to be faced with an "external onslaught" aiming at "nothing less than the political and moral subversion of the White Man" and then sailed on to this salving conclusion: "In countering an onslaught in which the enemy uses all methods available, it would be suicidal to deny oneself such methods." It is the ultimate Calvinist heresy: that he who has been saved by God's grace can be justified in whatever he does.

"You'll have to prepare many yeses," the former detainee had told me. If the South African experience is any guide, a system that has to justify to itself its use of harsh interrogation methods cannot easily reserve them for saboteurs and assassins, for it has a need to incriminate anyone it suspects in the seemingly illimitable conspiracy that threatens its continued operations. Once a suspect has been tortured, the interrogation has to be continued until some shred of evidence vindicating torture's use has been extracted. Some suspects may know where Soviet-made weapons are buried in the veld, but others may not. The man I knew claimed that statements that had no basis in fact had been dictated to him. Maybe I was naïve, but I could not imagine that he made up his story or feigned the reluctance and reserve with which he told it. If it is assumed to be true, it is interesting to ask what use such statements could possibly be to the interrogators who knew them to be false. Were they justifying themselves to their senior officers or enabling their senior officers to justify themselves to the government? In that case they were compromising the intelligence system. Or could it be that these statements were needed for display, on a confidential basis, to industrialists, diplomats, political figures at home and abroad who might occasionally raise their eyebrows over security police pressure on black trade unions or outspoken blacks such as Bishop Tutu? It was only a fantasy, but I could easily imagine an official in a pinstripe suit taking such a statement out of his attaché case, sliding it across a desk, and saying in calm, even tones, "No government can ignore evidence like this." If the "onslaught" isn't limited to bombs, if it is also conceived to be psychological—involving East and West, the churches and the media, financial interests and organized labor, both inside and outside the country, all aiming at the "political and moral subversion of the White Man"—then it is all the more obvious that the security police cannot confine themselves to the hunt for saboteurs. They have to go after "dangerous dissidents," too. And who are they? Those who are selected for interrogation, obviously. Otherwise they would not be selected.

The presumption of guilt is written into South African security laws; on some terrorism charges the onus is on the accused to prove his innocence. For those who have been detained but not charged, the possibility of innocence does not arise. This was explained in memorable terms by a notorious figure in the security police, Major Arthur Cronwright, at the inquest into the death of Neil Aggett, a young white doctor who had been serving as an official of a mainly black trade union. The detainee had been found hanging in his cell, an apparent suicide, after ten weeks in the custody of the security police. Of the 168 hours that made up the last of these weeks, he had spent 110 in the interrogation rooms on the tenth floor of John Vorster Square, the security police headquarters in Johannesburg, 62 of them at one stretch, although he had already made a statement. This was necessary, explained Major Cronwright, who had supervised Aggett's interrogators, because the authorities had information that he belonged to a cell of the African National Congress. Why was there no reference to that allegation in Aggett's statement? asked the lawyer for the dead man's family in cross-examination. Probably, Major Cronwright said, he was asked about it but failed to confirm the information the police had; in that case his answers would not have been recorded because, the witness explained, "They were in the negative, and the Commissioner of Police isn't interested in negative answers."

The commissioner of police is *not interested*. It is described as a condition, a state of mind, and as such it becomes a functional definition of fanaticism. Wrapped up in their racial holy war, not to mention their personal conflicts over the violence they inflict, the security police can only assimilate reality when it feeds their fantasies.

Among the government's white supporters who cared to address the question of why a man in detention might choose to kill himself, Aggett's suicide was immediately taken as confirmation of the worst suspicions of the police, whatever those might have been. "He died for his cause," I was told a few days after Aggett's death by F. W. de Klerk, one of the Cabinet's younger members, a confident power wielder. I asked the minister, who acknowledged that he had never heard of Aggett before his death, to try to recall his immediate reaction upon hearing the news that another detainee had died in police custody.

"Anger," he replied instantly.

"Why anger?"

"I knew how it would be used against us," he said.

An outsider cannot fail to become aware of unfocused anger as a by-product of South African life or the patterns of aggression and casual violence to which it gives rise among both blacks and whites. Even an American notices it, for despite all the obvious analogies between the two countries with their histories of racial conflict and frontier violence, the local pathology takes distinctive forms. Viewed against this background, the violence in the interrogation rooms can seem measured and purposeful, which is how, I imagine, the interrogators themselves would choose to view an occupation that is, necessarily, even more dehumanizing for them than it is for their victims. Engaged in a self-sacrifice that is fundamental and probably irrevocable, the interrogators have every reason to feel unappreciated.

Their encounters, overwhelmingly, are white versus black and, as such, a form of racial violence. In the society at large the menace of violence between the races may provide a framework or context for most other violence, but it is not in itself typical. Apartheid ensures that the victims of most black violence are black and the victims of most white violence white. That is one of its virtues, its supporters would contend.

Very occasionally a close reader of South African newspapers will come upon archetypal stories of the white madam who has been raped by a black servant or intruder or the white farmer or apartment dweller accused of murdering a black woman after she became pregnant with his child. Occasionally, too, there are stories of casual or random gunfire: A seventy-seven-year-old woman near Port Elizabeth wounds a nine-year-old black boy in the stomach when she finds him trespassing in her orchard; for being too "noisy," a fourteen-year-old black caddie in a town called Alexandria is shot in the head; two whites shoot up a black railway carriage near Pietersburg, killing three and wounding two ("I hate everything that is black," one of the accused then tells the magistrate); five white soldiers on furlough in the western Transvaal take a couple of potshots at a target of opportunity provided by two black schoolboys, one of whom dies. Or there was this report of a white farmer and his son practicing their marksmanship on a group of colored girls:

> PAARL—A farmer and his 13-year-old son are to appear in court on charges of attempted murder for allegedly shooting three young girls who were playing in a river adjoining his farm. A police spokesman said about 12 children were playing in the Hugo's River when the farmer arrived and fired two shots at them. He then allegedly handed his rifle to his son, who fired eight shots at the group. Eloise Swart (8), Joan Arries (10) and Diane Pegeur (8) were wounded in the arms and legs.

Least commonplace are the grotesqueries of racial sadism: the story, for instance, about the farmer in Bonnievale who was sentenced to eighteen months in jail for forcing a colored laborer to castrate himself as punishment for a sexual assault on a white woman. (Outraged by the sentence, which they regarded as unduly harsh, the farmer's white neighbors took up a collection on his behalf.) Or the stories about blacks who get savaged by guard dogs in white suburbs, including one especially horrifying report that the SPCA had been besieged with calls from whites who wanted to purchase two bull terriers after the morning's papers told how they had broken their chains and killed a twenty-year-old black woman who had been employed at the house as a servant. (The victim's employer had not known her name.)

Well, it must be acknowledged that every society has its peculiar forms of psychopathology. While I lived in South Africa, there were no American-style mass murders or unmotivated political assassinations there, so I'll pass over these examples without attempting to squeeze them further for a meaning. In South Africa the major arena of interracial violence remains the highways, where the death rate, measured on the basis of the number of vehicles or miles driven, is at least four times what it is in the United States, with blacks, who own fewer than 15 percent of the vehicles, accounting for more than 60 percent of the deaths—a statistic that can only partly be explained by the alleged carelessness of black pedestrians who are the main victims.

Perhaps that statistic reflects social pathology, too, but the point remains that self-destructive violence is far more typical. Among blacks it results from theft, drunken weekend brawling, and intratribal (especially Zulu) blood feuds labeled faction fights. In the township of

Soweto, where the number of cases of murder and manslaughter in a year is more than double what it is in the whole of Great Britain—so that the chances of meeting a violent end, calculated on a per capita basis, are at least 120 times higher than they would be there—a knife is the weapon in at least 85 percent of the cases. The funeral director with the largest patronage in Soweto, an Indian, told me that the majority of the persons he buried had met a violent end. Poverty, overcrowding, broken families all are part of the etiology that is usually outlined in explaining ghetto violence; so, too, in the case of Soweto, is the almost complete absence of preventive action by the police, who are preoccupied with protecting white neighborhoods and with surveillance of black politics.

Among whites, by contrast, the gun is usually the weapon, and the victims are typically relatives or friends. The number of guns held under license by the white population works out to about one for every adult male, and according to a private security agency called Fidelity Guards, "Out of every nine whites admitted to J. G. Strydom Hospital in Johannesburg with gunshot wounds, only one was wounded in the course of an armed robbery." Even if it is assumed that all robbers are black, it follows, under apartheid, that the finger on the trigger in eight out of nine of these cases was white. Often, as headlines regularly recount, it is that of a child who has come upon a loaded weapon a parent has kept at hand against the more remote danger of dusky intruders:

BOY DIES IN
SHOOTING ACCIDENT

BOY'S "GAME"
WITH PISTOL
ENDS IN DEATH

BOY, 6,
SHOT BY
BROTHER

GIRL (4) SHOOTS HERSELF IN CAR
DYING DAUGHTER FOUND BY ANXIOUS MUM

"I was bathing my youngest son, Mario," a Mrs. Venter of Kempton Park is quoted as saying in this last report, "when the maid called me and said Maureen had shot herself." The father apparently went nowhere unarmed. "I usually take the pistol out of the car and lock it up in the wardrobe," he said, "but I must have forgotten."

Guns are always at hand, too, in white neighborhoods to settle marital disputes:

WIFE SHOT HUSBAND
7 TIMES, COURT TOLD

CONSTABLE TELLS OF SHOOTING "UNFAITHFUL" WIFE

SHOOTING SEQUEL
TO TUG-OF-WAR
OVER CHILD

"DEVASTATED" DAD SLAYS TOTS
THEN TURNS GUN ON HIMSELF

WOMAN SHOT HUSBAND IN BED, COURT TOLD

In the last case, since the husband had a black woman next to him in the bed, there was no penalty at all. "In these circumstances, she was justified in shooting the scoundrel," Justice Human of the Rand Supreme Court declared. Normally the South African legal principle of diminished responsibility makes for light sentences when the surviving spouse can show that the deceased was unfaithful or otherwise responsible for raising the level of emotional stress. A Nelspruit magistrate levied a fine equivalent to $1,200 on a man who shot his wife in the head at point-blank range. The magistrate also suspended the man's right to own a firearm. "You were provoked by your wife's hitting and swearing at you," he told the man, "but you had no right to pull out a pistol and shoot her."

If this was what happened when whites killed their nearest and dearest, it seemed hardly any wonder that white interrogators fared well in South African courts when one of their prisoners died. Nor was it necessary, in such a violent country—when the total of political detainees known to have died in police custody averaged out to fewer than three a year over twenty years, almost exactly the same as the number of persons killed in "terrorist" attacks in the same period—to draw comparisons to El Salvador or Iran in order to demonstrate that the security police are subject to constraints. In fact, it is their boast that the rate of deaths among ordinary criminals is higher than it is among political prisoners.

The security police may not be licensed to kill detainees, but those officers who are inclined to viciousness have ample scope, both outside and inside the interrogation rooms. There is a long and sordid history of tricks being played against enemies of the regime even after they have been effectively neutralized: John Harris, the white who was sentenced to hang in 1964 for the bombing of the Johannesburg railway station, was spitefully told that his application for a reprieve had been granted when actually it had just been rejected by the president of the republic; the wife of a political detainee I knew was regularly terrorized while he was in jail by vandals in her driveway in the middle of the night smashing the windshields or windows of the family camper; Helen Joseph, a white woman who has become a kind of patron saint to the black cause after sixteen years spent under banning orders and house arrest, was past seventy-five, living alone, and partly infirm when shots were fired at her house, and as if that weren't enough, she remained a favorite target of practical jokes and threatening phone calls, including one when she reached seventy-seven from a heavy breather, who asked, "What kind of wood do you want for your coffin, Helen?"

Similarly, it has not been enough to banish Winnie Mandela, the wife of the imprisoned black leader, to the black "location" of a small Afrikaans farming community in the Orange Free State, where she is confined at nights and on weekends under house arrest in a house without electricity or plumbing; she has had to be subjected as well to a campaign of harassment that regularly results in her being charged with petty infractions of the banning orders under which she has been living for more than two decades. A woman of regal presence, Mrs. Mandela expects no quarter and gives none. And she says of the Afrikaner what the Afrikaner typically says of the black: "He knows only one language."

In a land of stereotypes, two-dimensional racial and political emblems are used, like mirrors catching the African sun, to shield and blind. Each side registers only the other's violence, not its own. Each side regards the other's violence as primordial. The potential for violence that is felt to exist within the society becomes for whites a justification for the violence of the state, which is presumed to be holding it in check. "South Africa could be worse than Belgium and Northern Ireland and Lebanon all rolled into one," an Afrikaner law professor told me, underscoring with a curious combination of pride and alarm the possibilities of racial and ethnic strife. Like most such prophecies, this one clearly had the potential to become self-fulfilling. In the same way, the idea that institutionalized white violence legitimizes revolutionary black violence is increasingly accepted—only sometimes regretfully—by blacks.

Whites complain with some reason of the world's "double standards" in judging the South African variety of repression more harshly than that of more murderous regimes, then pirouette on the spot and leap into a breathtaking display of double standards that any connoisseur would regard as unsurpassable. When the first accounts of torture started emerging from black-ruled Zimbabwe, where the government of Robert Mugabe was experimenting with laws and methods of control inherited from white-ruled Rhodesia, few South African whites were prepared to draw the trite lesson that violence begets violence. Zimbabwean torture was an outrage. It also, by some roundabout but inexorable logic, served to vindicate South Africa.

Driving through Zululand on an early summer afternoon in this period, I pulled off the road into a churchyard at a place called Elandskraal to jot down a few notes and there fell into conversation with an elderly farmer who had been visiting the graves of his German-speaking forebears. He wore bedroom slippers, threadbare trousers held up by gray galluses that looked as if they might give way with the effort, and a faded blue shirt with traces of recent meals; his skin, covered with liver spots and dry as parchment, seemed another old garment. Vic Dedekind was his name, and as he soon explained, he was descended from a German evangelist who had retreated to this place 120 years earlier from a point farther in the interior when the Zulus there "began to get dangerous." The mission this first Dedekind then founded at Elandskraal still existed but was now run solely by blacks. Dedekind outnumbered all other surnames in the small cemetery, which was surrounded by four rows of poplars that had topped out in the decades since his father's generation built the stone church. The epitaphs were all in German, and so were the services, even now when the tiny community, a "white spot" in Zululand, had dwindled to fewer than 150.

In this setting of piety and co-existence, Vic Dedekind was explaining why he would rather die than live under blacks. "The black man isn't fair," he said. "Look at Zambia, poor old Zambia. And look at Mugabe. Is he fair? Look at what he did to those three air force officers. Arrested them after they had been released by the court. Is that fair?" He was referring to a recent case of three white officers who had been acquitted on treason charges in Harare by a black judge after convincing evidence that their self-incriminating statements about complicity in a South African sabotage plot had been obtained by torture.

"A lot of countries have detention without trial," I commented mildly, not wanting to provoke an argument but giving him just a little bait. "This one, for instance."

"Of course, it must!" the evangelist's descendant exclaimed. "Look at that black man they caught with a bomb near the hall in Maritzburg where the prime minister was speaking. What would you do with him? If I were the government, I wouldn't waste time on a trial. I'd get a rope and string him up!"

To go to Zimbabwe in this period was, in this respect at least, to see mirror images. In Harare, I had asked Emmerson Munangagwa, the Cabinet minister who was regarded as Prime Minister Mugabe's most influential security adviser, about the reports that the white officers and numerous blacks had been tortured. He responded elliptically, avoiding a categorical answer but seeking to impress on me his own sense of revulsion over any use of torture, which was rooted in his experiences as a "freedom fighter." The first thing he did, he said, when he took over his department was to revisit a room in a police station where he had been tortured by white officers who hung him upside down by leg irons from butcher's hooks that ran along a track on the ceiling. This enabled his interrogators, the minister said, to bat his suspended body back and forth on the track from one end of the room to the other, as he if were the puck in an adaptation of hockey. The game continued until he lost consciousness. The day after the independence ceremonies, the butcher's hooks were still on the ceiling, and astonishingly, his former interrogators were now on his staff, as was another official who acknowledged having once sent him a letter bomb. They told him they had just been doing their jobs; he then promised they could start in independent Zimbabwe with a "clean slate." Some had later proved to be South African agents, but others still appeared to be loyal officers, the minister said. In the beginning he had no choice but to trust them, he explained. Zimbabwe could not have been expected to dismantle its only security agency.

As for the possibility that there were now black torturers, Munangagwa could only say that he deplored it. "People like myself and the prime minister who suffered in the past don't like to see people detained," he said. "We always said that if we ever got power, we won't allow those things to happen in Zimbabwe." Nevertheless, within a few months there were at least three times as many persons in detention without charge in Zimbabwe as there were in South Africa.

The same reasonable tone, the same elliptical allusions to the needs of security and shared human values were what I had gotten from the Zimbabwean's opposite number in Pretoria, Johan Coetzee. I had met several persons whom Coetzee had arrested and personally interrogated in his days as a younger officer. None of them was threatened with violence. A former member of the South African Communist party told me that Coetzee had made a point of reminding him that the police don't make the laws. "He said that if our side won, he would serve the government just as loyally," the former party member said. Interrogators say things like that, I suppose, to create an atmosphere of trust; then, occasionally, if Emmerson Munangagwa was to be believed, they turn out to be true. In fact, it wasn't at all hard for me to fantasize a situation in which a General Coetzee advised a Prime Minister Mandela.

But the General Coetzee I met was more intent on proving that Nelson Mandela was a Communist. Johan Coetzee, who was said to be preparing a doctoral dissertation on Trotskyism, fancied himself a student of Marxist ideologies. He had visited Nelson Mandela on Robben Island and spoken to him there. The Mandelas, husband and wife, had known him in the fifties, when he was a sergeant, sitting in and taking stenographic notes at public meetings of the African National Congress while it was still able to hold them. Johan Coetzee was there when the Freedom Charter was adopted. In conversation he held me at arm's length, alluding to these experiences, then swiftly dropped the curtain. None of the top white politicians had ever laid eyes on Mandela or any of the other black nationalist leaders they had proscribed as enemies. Coetzee was their link to that reality, the only man who could tell them what it was all about. Having infiltrated agents into the inner circles of the underground, he knew much of what there was to know; how much of what he knew he really understood I could not make out.

From the office of the commander of the South African security police in the center of Pretoria, I discovered on my first visit, the visitor looks across a rooftop terrace to the top floor of the American Embassy in an adjacent office building. The blinds on the embassy windows I could see were drawn. It was, I realized, a part of the embassy into which I had never been invited, the communications room perhaps or the offices of "the company." I wondered what kinds of listening devices were trained on those rooms.

"You've destroyed your CIA," the general was saying, perhaps sensing my thoughts. He had never been to America and didn't want to go, he said, because he knew that there was nothing he could learn there. He had heard from American police officers on visits to South Africa how crippled the FBI was by the federal system. America was returning to the jungle as a result. On top of a filing cabinet I noticed a plaque presented to him by the Dan Police District in Israel. I was curious to see whether he would allude in any way to my previous tour and expulsion from South Africa, but that was not the association evoked by my family's Dutch name. "Lelyveld," he said, the wings of his neatly clipped mustache spreading in a tight smile, "that's my wife's maiden name."

He gave it the correct Afrikaans pronunciation, broadening the *e*'s and honing the *v* to an *f* so it sounded unfamiliar to me. Unfortunately I was never invited home to meet the family, and it soon became apparent I never would be. My final exchange with the general came a year after I had started getting no response to my requests for interviews. By then, as a result of the Reagan administration's policy of "constructive engagement" with South Africa's white rulers, General Coetzee had been to Washington, where he had taken advantage of the chance to show off his knowledge of Communist tactics and ideology. My opportunity to speak to him came in a public hearing room, where that morning he had finished his reading of a 120-page statement on the place of the South African Council of Churches and Bishop Tutu in the web of subversive conspiracies facing South Africa. I told General Coetzee that I was sorry I hadn't been able to follow closely his Afrikaans responses to questions then posed by the bishop's lawyer, who examined the nation's highest ranking doctoral candidate on the history of church-state relations from the time of Thomas à Becket, that first "turbulent priest," to Desmond Tutu.

"*Ja,*" said the general with a withering look, "and then you could have made one of your whitewash with Omo comments."

He turned on his heel and walked away before I could figure out what he meant or frame a reply. He was referring, I realized belatedly, to a paragraph of an article I had written after the magistrate in the Aggett inquest had exonerated General Coetzee's men of criminal responsibility for the suicide in their custody of the young physician and trade unionist. The paragraph, tucked away at the end of a piece of analysis that followed my dispatch on the verdict, a kicker in newspaper parlance, had been inspired by an advertising slogan painted on a wall near where I had parked my car on the final day of the inquest. When my eye fell on it, I had just finished listening to a judgment that had taken the magistrate six and a half hours to read. The inquest itself had stretched over eight months so that a succession of former detainees could relate their experiences in the interrogation rooms. It had been a classic example of arbitrary police power being forced to unmask itself in the South African system, as if it were subject to judicial control. And the result had also been classic. Somehow the magistrate contrived to disbelieve virtually all the testimony of the former detainees about their observations of the dead man in the final weeks of his life or their own experiences in the custody of the security police. The testimony of the security police was virtually all accepted on grounds that it was corroborated by their fellow officers. The slogan on the wall, for a laundry bleach called Jik, seemed to encapsulate everything I could think of saying at that moment about this weird proceeding, in which the interrogators had been made vulnerable to public exposure and ridicule and then sent back to the interrogation rooms with a judicial seal of good housekeeping: "With controlled strength," it said, "for the world's whitest wash."

With none-too-subtle sarcasm, I wrote that the makers of the bleach were flirting with a contempt of court citation. Now, as I was left standing in General Coetzee's wake, I wanted to point out that he might have taken the first part of their slogan as a balanced judgment on his exercise of his command, if not an accolade. I wanted to point out, too, that Omo was a detergent. But the general was out of sight before I thought of shouting after him, "It was Jik."

CHAPTER 8

■

PART OF US

I t's an obscure but striking historical curiosity that the first white woman to die and be buried in the Transvaal, the region that was to become the country's economic and political heartland, wasn't an Afrikaner but an American. Jane Wilson was the wife of a minister in the first tiny group of missionaries dispatched to South Africa by the American Board of Commissioners for Foreign Missions. Her death in 1836 at the first American mission in the country (now a rail siding known as Sendelingspos—or "missionary's post"—outside the western Transvaal town of Zeerust) came a little more than a year before the earliest trekkers established their first settlement on the far side of the Vaal River. The Americans, who had been in South Africa for a year and a half, had come to Sendelingspos in hopes, as they might have expressed it, of taming the heathen heart and saving the soul of Mzilikazi, the renegade Zulu chieftain who broke away to establish the Ndebele nation. They found this South African Genghis surprisingly gracious and hospitable, but then, before they were fluent enough in his language to start proclaiming the gospel, they were struck down one after the other by a fever, which could have been typhus or malaria, and once they were diseased, they were shunned. As the Americans interpreted it, the superstitious heathens now imagined them to be under a curse, but of course, isolating them and their infection may also have served a hygienic purpose. The result was that Jane Wilson's grave was all the Americans had to show for their year among the Ndebeles, when they faced and made a melancholy choice that can be seen as a harbinger, if not the very model, of the political choices successive American administrations now face when they try to straddle the South African question. Put crudely, it boiled down to a choice between black and white.

The Ndebeles and Afrikaners had been moving into the same territory simultaneously, and after a couple of skirmishes, the trekkers decided that Mzilikazi had to be taught a lesson. The attacking Afrikaners then rode through the mission station, trampling its crops and shooting down Ndebeles who thought they might find refuge there. Each dead Ndebele was a heathen soul lost to the American Board of Commissioners for Foreign Missions, an interdenominational body that had yet to record its first conversion in South Africa. The Americans, fearing that Mzilikazi might be decidedly less welcoming to them after his humiliation at the hands of the Boers, that he might even react by imprisoning or killing them, agonized over whether they should take flight with the attackers. They didn't express themselves in terms of race when later they had to frame an explanation for abandoning their station, but it is evident that they were afraid to be the only whites left in the vicinity after the trekkers had withdrawn to their base on the other side of the Vaal. Daniel Lindley of Ten Mile Creek, Pennsylvania, by way of Athens, Ohio, where he went to the University of Ohio, and Rocky River, North Carolina, where he preached to both slaveholders and slaves, summed up the calculations and rationalizations that led the missionaries to desert the Ndebele chief and "the wicked people for whom we felt the deepest pity" in a report to his sponsors in Philadelphia:

> We did not like the idea of leaving him so abruptly and with a company of men who had shed the blood of so many of his people, lest our doing so might put an insuperable barrier in the way of other missionaries who might possibly wish hereafter to approach him for the purposes of giving instruction. Yet we thought the possibility of our doing mischief in this way very small for the time of his overthrow, we fully believed, had come.

Later it emerged quite plainly that the racial reaction had been that of the missionaries rather than the heathen king. Mzilikazi was deeply wounded by the decamping of the whites, who had kept none of the promises made on their arrival to impart great truths and useful skills. Giving his supposedly predestined overthrow the slip by re-establishing his nation in what is now Zimbabwe, Mzilikazi survived for more than three decades, displaying thereafter a healthy skepticism toward missionaries.

Daniel Lindley was another survivor. In a remarkable career that did not finally end in South Africa until 1873, he went on in the American way, pursuing his own ends on both sides of the racial divide without any sense that local circumstances might enmesh him in a significant contradiction. In the event, he left his faint but discernible mark on the main forces that are now in conflict: The Afrikaners, who had formally adopted him as their *predikant,* or parson, named a town in the Orange Free State after him as well as a Transvaal hamlet, Lindleyspoort ("Lindley's gate"), and a Zulu pastor of a church he founded became the first president of the African National Congress.

The American subtheme in South Africa's turbulent history doesn't really become apparent until nearly a century after Daniel Lindley was laid to rest in the Sleepy Hollow Cemetery in Tarrytown, New York, not until the United States was a nuclear superpower capable of seeing its interests at risk in any drastic political change anywhere. But it is worth teasing out, for it points to the proclivity for earnest but inconsistent dabbling that now gets dignified every four to eight years under the rubric "policy." In recent years we have seen the United States groping under Gerald Ford toward a policy of joint covert operations with the white regime in Pretoria; then, within twenty-four months, blithely, even offhandedly, proclaiming under Jimmy Carter its wish to see the speedy termination of that regime; then, when that brief impulse vanishes without a trace, promising Ronald Reagan's "constructive engagement." It is thesis and antithesis, never synthesis, and it is prefigured by the pious Presbyterian figure of Daniel Lindley cantering across the subcontinent after his flight from Mzilikazi to re-establish himself on the Indian Ocean coast on the outskirts of what was not yet Durban.

There at a place called Umlazi, now a major black township, he meets Piet Retief, the Afrikaner martyr-to-be, who is on his way to his fateful encounter with Dingane, the king of the Zulus. The missionary and the trekker both lack prescience, so much so that Lindley asks Retief to intercede on his behalf with Dingane. Obligingly the Afrikaner sits down and pens a letter to the man who is about to command his demise. "You may believe what these preachers will tell you of God and his Government of the world," he writes. Advised while he is stopping at Umlazi that it might be better not to take armed men with him into the Zulu kraal, Piet Retief gives a reply that foreigners in South Africa can still hear if they are too forward with their advice: He understands kaffirs, he says. Yet something Lindley tells him appears to stick in his mind, for in writing to Dingane, he holds up the Zulu's archenemy Mzilikazi as an example of what happens to wicked kings and repeats the American's erroneous forecast of the Ndebele's early death. In so doing, one eminent historian of the trek concluded, Piet Retief may have "countersigned his own death warrant" by appearing to threaten Dingane.*

Lindley goes off to Port Elizabeth to establish the Temperance Society, then returns to Natal to find that the situation has been transformed by Retief's murder, the Zulu defeat at Blood River, and the arrival of the main body of trekkers. He has now been in South Africa for four years and has yet to save a single black, but once again he pushes that project—the reason for his being there in the first place —to the back burner. He has had an insight that is prophetic in the secular sense, and it makes Daniel Lindley the first practitioner of "constructive engagement." Drawing an analogy from the fate of the Cherokees, who had been robbed of their land by aggressive white settlers and forcibly relocated in the United States, he foresees that a new order is going to come ineluctably into existence in the Zulu heartland in which "one part will be white and the other black." Daniel Lindley is no bleeding heart about the "savage creatures" he has come to save; he feels sure that like the Cherokees, they will "soon be compelled to give up to a better sort of mankind." But that "better sort" is none too good either. The "wickedness" of the whites, he argues, "can destroy the natives," who, once they have added the vices of the whites to those they already have, will be "two-fold more the children of hell than they were before."

And so he sends off an audacious proposal to the American Board of Commissioners for Foreign Missions. It is that he be allowed to focus his missionary efforts on the trekkers, who are already supposed to be Christians, rather than on the heathen Zulus. "Unless they come under religious instruction," he warns, with what after nearly a century and a half sounds like authentic divination, "they will overturn everything in this country." The conversion of the Zulus is still his aim, he writes, but "the cheapest, speediest, easiest way to convert the heathens here is to convert the white ones first." In other words, there is little hope of having influence with the blacks unless something can be done to

*Eric A. Walker, Emeritus Vere Harmsworth professor of imperial and naval history in the University of Cambridge and Sometime King George V professor of history in the University of Cape Town, in *The Great Trek.*

restrain the whites. The board in Philadelphia is as dubious about this proposition as many are today when it is advanced as a rationalization for a diplomacy that insists on dealing with the whites first because they hold power. There is, perhaps, a suspicion that Lindley in his frustration and eagerness to save souls ("show results," the diplomat would say) may be calculating that the odds will be better among the whites, a suspicion, too, that for all his moral strictures on them, he probably finds them more congenial. But Daniel Lindley is permitted to bring his mission to the Afrikaners in Pietermaritzburg, and in 1840 the *Volksraad* ("people's council," or Assembly) of the short-lived trekker republic in Natal formally invites the man from Ten Mile Creek, Pennsylvania, to serve as predikant to the community, which embarked on its exodus with no ordained minister of its own. And so he preaches to all the Afrikaner leaders of that time, including the military commander and hero of Blood River, Andries Pretorius. When after opening a school, the American starts to teach that the earth is round, there are some among the trekkers who have second thoughts, fearing that he may be a heretic.

Lindley's spiritual influence doesn't keep the Volksraad from formulating the first resettlement program when in 1843 it resolves to remove from its territory all blacks "except such Kafirs as may engage themselves for hire as laborers amongst the people." But by then Britain has already proclaimed its intention to annex the territory and impose under colonial authority a legal system that shall not grant or withhold rights "on mere distinctions of color, origin, language or creed." As happened in the Cape a decade earlier, some Afrikaners find this too much to swallow; they then start what has come to be known as the Second Trek into the interior, moving on like the Mormons and other frontier religious bands in America in the same period, without waiting to discover how little British practice would conform to British principles. The Afrikaners' predikant stays on, turning his attention back to the Zulus, and in 1849 finally establishes a church with nine black converts at a place called Inanda. One of the nine is a young Zulu of chiefly lineage named James Dube who, twenty-one years later, on what Daniel Lindley calls "the gladdest day of my life," is ordained as the pastor of the Inanda church. Lindley's view of Zulus appears to have softened under the influence of his protégé. Once he thought there was "nothing in them but pure, unmixed, unmitigated selfishness," but he adores James Dube for his "imposing appearance," which is matched, the American writes, by his "mind and religious convictions." James's son, John L. Dube, goes to Oberlin College, a destination that, just possibly, may have had something to do with the favorable impression Daniel Lindley brought back from a visit to Ohio in 1861 before John Dube was born. "I rather admired the harmony of colors," Lindley wrote after his first exposure to a racially mixed institution. Later at Inanda the Reverend John Dube founds a school called the Ohlange Institute, modeled on Booker T. Washington's Tuskegee. Still later—no longer a fan, it seems, of Booker T. Washington—he writes for the most militant black American publication of the day, W. E. B. Du Bois's *The Crisis.* In 1912, when the African National Congress comes into being in Bloemfontein as the South African Native National Congress, this Oberlin product is chosen as its president-general. Pixley ka I. Seme, a black lawyer who had attended Columbia, is chosen as treasurer.

In South African terms, it seems a fatuous or depraved flight of fantasy to imagine that a single divine could have blessed both Andries Pretorius and John Dube—the Boer commander at Blood River after whose son the Afrikaner capital was named and the Zulu aristocrat who embodied the black aspiration for equality in a modern state. The connection is too tenuous even to be noted. Such a divine couldn't possibly have been a South African. Probably he could have been nothing other than an American.

By the time John Dube returned from Oberlin, American influences were trickling and seeping into a peculiar array of South African psyches and enterprises, enough to provide raw material for a *Ragtime* pastiche set in the greatest boomtown the Southern Hemisphere had seen since the Aztecs. Johannesburg sprang into existence so fast, following the discovery of huge gold deposits within the borders of Paul Kruger's sleepy Boer republic in the Transvaal in 1886, that no one ever bothered to record which digger, speculator, or official had been honored when the city was named. American diggers and fortune hunters were among the *uitlanders* ("outlanders," or foreigners) drawn to the Witwatersrand, the long ridge that held within its bowels the world's richest gold reefs. They were followed, as Charles van Onselen has shown in his pioneering *Studies in the Economic and Social History of the Witwatersrand,* by squadrons of pimps and prostitutes fleeing an outbreak of civic virtue in Manhattan that had been set off by the anti-Tammany campaigner and cleric Charles Parkhurst. The Johannesburg underworld, Van Onselen writes, "was dominated by 50–70 'Bowery Boys' who preferred to refer to themselves as 'speculators.' " The young state attorney who ordered a crackdown on the Bowery Boys in 1898 was not casting himself as an Afrikaner Parkhurst. Jan Christiaan Smuts, then twenty-eight and recently returned from England, where he achieved results of unprecedented brilliance in Roman law at Cambridge, drew his moral inspiration from another American. While reading law at the Middle Temple in London, he had found time to write a book on Walt Whitman, who, he later said, taught him to appreciate the "Natural Man," liberating him from "conventional preconceptions due to my very pious upbringing." It was not much of a consolation to the whoremasters from Manhattan, but thanks to Whitman, Smuts later wrote, "Sin ceased to dominate my view of life."

Almost simultaneously the first black American missionaries started to arrive in South Africa at a time when black Christians there were beginning to question the need for white tutelage and white control of their churches. The African Methodist Episcopal (AME) Church, the largest of the independent black denominations in America, had sent missionaries to Liberia as early as 1820. In 1898, the year before the Boer War broke out, a black American bishop from Atlanta, Henry McNeal Turner, ordained sixty-five clergymen for the AME Church on a five-week tour of South Africa, during which he met President Kruger, who is reported to have told him, "You are the first black man whose hand I have ever shaken." Some historians seem to think that the slogan "Africa for the Africans" was introduced in this period into South Africa by black American churchmen. In any case, they helped prepare the ground through the independent black churches for the influence, a generation later, of Marcus Garvey, the West Indian campaigner who made "Africa for the Africans" a battle cry that ultimately resounded from Harlem to Johannesburg and Durban,* where it gave rise to a succession of black pride and Pan-Africanist movements; these, advancing the argument that blacks could not count on the support of well-meaning whites for their own liberation, shaped a black political tradition that has sometimes waned but never been extinguished in South Africa. In the early years of the century, whites

---

*And even in the remote rural areas of Transkei and Ciskei, where according to Mary Benson in *South Africa: The Struggle for a Birthright,* a popular expectation grew that Garvey was on his way, presumably by sea, to liberate blacks.

in Natal seemed to have a sense of what was to come and who was to blame. "An evil star rose in the American firmament and sent its satellites to preach sedition in Natal," a letter to the *Natal Mercury* proclaimed in 1906 following a Zulu rising against a new tax that was to be levied on each hut.

In terms of world history, the Zulu rising is memorable now mainly for the effect it had on an Indian lawyer who had been reading Thoreau on "civil disobedience." Mohandas K. Gandhi called on his community in Durban at the start of the suppression campaign to contribute to "a special fund for the soldiers who have gone to the front to fight the Kaffirs." The campaign against the Zulus, he wrote, gave Indians "a splendid opportunity for showing that they are appreciating the duties of citizenship" in a way that would leave "a very favorable impression on the minds of prominent whites." To that end Gandhi himself donned a uniform and, with the rank of sergeant major, led a unit of Indian stretcher-bearers into Zululand. "We are not overcome by fear when hundreds of thousands of men die of famine or plague in our country," he wrote in his sarcastic, hectoring vein when calling for Indian volunteers. "Why then should we fear the death that may perhaps overtake us on the battlefield?" The corps was disbanded after scarcely three weeks, but the themes of symbolic struggle and sacrifice pointed the way to what followed. Within two months, articulating for the first time his concept of *satyagraha* in a speech in a Johannesburg theater, the mahatma-to-be called his first campaign of nonviolent resistance.

By then the idea that the contagion had started on the other side of the Atlantic had become a matter of faith for many whites. A clergyman named John Scott declared at a public meeting that "one of the greatest dangers to the standing of the white men in South Africa" was the encouragement that various churches were giving young blacks to go to college in the United States. A pamphleteer warned of the danger of "missionaries, saturated with American democratic ideas," traveling "up and down the land telling the Kaffirs that South Africa is a black man's country, and that blacks must 'stand up for their rights.' "*

---

*In 1982, nearly eight decades after this appeared, these same warnings and themes were still being sounded, having become a hoary convention, almost a polemical genre, among some whites. A judicial commission formally reported to the white Parliament that the "potentially lethal theo-political force" known variously as Black Conscious-

In the aftermath of the Zulu rising, colonial Natal became so hysterical over the menace it perceived of independent black churches responding directly or indirectly to the exotic message of American blacks that it actually made it illegal "for any Native Minister or member of a religious movement not under European control" to address meetings of any description. "The Natives," an official commission had urged with a candor and clarity that almost seem admirable when contrasted with the obfuscation and doublethink in present-day pronouncements, "must be made clearly to understand and to realize that the presence and predominance of the White race will be preserved at all hazards."

In the Boer War itself, Americans could be found sympathizing with both sides and also fighting on both sides. Some of the Yankee uitlanders who had taken part in the initial gold rush to the Witwatersrand now signed on with the Imperial Light Horse, the uitlander regiment, which was also known, Thomas Pakenham informs us, as the "Imperial Light Looters." The British war effort had the tacit support of the administrations of William McKinley and Theodore Roosevelt, which allowed the British consul in New Orleans to recruit muleteers for Her Majesty's forces. Admiral Alfred Thayer Mahan, the great naval historian, assured Lord Roberts that the "best of my countrymen" knew that Britain was fighting for "equal rights and human welfare." *The New York Times* editorialized that "Tammany Hall is a magnificent illustration of freedom and majority rule" by comparison to the Boer regime in the Transvaal. The admiral and the editorial writer were probably talking about the rights of white uitlanders in Paul Kruger's republic rather than blacks, but church groups fostered the illusion that a British victory would lead to an improvement in the legal and social status of the "natives." By contrast, those who abhorred the *fin de siècle* imperialist vogue, especially as it was then manifesting itself in the American colonization of the Philippines, saw the Afrikaners as a sturdy, liberty-loving people battling for their independence. In this anticolonial perspective, paradoxically, South Africa's blacks were all

ness and Black Theology "had been introduced into South Africa from the outside . . . mainly from the cauldron of black thought and action in the United States of America." The report traced the hostility of various church movements to apartheid to a "fateful seed," the adoption by American Methodists in 1908 of a "social creed" calling for "equal rights and complete justice for all men in all stations of life." The judicial commission then singled out Bishop Tutu as "the prime exponent of American Black Theology in South Africa," stressing his "very close links with the anti-South African Black Establishment in the USA."

but invisible. Richard Harding Davis, the dashing American correspondent, appears to have noticed them seldom and only as a part of the background scenery during the time he spent with British forces and then the Boers, who were fighting, he wrote, "for a cause as old as the days of Pharaoh and the children of Israel, against an enemy ten times as mighty as was Washington's in his war for independence."

Davis maneuvered himself from one side of the conflict to the other by shipping out from Durban to Mozambique, where the Portuguese authorities had set up a series of complex procedures to filter out foreign sympathizers of the Boers intent on taking up arms in their cause. He then traveled from Lourenço Marques, the present-day Maputo, to Pretoria with a group of sixty volunteers from Chicago, all Irish-Americans, who had gotten through the net by pretending to be a Red Cross ambulance corps; in fact, Davis reported, the Portuguese authorities had confiscated "the chief part of their medical supplies" after discovering that it consisted mainly of malt spirits. For Irish nationalists, the Boer cause had irresistible appeal—the Afrikaners were, after all, their enemies' enemies—even though Irish troops were disproportionately represented on the British side, where they took some of the heaviest casualties. Richard Harding Davis watched as President Kruger reviewed the volunteers from Chicago, after they had shed their Red Cross insignia. He was present again when Oom Paul received a message of sympathy and support that had been signed by 2,900 Philadelphia schoolboys and hand-carried all the way to Pretoria by a sixteen-year-old liveried courier from a messenger service in New York. The renowned correspondent lives up to his reputation in his description of the scene as the nervous adolescent tries "in an excited, boyish treble" to unburden himself of a brief speech of presentation "he had rehearsed in the dark corners of the deck to the waves of the Red Sea and the Indian Ocean." The forbidding old patriarch "peered down at Jimmy Smith like a giant ogre," Davis wrote. "One almost expected to see him pinch Jimmy Smith to find out if he were properly fattened for eating. But instead he took Jimmy's hand and shook it gravely." Just three hours later President Kruger separated from his invalid wife, whom he would never see again, and rode out of his capital on the first stage of the journey that would carry him into exile. When he returned to Pretoria, four and a half years later, it was in his casket. He had died near Montreux, leaving a last testament to his people. "Look to the past," it said, "for it contains all which is fine and noble."

Jimmy Smith, presumably, read the news in Manhattan, where it would not have had much of an impact on anyone who had not shared his adventure. South Africa and its conflicts were never a preoccupation in the United States, but Americans kept popping up in South Africa in unlikely guises, and curious, sometimes funny connections kept being made. When the United States entered World War I, 1.75 million recruits into the American army were asked the following multiple-choice question on a battery of supposed intelligence tests: "The number of a Kaffir's legs is: 2, 4, 6, 8." As Stephen Jay Gould has shown, the inability of new immigrants from Eastern and Southern Europe to grapple with such queries was later offered in the debate over immigration as scientific proof of their intellectual inferiority. In a letter to Lloyd George in 1918, Jan Christiaan Smuts, then serving in the Imperial War Cabinet in London, expressed his concern that General John J. Pershing was not up to the command of his expeditionary force and suggested that President Wilson be pressed to give combat command to a more qualified foreigner. Smuts had just the candidate in mind. "I am naturally most reluctant to bring forward my own name as you can well understand," he wrote to the British prime minister. "But I have unusual experience and qualifications to lead a force such as the American army will be in an offensive campaign."

Little noticed in the midst of a world war, a tangible and serious connection was forged in this period between South Africa and the United States by Ernest Oppenheimer, the son of a Jewish cigar maker from Friedberg, Germany, who had been in South Africa for only fourteen years when he founded a company that was to become a dominant force in the gold-mining industry; then, after it had taken over the De Beers diamonds cartel, in the economy as a whole; then, having opened up the Copper Belt in what was to become Zambia, in the region; until, finally, when it started to reinvest its Central African assets in North America, it emerged as a fully fledged multi-national. The Anglo American Corporation drew half its initial capital from Wall Street interests, thanks in part to the persuasiveness of an American middleman, a former mining engineer named Herbert Hoover. Ford and General Motors were soon to follow, but this was the first major American stake in South Africa. Originally there was to have been no "Anglo" in the new corporation's name. "Anglo" was something of a misnomer, at best a patriotic gesture acknowledging South Africa's status as a dominion under the king-emperor. The original idea had been to herald the vital new connection across the Atlantic by calling it the African-American Corporation, but the American partners shot down that name as soon as they heard it.

"African-American," they cabled, "would suggest on this side our dark-skinned fellow countrymen and possibly result in ridicule."

A half century later, when I first went to Africa, contradiction and ambivalence continued to be the main themes of the American involvement in South Africa, such as it was and such as it would be. The realization that this was the case dawned on me slowly. It seemed fantastic to me (a conventional liberal from New York, beginning my assignment in the short, stormy season between the passage of the major civil rights acts and the large-scale commitment of American forces to Vietnam) to suggest that my country had any real complicity in the apartheid state but not fantastic to speculate that American power might one day make a difference in the region on the side of the disenfranchised. Puny Rhodesia had not yet gotten away with its defiance of a Labour party government in Britain; the first of the several Nigerian coups and its aftermath in Biafra had yet to occur; Tanzania was widely held to be some kind of model; Israeli forces had not occupied the West Bank; "terrorism" was a phenomenon of the nineteenth century; and the term "third world" had yet to set off in self-satisfied Western minds a rush of images of physical ruin and moral chaos, nor had anyone yet dismissed the United Nations as a "theater of the absurd." In other words, the liberal idea that Americans were on the same side as the world's poor still had some life. I drew no political conclusion from the fact that I flew with South African mercenaries on U.S. Air Force C-130's in what was then the Congo. The issue there, as I construed it, was not left versus right or East versus West or black versus white; it was, I would have said, a choice of catastrophes, something like death versus lingering malignancy.

It was an American ambassador in what was still called Léopoldville who revealed with a dry quip a fundamental element in the situation that might have served as the starting point of any analysis. G. McMurtrie Godley, who would later in Laos get involved in a bigger conflict than the one he was then managing in the Congo, was no mannequin in pinstripes pretending to be a strategist. He chomped cigars, had trouble keeping his shirttail in his trousers, and spoke English as if he knew it to be a living language. When I remarked that a crisis seemed to be in the making in southern Africa, with the issues of Rhodesian independence and South Africa's illegal occupation of the territory now known as Namibia possibly coming to a boil at the same time, he blew a cloud of smoke at the ceiling and then dismissed the idea that American power might be brought to bear against the white regimes. "The day has not yet come," Mac Godley said, "when white men will fight white men in Africa for the sake of black men."

This was close to what Daniel Lindley had discovered about himself in the western Transvaal in 1836, when he fled his mission station with the whites who had attacked it, instead of staying to succor the victims. Naturally it was a point that never found its way into American speeches in the General Assembly on the wickedness of apartheid or the sanctity of international law. But it could not have been lost on planners in Salisbury or Pretoria. They must have known that wherever American warships ventured—into the Gulf of Tonkin, the eastern Mediterranean, or the Persian Gulf—they would never blockade South African ports in order to uphold a United Nations resolution. Although I didn't think much about it at the time, I got another lesson in the ambiguity of the American position on South Africa at a breakfast after my expulsion at the London residence of Princess Lee Radziwill, where a small group of journalists and politicians had been invited to meet Robert Kennedy on his way to Johannesburg. This was the later Bobby Kennedy, the junior senator from New York and searching liberal who was breaking with Lyndon Johnson over the war his brother had bequeathed. His trip to South Africa, the first significant gesture of support that an American politician had made to beleaguered blacks and student liberals there, was supposed to evoke the hope that democracy could be a solution. "What should I say," Bobby Kennedy began, "if someone asks me about American investments in South Africa?"

"Do you want the truth, or do you want the political answer?" asked Colin Legum, a South African by birth who was then the *Observer*'s man on Africa. In an elegant dining room, at nine in the morning, when the scrambled eggs were yet to be served, Legum's question sounded unnecessarily challenging.

It was Senator Kennedy who broke the embarrassed silence. Everyone laughed when he replied, "I try to make them come out together."

Americans were still trying when, a full ten years later, I found myself running one December evening toward Park Avenue in New York to keep up with Representative Andrew Young, who had the habit of catching up on his exercise by breaking into a trot on city streets. A fellow Georgian had just been elected President, and I was traveling with Young that week to write a magazine article about the black congressman who had a chance to exercise more influence in the White House than any black before him. The announcement was still a day off, but Young had just accepted a job as ambassador to the United Nations. In fact, he had just come from his first meeting with Cyrus Vance, the President-elect's choice as secretary of state. They had not dwelt on the arms race, the Middle East, or mass poverty in the poor nations. They had talked mainly about South Africa. Vance, Young said as we rode uptown in a taxi, favored the use of sanctions. The black former preacher, who would have gone to southern Africa as a missionary when he left divinity school if the Portuguese authorities had given him a visa to Angola, said he disagreed with the white corporation lawyer. The taxi was taking us to a small private dinner where, inevitably, South Africa would again dominate the conversation, for the other main guest, aside from Young, would be Harry F. Oppenheimer, the corporate dynast from Johannesburg. I thought I had learned something about the world when I discovered that the South African had the ability to discern where influence on southern African policy would lodge in the new administration and to make his first contacts before an announcement and before specialists in the State Department could have known. Over dinner Oppenheimer raised complex issues with exquisite tact without eliciting anything that might be called a statement of a policy objective. Finally he was driven almost to the point of direct inquiry, asking in a diffident and donnish manner exactly what it was that Americans intended to signify when they used the term "majority rule."

The ambassador-to-be was obviously thinking of something else when the elaborate question was put. He did not seem to realize that it had been addressed to him, that the table was now waiting for his response. It might have been a minor turning point in American diplomatic history and a landmark in the meandering course of the American involvement in South Africa when the blank was finally filled in by Young's aide, Stoney Cooks. "Let's just say," the trim young black man softly replied to the septuagenarian magnate, whose head was now tilted to one side in polite expectation, "one man, one vote." In fact, it was just an anecdote, another snapshot from my memory book.

A few days later in Atlanta, I pressed the point for the purposes of my article with Young, who was now speaking on the record as ambassador-designate. Did he really think, I asked, that the new administration could bring about the start of a peaceful transition in South Africa to black majority rule? Yes, he really thought so. I think I whistled; then I said he must be calculating on eight years, assuming a second term for the new President. No, he thought it could be done in four.

"That's a short time," I said.

"It's not so short," said Andy Young.

Another anecdote, another snapshot. Having negotiated in Birmingham, Alabama, as a lieutenant to Martin Luther King, Jr., in 1963, Young thought it only natural that he should now go on to Pretoria, as if the two places were stops on the same line. A black American could speak to the fears of white South Africans better than any white, he believed. Andrew Young was Daniel Lindley's heir. It seemed a remarkable twist of history that he was able to make a small beginning in imposing his sense of destiny, that he actually made it to Pretoria. "I get along with those kind of folks," he told me when he returned from meeting Balthazar Johannes Vorster. Later the former prime minister gave me his own gloss on the encounter. "He loves himself, that boy," he said, fascination overcoming an undertone of distaste. "He must kiss himself every morning in the mirror."

Young would ultimately earn some credit for the independence of Zimbabwe, but of course, he was back in Atlanta when his four-year note came due unpaid. After having been indoctrinated with the view that they were targets of a "total onslaught" by both superpowers, with the Ford Foundation and the Trilateral Commission and the Council on Foreign Relations all conspiring to promote Black Consciousness on behalf of the CIA, white South Africans had suddenly to adjust to a less hostile world. The state broadcasting monopoly hailed the election of a new American President as a defeat for "pseudoliberalism, permissiveness, state intervention, appeasement, and antipatriotism." There was hope now, the commentary proclaimed, for "Western Christian culture." Western Christian culture, in its terms, had less than nothing to do with missionaries like Andrew Young or churches that are obsessed with apartheid.

In the event, it had to do with an American political scientist from Georgetown by way of Johns Hopkins and the Nixon White House, who possessed an American political scientist's faith in the "modernizing" aptitudes of military elites. Chester Crocker, the new assistant secretary of state for Africa, described the leaders of the South African armed forces as a "lobby of modernizing patriots." In America his name was known mainly to specialists and lobbyists; with a precisely trimmed mustache and a banker's caution with words, he was guarded, remote, resolutely nontelegenic. But in South Africa his name was dropped into conversations as if he, rather than Kissinger, had turned out to be the new Metternich. A magazine editor used the fact that he had once lunched with Chester Crocker in a libel suit in order to prove that he possessed the sort of standing that could be damaged by a scurrilous article. One of the best-informed operatives Washington had ever fielded in the region, Crocker had criticized Andrew Young for raising unrealistic expectations and trying to impose an American agenda on South Africa. Yet he himself, with a policy that amounted to a little bit of carrot and no stick, was ready to see South African military power used to impose an American agenda on the region. Through support of insurgencies and covert sabotage operations across its borders, Pretoria managed to force neighboring black states to recognize its hegemony, acknowledge their economic dependence, and act against South African black exiles. Washington occasionally moralized over the means, the secret training camps, clandestine movement of arms and men, the subsequent bombings and assassinations, but it warmly applauded the results, accepting the taming of black nationalism inside and outside South Africa as an advance toward regional stability and a setback to Soviet influence. The adenoidal voice that read the commentaries on Radio South Africa proclaimed a "Monroe Doctrine" for the region, based on the "joint commitment" of Pretoria and the Reagan administration. Chester Crocker would never have put it so nakedly, but it was he who coined the term "constructive engagement."

"It is not our task to choose between black and white," he said. The American task was to defend Western interests, which he listed as "economic, strategic, moral, and political," in that order. It was significant that the political interest, entangled with the question of who actually ruled South Africa, came last, not first, where Andrew Young had implicitly placed it. The reordering of priorities was more rigorously accurate as an expression of real relationships, but the change, once again, was mainly verbal. Crocker had resurrected the premise of a secret policy memorandum of the Nixon years: "The whites are here to stay and the only way that constructive change can come about is through them. There is no hope for the blacks to gain the political rights they seek through violence, which will only lead to chaos and increased opportunities for the communists." Even though the regimes of Mozambique, Angola, and Rhodesia, which had been included in that estimate, all had now fallen, it seemed more plausible than ever as a description of the situation in South Africa. And Crocker found a way to say it openly by balancing two axioms: The United States would not let South Africa be "destabilized," and it would not align itself with apartheid.

It would not align itself with apartheid, but it would depend on the whites who were now in power and still busy elaborating the apartheid system to bring about constructive change. The evident contradictions in this stance could be resolved only by a trusting or willfully blind acceptance of the assurances of change and reform that are offered wholesale to visitors like Chester Crocker in the offices of white generals, Cabinet ministers, and corporation executives. And this depended on not seeing what was going on in places like KwaNdebele and Ciskei. Not choosing between black and white meant, in practice, focusing on white politics and identifying American interests with the fortunes of the governing party. It meant writing off black nationalists, except as potential apostates who might be willing to accept junior partnerships in the apartheid state when the time came for its next renovation. Winnie Mandela put it perfectly the last time I visited her in her place of enforced exile, where she had been deposited initially so that she would be unavailable to meet Andrew Young on his first visit in 1977. "Constructive engagement," she said, meant telling blacks to call off their struggle because "the bosses are working it out."

Other blacks reached the same conclusion. For the first time in nearly twenty years, it was sometimes possible to find no blacks except servants at American diplomatic receptions. They were always invited, I was told, but often they stayed away. Important American officials sometimes visited the country without making even a token effort to seek out black opinion. The head of the CIA breezed through on a visit that was meant to be secret. Aside from his official contacts, which were never disclosed, he saw only a selection of Johannesburg businessmen, instigators of "change" in the view of Andrew Young as well as Chester Crocker.

Once, at a private luncheon, I heard one of those same businessmen make a remark that seemed to sum up the reformist program. "What this country needs," he said, "is a good multiracial oligarchy." Later, when it was announced that Gavin Relly, one of Harry Oppenheimer's lieutenants, would succeed him as chairman of the Anglo American Corporation, I asked him how he would express the comment he had made at the luncheon if he'd known he was speaking for publication. Relly paused, took a deep breath, and then declared with a puckish look that was not without self-mockery, "We need to get this country under some sort of multiracial oligarchy!"

But didn't there have to be an eventual outcome, I asked, to the South African conflict? "I used to think, rather simplistically, when I was much younger," he replied, "that, really, why do we go on with this bloody thing? Why don't we have one man, one vote and be done with it? I now no longer think like that at all. I don't believe in final solutions. One can go on in a state of permanent transition."

This was neither doctrinaire nor inhumane, but it assumed white dominance for decades to come and thus fell far short of black expectations. Apartheid would survive, but it would be apartheid with a human face that might now, on occasion, show itself to be brown or even black, enabling those who wanted to engage constructively with South Africa to do so with diminished embarrassment. Repression would still be necessary, but it would try to be discreet. The West would have to accept at face value and even magnify the good intentions of the whites, ignoring insofar as possible the central issue of power, in order to prevent a strategic vacuum and keep its supplies of gold and platinum, manganese, vanadium, and chromium, according to what was merely the latest stance in Washington. It would do so until the next swing of the political pendulum, when once again it would sound righteous to little or no avail. Constructive engagement might then be said to have set the stage for constructive disengagement.

The issues of policy were interesting to debate from an American standpoint, but it was hard to be sure that they had much or even any bearing on what really happened in South Africa, which would remain a land of immense human possibilities and immense human failures whatever Americans thought or said, especially since what Americans did never varied very much anyhow. There was more paradox and futility in the world than the policy planners knew how to acknowledge. Here, as elsewhere, America worked at cross-purposes with itself, looking during Jimmy Carter's time for ways to pressure Pretoria while its own economic policies were driving up the price of gold to unimagined levels, thereby rendering the white regime temporarily invulnerable; then, when high interest rates in the United States left gold in the doldrums and South Africa vulnerable, eschewing pressure tactics altogether under Reagan. A perverse case could be made that Carter unwittingly saved South Africa from the consequences of the Soweto unrest and the collapse in Rhodesia, giving white power the breathing space and wherewithal to approach self-sufficiency in arms and even in energy, while Reagan, far from influencing the course of events, was influenced himself to the point of not only tacitly accepting South Africa's tactics in Angola of supporting an insurgency to force a political shift but also imitating them in Nicaragua.

When British forces under Lord Roberts were marching to Pretoria in the Boer War, Richard Harding Davis asked President Kruger how the United States might help. "By intervention," Kruger shot back. "It can intervene." Kruger's heirs would recoil from any such suggestion today, but black leaders like Oliver Tambo, the exiled head of the African National Congress, might echo the old patriarch, who replied with a parable after Davis had pointed out "that it was not at all probable."

"Suppose a man walking in the street sees the big bully beating the boy and passes on without helping him," the president said, casting his tiny republic as the juvenile. "It is no excuse to say after the boy is dead, 'The boy did not call me for help.' We shall not ask for help. They can see for themselves." Kruger wasn't asking for an American army to fight the British. He wanted what diplomats rightly mistrust: a clear moral stand that dispensed with calculations of interest. He was sick of the balancing act. Richard Harding Davis, who believed that the Boers were fighting for "the principle for which our forefathers fought," leaves this as another anecdote, another snapshot. He passes a moral judgment on Britain for the brutality of the war—his judgment stands as proof of his rectitude—but never suggests that there were practical steps that his own country should have taken. Oom Paul, posing for Davis on the veranda of his house with his stovepipe hat on his head, glares out from the pages of the American's book. His expression is stolid and proud, not fatalistic but equal to his fate and, in that sense, unsurprised. The attitude to the man behind the camera and his audience across the ocean is harder to read. It may be indifference, or it may be reproach.

Some Americans set themselves up as arbiters of the South African conflict; others take sides. Out-of-office public figures shuttle to the tip of Africa, paying their way with gentle jeremiads and lectures on Western values, while disparate, self-selecting groups with different or conflicting concerns maintain the casual, distracted, yet historically ordained identification that connects America to all the major antagonists. And all the while, in seeking to renovate and preserve their system, South Africans tend to hold up a mirror to America so that Americans are struck, however ambivalently, by a weird family resemblance. It would be excessive to speak of the Americanization of apartheid, but a little imitation makes it possible for the envoys of American venture capital and enterprise to feel increasingly comfortable and optimistic in the environment apartheid shapes. If what is taken for normal in San Diego or Houston can be made to seem not abnormal in Durban or Johannesburg, then the problem can be presumed to be on its way, in whatever time scale, to resolution. The discovery that a black is sitting at the next table in a restaurant or holding down a skilled job at a decent wage— that the whole of South Africa is not necessarily a penal colony for all blacks all the time—flashes a message of hope to the American mind.

I experienced these small epiphanies myself, usually as a result of something that I could as an American regard as normal—a glimpse of middle-class life, a snatch of conversation in an amicable key, something ordinary and everyday that left me momentarily absorbed in the South African dream that the racial conflict might quietly fade away. Early one morning, walking downtown to my office, for instance, I saw a new Toyota pull to the curb with a well-dressed black couple inside; the woman got out and walked briskly away, presumably to her job, and then the man drove off, presumably to his. I knew nothing about them aside from what they were wearing that morning and what they were riding in, but that was enough to cause me to reflect that most people in the world, even most people in my own country, would find it hard to regard them as victims. Then, instantly carried away, I was seized by the hope that maybe, somehow, it all would work out. The same hope welled out of nowhere as I sat waiting for a hubcap for my wife's car in a Volkswagen parts department, where blacks and whites, drawn by their common devotion to their automobiles, made room for one another and exchanged bits of lore about mileage and prices and new models, without any trace of self-consciousness. Or there was an afternoon at an important soccer game, where the crowd, which was 99 percent black, was waited on and entertained almost entirely by whites: white scorecard and Coca-Cola vendors, white drum majorettes, white bandsmen, and white bagpipe players, who were promptly hooted off the field. The fleeting evidence that racial hierarchy could be dispelled for a moment or an afternoon put the grinding issues of South African life into a soft, blurry focus as for an ad for a new shampoo. Apartheid, too, could be milder, gentler, making the country easier to manage than the outsider might have imagined. But the dream of its fading away was like the Marxist vision of the withering away of the state, and no black could sustain it for long.

Americans were seldom there for long, and the idea that blacks might want more than piecemeal change involving a selective lowering of barriers for selected segments of their population was surprisingly easy to overlook. A false analogy was at work: We saw Jim Crow go away, so why can't apartheid? The reason is apparent to South African whites. It is because legal equality for blacks would lead swiftly and inevitably to the loss of white power. Whites as well as blacks understand that blacks will have to dominate the country as whites now do before they can tear down the whole apartheid edifice. Reasoning from American analogies, Americans tend to misconstrue the conflict, to talk about human rights and living standards while fuzzing the central issue of power. ("It is not our task to choose between black and white.") This makes it easy to suppose that whites who talk about "reform" and "change" are talking about an end to white dominance when often they are really searching for ways to make it more tolerable so it can endure.

Mike Rosholt, the chairman of Barlow Rand, South Africa's second-biggest conglomerate, went to the trouble of making a pilgrimage to the Reverend Leon Sullivan in Philadelphia to consult him on how to draw up a code of fair employment practices that would do for the 325 companies in his group what the Sullivan principles were supposed to be doing for American multinationals. Now no foreign visitor to Barlow Rand's American-style suburban headquarters in a parklike setting that could be Fairfield County or Westchester can get away without having at least one copy of the employment code thrust into his hands. It was not just for show. Rosholt demonstrated that he was in earnest about being an equal opportunity employer, monitoring his managers on their performance in upgrading the status of black workers and investing more heavily in training programs than the multinationals in South

Africa. But Mike Rosholt had to try three times when I asked my question about whether there didn't have to be an outcome to the South African conflict before he could come up with an answer that he thought would sound right in New York.

"Look," he began, "no one really wants to face an ultimate . . .

"I don't believe that any white person here really . . .

"Very few liberals want to face a situation where there's an immediate equality," he said finally, his voice pitched very low, "and I don't believe it is necessary. I'm a great believer in evolutionary stages. But there's got to be movement."

In terms of evolutionary stages, the enlightened South African industrialists of today are like the white "paternalists" of Central Africa, whom Doris Lessing ridiculed nearly thirty years ago, before the ruinous Rhodesian war. They would do everything in the world for the Africans, she wrote, "short of giving the Africans . . . an equal vote with the white man." The effect of Lessing's sarcasm has been somewhat blunted by the concept of democracy that has evolved in the independent black states, including Zimbabwe, Zambia, and Malawi, the components of the old Central African Federation she was lampooning. The postcolonial states pay an unconscious tribute to the white regimes they succeeded, for they also believe in the dominance and preservation of an elite, only now they are occasionally moved to characterize that elite as a "vanguard." Whatever it is called, like the white regimes it replaced, it has a tendency to suppress opposition movements and rival ethnic groups. It matters enormously, of course, that the constituencies of the new regimes are not limited to a racial minority and that rights are no longer defined in racial terms. But the functional difference between being disenfranchised and having an equal vote in a one-party state gets to be a little subtle.

Obviously the American multinationals that subscribe to the Sullivan code wouldn't want to be caught saying that "immediate equality" isn't necessary. That would be regarded as uncouth at home. Yet what they do say sometimes amounts to the same thing. Mobil, indulging in the same sort of corporate advocacy that it pioneered in its advertising in America, devotes a two-page color ad in South African magazines to the importance of upgrading what it calls Black Education. Not the education of blacks but "Black Education." The apartheid pattern is at least implied. Corporate advertising certainly doesn't cavil about it. Instead, it focuses on what it takes to be larger issues:

> If the Free Enterprise system is to prevail and grow, we need quality people and Whites alone cannot fill the additional 220 000 management and skilled or semi-skilled posts which must be created each year between now and the end of the century.
>
> Merely educating and training a greater number of people is not the answer—the quality of Black Education and its end product must be improved. . . . South Africa's future and yours depends on it.

The advertisement shows a black and a colored leaning disconsolately against a wall in a ghetto setting. Scrawled on the wall, over their shoulders, is graffiti that originated in an advertising copywriter's mind. "Black education needn't be a dead end street," the graffiti proclaims. The sentiment is not objectionable, but it identifies Mobil with half of the government's argument. The other half is all menace, contending that if whites are made to relax their grip on power, then strife and radical black despotism will ensue so that neither the "Free Enterprise System" nor "Black Education" can advance. Let things go on as they are going, the outside world is advised, and there will be hundreds of thousands of educated blacks, maybe millions, and perhaps then apartheid can be further eased. Probably Mobil has another philosophy of history. Probably it would not agree that this is an ineluctable either-or choice. The political issue of who controls "Black Education" is evaded in the ad. Still, if it is saying anything to blacks as well as whites, Mobil is saying, "Apartheid needn't be a dead-end street."

Making the best of apartheid means teaching a disenfranchised black how to deal as if he were an equal with a white supervisor and teaching the white how to take it. There are industrial consultants in South Africa specializing in this "interpersonal training." Usually they find their inspiration in the United States, repackaging American training "modules" for South African consumption. A firm called Contact Training in Johannesburg offers a program called Interaction Management, known to initiates as IM, that was developed originally by Development Dimensions, Inc. of Los Angeles. Interface Communication applies a technique called "behavior modeling" to white-black communication in an industrial setting in South Africa with the aim—according to an article ("Behavior Modeling as Social Technology in South Africa") in a journal published in Durham, North Carolina, called *Personnel Psychology*—of "improving the behavior and attitudes between white supervisors and black employees."

The idea of racial hierarchy is thus built into the design of the program. It is, after all, the reality with which the trainers must start if they are to perfect their "technique for helping people to act more positively to one another." The logo for Interface Communication shows two profiles in silhouette, one black and one white. Rod Spence, a South African with an M.S. in industrial psychology from New York University, explains that the technique of behavior modeling is analogous to sex therapy. In the South African context, he says, the aim is to break down an autocratic "parent-child" model of communication between the races that has been fashioned over the centuries and replace it with "adult-adult communication." The trick is to focus on behavior rather than attitudes. A white supervisor who starts off by thinking blacks are just "kaffirs and *tsotsis*" (hoodlums) will end up thinking, after role playing his way through a series of training sessions, that "kaffirs and *tsotsis* are still kaffirs and *tsotsis* but my guys are better." So Rod Spence expresses the process; only later, after this breach has been made, he says, will the white begin to generalize from his experience.

For the white supervisor, the training involves learning "to focus on the problem and not the person." He learns that in order to get results, he must be careful to "maintain the employee's self-esteem" while correcting his errors. For the black, Interface Communication offers a form of assertiveness training. He learns to ask questions, to seek fuller instructions when he is unsure, and even to voice his complaints. "Assertive, not aggressive," Spence is quick to point out. Offering these pointers as a managerial technique rather than a moral admonition apparently makes them easier for whites to ingest. They are not used to listening to blacks, but they can be conditioned to do so, it appears, if they are told that it is in the interest of production, profits, and their careers. The training sessions involve videotapes of "situationalized" exchanges between a supervisor and an employee, meaning an example of the behavior that is sought, which is acted out by a real supervisor and a real employee, recognizable people from the workplace. Then the trainees try it for themselves with the guidance only of a sheet of terse, numbered instructions: "Always be polite and constructive. . . . Accept your position without resentment. . . . Do not complain to other workers if you have a problem but talk to your supervisor." Or, "Express your confidence in the person. . . . Ask if he has any questions concerning the instructions and answer all the questions."

The latest videotape has been "situationalized" at the Kellogg plant in Springs, where South Africa's cornflakes are produced. The white and black call each other by their first names, John and Abner. "Can I ask a few questions, John, just to get clarification?" Abner asks. John beams. So does Coos van der Merwe, the industrial relations manager at Kellogg's, who is not only a bearer of an archetypal Afrikaans name but a product of the Waterberg, a corner of the Transvaal whose conservatism is usually described in geological similes such as granite-like, and not only a product of the Waterberg but a former official at the West Rand Administration Board, the apartheid apparatus that administers Soweto's blacks. Coos finds no contradiction between being a loyal supporter of the governing party and a loyal employee of an American company that needs to demonstrate its enthusiastic compliance with the Sullivan code. In fact, having just selected the first fifty workers and six supervisors from the plant at Springs for training by Interface, Coos seems to be generating much of the enthusiasm. Despite the name of the program, the two groups won't be mixed in the training sessions in order to minimize suspicion and tension. Whites will take the roles of blacks, and blacks will take the roles of whites in their separate sessions. The results, it is expected, will become evident in their day-to-day contacts on the shop floor. Kellogg hopes this will help ease tensions that have been evident among white supervisors since it recognized a black trade union in 1981. The day in which a white supervisor could threaten to dismiss a black worker on the spot has now passed, and many supervisors have had a hard time adjusting to the loss of authority. The Interface program will also look good, Coos knows, in the next audit of Kellogg's performance under the Sullivan principles. In reports to the head office in Battle Creek, Michigan, it will snap, crackle, and pop.

The article in *Personnel Psychology*, based on a pilot program at a pharmaceutical company in South Africa, points out a potential problem, however. "The training of supervisors was easier than the training of employees," it acknowledges. The employees tended to concentrate "more on preparing their own case than listening to their supervisors." The article doesn't touch on the question of why this might have been, just as it doesn't touch on the question of why there were no "modules" to instruct whites on how to take instructions from blacks. Was it that the black employees were slower learners than the whites or deficient in education? Or could it be that the Interface trainers had failed to convince them that they as well as the company and supervisors would benefit from the program? Could it even be that they found it hard to accept their position "without resentment"? I could only speculate; Kellogg's foray into "social technology" was to start only after my departure from South Africa. But it didn't do to be snide about such an effort, for it pointed to an obvious need that was not only overlooked but denied in the grand scheme of apartheid. It's true, if anything is in South Africa, that blacks and whites need to learn how to communicate. "The objective is interracial harmony—the alternative is tragedy," says the article in *Personnel Psychology* of Durham, North Carolina. But before "interracial harmony" is talked about, it might be pointed out that the possibilities of communication are not exhausted by the giving, taking, or even questioning of instructions.

"Historically," Chester Crocker once wrote, "South Africa is by its nature a part of us."

Crocker was talking about how we see it, leaving aside the question of how the majority of South Africans would see it if anyone tried to ask them. That may sound arrogant, but it was a subtle argument advanced by a subtle man. We have principles and interests that we have to try to reconcile, he was saying. Therefore, we must be simultaneously for stability and change, if that is possible, and maybe even if it is not. But then Inanda "by its nature" must also be a part of us, if any place in South Africa is. Inanda is the black area near Durban where Daniel Lindley started to save black souls and John Dube, Oberlin product and ANC founder, passed most of a long life. Inanda grew up around Lindley's mission. Americans were working there a quarter of a century before there even was a Johannesburg. When Lindley was ready to go home, having spent the last twenty-four of his thirty-seven years in South Africa there, the Zulus of Inanda took up a collection to be held in trust for his eventual funeral expenses in America. Twenty pounds, the equivalent then of about $100, was collected. "We will send the money over the seas so that others may not bury him," it was said.

John Dube acquired land in Inanda, less than a mile from the spot where Mohandas Gandhi, inspired by Tolstoy, established a kind of rural commune so that whites and Indians could live in interracial harmony. Gandhi published a paper called *Indian Opinion* from his Phoenix Settlement starting in 1904, the same year that Dube founded a Zulu paper called *Ilanga*. When I first visited the Phoenix Settlement in 1965, it was still set in the midst of sugarcane fields and rural small holdings of both Zulus and Indians who had been living peacefully together since the days of Dube and Gandhi. When I went there seventeen years later, most of the vacant space had been filled in by black and Indian refugees from Durban neighborhoods that apartheid had leveled. Gandhi's settlement still survived as a memorial, but interracial harmony was now a subject for a small museum that had been erected there in memory of the mahatma he became. A new Phoenix had meanwhile risen from the ashes of Gandhi's dream, a segregated Indian township—the very antithesis of what he had hoped to build, cynically or uncomprehendingly sanctified by the name he had chosen. Phoenix, the township, now spilled over one hill; Inanda, the black area, extended over the others. Gandhi's tiny Phoenix lay squeezed in between in the apartheid vise, a landmark to a South Africa that never was.

Where blacks were still living on Indian-owned land, the authorities were busy getting them expelled. The racial boundaries were being firmed up, not eased. To that end Inanda had been dropped into a legal limbo between South Africa and the Zulu homeland. It was no longer a part of the one exactly, but not yet a part of the other, so neither was responsible for building a proper water supply system when the area's population soared by 153 percent in the 1970's with black refugees from the white areas. Outbreaks of typhoid and cholera followed, only fifteen miles from the center of Durban, a major industrial city. All this was going on while Chester Crocker was writing about the prospect of "purposeful change."

And of course, it was purposeful. But then, to confuse my parable, the kind of change Crocker meant came to Inanda. It came first in khaki as the army mobilized an emergency supply of clean water for the stricken area. Then it came in pinstripes as the business community, lobbying through the Urban Foundation, its privately endowed department of good works, demanded not only a proper water supply system but a reasonable plan for housing in an area of rapidly rising population, not the usual state-owned, state-administered township but a demonstration project for the free-enterprise system in which the employees of the foundation's corporate sponsors might own their homes. The result was a model "self-help" scheme in which building sites, along with piped water, decent roads, and various community facilities, were provided to families that also got the credit, building materials, and technical advice they needed to put up houses. When I visited the place, about seventy houses had been rising every month for two years, and Inanda now had a small corps of private black building contractors.

Obviously it was a showpiece. I didn't have to drive very far to find the remnant of a squatter colony where whole families were crowded into wooden shipping crates marked "Toyota" or "Renault" with the initials CKD (for "completely knocked down") stenciled on their sides. I knew, too, that lots of ambiguities still clouded the legal status of the residents and that none of them, at this stage, yet owned the land on which their houses stood. Still, it was a grass-roots project that would be acclaimed anywhere in the world, proof of a wealthy land's capacity to tackle the problems of human wretchedness it had largely invented and legislated for itself. And it brought to my mind a contrast that was full of poignancy and ambiguity. Several weeks earlier I had visited the barrios, the crowded shanty areas that ring the Mozambican capital of Maputo farther up the Indian Ocean coast, no farther on the map from Durban than Johannesburg is, but a world away. Here a radical political movement had been mobilizing the masses for nearly a decade, but on the afternoon of my tour that meant mobilizing them to stand on line for water rations, in a context in which equality had come to mean scarcity and equality of need. In South Africa, meantime, a system that went about producing refugees, occasional epidemics, and gross inequalities, that routinely turned efforts at mass action and economic enterprise into criminal offenses, could incidentally, as an experimental digression from its usual pursuits, start to house and feed some of its people as the political leadership in Maputo had earnestly wanted to do all along.

If I had seen a development like the Inanda project attributed to Frelimo, the revolutionary party in Mozambique, rather than to a foundation backed by an oligopoly, I would certainly have been impressed. It seemed only reasonable to be impressed in South Africa as well, even though the framework of racial law hadn't buckled at all. In fact, while the new houses were rising, the authorities were busily trying to purge Inanda of tens of thousands of "illegals." They were also said to be requiring that no loans for houses in the development area be given to blacks who had failed to begin the process of their own alienation as South Africans by registering as citizens of the homeland.

In the name of "self-help," apartheid was thus spinning off yet another subcaste in Inanda. Just the opposite had happened 300 miles away in Maputo at the time of "liberation" from Portugal, when the *cidade di cimento* (the modern "cement city") had been thrown open to the black masses with the nationalization of all housing that wasn't actually occupied by its owners. Many still dream of such a liberation coming to Durban, but in Maputo it spurred a cataclysmic flight of the entrepreneurial and managerial Portuguese classes, leading, with a further push from South African-backed insurgents, to the conditions of economic collapse I had glimpsed. And now socialist Mozambique was busy evicting unemployed blacks from the center of Maputo faster than the white authorities in Durban were evicting them from Inanda. Moreover, those same socialists, who sometimes still described themselves as Marxist-Leninists, were looking to white South Africa, the hated apartheid state, to come to the rescue with investment and skills. That black Mozambican officials might one day visit Inanda to draw pointers from the housing scheme there for the barrios of Maputo was no longer unimaginable. These twists, inversions, and reversals left me feeling a little dizzy. For a brief historical moment that threatened to stretch into an era, white South Africa seemed able to say to its own blacks and its black neighbors, *Do it our way or not at all. On your own you'll only make a mess of it. We'll make sure of that.* A neologism that had once popped into my mind was there again. You could call this whitemail, I thought.

Standing in Inanda, I looked around at the crazy quilt apartheid had thrown over the land, at the Indian township, the squatter colonies, the new Inanda development, and a conventional black township called KwaMashu on the other side of a gully. "I can't make any sense of it," I remarked to my Soweto friend Chris More.

"I'm not trying," Chris answered with a laugh.

Inanda was part of us, presumably, because 134 years after the arrival of Daniel Lindley a section of it had finally benefited from the free-enterprise system as it is practiced in South Africa and therefore from the Western economic order. But its inhabitants would not be able to purchase freehold title to their land, as John Dube had done before the passage of the Native Lands Act in 1913, not at least until Inanda had been formally merged into the homeland. Then it would be part of us but not of Durban, where its inhabitants worked and most of them once lived, and someday, if the Zulu leadership were finally cajoled into accepting the independence it had so far firmly rejected, it would not be a part of South Africa. That was what Chris saw.

On the other hand, if "liberation" would do to Durban what it had now done to Maputo, would it be worth it in Chris's eyes or those of Inanda's residents? My opinion, which didn't matter, was that it would be worth it, even then, but the issues blurred. If, by some miracle, democracy could suddenly come into existence in a society as skewed and riven, economically and socially, as South Africa, how could its leaders fail to respond to pressure for radical change in the name of equality? And how could such changes, given the near monopoly of managerial and entrepreneurial skills by a racial caste, fail to bring about economic collapse? With such prospects and probabilities, how could a prudent black government run the risk of political democracy? Would it, too, not be tempted to go on in a state of "permanent transition" in order to preserve a multiracial, mainly white, oligarchy that kept the mines, farms, and factories producing? I had always believed that my country should be on the side of political and social democracy in South Africa. Standing in Inanda and thinking of Maputo, I was left wondering whether such a side could really exist or, rather, since I knew that it existed, that it was imperishable in the sentiments of many black and some white South Africans, whether it could ever make its mark on the land apartheid had shaped.

Chris and I cut short our visit to Inanda because we were due at a spectacle that had a roundabout relevance to these issues. It was the national championship of a ballroom dancing competition for blacks and browns in which the contestants, responding on some level to the idea that they were part of us, would be graded on their ability to do it our way. Hundreds of them had been drawn from all over the country, to the regimental hall of the Durban Light Infantry, which had been rented for the occasion from the South African Defense Force by the makers of a cheap white wine, the sponsors of the event. In both New York and Johannesburg, I had seen Athol Fugard's *Master Harold . . . and the Boys,* in which two black waiters in a teahouse prepare for such a contest in the township. The hall of the Durban Light Infantry was where they would have dreamed of arriving, the final perilous crest on the mountain they were attempting to scale.

A small combo, sitting under the regimental altarpiece, a wooden hoarding topped by the unit's coat of arms and cataloging its campaigns

from Ladysmith to Cassino, listlessly banged and blew its way through
a succession of tunes that were played, it seemed to me, at high school
dances in the Bronx thirty years earlier. In no sense was this the music
or rhythm of the townships, which were Motown and disco, imported
and Africanized, not the death rattle of Jimmy Dorsey as transmitted
over all those years and miles. Tango, samba, rumba, cha-cha, what we
used to call the lindy and what they now called jive—all had their
adherents, along with the waltz, starting with contestants in the five-
to seven-year-old category, who were pushed out onto the dance floor
by ambitious mothers and fathers. The dress was formal, resplendent
in the case of the adults in the advanced categories, where the men
wore white tie and tails and the women gowns of gauze and taffeta in
lime green or raspberry, lemon or shocking pink, with sequins on the
skirts and sparkle in their hair to catch the light. A single white troopie
in fatigues, with an Uzi submachine gun slung under his arm, stood
transfixed and astonished at the door, where he was supposed to be on
guard to protect the army's property. The judges were whites, including
a couple that had recently danced off, I was told, with "the gold cup
for whites" in their separate, reputedly more advanced league.

The man, a platinum blond who wore elevator shoes, was named
Trevor. His partner, whose frozen smiles had a way of melting into
expressions of boredom and disdain, was Mandy. When the juvenile,
novice, and intermediate championships all had been settled, the lights
dimmed, and the combo took a break so that Trevor and Mandy,
dancing not to the colored combo but to strings on a cassette recording
they had brought, could offer a "demonstration." On the wall the
regiment's coat of arms carried the legend "Primus in Africa." Trevor
and Mandy were presumed to be primus in Africa, too, in another kind
of Latin. Its intensity was transmuted into English hauteur in their
rendition of the tango. No connoisseur of the art, I found their sudden
chin thrusts and sideways stares comical. But there were "oohs" and
"ahs" from a group of Zululand nurses and teachers with whom I was
standing. "Thank you," said Trevor, taking the microphone and gently
patting his perfectly unmussed hair, "I know that you people enjoy the
tango from the applause you give your own couples when they dance."
You people, your own couples. In white ties and tails and sequined
gowns, they still didn't come close to making it in his eyes, the distant
blue eyes of a colonial subaltern.

It was past two in the morning when the last of the big trophies had been handed out to the new black ballroom dancing champions. The troopie at the door had locked away his weapon and changed into his street clothes so that he could split as soon as the hall was empty. And Mandy had long since left in a taxi when Trevor next took the microphone to offer a final critique of the performances he had been judging. "I would like to say the standard has improved tremendously," he said, pronouncing his verdict from on high. "Just keep working on your basics, and I hope to see another improvement next year."

This, too, was "social technology." The tone was that of a man who had done his duty. There was no hint that he might have enjoyed himself for a moment. But Steward Dephoko, a machine operator from Sasolburg who had just taken the prize in advanced Latin dancing with his partner, Alinhal Mareletsa, didn't hear the condescension I thought I heard. His own performance had been full of fun and verve and daring gymnastics; I thought he could teach Trevor. But the new champion had danced in a multiracial competition at the Carlton Hotel in Johannesburg, where he had come in only fourth. "I was no match for the white guy," he acknowledged. So he was not offended by what Trevor had said or the way he had said it. "If he tells me to work on the basics," Steward Dephoko said, "that's exactly what I'm going to do."

So Trevor's way is Steward Dephoko's. One day, with violins playing and soft lights casting beguiling shadows, they may appear in their patent leather dancing shoes, each immaculately attired, at the same ballroom dancing contest and dance as equals. It is the dream of a happy ending to apartheid. And South Africa, as the credits roll up on the screen to all the strategists and officials and industrialists who never lost faith, will still be a part of us.

CHAPTER 9

■

COMMON RESPECT

The sign was peeling, but it still managed to scream, "ALL LIARS, ATHEISTS, SKEPTICS AND FOOLS MUST PLEASE KEEP OUT!" I was reasonably sure I was not a liar and didn't want to think about the other categories, so I stepped forward to read the small print. "A curse lasting seven years shall fall on all who destroy any part of this place," it said. "They will be unlucky in all they do, be hunted like beasts and finally die in agony in lonely places! BE-WARE!"

Risking all, I continued on, entering the precincts of a shrine that seemed to derive its inspiration partly from the cult of the avenging Hindu goddess Kali and partly from Disney World. Ostensibly it was an African kraal, but the roofs of the whitewashed round huts bristled with religious symbols that were not primarily associated with Africa, including the Muslim crescent moon and the Hindu swastika. In open spaces between the huts, outsize, crudely formed sculptures, molded in cement and covered with plaster, looked as if they were meant to embody the iconography of schizophrenia. Painted in Day-Glo colors that mostly struck the eye as bilious rather than as lustrous, this pantheon included a dinosaur, a tiger, a green earth mother with the heft of an ox, a Martian or other extraterrestrial visitor with an overextended brow of an orange hue, and a mechanical figure that may only have appeared to have been inspired by the Tin Woodman of Oz.

An unprepared onlooker, happening upon these totems without any explanations beyond the warnings at the entrance, would tend to conclude, I think, that they were products of a sensibility that was idiosyncratic, not a little obsessive, and possibly disturbed. In that case the unprepared onlooker would be far removed from the reflections that the white officials of the West Rand Administration Board, the sponsors of the display, hoped it would inspire when they underwrote its construction and arranged for it to be included as the major cultural attraction on their guided bus tour through the township of Soweto. The board, the arm of the white bureaucracy that manages the largest black settlement in the land, was not responding to popular clamor, nor was it moved by spurious aesthetic values, when it allowed this singular shrine to be erected in a park that had been donated several decades earlier to the blacks of Johannesburg by Sir Ernest Oppenheimer, the mining magnate. Instead, it was enabling a statement to be made about what it saw as the authentic qualities of African culture. To judge from the result, these were its weirdness, veneration for the grotesque, and remoteness from any religious tradition that the white tourist might seek to connect to the strange apparition called Soweto. It was there to proclaim to the visitor, *These people really are different, in more ways than you can imagine. They really want to live apart, not with whites in cities, not in cities at all.* And beyond that, to say, *If you can't make sense of this, don't tell us how to run this country.* In other words, to whites who didn't participate in its rituals, whatever they were, the shrine was presented as a political argument and, more than that, a justification.

But if that is what it meant to the whites who gave it their protection, what did it mean to blacks? The question pointed to the oddest feature of the place, odder than the minatory signs or Day-Glo icons, and that was the fact that it was not easily accessible to blacks. It had been created as an evocation of African culture for white tourists, not for Africans, and until recently the park was closed, I was told, to anyone who didn't arrive on the tour bus. Imagine a Mecca that barred Muslims. The anomaly finally registered, and now there was a sign saying, "City of Soweto. Museum, village and tea garden. Admission 5 rands." But the fee, which meant the typical Soweto family would have to shell out half the month's rent to pass fifteen minutes there, was obviously intended to limit rather than invite local curiosity. So the question of what the shrine meant to blacks had to be refashioned and refined. What did it mean to the black who had conceived it? To whom was he speaking?

Credo Vusamazulu Mutwa, a traditional healer or witch doctor with a flair for polemics in English that showed flashes of undeniable brilliance, had made a notable career of interpreting the unknowable Bantu to

whites. At his best he wrote scathingly of the presumptions and smug-
ness of the colonial culture, of the white man's enduring ignorance of
Africa and its ways. But he traded in mystification more than demystifi-
cation and, having taken his stance as the authentic voice of an Africa
that was despised, fitted his narratives to the stereotypes of his white
audience with all the shrewdness and astuteness of a salesman who
knows his market. I don't mean to imply that Credo Mutwa occasionally
pandered to white prejudice. I mean to say that had become his essential
business, so that finally the Africa he portrayed was an almost perfect
reflection of the Africa whites wanted to see.

In his writings* Mutwa entertains with tribal sagas and clever rein-
terpretations from a black perspective of historical episodes such as Piet
Retief's demise or the so-called kaffir wars, all supposedly handed down
by revered black holy men. He also teaches that blacks are universally
great fatalists, that they lose their souls in cities, have no aptitude for
anything mechanical, are prone to bribery as a matter of cultural
predestination, that they are ruled by the passion of revenge but dare
not look a white man in the eye. ("To the Bantu, pale green or blue
eyes seem supernatural, able to pierce the very soul," Mutwa declares.
"When a Bantu can manage to look a white man straight in the eyes,
two conclusions can be drawn: firstly, he has lost all contact with his
tribal customs; secondly, he has lost all fear and reverence for the white
man and he despises him.") To the Bantu also, Mutwa tells us, Christianity has been "one of the worst plagues ever," for vitiating his own
tribal traditions, it has produced a race of detribalized blacks ("empty,
bleak Godless zombies, ripe for conversion to any subversive creed").
The political implications of these themes are not always oblique.
"Apartheid is a law of nature," Mutwa writes. "Apartheid is what we
want and need." By this, he tells us, he means a system that will leave
him at peace in his kraal, that will preserve him from both black
despotism and white bigotry, from the savagery and horrors of the race
war that his more sibylline utterances constantly promise.

Some of the ingredients tossed into this stew have a potential for
nourishment. Of course, Africans want to heal the cultural wounds that
have been inflicted on them and revive lost values; of course, there are

*His two books, *Indaba, My Children* and *Africa Is My Witness*, were excerpted in
a collection that Penguin Books published in London under the title *My People: The
Incredible Writings of a Zulu Witch-Doctor*. In the United States the collection was
titled *My People, My Africa*.

empty, bleak zombies—white as well as black—who can be led into unspeakable acts of violence; and of course, there is no instant political fix in the white world—meaning the modern, industrial, urbanized world with its overlay of racial laws—for all that blacks have suffered in South Africa. A profound reflection on politics and culture could be spun from such themes for the present generation of blacks. But this Zulu shaman is up to something else, not telling blacks what they need to hear but whites what they want to hear: that any black who speaks of democratic values, Christianity, the modern world, and the rightful place of his people in it is by definition nothing but an imitation white, a fraud, or a lost soul, estranged from his people, adrift and doomed. You can spot him when he looks you in the eye. It's not the Nelson Mandelas or Steve Bikos or Desmond Tutus who express black aspirations, then, or the thousands of exiles in London or East Germany or Dar-es-Salaam; it's not the literary figures or the occasional professor with a foreign degree. It's the *songomas,* the traditional seers and witch doctors. The real Africa is deep, dark, and, yes, savage; forever alien. Listen for the drums. Or, better yet, take the Soweto tour—Credo Mutwa will explain it all.

In fact, I discovered when I set out to meet him, he was on the public payroll for that purpose. Given a phone number where I was told he could be reached, I found I was calling the offices of the Soweto Parks and Recreation Department, a white official of which intercepted the call, brusquely informing me that it would be impossible for Mr. Mutwa to speak to me for at least a month. "He is an employee and runs a facility for us," the official said, referring to the shrine I had visited. "He has very little time." A couple of hours later, when I guessed the white official might be out to lunch, I tried again. This time I was put straight through to Credo Mutwa, who said he would see me, but only on the condition that I took an oath not to injure South Africa in anything I wrote. "I'm not trying to injure anyone," I answered piously. "I just try to write the truth."

He was not at the shrine at the appointed hour, but a young man, who was evidently expecting me, provided an escort to lead me to his residence. Following the escort's directions, I then drove back across Soweto and, to my surprise, through the gate of a compound of the Parks and Recreation Department. At first I was sure there had been a misunderstanding; then I wondered whether I was about to be screened by the white official who had intercepted my call. Both suspicions turned out to be wrong. Credo Mutwa actually lived in this place, separated from the rest of Soweto by a high security fence. The department's own sorcerer had been living here ever since the disturbances of 1976. In effect, he was in the safekeeping of his white employers, who had installed him in a tiny brick shed that bore every resemblance to the servants' quarters that may be found in the backyards of the humblest white neighborhoods. The refuge had been provided after his former home had been gutted by fire bombs, an attack by young blacks that came swiftly as retribution for his testimony to an official commission in Pretoria that had been assigned to discover the causes of the violence. The white authorities had pushed the witch doctor forward as an expert witness, not only on the causes but on what blacks really thought and wanted. His testimony had been reported at length in the Afrikaans and English press. Most blacks were not capable of holding power, he had said. They also were not capable of making the kinds of bombs being used in Soweto; therefore, it was obvious that white subversives were masterminding the protests. The government was not reacting strongly enough; it should call out the army, for blacks respect strength. "Our ancestors are looking down on us with shame," the seer had said in Pretoria. A few weeks after the attack on his house, his holy village had also been burned. More than a year then passed before the buses were stopping there again so that white tourists could be astonished and given pause by the secrets of Africa.

I had assumed this all was ancient history, but the accusation that he was a sellout still cast a heavy shadow on Credo Mutwa's life; in fact, he regarded himself as a marked man. At the same time, after seven years in the backyard of the Parks and Recreation Department, he was not exactly overflowing with gratitude to the white officials who had sought to domesticate him. Credo Mutwa had a deeply rooted ambivalence to all his white patrons and the phenomenon of white patronage, which was especially severe, it seemed, because he also felt himself to be unable to survive without it. "All I ask," he had written, "is to be granted the opportunity to live again in a Zulu kraal." Yet here he was, still stranded in Soweto, taking refuge behind a government security fence but keeping his own private, and sometimes not so private, account of the opportunities that had been denied him by whites he had trusted.

It made for a sad story, the one he ought really to sit down and write in meticulous detail. He had worked for years in a curio shop on Eloff

Street in Johannesburg, where he would testify to the deep significance of various artifacts, baubles, and knickknacks, which he helped his employer to gather or sometimes simply manufactured himself. Later, when the first edition of his first book was published, it contained a photograph as a frontispiece showing Mutwa with the shopkeeper, described there as his "sponsor," and with another white, a professor, described as his editor. Still later he complained that the text had been altered in ways he had not approved and that he had never received his fair share of the royalties; for these reasons, he said, he had quit writing books. A subsequent employer was accused of stealing a brass necklace that Mutwa, now practiced in the business of dubious authentications, claimed had been worn by the founder of the Zulu dynasty, Shaka.

His experiences with official sponsors had not been much happier. From a tin box on a shelf, he took his worn and tattered "reference book"—for even a seer must carry this passport in the "white area" if he is black—and showed me where his occupation had been listed as "painter" because an Afrikaner official had refused to allow a black man to describe himself as an author. Later, when the white authorities agreed to sponsor his shrine as a museum, this was crossed out in red ink, and he was listed as an employee of the Administration Board. There, too, he indicated, his confidence in whites had been misplaced. He had assumed, he said, that the board was lending him the money to build the shrine and that he would then be able to pay it back with the admission charges that were included in the fees for the bus tour. Instead, he got his meager wages and the hovel he was now inhabiting as a servant of the Department of Parks and Recreation, which counted as revenue the admission fees he felt to be rightly his. "Last year it was ninety-one thousand rands," he said.

To get to this point in his story, I had to pass muster again, only this time, confusingly, it was not an oath that I refrain from doing any damage to South Africa that he required but some evidence that I was not functioning as an agent for the security police. "How can I be sure, Mr. Lillydale?" he asked. "They're very good at faking American accents, you know." The man who sat before me in the dimness of the crowded little room was partially obscured by the bottle glass lenses of his spectacles and outsize white overalls that hid his corpulence like a sack. But his voice was a lovely instrument, brightly mellifluous and full of play, with a range of tones that included humor, indignation, and hurt. His conversation was a one-man oratorio, designed to entertain and instruct. Credo Mutwa quickly made me feel that he knew my type, that he knew all our types. What dispelled his initial suspicion, he let me know, was my answer to his question about my religious antecedents. "I can speak to you more openly, Mr. Lillydale," he said, "because you are an Israelite. We Africans call them the holy people."

Elaborating on this theme, he now reached up to a shelf above my head and pulled down several stone artifacts. One connected to a harness of well-scoured copper, and carved out of a jade green stone, probably malachite, was unambiguously a tumescent penis. Another was a soapstone tablet. All were inscribed with symbols: some that looked like hieroglyphics; others that might have been renderings in miniature of the pictographs that Bushmen drew on the walls of caves. Those on the soapstone, cut into the surface with a spastic angularity, were crudely copied Hebrew. If I had been asked to hazard a guess as to the ages of these objects, I might have said two weeks to two years. Mutwa informed me they could be estimated in millennia. Slowly, with histrionic laboriousness, he then translated one of the inscriptions. "You . . . must . . . love . . . your . . . neighbor . . . as . . . yourself," he said, reading the symbols with his index finger, as if they were Braille. "This was known, as so much was known, to our ancestors," he said solemnly.

As forgeries go, these were obviously not in the same class as the Piltdown man or Hitler diaries, but the performance was entrancing. I learned that one of the lost tribes of Israel had settled in Venda, a tiny black homeland that was now supposedly independent. The Israelites were Venda's traders, it seems. Then, leapfrogging to the present, I learned about Africa's "real leaders," who were "not the tin pot, jackrabbit politicians; windsurfers riding a wave of sentiment; shitheads, as you Americans say, who are only turned on, as you Americans also say, by the flash of a flashbulb." The real leaders were unknown. They were Africa's priests, "the people called witch doctors." All of Africa's wars were religious, and only they could lead. But they were lying low for now, hiding out, I was to surmise, in places like the compound of the Parks and Recreation Department in Soweto. The point was not made directly, but I was left in no doubt that I was in the presence.

We had been talking for more than two hours when, suddenly, I heard a peremptory shout and a figure appeared in the sunlit frame of the doorway. He was a pale, youngish Afrikaner, wearing short shorts and knee socks that drooped, and he was demanding to know why some task that Mutwa had been supposed to perform at the office was still undone. Credo Mutwa, who was the white man's elder by at least twenty years, was now on his feet, wringing his hands and speaking in a voice that I had not previously heard. It was simpering, whiny, the voice of a child exhausted by sobbing. But he was not so distraught as to fail to address the white man in the third person. Had the *baas* not read the newspapers that morning? Had the *baas* not seen the headlines about the fighting at the University of Zululand? Had the *baas* not heard how our children have been killing each other with spears? Did he not remember that Mutwa's own son was a student there? Now the white man's voice underwent as sudden a change. Where he had been peremptory, he was all sympathy, almost singing, cooing, like a parent wiping away tears. "Oh, Credo, oh, Credo," he murmured soothingly. He had heard about the fighting but had forgotten about Credo's son. Oh, he hoped it would be all right. It would be all right. He knew it.

"Baie dankie, baas," Mutwa said in a choked voice, thanking the official.

"Baie dankie, Credo," the Afrikaner sang in response.

Once his departure had ended this touching scene, I asked Mutwa whether the white really insisted on being called master by him. It seemed a little odd, I said, since it was obvious that he was older, more cultivated, better traveled, an author of renown. "We don't know how to speak to one another in this country," he replied somberly. Our conversation then lagged. It took a few moments before he recovered his prophetic voice. When I made a move that indicated I might be ready to leave, he abruptly stopped speaking, as if I had pulled a plug. I then apologized for having to run. "I am not a sellout. I am not a traitor," he said as we stood at the door, in a voice that affected neither pathos nor pride. Perhaps there was even a touch of humor, the verbal counterpart of a quick wink, when he added, "I am just an old man who knows how to talk to Afrikaners."

"You can always hear them talking," said Valerie du Plessis, an Afrikaner farmer's wife in the remote Free State town of Luckhoff. "Even when they work, they are always talking. 'You can't talk and work at the same time,' I tell them. They stop a little, and then they start again, just like children. I don't know what they talk to each other about, I don't know."

Midway in an explanation of the racial order in South Africa as it was reflected on the family farm, she was trying to explain the place of the whites. Her point, basically, was that it was natural, not imposed. Someone has to think; someone has to lead. Who else on the farm or in the country could do it? The blacks depend on whites. That folk belief of the whites is the armature around which all the fancy ideological and managerial and sociological arguments get wrapped. Self-esteem thus becomes an ethical principle. Without it there is only strife and the struggle for survival. Belief in struggle and the sanctity of strength is fundamental in the outlook of most Afrikaners, but only extremists take this firewater straight. Adding a dash of altruism is a sign of good breeding.

"You always give; they always receive," the farmer's wife went on, finding the words she wanted. "That's how we know them."

The social order is founded on this one-way flow, not of material benefits, obviously, but of authority and foresight. Mrs. du Plessis would have caught the essence of this folk belief had she said, "That's how we want to know them." As a description of reality in South Africa, the sentimental view of a rural order that remains essentially feudal in its insistence on loyalty and dependence as the currency of healthy race relations was always questionable. Industrialization and urbanization have now cut it adrift from its moorings, but it hasn't yet sunk. In the conversation of those Afrikaners, self-described as "enlightened," who want to mold the racial order into a new and more pleasing shape, the sentimental view of a pastoral order floats as near to the surface as it does in the talk of farm wives.

"The time will come," Prime Minister P. W. Botha assured me in his office in the Hendrik Verwoerd Building in Cape Town, "when the colored people and the black people will admit that the National party was the catalyst to bring them to their own in southern Africa." That the colored people and the black people, who are, of course, ineligible for membership in the National party, might get there *on their own* was more than was dreamed of in his philosophy. Or, more precisely, it was his nightmare. The Afrikaners might be outnumbered by more than ten to one in the country they regarded as their own, but it was their place to determine for all the others the destination, the route, and the timetable. And when finally in the fullness of time they got to wherever it was they were going, all the others would have learned to be grateful.

This prime minister* was known as a truculent machine politician and short-tempered bully when he took office, a man who needed to be dosed up on tranquilizers to hold a civil conversation with anyone from a political culture other than his own. In practice he had shown himself to be the first Afrikaner nationalist leader with any aptitude for taking other viewpoints into account, a skilled political manager who had the courage to make demands on his own people, urging them "to tame your hearts with your minds." Yet what he knew of black reality in his own country, he knew from intelligence reports and carefully planned official tours in helicopters and ministerial limousines, plus an occasional encounter, maybe once every two or three years, with a black churchman or homeland leader who was prepared to be a little out-spoken. P. W. Botha was ready to meet black nationalist leaders from Mozambique, Zimbabwe, and even Namibia; he found it hard not to be boastful about his friendship with the Angolan insurgent Jonas Savimbi. He would travel anywhere in Africa to make another breach in the tattered boycott of the Organization of African Unity. But he was not prepared to acknowledge the existence of black nationalist leaders in South Africa, except as common criminals. There was no reason to imagine that this hard-bitten politician ever felt a temptation to drive thirty minutes in the middle of the night and take a peek at Nelson Mandela through a cell door or one-way mirror, let alone arrange an off-the-record conversation, just to satisfy his own curiosity. Beyond the practical questions of power politics, such curiosity was more than he could afford. Geography rather than ideology obviously made all the difference. If Mandela had been born in Angola, he might have been as eligible a partner as Savimbi in Botha's eyes. Since he insisted on regarding himself as South African, he had to be counter-feit, a surrogate for a sinister foreign foe, incapable of acting on his own for reasons of his own and, therefore, not a fit object for a prime minister's curiosity, not at least in this epoch.

It was altogether natural, then, that when he talked about basic values, P. W. Botha led me back across six decades to the Free State farm on which he was reared. "I grew up on a farm where I came to know black people very well. I played with them, I worked with them,"

---

*In 1984 he became president under a new constitution that armed him with poten-tially authoritarian powers.

he said. "I was taught by my father to be strict with them but to be just." The child learns to be strict with other children; the child then grows up, becomes an adult, and leaves the farm, but in his mind the other children remain children forever. This excursion back to childhood is almost automatic, the visitor discovers, in conversations about blacks with Afrikaner public officials, few of whom, it seems, have found it possible to learn anything worth mentioning on the subject in their adult years.

I had heard that in private conversations P. W. Botha had been known to relate his readiness to seek a political accommodation with the mixed-race coloreds to an experience his mother had during the Boer War, long before his own birth. Yes, he said, speaking solemnly, there was such an incident. She was a young married woman of twenty-six, living on the farm with three small children and a sister of only thirteen, when she was awakened in the middle of the night by an armed intruder from the enemy force who demanded money and threatened her life.

"They succeeded to escape and fled to a nearby colored family, who lived on the farm as gardeners," the prime minister went on. "After they left the farmhouse, it was set on fire. The next morning enemy forces came up to the farm and took away all the cattle and sheep, but the colored family helped my mother and the children to hide in a nearby cave. There this colored gardener and his wife protected my mother and the children for more than three months, while during the day collecting food for them. Then, by sheer accident, she was discovered by enemy forces and taken to a concentration camp."

The prime minister now paused, raised his chin and gave me a long, faintly challenging look. On the podium or in Parliament, this was his way of signaling that he was about to make a telling point. "When she returned to the farm after the war," he then said, "this colored family was still there, tending the gardens." In his own mind it was a lesson about trust, loyalty, and mutual dependence, rather than subordination. Subordination was assumed.

There must be thousands, even millions, of young coloreds and blacks whose political values have been shaped by the experiences of their mothers—by having seen their homes destroyed and their families separated by policies his government still upheld—but that obvious idea was not readily accessible to P. W. Botha. In this sense he was careful to remain blinkered. And yet he believed himself to be responding to moral imperatives, at least some of the time. The farmer, after all, has obligations as well as privileges, and the frontier farm remains a model. Challenged once at a party congress to defend the army's new practice of putting blacks and whites in the same combat units, Defense Minister Magnus Malan, a Botha protégé, heatedly denied that it had embraced a policy of "integration" between the races. "It is not integration if a farmer works with his black laborers or a housewife works with her servant," he said. "Why is it integration if there are blacks in the Defense Force?"

The gardener is still tending the garden, but now, so he doesn't feel a temptation to stray, it is important to ensure that his loyalty is repaid. The rural metaphor that politicians half-cynically manipulate for reasons of power can also be embraced. A farm may be a poor metaphor for a modern industrial society, but it can also be a farm.

Jan Boland Coetzee is trying to turn his Cape farm into a model of a new South Africa in much the same way that the Welsh visionary Robert Owen tried in the early nineteenth century to provide a model for newly industrial Scotland by establishing his own little utopia at New Lanark. A former Springbok rugby hero, Coetzee is now widely held to be the country's most serious and able winemaker. Initially he managed vineyards that had belonged to an Afrikaner politician named Paul Sauer who was reputedly the man who coined the word "apartheid." It was a matter, you might say, of putting new wine in old bottles. On the Sauer family estates, Jan Boland Coetzee methodically set about improving the living standards of the colored farm laborers, with carefully planned investments coordinated with those he was making in upgrading the cabernets, until finally, it was said, his employers put a lid on his capital spending.

Not one to cut corners, he then quit and took his family off to Burgundy in order to refine his art and his ideal of a Cape wine estate, which was as much a social ideal as a vinicultural one. Back in South Africa he found the money he needed to build that estate, literally from the ground up, by entering into a partnership with a man who had made a fortune in the high-risk business of trucking supplies to Savimbi's rebels in the Angolan combat zone. Before he laid down his vines, Coetzee had perfectly contoured the mountainside near Stellenbosch on which they would be cultivated, seasoning the soil as he shaped it with 10,000 tons of lime and 5,000 tons of phosphate. In the same careful and prodigal manner, he designed a housing estate for his laborers with as much attention to the architectural details as they bore on convenience, comfort, and family life—modern plumbing, fireplaces, solar reflectors, laundry rooms, the layout of bedrooms and dining space—as he was putting into his own home. Jan Boland Coetzee wasn't just talking architecture; he was talking nutrition, education, and "community development," conceiving a miniature welfare state. Already he was a force in something called the Rural Development Foundation, which offered the services of social workers and sports instructors to Afrikaner farmers who felt they ought to get serious about the business of uplift.

A solid block of a man with a neck like a newel post and legs as thick and firm as the trunk from which it was carved, he was frugal only with words. What he was doing was as new to the Cape as New Lanark was to Scotland in Owen's day, but he hadn't yet found it useful or necessary to learn a new vocabulary. He spoke softly and gently, saying just a little at a time, laying himself open to argument and waiting, not warily but watchfully, to see whether he would get it. The laugh lines around his eyes suggested that he derived a small pleasure from playing the white political primitive, that he was not above baiting his visitors. His colored laborers were like children, he said, didn't know what was good for them, only wanted their daily *dop* (tot) of wine, would never have thought to ask for any of the things they were getting. As for blacks, they didn't even have words in their languages to distinguish the different parts of a vine, had no technological sense, had invented nothing, "couldn't even make a match." They could be uplifted, maybe, but there weren't enough whites who saw the need, not enough to do it in any case; that was the problem in South Africa. Yet when I asked whether he thought Afrikaners and coloreds were essentially different peoples, he replied laconically, "We made them." And when he showed me the label for the first of his new wines, it was an etching of his son playing with a brown friend in front of the house he had not yet finished building—an image ambiguously balanced between the sentimental Afrikaner notion of a rough, transitory equality among *klonkies* (playmates), with a fixed expiration at puberty, and the broader social regeneration for which he seemed ready but had not learned the words. And so, cultivating his vineyards and building his little New Jerusalem, he continued to sing the same old lyrics as the farmers in the Free State.

"They can't take decisions all by themselves," Valerie du Plessis, the farmer's wife in Luckhoff, had said as we sat chatting at dusk in her garden. "Some of them are a little intelligent. They try to think, really they try. But you must tell them everything." Oh, the poor, hapless, lovable blacks; if only the world could understand how contentedly they lived side by side with whites on the farms of the Free State! I was in my last month in the country in 1983. It could have been my first month in 1965; it could have been eighty years earlier. I was talking not to crazed fanatics or ideologues but to decent, upstanding citizens, supporters of the prime minister's constitutional initiatives, believers in "reform," who seemed to imagine, nevertheless, that they inhabited the New Jerusalem already. Gerrit du Plessis, Valerie's husband, fondly trotted out his best example, Ou Skilpad ("Old Tortoise"), an aging farmhand he had known since he was a youngster, who still called him *klein baas* ("little master"), never having chosen to recognize the succession of generations that had long since taken place on the farm. "I'm like a child to him," the middle-aged farmer was saying. "I call him *outa.*" The term, meaning "old father" or "old man," is used only for a black or a brown in Afrikaans. "I've known him all my life, but we don't mix socially. He won't come into this house, and I don't go into his. I don't even know his native name, actually, but there's a common respect. We live side by side.

"Of course, if this light is out, I want silence," the farmer added, pointing to his bedroom window. "I'm still the owner of this farm. It's common respect."

In one of his stories, Can Themba prays for "a little respite, brother, just a little respite from the huge responsibility of being a nice kaffir." The paternalistic white idea of "common respect," of blacks who will always be dependent on them for guidance and support, lies on black South Africa like a collapsed circus tent. Most whites and most blacks have long since left the farms, but new forms of address have been slow to evolve. "Behavior modeling" isn't new to South Africa; it has been going on for generations.

"Has master got a girl?" asked a young black woman who was laboring like a stevedore in the crew of movers that came to carry off the last lot of furniture from our apartment.

"I'm not a master," I said wearily, raising for the hundredth or thousandth time the ontological question of what I thought myself to be inside my white skin in South Africa.

"Oooh," said the young woman in an uncertain voice. Tired of lugging boxes, she had been looking for a job as a domestic, not an apologia. If I was not a master, I could be of no use.

What many whites take to be natural deference or common respect is usually a measure of economic necessity, a humoring and mirroring of their own self-love, a way around their petulance. It's a matter of white folklore that blacks show respect by not addressing them by their names, a matter of black folklore that whites resent being called by their names. Both sides therefore know, without knowing anymore how it started, that direct address can be taken as an insult. In a remote corner of Zululand called Bergville, I tried again to duck the title *baas* when it was lobbed my way by an elderly black who was working by the side of the road in a rag that had once been an Eisenhower jacket.

"What must I say when I meet you?" he asked after a friend had explained in Zulu that I was a foreigner who didn't like the word.

"Hello, Joe," the friend suggested.

"Hello, Joe!" the old man exclaimed, laughing at the joke as he pumped my hand. Here, too, of course, I was still a white man having his way. The predicament seemed inescapable.

"*Hel-lo, mas-ter!*" a black woman who worked as a maid in our apartment building would say tauntingly when we met, watching to see if I flinched and then snickering when I did.

"Evelyn," I would plead, "I've told you I'm not from this place. I have a name."

"Oh, no, *mas-ter,*" she would reply. "This is not America. I can't call you by your name."

Ou Skilpad in Luckhoff, I imagine, would be surprised but not offended if his *klein baas* suddenly insisted on being called Gerrit. He would be even more surprised if Gerrit, after all these years, asked him his name. But such meddling with tradition would not by itself change their relationship in any fundamental way.

These are the crudest examples of the problem of communication under a system designed to minimize it. Relatively few whites know how to address blacks as equals without seeming to patronize them. Relatively few blacks choose to be patronized when they have the choice. It is a matter, in the first instance, of law rather than culture or manners, for when legal equality is only an aspiration, it tends to be mimicked. Even when blacks and whites are on the same side of the political fence, the imbalance in legal rights and privileges can poison the possibility of friendship. Few township blacks are eager to sit in a white garden on Sunday afternoons; few whites feel comfortable in the townships. The reality is that they inhabit different worlds, so even if they long for friendship as a confirmation of the possibility of common citizenship, they seldom feel they can trust it: neither the whites nor the blacks. The staunchest white liberals I knew had a wide acquaintance among blacks, cultivated at quasi-diplomatic and philanthropic functions; few of them, it seemed to me, had active black friendships.

As a foreigner and journalist, I was somewhat less shackled by my racial status and soon had more black friends in Johannesburg than I could claim to have in New York. Yet, inevitably, I lived the overwhelming proportion of my life in the white world. If I had been born there, I might have felt desperate and cut off. Since I was on an excursion, full time, I could come to terms with the country. But it was easier to cross the racial boundary than to straddle it, easier, for example, to meet blacks on their own ground than to stage-manage mixed parties in the "white area." There was a sense in which most of the whites and most of the blacks I knew went along with apartheid, for all their moral aversion to it. They had grown tired of each other, not as individuals but as symbols. It was a strain always to be apologizing for your privileges or acknowledging another's status as a victim; a greater strain, of course, to be the victim and to try, however briefly, to inhabit the reality from which you were barred. They were too alive to each other's hypocrisy: the blacks too quick to note that the whites hadn't sacrificed or suffered; the whites too quick to wonder if the blacks had "sold out."

Just a little respite, brother. It was a weekend in an industrial port, and a black doctor, a friend of a friend, told me that I could find him on Sunday afternoon at a hotel for nonwhites on the fringe of the downtown area; he would be attending a meeting with some colleagues, he said. The desk clerk directed me to a reception room one flight up. It was musty and unlit, and all the furniture had been shoved to the wall as if for a dance. Seven men, each dressed in expensive and fashionable sports clothes and each introduced as Doctor, lolled on chairs set close together in a corner so that they were mostly sitting side by side, rather than facing each other. It was only two in the afternoon, but the "meeting," I was told, was about to adjourn; the agenda, manifested in empty bottles on the floor, had been exhausted. A couple of the doctors were in a drunken stupor; the rest, as any layman could diagnose, were on their way. My friend's friend, a large and commanding presence in brown overalls and soft Florentine boots, could not remember our phone conversation but readily accepted my explanation that I was there at his invitation. The meeting would resume, he said, as soon as a new agenda could be organized.

With a pale green Mercedes leading the way, followed by a blue one and then a silver BMW, a cortege worthy of a state occasion then set out from the run-down fringe neighborhood on what amounted to a foraging mission. I brought up the rear, breaking caste in a rented Volkswagen Jetta. My friend's friend rode with me. "A lot is happening underneath," he said, talking politics as the convoy headed into a colored slum.

We idled our engines and stopped for only an instant at a shebeen, where the supplies were evidently not equal to our demand. At a second shebeen, in an area of shanties, we locked up and went inside. Two young shebeen girls came to life at the arrival of so much affluence. With my white skin, I could be nothing but trouble, so they made sure that their glances didn't include me, affording me the experience of invisibility. The more vivacious of the two, in checked slacks and a maroon sweater, climbed up my friend's friend as if he were a tree. A man who was in the shebeen when we entered quietly grilled the American, in speech that was not in the least slurred, on fine points of Ronald Reagan's stance on South Africa, with particular reference to nuclear energy. One of the doctors came crashing into that conversation on his own bleary tangent. Did I think, he wanted to know, that racism was the reason that his young Australian colleague at the hospital ignored his instructions? Vodka, brandy, and beer had meanwhile emerged from their place of sequestering—they would not have been kept on the premises in any quantity because of the danger of a raid —and the convoy now wove its way out of the slum, then headed out of town on the national road.

Our destination this time was a parking lot behind the dunes of a remote beach that was segregated for black use. It was not a day for swimming, and the beach was practically empty, but there were about a dozen cars in the parking lot and forty or fifty persons reeling around in various stages of intoxication. The scene was very South African; a parking lot outside a stadium where a rugby match had just been played would have looked the same, except for the epidermal characteristics of the careening figures. White or black, someone was bound to have a *braai* going; in the middle of the parking lot, chops, ribs, and slabs of beef were sizzling over a fire. A young man, bare-chested under a checked vest, locked me in a bear hug and asked, shouting out the words, if I was an agent of the ANC, the underground movement. He then insisted on having his photo taken with me. Inevitably I wondered as it was snapped how long it would take to fall into the hands of the security police. My friend's friend may have had the same thought, for he now suggested that we continue our party inside a red Mercedes, which was there when we arrived. The owner of the car told me about a trip to New York, where he stayed at the Edison Hotel off Times Square; he also remembered Bloomingdale's. "What's the name of that other store?" he asked. "Lord and—?" A siren blasted away all other sound, and everyone seemed to freeze momentarily, but no cops appeared, and the transistors and cassette players went on playing, almost but not quite drowning out the breakers on the other side of the dunes. "You've got to have a program," my friend's friend said, resuming a conversation that seemed to have been playing in his mind since we drove away from the hotel in town. Then before he could pursue the thought, he dozed off.

"I think you'd better leave," the man who stayed at the Edison quietly advised me. He guided me from his Mercedes to my Jetta, where a woman was crouched down, next to the driver's door, relieving herself. Later, on other trips to that city, I thought of calling my friend's friend again but was always stopped by the realization that he would have no recollection of ever having met me.

A little respite. "This is our liberty; this is our freedom," the regulars at the shebeens proclaim, saluting each other sardonically with their drinks. Shebeen wit has a quality all its own, with more cutting edges than a reaper. It is too sharp, too knowing, to let either bravado or self-pity hold sway. "This is our liberty," pronounced as a mocking benediction over a concoction based on brandy or cane spirits, manages to be a judgment both on the system and on those who only talk of overthrowing it. It manages, too, to describe reality, for aside from the churches, the shebeens are the only readily available outlets for the need to belong and be heard. The promise of communion they offer may be short-lived, but for many, migrants from the crowded hostels or township dwellers who cannot possibly handle all the demands of their extended families that are likely to await them in their equally crowded homes, it can be all that makes life bearable. Obviously, if anyone needs drink as an anodyne and a release, it is the South African black. Yet drink is also a conspicuous part of his political economy, part of his bondage. This is not only a matter of historical record or religious and political sermonizing; it is a matter of shebeen lore. A black friend deciphered the writing on a can of Lion Lager for me as if it were a cabalistic message. The beer can said:

O.C.B. LTD.

L I O N

L A G E R

S.A.B.

According to my friend, the first line meant, "Our colored brothers live to drink." The next line adjured: "Let Indians Own Nothing." L-A-G-E-R was the heart of the message: "Let Africans Gain Equal Rights." And S.A.B. was the signature, not of South African Breweries but South Africa's blacks. If you managed to decode it, there wasn't only the demand for rights on the beer can but a measured and mordant tribute to the effectiveness of the divide-and-rule tactics of the country's rulers.

And those tactics have involved the sale of booze for a century now. The historian Charles van Onselen traces the origins of the liquor trade in the Transvaal to a distillery called Volkshoop ("People's Hope") that opened in 1883 on a charter granting it a monopoly within the borders of the Boer republic. Needless to say, the *volk* were the Afrikaners, who found in the new enterprise a market for their surplus grain and fruit. Within a decade the people's *hoop* was heavily dependent on the thirsts of black "mineboys" recruited for the new gold mines. Up to a point black drunkenness served the interests of the mine owners, who calculated that blacks returned to their tribal areas once they had accumulated a little cash. The more they spent on drink, the longer they stayed, limiting the turnover in the work force. But by 1895 at least 15 percent and possibly 25 percent of the black work force was disabled by drink on any given day. The mineowners then became converted to the righteous cause of total prohibition—for blacks only —which was put on the statute books but never enforced by Kruger, who retained his alliance with the mainly Jewish liquor interests. By

1899, on the eve of the Boer War, emerging black church leaders were holding meetings of "educated natives" in Johannesburg to demand enforcement as a way of saving their people from the poisonous spirits sold as "Kaffir Whisky."

Some of the churchmen who campaigned then against booze later campaigned for political rights, forging the idea early on among politically conscious blacks that alcohol was one of the instruments of their oppression. The connection was not merely symbolic. By 1908 the city of Durban had discovered that the cost of policing blacks and running the black "locations" could be shifted from white taxpayers to the blacks themselves by the establishment of a municipal monopoly on the brewing and sale of beer for blacks. This was really ingenious. Beer became the solvent that recycled black wages into black administration. In 1929 political activists in an early black trade union and the Communist party organized a boycott of Durban beer halls. A front called the Anti Kaffir Beer Manufacturing League issued a pamphlet calling on blacks to "part company with Kaffir beer" because the profits from the trade were used "to build compounds and barracks which are full of bad laws and disagreeable control." The 1929 protest started nonviolently, with a brass band marching behind a Union Jack and a Soviet flag at an early demonstration, but ended in bloodshed when black workers clashed with white vigilantes.

Nearly half a century later, during the Soweto student protests, the municipal beer halls once again seemed an obvious target for black anger. In the eyes of the students, it was drink that unmanned their fathers, that helped them adapt to a racial humiliation they should have resisted. The state's liquor outlets were burned and sacked, and the 4,000 illegal shebeens in the township were ordered to close down by the students' committee that functioned briefly as its invisible government. The shebeens, the students said, were where their parents went "to forget the problems facing blacks." They were also the most conspicuous form of black private enterprise in the townships, but the students were uncompromisingly puritanical. "Nothing good has ever come out of them," their diatribe said. "Many of our fathers and brothers have been killed in or out of them. Hundreds of our colleagues have become delinquents, beggars or orphans as shebeen kings and queens have become capitalists. We can no longer tolerate seeing our fathers' pay packets emptied in shebeens."

But Soweto in 1976 was not the Paris Commune of 1871, let alone the Petrograd Soviet of 1917. Some of the black students who were

behind such manifestos left the country to join the underground movements; some went to jail. Of those who remained, many inevitably
drifted back to the shebeens, which flourished again as the fires of
rebellion died down. "Our leaders are fighting one another, but for
who?" asked a letter in the *Sowetan,* the black newspaper. "The answer
seems to be for a drunken nation." In the agitprop that the "struggle"
now often inspires, black drunkenness remains a symbol of black acquiescence, of wasted strength:

> *Friday night*
> *Shebeens house-full*
> *The beautiful night once more is come*
> *We drink*
> *Baas liquor*
> *Baas prison*
> *Waters of immortality*
> *In Lion Lager our lives enclosed*
> *We search*
> *Black Label joyous we drink*
> *In shebeens white ghosts rejoice . . .*
> *Our eyes red blind dusty smoky*
> *Baas toxin*
> *Waters of the white man.*

But this half-choked cry can rarely be heard over the more prevalent
doggerel that sells the "toxin," which can be presented now, blacks
having achieved equality of a kind on the barstool, as the waters of the
black man. "An Old Buck man always wins!" a black boxer, girdled in
his Old Buck Championship belt, a symbol not only of gin but of
triumph over whites, flexes his muscles in the advertisement. "Cinza-
tional you!" Cinzano, "the chic international drink," belongs to a
young black woman whose hair, tightly braided in what are called corn
rows, glistens with beads. She opens her mouth to shout and raises her
right hand, which isn't clenched in a fist but is curled around a frosty
highball. Or there's "Swing to Pink!" Here the black model, in a gauzy
pastel, reclines in a hammock on her seaside terrace, lifting a glass of
Campari, which is "always delightfully pink and delectably dry." The
linkage between "liberation" and abstinence must be snapped; liberation in a mass consumer society, after all, means the opposite of discipline and denial. To complicate matters even further, the black versifi-
ers who declaim the poetry of "struggle" occasionally find employment
in ad agencies; also, among them are some who are often drunk.

The prime minister boasted that his party would bring the coloreds and blacks "into their own." His reform plan includes the legalization of shebeens. The shebeen queens and kings, former targets of rebellious black youth, have started to molt into licensed entrepreneurs. Their national association, underwritten by the liquor lobby, held its first banquet in the grand ballroom of Johannesburg's Carlton Hotel. Technically they all were still liable for arrest as bootleggers under South African law, but they were expected to serve now as the vanguard for the black advance to capitalism. In their tuxedoes and evening gowns, they talked of the day when their association would control not only the sale but the distribution of liquor in the black areas. In the mass consumer society, they seemed to be saying, blacks will finally win out by consuming most. Already in alcoholic spirits they are nearly holding their own, accounting for 60 percent of the market. The prospect seems to frighten neither the liquor companies nor the white authorities. There is no reason why it should; the shebeeners are still small-time operators, hustling and being hustled by the competing liquor companies. Stellenbosch Farmers' Winery, a cooperative representing the Afrikaner farmers of the Cape, picked up the tab for their dinner at the Carlton, making sure its own labels were conspicuous on the tables —exactly one century and four months after President Kruger had dedicated a distillery called the "People's Hope."

"Oh, God," another letter to the *Sowetan* implored a few weeks after the banquet, "help the African Azanian to leave liquor and there will be change from the highest zone to the lowest. Boycott liquor until you achieve equal rights. Then drink to your death."

The consummation of "liberation" may be imagined in various ways; it may even be regarded as inevitable. But no black South African who is old enough to have entered the workaday world, on whatever kind of official authorization, can really count on seeing it in time to make a difference in his life. How then can a black who aspires to normal autonomy for himself and his family, who is drawn to neither the discipline of revolutionary politics nor the indiscipline of the nightly shebeen crawl, put some distance between himself and the grinding conflict that insists, in so many ways, on defining his existence? What exit is there from the tent of white paternalism and control? The system offers him a little respite in the form of a deal: It will leave him alone if he accepts its basic premise, confines himself to the black world, and tries to make a living off blacks.

Like the shebeeners, he tells himself that it is better that the profits that are wrung from blacks end up in the hands of blacks, that he is doing his best, by means of capital accumulation, to close the gap. And in the meantime—however long that meantime stretches—he can offer his children an opportunity to live with a little dignity and ease. This isn't shameful, but it is bound to be uncomfortable, for in his success he sets himself apart as one who is prepared to tap black misery for his own purposes. Like the ghetto doctor who buys a fancy car with the fees of the poor, or the successful shebeen operator, he is doing only what is expected. Few begrudge him the advantages for which he has scrambled. Yet like them, he achieves isolation.

One of the most appealing homes I visited in South Africa was also one of the eeriest. It belonged to a Soweto physician named Johnny Mosendane, who was sufficiently well-to-do to keep a Mercedes station wagon and a new Porsche in his two-car garage. There was scarcely another dwelling in the whole vast encampment, South Africa's most populous single settlement, that was worth as much as his cars, let alone his house. The high-style architect he had engaged had been ingenious in arraying skylights, windows, and an interior courtyard so as to achieve a flow of natural light through rooms that were vaulted and domed. The effect was vaguely Aegean, but there was also no getting away from the fact that the building was conceived as a fortress. Seen from the ghetto street, it was a windowless brick rampart with a big steel door over the garage, set in as inconspicuously as possible, virtually hugging the ground, among the tiny, uniform township houses that pressed against it. The physician had built his dream house before developers had started to demarcate middle-class enclaves in this vast proletarian Levittown, marketing them with names like Prestige Park or Selection Park so that here and there an upwardly mobile black might sustain the illusion that he lives where he does as a matter of personal choice rather than as the result of the sufferance of a remote and alien authority. Yet outside those few enclaves, which probably amount to fewer than five square miles in the whole of South Africa, the isolation that can enclose a prosperous black man is not just psychological.

For Tony Dube, the enterprising operator of Tony's Supermarket in a Zululand town called Nqutu that is the epicenter of a homeland social disaster, it was represented by a high chain-metal security fence on a ravaged landscape. Outside the fence Nqutu was a sea of squalid mud

and cinder-block hovels in which a former missionary hospital with a
pediatric ward that was perenially crowded with malnutrition cases
formed one island, adjoining another that contained the tiny commercial center with the supermarket standing across from the dusty square
where buses from the "white areas," or outlying resettlement sites,
disgorged their passengers. Inside the fence Tony Dube had built a
house worthy of Johannesburg's fanciest white suburbs; there wasn't
another dwelling remotely like it within thirty miles. Someday there
would be trees and shrubbery to provide some privacy, but now, with
just the barrier of the fence and the beginnings of a lawn, he seemed
a prisoner of his own success. Talk of eeriness. The house was only a
few hundred yards from the store, but morning and afternoon Tony
Dube made the trip in his shiny Mercedes 380 SE. Experienced criminals prey on half-forgotten places like Nqutu, he said, so he traveled
armed. His concern for security helped explain why he lived so near the
store, but it made him doubly a prisoner. The supermarket owner had
little for which to apologize. He achieved a rapid turnover on a large
and carefully selected stock with prices that were sufficiently low to
compete with the huge chain stores in the nearest white towns, provided employment, and got the profits that had previously gone to a
white man named Wilmot. But he was as isolated and vulnerable in
Nqutu as an Anglo-Irish lord in the midst of the great famine.

Benjamin Silanda also stood outside the tent of white paternalism
and control. A faith healer and revivalist, he had a tent of his own, for
which he had paid $25,000. In addition, he had the only custom-built
Cadillac Fleetwood Brougham in the whole of South Africa. The
interior was white leather, and there was a sliding panel in the roof that
was kept closed so as not to interfere with the "electronic climate
control," a feature that enabled his chauffeur to regulate the air conditioning. The Silanda Cadillac had its own computer, which adjusted
the position of the seats, dimmed its lights on the approach of another
car, and constantly flashed the latest fuel data, showing the vehicle's
rate of consumption, on a little screen. In less than half a minute the
numerals dancing in red illumination in the screen might skitter from
47 to 33 to 29 to 21. The car's owner, who liked riding in the front
seat next to his driver, never bothered to find out whether these were
miles per gallon, kilometers per liter, or what; he left such details to the
chauffeur, a tall, laconic man who wore a long white lab coat and a
peaked cap, lacking only goggles to complete the authentic outfit for

an exceptional touring car. Cadillacs were rare in Johannesburg, unknown until this one came along in the eastern Transvaal, where Benjamin Silanda had his businesses, a large trading store and the center of his revivalist's crusade, in a black homeland called Gazankulu. There are merchant bankers; he was a merchant evangelist. When I asked what had inspired him to spend nearly $100,000 to import his car, he was neither boastful nor defensive. "I like the grille," he replied.

Considering that a Rolls-Royce or Mercedes would have had more prestige in the eastern Transvaal, it had to be acknowledged that the statement he was making with his Cadillac was, in some sense, a private one. Perhaps the car was a souvenir, an evocation of America, for he had first seen it outside a hotel in Miami Beach while attending a religious conference. Nothing else about the merchant evangelist seemed ostentatious. In fact, when I first met him by appointment that morning at his bank in the town of Nelspruit, he looked unimposing, even meek as he waited at the teller's window in a shapeless brown suit, clutching an old paper shopping bag that was held together with tape. Benjamin Silanda was past middle age; most of his teeth were missing; little patches of gray stubble on his jowls and cheeks suggested that he should have worn his glasses while shaving. The teller, a white woman who addressed him in Afrikaans, seemed to regard him not only as a black and therefore a juvenile in the guise of an old man but also as a nuisance. In an impatient tone that stopped just short of open rudeness, she sent him trudging off to another department. That department sent him trudging back. The black man wasn't pounding the counter or shouting, but he was now being more pertinacious than a black man is expected to be in Nelspruit. So this time the teller, turning red in the face, summoned an assistant manager, who reacted with a start, then exaggerated courtesy, as if it had been a director of the bank who had been getting this runaround. All the black man had been requesting for half an hour were some paper clips and rubber bands, which he used when he counted out his cash into little stacks and then joined the little stacks in rolls before piling them into a shopping bag and carrying them to the bank in his Cadillac Fleetwood Brougham on Mondays. Ushered finally into the manager's office, he was inundated with paper clips and rubber bands. As he scooped them up and left on other errands in Nelspruit, I noticed the assistant manager speaking sternly to the teller.

We met again in the afternoon at an Indian shop, where the merchant evangelist was acquiring some bolts of cloth. These, along with the groceries that now filled the back seat of the Cadillac, were put into the trunk, which already contained five new cash registers that he had ordered for the check-out lanes at his store. The back seat was then clear for me to ride in it to his headquarters in the homeland, at a place called Acornhoek on the edge of the Kruger National Park, about eighty miles to the north. "Will I get into trouble for carrying a white in the car?" the merchant evangelist asked nervously. "It's not like overseas."

On the way out of the "white area," we stopped at a fast-food chicken stand. Nelspruit now had a couple of places where a black could be seated and served, but pushiness, going where he wasn't really wanted, was not his way. He had skipped lunch in Nelspruit, and now, on his way home, he had his chicken and diet Coke in the front seat of his Cadillac.

Finally we were back on the tribal checkerboard of the homelands —with Lebowa to the right of the ribbon of asphalt along which we were proceeding and KaNgwane, followed by Gazankulu, to the left— cruising at dusk through these putative nation-states, which struck the eye as one undifferentiated rural slum, toward purple mountains in the custom-built chariot. Benjamin Silanda visibly relaxed into its white leather cushions. His church, the Nazarene Revival Crusade, had split off from a movement of the same name that been founded by white missionaries from Kansas City. At issue was his exercise of healing powers. "The healing was from Jesus; the owner of the healing was Jesus," he said. He was merely the means. Since the schism he had continued healing, and his church had rapidly expanded. It now had 15 pastors and its own Bible school to train more, a sanctuary that could seat 2,000 worshipers at a time and the new blue-and-white striped tent, which could hold an additional 3,000; it also had four trucks, three buses, and two vans. The 30 employees at the store all belonged, and business there started with half an hour of prayer every morning. The church followed the practice of total immersion when it received con- verts. "We don't sprinkle," its leader said, laughing for the first time since I had intruded myself into his day.

Did the Nazarene Revival Crusade have any particular message, I now asked, for South Africa's black people? "There's no problem for those who repent, those who are Christians," the merchant evangelist said. "To be a Christian is a hundred percent. The Holy Spirit is looking after them. The ones who get problems are the people who are not praying."

The light was failing and they were just beginning the evening prayers when the Cadillac nosed into Acornhoek, parking near buses that promised in enlarged script on their sides, "Jesus is coming" and "Jesus heals." That put us outside a curious building, unlike any I had seen, that had something of the profile of a cruise ship riding low in the waves. The enormous sanctuary was only one story high, without any attempt at vaulting; studded with pillars, it was, in effect, a long, low chamber made up of many smaller rooms that had no walls. A spiral staircase on the outside led to a smaller section of two floors, which sat amidships like the deckhouse. These floors housed pilgrims, my host explained, including the relatives of the sick and lame who come for healing. Set on top was a smaller room, a kind of pilothouse, that was temporarily unreachable, not having been connected as yet to the lower portions of the structure by stairs or even a ladder. I asked if his builders had worked from a plan. "There was no plan," he said proudly. "We just built."

He had preached in the morning in the store before leaving for Nelspruit and would preach there again tomorrow; he was too tired, he said, to preach in the church tonight. Inside the sanctuary, where a young minister in a black robe was now energetically leading a hymn of many verses from behind a harmonium, a high proportion of the worshipers had conspicuous deformities, such as bent spines or misshapen limbs. Nearly all of them, Benjamin Silanda said, would recover the next time he preached. The problems of those who were emotionally deranged took longer, as long sometimes as five days, he said. The claims he was making, I knew, were no more fantastic than those made by American and American-trained faith healers, who find a large following among South African whites. A few weeks earlier, in a former discount house in Johannesburg that had been converted into an evangelical headquarters by an organization called the Rhema Church, I had heard a white South African revivalist promise to cure cancer and diseases of the kidney through the miracle of faith. The white revivalist was dressed in a navy blazer and white duck trousers, like a television sportscaster at a lawn tennis tournament; a video camera was, in fact, trained on him, capturing his every gesture and word. His own salvation, so he said, had occurred in Tulsa, Oklahoma, the home, of course, of Oral Roberts's fabulously successful television ministry. From that flat Sinai he had brought back the Word, which included the word that these were the "last days." Others have preached that the Apocalypse will come in South Africa or, alternatively, that South Africa has been divinely chosen as a latter-day Noah's Ark, preserved by God's grace in order to survive the inevitable nuclear catastrophe that the satanic superpowers were destined to unleash on the world. In occult symbiosis, the lunatic fringe in South Africa and the American lunatic fringe shared the insight that Jimmy Carter, the born-again Christian who harped on human rights, was in fact the Antichrist; his failure to perceive the divine plan for South Africa was part of the proof. Doesn't the prophet Zephaniah speak of the Lord's receiving offerings "from beyond the rivers of Ethiopia"? Hadn't Billy James Hargis come forth from Oklahoma to declare that Satan had chosen South Africa as his battlefield? I wondered what permutations of these formulations were now seeping, far beyond the rivers of Ethiopia, into Gazankulu.

"The world is coming to an end now, very soon," the merchant evangelist affirmed cheerfully as soon as I edged the conversation around to the question of the end of time. "Most people who are living now will die, but the younger ones, they will see it."

CHAPTER 10

■

PILGRIMS

The fact that South Africa is a large country with an inviting climate sets limits on the ability of the state's intelligence arms to monitor conversation. Anyone who is sufficiently paranoid or circumspect—the distinction is seldom obvious—to fear that miniaturized listening devices may be lurking in a phone or other appliance has only to step outside into the golden sunshine to converse with greater ease. The same goes for evading the ears of informers, provided the interlocutor is really beyond suspicion. So serious political conversations tend to take place not in basements or garrets but in gardens, as if revolution were a neglected branch of horticulture involving plants that germinate only slowly. On a mild but overcast winter's afternoon in a Cape Town garden, a political figure of radical views made the point that sometimes the plants never flower. The world might imagine that a revolution in South Africa was long overdue and inevitable, he said, but that would be a dangerous delusion for anyone who seriously wanted to engineer the collapse of white power. The state's enemies had to recognize that it had available to it a strategy to forestall or prevent revolution and thereby to preserve the existing racial system with only minor adjustments; that was gradually to deracialize the hierarchy of oppression so that substantial numbers of nonwhites benefited from it. In other words, it was to make collaboration respectable. At this stage it was the greed and inbred racism of the whites, rather than the uncompromising demand of an aroused people for full equality, that made the failure of this strategy seem likely. "But," this serious-minded horticulturalist observed, "revolutions sometimes fail."

He was talking about not only the struggle for power but what happened afterward. There was no single answer to the question of what "liberation" in South Africa might mean. Was it a process, a political goal, or an ideological dream? Did it entail Africanizing the country or Westernizing its majority? Would freedom from racial oppression mean freedom for them in any recognizable sense or a different form of regimentation? Was "liberation" something that came after the revolution, or could it be the other way around? Could it be, as Gandhi, Mao, and Frantz Fanon each had preached in different settings and ways, that revolution came only when some critical mass of the oppressed had liberated itself from its sense of impotence and inferiority?

Being neither a theorist nor a South African, I had no clear stake in this discussion and little appreciation for its nuances. But listening in, I was occasionally reminded that Gandhi had hoped to bring about India's freedom as the moral achievement of millions of individual Indians, as the result of a social revolution in which the collapse of alien rule would be little more than a by-product of a struggle for self-reliance and economic equality. Foreign rule collapsed, but strife and inequality among Indians worsened. "This is a sorry affair," the mahatma then said, surveying the independent India he had achieved. I saw this as a possible lesson for South Africa, and not necessarily a discouraging one. If the collapse of apartheid had to depend on the moral achievement of millions, on the simultaneous mass conversion of the oppressors and oppressed, it would probably never happen. I mistrusted political mysticism and the religious instinct in politics, and yet as I traveled the country, I had a series of encounters with religiously inspired blacks, browns, and whites who couldn't wait for liberation to be liberated. They had an instinct that could be undervalued as romantic or utopian, but I learned to regard them as South Africa's glory, if not its hope; its moral, if not its political, center. They were members of the smallest minority in the country, these liberated South Africans, for they were those who defined themselves as South African before they mentioned a color, tribe, or ethnic group. I don't mean to suggest that they were the only decent people in the land or that they were likely to be the ones who would finally resolve its conflicts. I mention these free South Africans because not to do so would be to take no account of the positive moral energies that invigorate and partially redeem the present, keeping alive a sense of a South Africa that could be: not an inevitable South Africa being brought into existence by unseen forces of historical necessity but not entirely a mirage either, for it exists in tiny outcroppings—in these lives, in lives like these, in the lives that they, and those like them, touch.

Joe Seremane was sent into internal exile by the state's security apparatus and arbitrarily transmogrified there from a black South African with no rights into a Bophuthatswanan with rights existing on paper like assets in a frozen account. As a black man who had once dared to take a political stance, he was expected to learn the lesson that his fate was controlled by invisible and anonymous officials, that destiny was what they said it was. But Joe Seremane had a sense of humor as well as a sense of the absurd. The South African system, as he experienced it, was a practical joke played on his personality. And his personality was simply too large and expansive to stay bottled up in a dusty township called Montshiwa, where he had been dumped, a place of total obscurity in the western Transvaal.

An alert reader of the letters columns in the English-language newspapers of Johannesburg or the nearer-to-hand *Mafeking* (after an orthographic reform, *Mafikeng*) *Mail* might have noticed a few years ago that Montshiwa had suddenly become the unlikely platform for a whole chorus of unintimidated, sometimes mocking black voices. There were Pax Patria and Domus Vero, Justice Lover, and Black Savage; Kubu Segathlhe, and Jack Senwamadi (a surname ominously translatable as "one who drinks blood"), not to mention an urbane and chatty Montshiwa-based jazz critic named Monty Simon and, coming closer to the source of this din of free and unsolicited opinion, a certain Wetsho-O-tsile Seremane, who playfully ended one of his many letters by declaring, "Pens such as Domus Vero, Justice Lover, Kubu Segathlhe, Pax Patria, Jack Senwamadi and Black Savage have said it all for me." That was as close as Joe Seremane ever came to acknowledging that he was all of the above. Wetsho-O-tsile meant "our fellowman has arrived." It was one of Joe's ways of signaling that he couldn't and wouldn't wait.

The editors of the letters columns were slow to catch on. On one glorious morning, two of Joe's epistolary alter egos managed to make themselves heard in the *Rand Daily Mail.* Addressing whites under his various aliases, Joe Seremane could be both caustic and tender. Sometimes he was not above taking on the black man's burden and seeking to uplift his readers from their slough of racial superstitions and fears. At his best he could be caustic, tender, and uplifting, all at once. Addressing the white hope South African pugilism was offering to heavyweight boxing, Gerrie Coetzee, Justice Lover explained his reasons for rooting for one of his fellow South African's black American opponents. "Gerrie, you and I and all of us are caught up in a nasty historical trap!" his open letter began, making the point, in terms the boxer could hardly be expected to grasp, that there was nothing personal about his hostility. He then drew Gerrie Coetzee's attention to a controversy aroused by a decision to desegregate the Pretoria stadium where the fight was to be held. What had the local authorities been trying to avoid? "My black body," answered Justice Lover, "totally disregarding my beautiful, tolerant and patient soul." How could he root for a white South African boxer while he himself was not accepted as a South African? "No, Gerrie," he concluded, "I'll back you the day that you and I are Azanians in a unitary non-racial and non-discriminatory state."

"My beautiful, tolerant and patient soul." There was a touch of self-mockery in the words perhaps, but they should have melted the hardest white heart. Pax Patria could also spread the balm of black compassion for whites, assuring his "white brothers" that blacks were not reared to hate, even those who "have suffered terrible pains which we would never want to recount—because it hurts—in the police cells and prisons." The casual reader could take this as a rhetorical device, but the testimony was autobiographical. "Are we going to be denied what is rightfully ours because of your fears that are really unfounded?" Pax Patria asked. "I'll keep trying to forgive," Justice Lover was writing in his next published effort a couple of weeks later, "but for how long?"

Forgiveness was soon strained by a letter signed simply "Anglican" from a white suburb called Berea. Anglican had warned blacks against "being taken for a ride" by Communists, who would exploit their grievances under apartheid, "then push you into a farm, together with a hundred others, and make you work for nothing." Justice Lover laid into Anglican. "Has Anglican of Berea, with all the comforts, privileges and protection of white South Africa," he asked, "tasted what it means to be branded a communist or terrorist simply because one refuses to endorse the unjust apartheid system?" Did Anglican of Berea ever speak up for black political rights, the release of black political prisoners, or the right of black children to attend his own children's schools? "Anglican brother," Justice Lover said, "we have already been 'pushed into farms' right here in South Africa—forced to be citizens of homelands. I also know what it is to work for nothing—the experience I gathered right here under your system of government and worse still I know what it means not to work at all because of influx control." That, too, was autobiography, not rhetoric. At about the same time, Jack Senwamadi got a little note of congratulations for having won five rands, in those days nearly $8, for "a best Extra-Forum letter" in the *Rand Daily Mail*. Then the *Mail* became noticeably less receptive to the letters; the voice of Montshiwa, it seems, had become too recognizable or perhaps too insistent.

By the time I met him, Joe Seremane and his entire cast had been virtually frozen out of the Johannesburg letters columns, but their, or his, epistolary spree was still gathering momentum. Now he was speaking mainly to blacks, especially blacks who were learning to think of themselves as Bophuthatswanans. When even the *Mafikeng Mail* showed signs that it might have heard enough from Domus Vero, Kubu Segathlhe stepped into the breach and started to run off his own home-typed newsletters for circulation in the townships. The man would not be turned off or silenced. "The Rustic's Viewpoint" these latest screeds were called.

Some rustic. Joe didn't grow up in the bush but in a township near Johannesburg; from adolescence on, he made himself a part of the history of his time and paid the price. He had traveled through southern Africa; his restless and inquiring mind had traveled the world. Yet cast adrift in a homeland, he became haunted by the perception that the homeland blacks—the biggest, fastest-growing segment of black South Africa, after all—were being written off by blacks who imagined themselves to be in the "struggle" as surely and completely as they were being written off by whites. To assail the policies and depredations of the Tinkertoy homeland regimes, to try to keep black nationalist sentiments alive inside the arbitrary and invisible borders of the tribal states, was to run the risk of conceding them a measure of recognition. Or so orthodox black nationalists seemed to imagine; if the struggle were to be saved from a possibly fatal compromise, in their view, Bophuthatswana could not be seen to exist, and neither could Bophuthatswanans. It thus followed that there could be no alliance with anyone involved in opposition politics in the homeland. Yet someone, Joe saw, had to keep a spirit of debate and quest alive in these stagnant satrapies, someone like Domus Vero or Kubu Segathlhe, two of his personae who became especially adept at playing the bumpkin with a sly sense of mischief as well as mission. "In our toothy laughter and seemingly conformist stance," the latter writes in an unsolicited commentary on the intellectual climate at the new university in the homeland capital of Mmabatho, "we shall be closely watching to see whether the words of assurance given us are not the same pie-in-the-sky rhetoric we have been fed on throughout our pathetic and miserable lives. . . . Please don't stifle my burning passion and hunger for knowledge and wisdom. Don't trap me in academic protocol and garb. The rustic spirit was born of the lush, free jungles and grasslands of Africa where even the wind is questioned when singing in the reeds."

It all boiled down to a refusal to be satisfied with white paternalism and white definitions of black goals, and it all was pouring forth in a steady flow from a little study this self-liberated black man had built for himself in the backyard of his township house in a homeland. The first time I visited there, he showed me the scrapbook in which he had compiled his missives. "Mightier than the Sword," he had written on the cover. I knew Joe then only as a fieldworker of the South African Council of Churches, responsible primarily for staying in touch with various communities of rural blacks who had been forcibly resettled in the homeland. But he overflowed that role, that definition, too. The letters he dashed off only hinted at the energy, wit, and amplitude of his conversation, in which his whole body seemed engaged, his long fingers eloquently playing to the rhythm of the words and his long face catching and reflecting every shading of humor.

He also had one of those South African laughs that are not merely rich and full-throated but become a kind of statement, a small triumph of personality, the response of strong individuals to the ridiculousness of having to pass a whole life trapped in someone else's dream. The blacks I knew who had suffered most seemed to laugh best, while the whites who had suffered least were always lapsing into self-pitying laments about the tragedy of *their* dilemma and how grievously *they* were misunderstood. Winnie Mandela laughed when she spoke about her visits to her husband, with whom she had not had a truly private moment in twenty-one years; how on her last visit he had upended himself on the other side of the Plexiglas window in the prison visiting room in order to show her a toe that had required an operation because of an ill-fitting shoe. "I saw the foot for the first time in twenty-one years," she said, laughing. Mamphela Ramphele, a political coworker of Steve Biko and the mother of his child born four months after his death, laughed when she spoke about the stunting of black political efforts that followed his removal from the scene. "That is why the Boers really scored," she said, laughing. In each case it was a bright laugh, unforced and unaffected, that did not deny a crushing personal tragedy but seemed, somehow, to subsume it. These women were heroines worthy of Tolstoy. Joe Seremane's laugh had that heroic quality, too.

The crucial fact about Joe's letters, I discovered on my next visit, was that they had started soon after his release from a period of detention in which he had been tortured. The garrison state had fallen on him with its full weight, and he had then stood up, dusted himself off, and spoken out. Justice Lover, Pax Patria, and Domus Vero had first felt the urge to preach to whites in 1976 in an interrogation room in Pietermaritzburg. There he was subjected to what is sometimes known as the helicopter, the torture in which the naked detainee has his wrists handcuffed to his ankles and then is suspended from an iron bar. "My reaction, my physical response, I'm unable to say to the closest person in my life, even my wife," he said. But his emotional reaction, a sense of revulsion that expressed itself as a kind of pity for his interrogators, was too strong to stay contained, and finally he made the mistake of telling a high security police officer that he had tried to understand the hate and bitterness he saw in his questioners and only hoped he never experienced anything like that himself. "You've preached enough, Joe," the officer said brusquely, either because he knew his duty and feared to meet the black man on that plane or because he was truly contemptuous of the weakness that such a moralizing response signified to him.

Joe, who was then nearly forty, hadn't waited that long to discover that he was as good as whites, that their categories and definitions didn't work for him. His father was a stern, self-disciplined Shona from the then Rhodesia who worked as a clerk on a gold mine near the town of Randfontein; his mother's origins were Tswana, but she would smack her children for referring to a playmate as an Ndebele or a Xhosa. "Those are your people," she would say. So he had never thought of himself as a Shona or Tswana, only as an African. The sharp cutting edge of apartheid was just beginning to slice into the land, and he was of the last generation of urban black children who sometimes played with whites. "The mine dumps were the no-man's-land where we played," he told me. "It was maybe there that we gauged ourselves against our masters and thought that we had no right to feel inferior."

Incredibly there was even an opportunity for a brief flirtation with the daughter of an Australian mining engineer.

His first taste of political struggle came at the same time, during what was known as the Defiance Campaign in the early fifties when the congress movement, adopting the Gandhian tactic of civil disobedience, dispatched its supporters into segregated "whites only" facilities. The congress was operating on a timetable that placed it well ahead of the civil rights movement in the United States, but it faced a national government that was ready to use force as ruthlessly as necessary to crush it. Joe Seremane and his teenage friends in Randfontein were never recruited or trained for civil disobedience, but they got the idea as soon as they heard about it and headed straight down to the post office to shout, "This is our country!" and other slogans on the white side of the barrier, until a police van arrived and they were hauled off to the station for a caning and, finally, sent home with a warning to behave like good little *kaffertjies* ("piccanins," a cloying racial diminutive used by English-speaking paternalists, would be the nearest translation). The police were less indulgent when they picked him up, a decade later, for agitation on behalf of the banned Pan-Africanist Congress. In 1963 he was sent to prison on Robben Island in Cape Town's Table Bay with the most stalwart blacks of his generation, to break rocks and carry night soil for six years.

It was another opportunity to gauge himself against whites, and Joe remembers it with a certain exhilaration. "Sometimes, late at night, when my thinking gets reckless and crazy," he said, "I find myself wishing that my sons will have an opportunity to experience it. I don't really mean that, but when I look around at my contemporaries, seventy or eighty percent of them are washed out, done in, defeated by the system. The ones who survive, the reborn lot, the people who have been regenerated and re-energized are the ones who came off the island."

In that lot Joe included his best friend from the Randfontein mine dumps, the number two accused in the trial in which he was number one, who found his way, in an incredible odyssey, from the island to business school in Muncie, Indiana, and then a trainee job on Park Avenue in New York with a banking multinational. The Robben Island man then lived on Roosevelt Island in the East River until, his odyssey still not complete, his bank assigned him to Johannesburg, where he now resided in a new custom-built house in Soweto's Prestige Park. It was not that Joe regarded multinational banking and Prestige Park as a happier ending than welfare work and Montshiwa, to which he was restricted after he left the island. What mattered to him was the striving, the insistence on self-definition. It sent some people into exile to write or to undergo military training or endlessly to wait, some into the church, and others who never found a way out of the townships on binges of acquisitiveness as if a black man, finally, could prove his worth only the way whites seemed to do it, by the car he drove or the house he built. A black man of Joe's generation could be dazed when he contemplated the various destinations reached by his contemporaries, all of whom had started out with a confident expectation that they would live to be free men in their country. The dispersal of energies and commitment testified to the power of the system, but a single man, Joe Seremane believed, could still show the limitations on that power through clear thinking and plain speaking. So, when his peregrinations through the country as a cigarette company salesman led the authorities to suspect that this Robben Island alumnus might be traveling to forge clandestine links between the rebellious Soweto students and the underground, he found himself preaching about the problem of bitterness to an officer of the security police.

He had not meant to end up a Christian. In his youth the example of the way the whites in the country practiced their faith had led him to consider conversion to Islam. On Robben Island he went to church only because Robert Sobukwe, the Pan-Africanist leader, was being detained in a cottage near the chapel and it was sometimes possible to glimpse him and even show him a clenched fist as a gesture of support on the way to worship. Even now he wonders about the Christian patience and forgiveness of his people. "If it's such a good thing," he asked, "why don't they see it?" But it's not the old story of what whites fail to see that goads him, living in a homeland, but the parody that these little black despotisms make of the Pan-Africanist dream he carried to prison; it's the spectacle of other blacks' accepting as a kind of fulfillment this sham democracy in a supposedly multiracial state that just happens to be more than 99 percent black, the spectacle, too, of township drunkenness. In his letters Domus Vero rails against "the evil and nation-killing shebeens," against filth and squalor, the absence of public hygiene and social vision. He finds "moral decadence" in the black public service and "social degradation" in the people. "Everywhere that the people are gathered you feel that uneasy silence on things that matter, and the shallow semblance of approval," he writes. "Is it treason to reason?" he asks.

His jeremiads go unheeded. He is the village scold. Some of his old cohorts may even feel that by staying in Bophuthatswana, he has opted out of the struggle. But he is his own liberation struggle, and at least he has liberated himself. On my last afternoon with him, we drove through Mmabatho, the showcase capital, on Lucas Mangope Highway, named after the homeland's president. Black gardeners were working in the gardens of high officials as they do in Bloemfontein or Pretoria; only here many of the officials were black. Joe Seremane was recalling with pride a jazz combo in which he played on Robben Island.

"Where did you get the instruments?" I asked in astonishment.

"There were no instruments," he replied. "We were bop scatting; we did it by voice. Each guy played two or three instruments. There were guys there with fantastic musical memories. We had the cream."

The Robben Island memory regenerates and re-energizes, just as he said. There wasn't the slightest suggestion that he now felt left out in Mmabatho. His idea of freedom had nothing to do with watching a black man manicure a black official's garden, but he could be driven almost frantic by his sense that such an idea was catching on. "The most painful thing is that people don't know it's working," Joe Seremane said. Apartheid was working, he meant. "They have to get in here and fight it."

I'm trying to talk about moral courage and its origins, not to engage in hagiography. But I will have to run the risk of relating my next example as if it were an allegory, omitting the real name of my subject, who could still be a target of reprisals from the South African military authorities. I will call him Dominee Eerlik, appropriating the Afrikaans word for "honest" and "upright." Apart from the name, I have taken no license with his story.

He grew up in the remote hinterland of the Cape, where his sense of what was appropriate in race relations was shaped, in part, by fistfights with young coloreds. It wasn't until he was studying theology at the university that he first became aware that it might be difficult to dismiss the criticisms of apartheid on moral grounds. Eventually, as the certainties on which he had been reared slowly dissolved, he was forced to acknowledge that he was no longer politically orthodox or reliable. It was not a discovery that he advertised, nor did it make him reconsider his choice of vocation as a minister of the dominant branch of the Dutch Reformed Church, one of the pillars of the system he questioned. A sense of strain came quickly, however, for his first assignment was to serve as a chaplain in the army, where the gospel he was expected to preach had political overtones. The only way to manage the strain, he found, was to keep his doubts to himself and restrict his preaching to religious themes. Then, after working as a missionary in a black country, he was rewarded with a choice assignment in a white suburb of Cape Town. There his political evasions, his failure to uphold and justify, were soon detected, and although he tried to keep his preaching apolitical, the ideologues in his congregation found something soft and not to their liking in his carefully balanced homilies. Their suspicions finally erupted after he had preached a sermon on the awkwardness of the Christian faith, the difficult demands it makes— for instance, the young preacher said, the demand that you love your enemy. "What is this new kind of message?" an elder of the church demanded the next day, suggesting that it had been insinuated into the sermon as a calculated attack on Afrikaners. A second elder, reading even more into the sermon, declared that he did not want his daughter to marry a black.

At his next church he went through the same cycle. At first the congregation liked the young dominee, and then it began to feel uncomfortable. He found a job in teaching, but that did not ease his sense of strain, for he was still a member of a church that upheld apartheid. His own inconsistency dogged him, especially after he had started to extend his contacts with nonwhite Christians. Finally, he felt that he could live with himself only if he followed the example of a handful of white dominees who had resigned from their church and taken up membership in its colored branch, which had just rejected the principle of segregation on which it had been initially founded by whites.

It happens that membership in the Dutch Reformed Church is not merely a notional affiliation; it is also something palpable, a document certifying the individual's standing as a Christian. Dominee Eerlik carried that document to the council of his last congregation, along with the membership papers of his wife and three children and a two-and-one-half-page letter explaining his reasons for returning them. The letter, which was read out to the council in his presence, said that the menace South Africa faced was apartheid, not communism, and that he and his family could no longer associate themselves with a church that had cut itself off from the body of Christ. None of the elders or deacons made any comment when the reading of the letter ended. In that silence Dominee Eerlik left the room.

This was an act of self-liberation, but it meant shouldering a heavy burden of isolation from those he had been reared to think of as his own people. Even if he now had an easier and less claustrophobic sense of who his people were, even if he could now call himself a South African without qualification, the law still required him to live as a white. In fact, it wasted no time in driving that lesson home. Almost immediately after he had severed his ties to his church, he received military call-up papers, ordering him to go to the "border" during the Christmas season as a chaplain. An incredulous Dominee Eerlik explained to a senior chaplain that they no longer belonged to the same church. Military orders were military orders, he was told. He was in an absurd position, but he knew that the law did not recognize his reality; he would be breaking it if he didn't go. Suddenly jail for himself and notoriety and penury for his family all were possibilities that he had to consider; he thought he had a duty as a Christian to refuse to serve, but he also had a Christian duty to his wife and children. So out of a combination of naïveté and desperation, he proposed a compromise that had the effect of turning the absurdity back on the military: He would go to the border, he said, but in his preaching there he would say what he believed.

No one got around to asking him what that was until he reached Oshakati, the military headquarters of the South African forces operating in the region of Namibia called Ovamboland and, across an international border, in Angola. There, in the combat zone, 1,200 miles from his family, the young dominee declared that insofar as the insurgents of the South-West Africa People's Organization, commonly known as SWAPO, were fighting against apartheid, he was able to understand their frustration. Saying what he believed in his Christmas sermon to Afrikaner troops would mean saying, "You have to try to love SWAPO, and if you can't do that, you have to try to understand them."

Dominee Eerlik didn't mean to be excessive; he had no intention, he explained, of giving a political sermon. All he wanted, so that he could go on living with his conscience, was the right to include that single sentence, or some version of it, in any sermon he gave. What happened for the next two days at military headquarters in Ovamboland will remain beyond the comprehension of anyone, like myself, who has not been steeped in some Calvinist or other Puritan tradition. Dominee Eerlik wasn't clapped into the stockade for insubordination verging on treason. Instead, like New England Puritans of the seventeenth century or Chinese Maoists on a "rectification" binge, the Afrikaner military officers he confronted engaged in a two-day struggle for the soul of this blond, blue-eyed, hopelessly wayward dominee.

On his first evening in Oshakati—which happened, I suppose providentially, to be December 16th, the Afrikaner Day of the Covenant —he found himself in earnest disputation with a senior chaplain. The older cleric said he couldn't understand why Dominee Eerlik kept harping on apartheid as the reason for his stand. "Apartheid doesn't exist," he said. "It has been dead for ten years. Apartheid isn't even a hundred and twentieth on the list of priorities for which we're fighting here." On a subsequent evening a couple of lieutenant colonels with combat commands jumped in, too, with all the passion they brought to any engagement with the enemy. One of them reverted to the discredited argument that there was justification for apartheid in the Bible. "I asked him please to show it to me," Dominee Eerlik recalled, "because if it was there, I wanted to preach it as well." For a moment the young dominee thought he was going to be assaulted, but, heedless of contradiction, the other officer tried to bury apartheid again. "Black and white fight together on the border," he said. "Do you call that apartheid? We eat together. Is that apartheid? And at night when we are are finished, we go to our own tents and sleep. Is that apartheid?"

"Yes, of course," Dominee Eerlik said, re-enacting the debate for my benefit. "Why must they sleep in their own tents?"

Later the senior chaplain tried to move the discussion back to a theological plane. The Bible nowhere teaches, he said, that you must serve the interests of other peoples to the point of neglecting those of your own. "We cannot duplicate Jesus," he declared. It was not, therefore, the Christian duty of the soldier to imagine the viewpoint of his enemy any more than it was the duty of the executioner to consider the viewpoint of a condemned man. The Christian duty of a soldier or an executioner was to perform efficiently, the chaplain maintained. Dominee Eerlik paused in his re-enactment. "Do you see," he asked, almost wearily, "why I couldn't preach there?"

The struggle for his soul didn't end with these debates, which ran on in one case for nearly five hours. He was also sent to hear the story of a repentant SWAPO "terrorist," who recited a set piece about how he was forbidden to read his Bible by "Communists" while fighting with the insurgents. An escort then made the mistake of mentioning that the man was a SWAPO deserter, not a captive. Dominee Eerlik asked to see a prisoner who remained loyal to SWAPO. The second man testified that he had his own Bible all the time he was with the guerrillas, attended services, heard sermons, and never was prevented from practicing his religion. Finally an impasse was recognized; the young dominee's soul was deemed to be irretrievable, and he was summoned for a brief interview with the commanding officer, who informed him he was being flown to Pretoria. This officer's tone was formal but not unfriendly, tinged slightly by curiosity. What would Dominee Eerlik do, he asked, if he were called up as an ordinary soldier? Dominee Eerlik replied that he would have to struggle with his conscience.

In Pretoria he was put through another theological discussion with a senior chaplain, then sent home to the Cape. I met him for the first time several weeks later. He did not know how the authorities were going to react; there would have to be some consequences, he thought. A year and a half passed before I met Dominee Eerlik again. He was serving a colored congregation in a Cape community where his grandfather had once been dominee of the white church. The army had kept in touch intermittently, warning that he still had an obligation as a white South African to do military service, but there had been no summons.

It was easy enough to guess at a reason for the hesitation. Obviously Dominee Eerlik could not be called to serve again as a chaplain, but if he were drafted for routine military duties, there was always the risk that he would refuse. The South African Defense Force has a policy on conscientious objectors. It knows how to handle Jehovah's Witnesses, holier-than-thou Anglicans, and Jews. It can handle the occasional Afrikaner renegade, too. But a dominee who wouldn't serve and who sought to explain his reasons to a military court could send a shiver of doubt through the Afrikaans universities and churches that might not easily be shaken off. He deserved to be punished, but how could he be punished without being turned into a symbol? For the moment, at least, the wayward dominee appeared to have battled Africa's mightiest army to a standoff.

"I know what I will do if they call me," he said mildly. "I will never again wear that uniform."

There are not all that many stories of Afrikaner apostasy, but there are enough to form a pattern. It would be wishful thinking to present them as portents, but it is impossible to dismiss them as aberrant and inconsequential. If there are still Afrikaners interested in writing their own history sixty or eighty years from now, I imagine that there is a better than even chance that they will find their heroes from this period among those who turned their backs on the dream of an enduring racial order, that they will then find meaning in the short life of Frikkie Conradie.

Frikkie, who was brought up on a farm in the western Transvaal, never in his youth heard anyone question the divinely ordained right and need of whites to rule over blacks. Ruling on his father's farm was a physical thing. He could remember the children in the family scream-ing in fear when his father applied his boot to the stomach or ribs or head of a prostrate laborer, or chased black trespassers across the veld in his *bakkie* as if they were game, or, having cornered a reprobate, dragged him around the farm on a leather thong as if it were a leash. And he could remember the racial catechisms the white children got in explanation of what it was that made such stressful dominance a part of the natural order: how it was the Afrikaner's duty to raise blacks to the level of human beings but, since they were now more like animals, how it was necessary first to break them in. The children absorbed the lesson but, Frikkie recalled, continued to scream every time there was an incident, in fear that they would see a man die.

It's not an easy country, he was taught. It requires discipline, im-posed by one generation on the next, accepted, and passed on in the usually unspoken assumption that discipline and morality are one; that indiscipline—a breaking of ranks, a doubt too persistently or openly expressed—is immorality, which can only lead in South Africa to a breakdown of social order. It is an ethos rather than a creed, and in Frikkie Conradie's case, it co-existed without conscious strain with the abstract, intellectualized lessons in ethics and theology he received on his way to becoming a dominee, until it cracked and disintegrated in a single night. That was his first night in Holland, where he had gone for graduate studies in theology, and all it took was an encounter in Afrikaans with a fellow South African who was there for the same purpose. The fellow South African was not white. His name was Allan Boesak, and he went on to become the leader of a movement of dissident ministers in the nonwhite branches of the Dutch Reformed

Church and, in the secular sphere, probably the most eloquent voice of protest that had ever come from the colored community. On that night of their first meeting, however, Allan Boesak didn't debate Frikkie Conradie; he simply asked Frikkie what he thought of apartheid and then, after getting a guarded, conventional answer about how it was not necessarily inconsistent with Christian precepts, proceeded to recount his own family's experiences in a series of forced removals under the Group Areas Act from homes in Cape Province. "I met Allan, and that's where the whole story starts," Frikkie told me. "Blacks succeed in getting through to us, and then we begin to understand what is happening."

Frikkie wasn't sure where it was that he learned to listen the way he listened that night, but once he started, he never stopped. Back in South Africa, he refused the ordination for which he had been trained in the white branch of his church and took it instead in the black branch, becoming the first white minister to take this step. Then he went to serve a black congregation in a dilapidated township called Alexandra, receiving the salary a black minister would get without the subsidy normally made available to white missionaries. He did not regard himself as a missionary bringing the light but as one who was receiving it from the people he served. "They take you as a racist and a paternalist," he said, "and they make you into a human being."

A lean man, pale and bearded, with none of the prim decorum in which Afrikaner dominees learn to encase themselves, he was speaking sorrowfully yet passionately about family when he said this. A smile flickered at the corners of his mouth, never quite extinguishing itself while he spoke. His whole life had been shaped by the stunning discovery he had made, and now, like some poet who has suddenly found his voice, he spoke with quiet confidence, mixing urgency with humor. He still didn't know much about Christianity, Frikkie said, but he understood what Jesus meant when he asked who is his real mother, his real brother. That much he had experienced, for he had more fathers and brothers and sisters in the real sense of those words among blacks than he had blood brothers and sisters. His defection had caused his mother and father great suffering, had led his brother and sister to shun him. He could only feel sorry for them. Afrikaners worry so much about what they stand for, about their precious identity, that they never experience life. "We ban people," he said, speaking softly, "and in the same process we also ban life out of our lives." When he felt the solidarity he had found among blacks, he said, he had only one fear. It was the fear of being again cut off from them, of finding himself alone.

His words sat in my notebook for a week. I didn't fully understand what they meant or how I might use them. And of course, I had no way of knowing that it would be the last week of Frikkie Conradie's life. Then, at age thirty-five Frikkie took a curve too fast on the way to the western Transvaal to visit his father's farm and died, barely twelve hours before his wife gave birth to their first child. Simultaneously a widow and mother, she immediately came under intense family pressure to have the funeral in the church Frikkie had left, for the sake of his aging parents. A mutual friend asked whether there was anything that might guide her in this extremity in my interview with him. I got out my notebook and typed up my notes, including the sentences "I have more fathers and brothers and sisters in the real sense of the word among blacks than I have blood brothers and sisters. I only really feel sorry for them because what they are not experiencing is life."

The funeral service was at the church in Alexandra, followed by burial in the black cemetery, where Frikkie, once again, crossed a barrier no other white had crossed. His old family was there in the small black church, and so was his new family, which overflowed in the hundreds into the churchyard. The eulogies became prayers for freedom and reconciliation. Wondering what the words they were hearing meant to them, I found it hard to tear my eyes away from Frikkie's white relatives, who were having to share their grief with Bishop Tutu and others who were notorious in the Afrikaans newspapers they read as agents or dupes of Soviet subversion. Then a brother got up to speak on behalf of the family. "My Broederbond brother" Frikkie had called him. A large middle-aged man, he spoke in Afrikaans with careful courtesy, saying he trusted the people of Alexandra would always remember the message his brother had brought them. Frikkie Conradie, of course, would have instantly reacted to the condescension; he would have said that this was getting the meaning of his life exactly wrong.

Allan Boesak, who was there when the whole story began, came much closer. "Frikkie Conradie," he said of his friend, "lived and died a free man."

For a self-liberated black the question is not how to take sides or surmount isolation. It is how to make a commitment that will be more than a gesture, more than a sacrifice. It is easy enough to flash and vanish like a shooting star, to burn out or crash, achieving the status of victim. The authorities stand ready to provide a quick, dirty lesson on power to any young black who needs to test it for himself. It is harder to choose exile, but what appears, at first, to be a heroic, all-or-nothing commitment can fade into a callow compromise, in the lengthening retrospect of a lifetime passed in dusty refugee camps and alien cities. What is obviously hardest is to stay and remain effective, staying not just to keep faith but to advance the cause of equality.

Malusi Mpumlwana, a political lieutenant and heir to Steve Biko, started to struggle with the question of commitment—of whether there was something required beyond courage and astuteness—shortly before his friend died. Malusi was then in the same Pietermaritzburg prison in which Joe Seremane had been interrogated and tortured, undergoing much the same treatment in what appears to have been an ongoing security police search for links between the old banned organizations that had gone underground or into exile and the new movements of black youth that had yet to be banned. In Malusi's case the treatment generally known as the helicopter was introduced as the horse. Sometimes, when his contorted body was dangling from the bar, his interrogators would break for tea, leaving him alone with his pain. Sometimes they would cane him on his bare feet, which burned with each cut, then loosen his manacles and insist that he stand—and go on standing for hours—on his flayed soles and heels. "They enjoyed it," he recalled. "There was one guy who was really having a great time of it." The man had served with a clandestine South African police unit in Rhodesia and had been captured on a foray into Zambia. "He said," Malusi continued, "that what he was doing was only a little of what he had been taught by the Zambians." The heaviest interrogation lasted about three weeks; for long stretches he was not allowed to sleep or use the toilet. "The methods they used were tough methods," he said, "but I expected worse things. So from day to day I told myself, 'This is not the worst yet.' I was able to keep my cool because I always said, 'It's not yet. The real bad things are still to come.' And then it was a surprise when it was all over."

Malusi had every reason to take seriously the threats that he might be discovered some morning at the bottom of the Umgeni River. Biko was still alive, but another close friend of theirs, Mapetla Mohapi, had died in detention, an alleged suicide. The context of what had happened and would happen was not, however, the main reason I found his account of interrogation more chilling than the others I had heard. The reason had to do with Malusi himself. I could think of very few people I had known whose demeanor so perfectly reflected character and intelligence. Malusi Mpumlwana spoke softly, with a natural reserve, yet had a ready and wholehearted laugh. He was modest to the point of selflessness, yet he conveyed confidence and authority. He was alert without seeming wary, direct without seeming assertive. I was obviously biased, but I thought he walked in a special light; it was as if you could see it in his eyes, which took on a vaguely Oriental cast from his high cheekbones and wispy mandarin beard. Any interrogator, it seemed to me, who wasn't already stupefied by hate, violence, or drink would have to view him with respect. A system that could make the confession about itself that was implicit in the attempt to humiliate and break a young man like this, I thought, showed that it was fundamentally resigned to its own moral rancidness.

Of course, it was late to be drawing this lesson, six years after Biko had gone to his grave, but then Biko's character was known to me only from words on paper or the memories of his friends, while I had known Malusi Mpumlwana for three years before I heard his experiences of detention in any detail. It was two different kinds of knowing so that while his story was by no means the worst I heard, it moved me most. There are those in what is called "the movement" who might say that Malusi lost his political bearings in jail in Pietermaritzburg. It was not that he was less committed or reliable or energetic when he emerged, but he seemed full of a mystical—and therefore politically suspect— insight that he needed to impart; even more than tactics, he now felt an urgent need to discuss basic theological issues of good and evil and what it meant in the South African situation to be doing God's will. Interrogation hadn't changed him in any visible way, but it had jolted him into a sequence of reflections and that others found hard to follow.

Late one evening, after a long conversation, he summarized them for my benefit: "What happened is I said, 'Exactly what is going on? What does God believe in? Look, we are very honest men, and we are committed to something which we think is really honest to goodness. It *should* be done! Somebody has got to do it! We are committing ourselves to something that is very important. And I believe that no self-respecting, loving God can fight against this or allow this stupid nonsense to happen.' And this happened to me, and I began to think about it and said to myself, 'Perhaps what is happening is that I plan and expect God to bless. I don't say I am on God's side; I say God is on my side or should be on my side.' And I began to sit back and reflect, 'If God wills good to happen, and I also will good to happen, where is our difference?' And then I thought that perhaps I should take more trouble to align myself with what might be God's wisdom. And since I have done that, I have become more than ever convinced that there is no greater foundation for a struggle for change and emancipation in this land than a conviction that it is God's will.

"But then, of course, you don't co-opt God into your will." Here Malusi laughed, a deep laugh from his chest. "You participate in His will and make your little contribution. Part of the trick is that you must be in constant communication with Him about it. Your everyday action must be in response to a feeling that this is the direction God wants you to take. Not only should this be the case, but I think you've got to know that *all* these people are God's people. Good and bad alike. He loves them all but hates the evil that they do. And therefore, you can smash evil with all the power that you can muster, but you've got to save every last soul of them."

Again Malusi laughed, not self-consciously but as if he had been caught unawares by the immensity of this demand or commandment, whichever he took it to be. And once again, I have to acknowledge that the meaning of his words, as I heard them in my living room in Johannesburg and as I think about them now, was and is beyond me. But knowing Malusi Mpumlwana, I knew they were not for him a summons to any kind of pietistic quietism or fatalism, nor did they represent in any sense a renunciation of the struggle in which he had been engaged. In a mundane sense, I imagine, they meant that those who sought to lead had to involve themselves more deeply than they had done so far in the lives and sufferings of the people, that their sense of urgency should express itself more in the intensity of that involvement than in their pronouncement of political demands and timetables. But that vague formulation is nothing more than one skeptic's attempt to put into words the commitment Malusi was trying to put into his life. In another sense, I also imagine, his reflections may have involved a premonition about what it might take to stay the course, to endure so that the struggle went on as more than a series of new beginnings and laments.

Biko and his friends had discovered in the movement they called Black Consciousness that each individual had the capacity to liberate himself. "It let us be free," Malusi said. "Very, very liberated, to the extent that even if you went into a town like Bloemfontein where you would have cringed in the past, suddenly you felt like you could challenge the whole white commando. Suddenly the world looked different. Biko's thrust was that political emancipation would not make sense without psychological emancipation because even if you had a change of government with people who felt inferior, what country could you run? So his view was that 'Black man, you're probably the greatest contributor to your own oppression,' that 'The white man has only to set the machine and leave it on automatic and you run it yourself.' So that what you really need to realize is that you must jump out of the train."

Malusi had jumped as soon as he came to know Biko as a young student in Natal and had never looked back. But the theological questions that preoccupied him in detention eventually carried this self-liberated activist to a new kind of concern for those left behind. "The measure of your freedom," Malusi said, "is to what extent you are able to recognize the unfreedom of others and battle to undo it. And then, while you're doing that, you get unfree again." Here he laughed at a paradox Black Consciousness had not foreseen. "I feel terribly unfree when I move into a situation of people who are very unfree—I'm talking about a simple situation of poverty—because I know they can't afford the good food they offer me. I feel unfree to eat it."

Only two brief weeks intervened between his release from detention in July 1977 and Steve Biko's last arrest. There was time for only one long and speculative conversation. Malusi tried to impart his sense of urgency about the need to consider the "role of God in this situation." Biko, a believer, was troubled by the theological problem of evil. Africa knew God, he felt, but God somehow overlooked Africa's suffering. The conversation reached no conclusion, and then Biko left on the trip from which he never returned.

It would be hard to exaggerate this irony: two close friends—one who had just been tortured, the other about to be tortured to death on behalf of what is supposed to be Christian civilization in South Africa —and in the little time left to them, they talk about the "role of God in this situation." The news of Biko's death came fewer than forty-eight hours after Malusi had learned about the death of his own father. With no time to mourn either of the two most important men in his life, he had to make arrangements for two funerals on successive days. The second, Biko's, had to succeed as a political statement, an expression at once of outrage and renewal. There were 20,000 mourners that afternoon in King William's Town, several hundred of them whites, the rest blacks. As the casket was lowered into the grave in the segregated cemetery next to the railway track, their protest and conviction seemed to reverberate throughout the country. The authorities reacted reflexively by taking the offensive with mass arrests, bannings of organizations, bannings of individuals. Malusi Mpumlwana went back to jail, which gave him a chance to deal with his emotions, the strongest of which was outrage over the injustice of the latest wave of suppression: Biko's killers went free, while his friends and followers went to jail.

Released finally under a banning order that made him a political nonperson, he found the movement he had helped build effectively obliterated. Many of its adherents had fled the country, responding to what they took to be the call of struggle. Malusi had talked about aligning himself with God's will. Attempting to do that, he resolved to stay.

His decision to become a priest in a black branch of the Anglican Church, which his father and grandfather had served as ministers, was not swiftly or easily made. It had not yet been taken when I met him, three years after Biko's death, at the time of Ciskei's hokey referendum on its hokey independence. Malusi by then had the status of an apostle because of his relation to the martyred Biko, but he was supporting his wife and children by working as a furniture salesman, an occupation that was moral in his eyes only by comparison to the jobs in the homeland government that some of his contemporaries had taken. "Compared to them, I am a free man," he said.

We drove to a clinic spawned as part of the community programs Biko's movement had fostered as an initiative in black self-reliance. It now belonged to the homeland. We went to a tannery near the town of Alice that had been part of the same effort. All that was left was the cement foundation; the authorities had razed the building, eliminating the livelihoods of the laborers in the process of demolishing the Biko legacy. They had done their work well. Malusi did not pretend that the vision of Black Consciousness was still smoldering in the hearts of the soon-to-be-Ciskeians. In the cemetery, to which he brought me, Biko's grave had the largest headstone but did not appear to be better tended than any of the others. It had not become a place of pilgrimage.

He recognized reality, but he didn't speak that evening as if the movement had failed or lost its way; in his view, Black Consciousness had been another chapter in the long saga of black resistance. He was then just thirty, still banned and under surveillance. Although he had been through more than most men experience in a lifetime, he was in the position of having to make a new beginning. It was not the restrictions on him but the questions he had started to raise in prison that gave him pause in that hiatus. I might have been put off had he voiced them in so many words, expressing his sense that there was a divine purpose in South Africa he had to serve. Instead, I was struck by his quiet confidence, the lightheartedness that seemed to co-exist with earnestness, not uneasily but as if they were somehow part of the same impulse.

That evening, as we were being seated in a steak house with "international" status, Malusi excused himself and went up to greet a white man at the bar, who seemed less than overjoyed to see him. Stiffly the man introduced his black acquaintance to the blonde with whom he was drinking. Returning to our table, Malusi explained that the man was an officer in the security police who had once been his shadow. In that role he had displayed an exceptional lack of subtlety and often managed inadvertently to tip the black activists off about police tactics and intelligence. That made him a favorite, and Malusi had developed a protective instinct for him, not wanting to see him replaced by someone more efficient.

"I don't think I've deliberately not hated," he remarked later when I told him how astonished I had been. "It's not part of my nature to be hateful, I think, but I can be quite indignant, and I detest evil. I can see the security police as individuals because I've come to know that you can get chaps working themselves up to be very bad. But I also see them as part of a culture, part of a system, which makes them very dangerous animals to be let loose."

On another of my visits following the homeland's independence, he managed to laugh when he showed me a formal letter he had just received from the Ministry of Internal Affairs in Pretoria, informing him that he would henceforth need a visa to visit the Republic of South Africa. "Should you arrive at a South African port of entry without a visa," the letter said, "you will not be permitted to enter."

By then he was in his first year of divinity studies near Pietermaritzburg, where he had once been detained; the letter therefore meant he needed a visa to continue in theology, Greek, and church history. If taken literally, it also meant that he could not drive out of the township of Zwelitsha, to which he had returned on vacation, to go to the bank or get gas for his car because the bank and gas station were across the unmarked border in what was deemed to be South Africa. He still thought of himself as a South African living in South Africa, of course, but he was now officially an exile in his own country. The more we worked out the implications of the predicament the white bureaucrats had devised in recognition of his service to the black cause and his potential for leadership, the more uproarious our laughter became. Technically, it seemed, he needed a visa to apply for a visa because the South African Embassy to Ciskei was still in white King William's Town. If he wanted to continue his studies, he could go into exile overseas, which would mean applying for a South African visa to reach a port of exit, or apply for a visa to stay home. Malusi had decided to apply because there was no purpose that could be served by his rotting in the township. "I'm not an alien, I can't possibly be an alien, but they've made me acknowledge that I'm a foreigner," he said. "They've succeeded beyond their wildest dreams."

Eventually this black South African living in South Africa got his visa to South Africa, and it was only then, five years after Steve Biko's death, that he made the decision to become a priest. He was moved not by any impulse to renounce political activism, he explained, but a belief that a strong political commitment, by which he seemed to mean an ideological commitment, was not as powerful as a strong religious commitment.

"Do you believe the churches can actually bring this regime down?" I asked incredulously.

"No, not the church," he replied, "but Christian conviction. Not the church as an institution but Christian conviction, which is my mainstay." As I understood him, he was talking about a conviction that grew not merely from a will to overcome the personal humiliation of apartheid but from a deeper sense of how it distorts the lives and increases the suffering of the masses of poor blacks. "It is very important to understand how people live so that becomes the driving force behind you," he said. "I identify in every way with an intention to liberate oneself from the self-perpetuation of oppression, but at the same time, I don't think that for me it means that you must be married to a particular political ideology. What's important is a burning decision to change the situation in every way possible."

Having just started parish work in the poorest of Durban's townships, Biko's heir said he didn't side with any one of the political sects fighting apartheid but with all of them. "I recognize all good as my pursuit," he explained, laughing again from the chest, "not just so-and-so's good." For that very reason there were some who now counted him as lost to "the movement."

In the same week that he had his last serious conversation with his friend Malusi Mpumlwana, who was then at the start of his own pilgrimage to the priesthood, Steve Biko had another long conversation with a white pastor, whose spiritual and political pilgrimage had been perhaps the most remarkable any South African had taken. The young black man, who had given himself to political struggle, talked to Biko about "the role of God." The Reverend Christiaan Frederick Beyers Naudé, who was then in his seventh decade and only a few months away from being silenced by a banning order, had talked politics rather than theology. Near the end of an arduous quest, he had come to believe that for a white South African, especially an Afrikaner, doing God's will meant supporting black political initiatives. There is no way of knowing if Biko had time to reflect on the contrast, but a kind of parallax was occurring in his orbit. Where the young black was now inclined to seek a political fulfillment through religion, the older white sought a spiritual fulfillment through politics. Specifically Beyers Naudé was preoccupied then by the question of what could be done to harness the fractious black movements into something like a unified force.

The trajectory he had traveled to reach this point, where he was beyond any doubt a traitor and heretic in the eyes of most Afrikaners, had carried Beyers Naudé from one end of the South African political firmament to the other. If he were to be compared to any contemporary figure of conscience, it would have to be the dissident Soviet physicist Andrei Sakharov. Naudé's apostasy, like Sakharov's, was especially galling and unforgivable because it had occurred at the very heart of a power elite. Once he had been the most highly regarded Afrikaner clergyman of his generation; any position his church or people had to offer could have been within his reach. Now, or so the top security officials contended, he was an agent of the underground. That charge had never been proved, but like the charge that Sakharov had illicit ties with the Americans, it could not be dismissed as altogether beyond belief. Contained within the smear was a germ of plausibility, for Beyers Naudé had unquestionably aligned himself with a cause most Afrikaners viewed as revolutionary. Not content to be merely a voice of conscience, he had crossed the invisible line that separates liberals from radicals in the eyes of most whites: He had sided with blacks. It did no good to argue that he was still more accurately described as a Calvinist than a Marxist, that he explained himself in terms of biblical injunctions and theological concepts of justice. Where he came from, a white who believed in black power had to be at least a Communist, if he was not even more depraved.

Yet the man was more remarkable than the story of his life. It wasn't only the distance he had traveled but his readiness at every stage to go on traveling, to find some new injunction in any new set of circumstances, that set him apart. From the outside it could appear as if his moral machinery were put together without a brake, as if the accelerator had got stuck, or, as if, in imbibing the stern sense of duty on which Afrikaners are supposed to be reared, he had overdosed. If that were all, if he had merely followed the dictates of his conscience, subjecting the primordial value of Afrikaner survival to earnest theological scrutiny, his entire journey could have been summed up in a sermon, and he would today be seen as an example, not as a threat. His principles only began the process of his detachment from his Afrikaner patriarchy. What did him in was his openness to experience, his readiness to step across the racial barrier and see for himself what it was really like over there.

Initially he had no appetite for confrontation or rebellion; when he was breaking with his people on issues they regarded as fundamental, he found ways to sidestep them in his preaching. He could tailor principles, like most preachers, but he could not deny facts. Starting in late middle age, he taught himself to embrace them. The urgency came from this openness; the more he knew, the more he felt was demanded of him. Even after he had been placed under a banning order and confined to a single district, he managed to travel deeper into the heart of South Africa than practically any other white, traveling with zest as well as zeal. Ostracized by Afrikaners, he sought a wider community, and yet, even after leaving his church so he could worship with blacks, he never ceased to be an Afrikaner dominee in his unfailing courtesy and pastoral manner, even in his grooming. The safari suits he wore in summer always looked freshly pressed; his hair, always was neatly combed and never, it seemed, in need of cutting. His days were crammed with appointments, but he never allowed himself to seem rushed or distracted. Some worried that he was politically naïve or reckless; none could question his courage. Yet whenever I spent an hour or two in his company, it was not so much his personal history or righteousness that struck me as his directness, his ability to fasten his attention on a person or issue. Being in politics, a risky branch of moral theology, especially for one who was under heavy surveillance, he could not afford to be entirely guileless. But he had overcome patriarchal aloofness, unbending and mellowing even as he became more intense. "You can always find something to laugh about in this country," he said to me once, "and you can always, always cry."

Beyers Naudé doesn't mention his father, a severe and distant figure in the patriarchal mode, as a model for the life he has led. But it is hard not to notice a rough symmetry between the journeys of father and son, although they traveled in opposite directions politically. The elder Naudé was never a man for easy compromises. Jozua François Naudé was one of only six out of sixty delegates who refused at the peace conference that ended the Boer War to affix their signatures to a treaty that gave the losing side a chance to win the peace under the Union Jack and the distant suzerainty of the British crown. In the face of certain defeat, he would have preferred to go on fighting. He then became a dominee but still wasn't resigned to the loss of Afrikaner sovereignty when, thirteen years later, in 1915, the fourth of his eight children and second son was born and named after another uncompromising Afrikaner. General C. F. Beyers, a Boer War hero, had died the year before in a brief rebellion provoked by the decision of some of his old comrades, who now held authority in Pretoria, to take South Africa into the World War on Britain's side. In the same period Jozua Naudé became one of the half dozen founders of a secret society that swore an oath to advance the cause of Afrikaner nationhood and dominance in all spheres of South African life. This was the Broederbond, which slowly amassed influence and power over the next three decades in what outsiders, including many Afrikaners, came to see as a sinister conspiracy. When Beyers Naudé, a half century after the founding of the Broederbond, broke with it to found an organization called the Christian Institute, his initial idea was that an elite group of idealistic Afrikaner clergymen could gradually change the outlook of their people through mutual consultation in private on the issues they faced. The

Broederbond was quick to condemn the institute, and eventually it was banned. But different as his aims and methods would become, the son's instinct in searching for a way to return his people to the path of righteousness may have been nearer to that of his father at the outset than he or orthodox Afrikaners would have imagined.

So much for symmetry. What is striking about Beyers Naudé's formative years is not the indoctrination he received but his complete insulation from the issues he was later to accept as central to the moral existence of every South African. He has no recollection of hearing his father say anything about blacks. No one told him that blacks were inferior or culturally backward or unfathomably different or destined to play a subservient role. No one explained the reasons for their exclusion from society. All of this went without saying, all of it was there to be absorbed by osmosis. Years later Beyers Naudé discovered that Robert Sobukwe, the university lecturer who founded the Pan-Africanist Congress, was growing up in Graaff Reinet while he was living there in his parents' home. But then Sobukwe, nine years his junior, lived in the dusty African "location," which Naudé cannot remember having visited. "It never entered my mind," he remarked, reflecting on his life up to the age of thirty, "that blacks were to be seen as a part of South Africa."

The issue of race grazed his consciousness for the first time in the form of a small, seemingly negligible question, provoked by the seemingly anomalous presence every Sunday of a handful of elderly coloreds at the rear of his father's church. The elder Naudé, who occasionally preached to a segregated colored congregation, explained that the old coloreds had been members of the white church before the traditional patterns of segregation had been found to be inadequate, before it was deemed necessary, in the interest of preserving the identity of Afrikaners as a white people, to set up an absolute bar to nonwhites' worshiping in the white church. The older coloreds, who had refused to relinquish their membership, were still allowed to sit apart at services, but their deaths would remove the last vestiges of racial laxity and perfect the exclusion of their people. The fact that it had once been a little different would then be conveniently forgotten, so the pattern of absolute separation could be elevated as the traditional way of life. Afrikaners did their duty to coloreds and blacks, the son was taught, by sending them missionaries.

That seemed to settle the business of race as far as he was then concerned. At the University of Stellenbosch, where he excelled in Hendrik Verwoerd's social science course, it never preoccupied him. There came another slight flutter of doubt when he started visiting a German mission station in the Cape called Genadendal after becoming engaged to a daughter of one of the missionaries. There coloreds and whites met in one another's homes on the basis of equality, the first such contacts across the color line he had experienced. Until then it had never occurred to him that this was possible; it was as if he had been reared in a teetotaling sect and had now allowed himself to sip a little wine. He was left with the guilty knowledge that it could be done, that there was a contradiction that probably needed some rationalizing between the kind of Christianity on which he had been reared and the kind practiced by his prospective in-laws, but it was nothing he allowed to burden his conscience.

To do so would have been to throw a shadow over his future, which seemed so tidily arranged. At the age of twenty-five, when he was serving his first congregation, he was approached in private by some of the elders and invited to join the Broederbond. Twenty-five was the minimum age for membership; the founder's son was right on course as one of the elect. The all-male monthly meetings of his "circle," or cell, became the main source of intellectual stimulation and fellowship in his life outside the church; here, too, he felt himself to be engaged in a sacred enterprise. Then, at thirty, he was called to a congregation near Pretoria, which meant moving to the Transvaal from the Cape, where the numerically predominant coloreds had seemed to blend into the landscape. In the Transvaal it was impossible not to notice that there was a huge black community physically present in the white heartland. For the first time, he acknowledged that there was a problem. It was something to think about, he thought—something to think about later.

The year 1948 comes, and Beyers Naudé votes for the National party and feels, when it squeaks into power on its apartheid platform, a deep sense of fulfillment tinged only by a filial regret that his dominee father, who died a few months before the election, had not lived to see this realization of his dreams. In the new government's first year, he becomes a minister in the Pretoria congregation that most of the Cabinet members attend, also a chaplain at Pretoria University, where, because even the most carefully indoctrinated students occasionally ask questions, he senses a need for the first time to have some answers on political issues. These he gets at Broederbond meetings, which in the capital now bring him into contact with key officials. If there is any injustice in the land, he feels confident, it is a reflection of man's sinful nature that can be addressed within the framework of apartheid. The vigor and obvious sincerity of his preaching win him a growing reputation, and he moves, with appropriate deference and decorum for one so young, in social circles that include the most powerful figures in the Afrikaner church and state. He is nearly forty before this picture starts to change significantly. Then, as a result of a half-year tour of Europe and North America as an emissary for the Dutch Reformed Church, he wakes up to the fact that his knowledge of what goes on in his own country is riddled with blanks. In Holland and England, Canada and the United States, churchmen ask him about the Defiance Campaign, which the congress movement has been waging. He has heard of it only vaguely and ignored what he has heard, so it is as remote to him as a report of a clash in Sumatra. Names of black leaders such as Albert Lutuli and Z. K. Matthews are mentioned in his presence; he avoids acknowledging, insofar as he can without actually lying, that he has never heard of them. He is asked what he thought of Alan Paton's *Cry, the Beloved Country,* which has had a secure reputation by then throughout the English-speaking world for five years. He confesses that he has heard of neither the author nor his book.

The trip teaches him a lesson about his own insularity; it also provokes him to undertake a private study of the biblical, theological, and historical justifications his church has advanced for the South African system. "It was a highly intellectual and academic exercise," he told me. "It had nothing to do with any personal experience." Yet the result is devastating. None of the justifications, he has to acknowledge to himself, can be honestly defended. He then widens his reading, allowing himself the forbidden fruit of studies of apartheid by English-speaking writers who frame the issues of inequality and dispossession. Now, in his early forties, he finds himself burdened with an incubus of doubt on his ministerial and social rounds. It is invisible to his congregants, for he confines his preaching to pietistic and evangelical themes. It is even invisible to his wife and children, for he deliberately shields them from it and the problems it would instantly raise for them, should they be similarly infected, in their contacts in the community or at school. Very cautiously he voices some of the questions on his mind to fellow members of the Broederbond, who acknowledge the seriousness of the questions but urge him to be careful not to raise them in the wrong place, at the wrong time. The warning seems superfluous; the thought of voicing his doubts openly has yet to occur to him as a real possibility.

"I was afraid," he said. "I just couldn't face it." Then in a period of five years, which brings him to the age of forty-eight and his first experiences as a pariah, reality rapidly catches up with him. Two kinds of history are occurring, public and personal. As Beyers Naudé seeks to reconcile his secular and religious faiths, apartheid gets steadily harsher and more aggressive ideologically as a result of the ascent to power of his old teacher Verwoerd, and as most Afrikaners learn to march in lockstep, the consequences for those who stumble or break ranks on racial issues become clearer and more severe. At first these conspicuous trends are only a small cloud on his horizon, but then his reputation for integrity and his high position in the church—he has become acting moderator of his synod—make him a sounding board for the private anxieties of three white pastors who have been meeting rising resistance to their missionary efforts in black communities as a result of the sufferings imposed by Afrikanerdom's quasi-theocracy. At this point he makes his first misstep on the slippery slope of Christian action. Had he told his colleagues that he was troubled by their testimony, had he prayed with them or even offered to initiate a study group under some respected professor of theology at an Afrikaner seat of learning, Beyers Naudé would probably have satisfied their expectations and preserved the margin of safety his conscience required. Instead, saying he knows there are problems but cannot imagine that conditions are really so bad, he resolves to do the one thing that a shrewder, more self-protective man would avoid at all costs: to go and see for himself. In middle age, for the first time in his life, he enters black townships and the hostels reserved for migrant laborers. For the first time he allows himself to speak to blacks about what it is like to be black in white South Africa. These are not outspoken political people but the deferential, pathetically moderate elders of Dutch Reformed mission churches. Yet once he knows the circumstances of their lives, the weight of his doubt becomes almost too heavy to bear.

At this point his personal history starts to converge with the history of his times, for he is chosen as one of the representatives from his synod to an ecumenical conference on apartheid that brings the major denominations in South Africa together under the auspices of the

World Council of Churches. Partly as the result of his efforts, the delegation from the Dutch Reformed Church manages to find common ground there on racial issues with the English-speaking churches, but that common ground is a retreat from apartheid and an affirmation that members of all racial groups have an equal right to share the "responsibilities, rewards and privileges" of citizenship. First Verwoerd and then the synods of Naudé's church repudiate the key resolutions. But when the time comes for him to recant, as the other delegates from his synod have done, Beyers Naudé refuses.

He has shown that he is undependable, a potential dissident, but he is not yet ostracized. In fact, he remains the senior minister of the most prestigious Dutch Reformed congregation in Johannesburg for two and one-half years and a member of the Broederbond. He is like a man on the ledge of a building high above a busy thoroughfare deciding whether he should leap, but he does not become an object of horror and pity. The shell of Afrikaner decorum never cracks; he loses his synodical office, of course, but viewed from outside, his life proceeds as if nothing has happened. Individual brethren in the Broederbond take him aside for earnest discussion and entreaty, sometimes couched in idealistic or theological terms and sometimes more frankly menacing. He meets privately with a small group of dominees who are similarly troubled but in his preaching continues to avoid the issues that preoccupy him. Direct speech on social justice would inspire panic, turning instantly into resistance, he believes. His training has made him an instinctive elitist; to move his people, he feels, he must move their church, and to move their church, he must move its leaders. But his discussion group shrinks rather than expands as individual dominees, fearful of being typed as dissidents, swallow their doubts. Beyers Naudé, who still has not been able to face his family on these issues, finds something inside himself that needs to resist the gathering silence. He begins publication of a journal called *Pro Veritate* that addresses itself to the church's role in society and the questions it has evaded and finally gives up his pulpit to found his Christian Institute as an ecumenical movement aimed primarily at influencing the white churches. His own church condemns the institute, before it has had time to do anything, and subsequently proscribes it formally as an heretical organization.

Yet at this point, having overturned his life, he has merely broken ranks. He still has never talked politics with a black nationalist, still knows next to nothing of the history of black politics. In fact, he has not even had English-speaking friends or gone to dinner in a non-Afrikaans home. He has traveled far, but if pressed at this point about his own politics, he still describes himself as a critical Nationalist. Nevertheless, by the age of fifty Beyers Naudé has been condemned as a traitor and almost wholly isolated within Afrikanerdom. In his family his motives and conduct are a source of bewilderment. Two sisters stop speaking to him, one permanently. Suddenly he has to learn to speak to his wife, his three sons, and his young daughter in a new way, not as the patriarch whose judgment on moral issues is final but as an equal trying to explain and persuade. Family love survives because he learns to accept debate, but that means accepting the reality that his elder sons will not follow him politically; only his wife, finally, manages to make that adjustment and go on making it as he blazes a new trail.

In this period, when his journey was still beginning, I encountered Beyers Naudé. It was 1965, and he was on the verge of liberalism. He still believed that initiatives for change would have to come from enlightened whites, that the Afrikaner people would not be able to go on negating the "voice of conscience." If the church moved, the people would follow, he said. Implicitly he was saying that he had managed to adjust his own position after discovering that his understanding of the racial situation was flawed and that other whites in growing numbers would manage to do the same; the churches could be the vehicle for clearing up what was basically a misunderstanding. My recollection is that there was something brittle and withheld in his conversation then, a point beyond which he could not be pressed, as if he recognized the weakness of his premise even as he stated it. He claimed that there were about 120 dominees in the Dutch Reformed Church who were silently sympathetic with his position. Soon it was only their silence, not their sympathy, that he experienced.

But he was now launched and reaching out to black and colored churchmen, and this introduced him to a basic law of South African social dynamics: The more a movement for change seeks the serious involvement of blacks, the less it appeals to whites. It took only a few years for him to hurtle across the political spectrum, moving from critical Nationalist and reluctant dissident to active white supporter of black initiatives. Few black groups were too small and exotic for him to find within them seeds of promise and growth. The former leader of the white synod devoted himself to fostering the independence of its black missionary offspring. Moving farther afield, he prayed with the impoverished members of the despised Zionist and Ethiopian sects that resolutely held themselves apart from the white-led churches. "He was not pretending," a black man who accompanied him to these meetings told me, drawing a comparison between Naudé and other white clerics who had tried to get to know the members of these sects. "You could see this man. He understands what love means."

When Biko and other black students flaunted the banner of Black Consciousness and seemed to be turning their backs on white liberals, the Christian Institute was the one white-led organization that wasn't offended. On the contrary, it rushed to offer organizational support and to introduce this new black leadership to potential financial backers in Western churches. Beyers Naudé, like an explorer on uncharted seas, pressed ahead with a singular combination of earnestness and recklessness; one after another, the institute raised such high-voltage questions as civil disobedience, conscientious objection, boycotts, and economic sanctions. Inevitably, its white membership dwindled, liberal white businessmen stopped writing checks, and the authorities stepped up their pressure, seizing Naudé's passport and declaring the Christian Institute an "affected organization"—in effect, subversive—which meant it could no longer be the conduit for overseas funds for movements of South African resistance.

And still this was not the end of his journey. In 1976 the Christian Institute expressed its support for the aims of the "liberation" movements so long as these did not conflict with the gospel. A month after that, Naudé spent a night in jail for refusing to testify to an official commission that had advised the authorities to act against the Christian Institute on grounds that it promoted black dominance and socialism. Beyers Naudé by then had told an audience at the University of Cape Town that whites should seriously consider black criticism of the capitalist system and ask themselves whether economic justice might not be promoted under some homegrown form of "African socialism." What churchmen describe as his prophetic ministry had now carried him to an unabashedly radical stance, but he expressed himself that day in terms of moral urgency, not political jargon:

> If you truly love your country, then decide now—once and for all
> —what kind of country you wish to give yourself to and then
> commit yourself to see to it that you have a share in the way such

a country is being created and built—even if it eventually has to be built from the ashes of a society which has destroyed itself through its own blindness, its avarice and its fear. For whatever is going to happen in between, one thing I know: A new South Africa is being born—a South Africa in which I wish to live . . . a South Africa in which I wish to give of myself to all the people of our land.

The next year, in the aftermath of Steve Biko's death, it became a criminal offense to print those words: The Christian Institute was banned as an organization, and Naudé was banned as an individual; that meant it was illegal for him to travel in the country, enter black areas, attend meetings, or be quoted in any publication.

And still that was not the end. Despite his restriction, which wasn't lifted until 1984, Beyers Naudé stayed in circulation, still maintaining, it seemed, a wider circle of contacts among black churchmen and activists than any other white in the country. If nothing else, his example demonstrated that it could be done. Younger Afrikaner renegades might never have seen him or heard him—Dominee Eerlik and Frikkie Conradie hadn't—when they broke away, but they were intensely aware that they were walking in his footsteps. And as he went on, he showed them where these led. His political effectiveness was hard to assess and easy to belittle, but there was really no way of calculating how many lives he might have touched. For blacks he remained, Desmond Tutu wrote, "the most resplendent sign of hope in South Africa today." The authorities seemed to endorse this tribute, for they paid Beyers Naudé the unusual homage of declaring him to be, under their security laws, a "listed" as well as a "banned" person. At the age of sixty-eight, he was still regarded as dangerous; had his "listing" remained in force, it would have been illegal to quote his words even if he died. Scarcely a month later a political movement called the United Democratic Front came into existence, resurrecting the slogans and themes of the outlawed African National Congress. The new front named Christiaan Frederick Beyers Naudé as one of its patrons, along with the imprisoned Nelson Mandela.

It was easier to understand why blacks chose to honor Beyers Naudé than it was to see why the security police persisted in regarding him as a threat. Was their need to proscribe him explained simply by the old bitterness over his treason to the Broederbond? Or was there a touch here of ethnic pride, a sense that a little Afrikaner backbone was what the forces of resistance required to become really threatening? He rejected suggestions such as Bishop Tutu's that his personal history might in some sense prove to be prototypical, not just for a few spiritual misfits among Afrikaners but for his people as a whole. This was not Christian humility speaking but hard experience. He had tried to pierce the racial cocoon that the Afrikaner spins for his own protection and had acknowledged, long ago, that he had failed. So why couldn't his voice be heard? Whom would it move? It wasn't as if thousands of black youths were going to follow a near-septuagenarian Afrikaner dominee over the barricades.

This mystery was partly dispelled for me when, toward the end of my stay in South Africa, I finally heard Beyers Naudé preach. I had talked to him many times in his garden but had never actually heard the public voice that had been stilled. Then one afternoon, when I was busy working, I learned that he was due to show up at a vigil on the issue of resettlement in the homelands that was being conducted by the Black Sash, an organization of white women that seeks to serve blacks caught in the coils of apartheid. His name was not on the printed program, but I was told he would deliver what amounted to a sneak sermon, testing the limits of his banning order, as he occasionally did, by challenging the authorities to charge him for preaching on a biblical text in the course of a worship service. I raced to get there in time and found myself listening to the emotional testimony of a white woman who had been shocked by what she had seen and heard on a visit to a "black spot" that was about to be cut out of the "white area" as if it were a malignancy. It was necessary to bring this to the "attention of the public," the good woman said, in a voice that sounded helpless with grief. She meant, of course, the white public, which had resolutely ignored the spectacle of the forced removal of blacks for more than three decades. I looked around the whitewashed chapel in which the vigil was being held. There were fewer than fifty persons, maybe thirty of them whites. There was also a press table, but it emptied before Beyers Naudé rose to speak; he still could not be quoted, so this was, strictly speaking, a nonevent. It was early evening in Johannesburg, and the reporters had deadlines; outside, offices and stores were emptying, sending whites and blacks scurrying to the separate buses that would take them to their separate group areas; escort agencies and restaurants were opening their doors on nearby streets in safe expectation of a better turnout than this. The organizers of the vigil had been recording the talks of all the other speakers, but now, as Naudé covered the short distance from his seat in the front row to the lectern in a few loping strides, his back bent slightly as if he were walking uphill, the tape recorder was switched off.

His text was I Kings 21, the story of Ahab, king of Samaria, who coveted the vineyard of Naboth the Jezreelite. Standing under a simple wooden cross, he read from his Bible only once, near the end of his narrative, which he related with the simplicity and immediacy of a fresh, cleanly told news report: how Ahab offered Naboth the choice of money for his vineyard or a better vineyard somewhere else; how Naboth replied that he couldn't surrender his patrimony; how Ahab then returned to his palace and sulked until his wife, Jezebel, promised to find a way to separate Naboth from his land; and how Jezebel then made illicit use of the royal seals to send an order to the elders of Jezreel so that Naboth would be hauled up on fabricated charges of blasphemy.

There was no straining after comparisons, but in Naudé's telling, Naboth's vineyard became as real an agricultural enterprise as any small holding in the Transvaal, and Naboth emerged as a worthy cultivator whose love of his land was strong enough to overcome the temptation of silver. Jezebel's abuse of authority, her use of the royal seals and suborning of witnesses, was what he stressed. How did the queen, he asked, get Belial's sons to testify falsely against Naboth? "I don't know. It must have been," Naudé said, rubbing his thumb and forefinger together, "something like this." He didn't interrupt his narrative again to comment on the outrage of Naboth's death by stoning or the subsequent seizure of the vineyard; he let the story tell itself. It had probably been many Sundays since he had last preached, and at first, he kept poking the black rim of his eyeglasses up the bridge of his nose with an index finger in what seemed to be a slight gesture of nervousness. But his voice had a bright resonance, which carried through to the one passage that he read, in which the Lord—taking note of the penance of Ahab, who tears his clothes, puts on sackcloth, and goes on a fast—tells Elijah the Tishbite, "I will not bring the evil in his days: but in his son's days will I bring the evil upon his house."

The voice softened when the time came to reflect on the portion's meaning. The words "South Africa" and "resettlement" had yet to be spoken; there was no need to speak them now. There are many parallels in our land, Naudé said, but there are also differences. There it was just a case of Ahab and Jezebel's getting overcome by a greedy wish to own a particular vineyard; here it is a matter of state policy. In the same spare terms in which he had recounted the stoning of Naboth, he now described the agony and weeping of those who lost their land. In his telling, their suffering became a palpable fact, not a remote, subjective experience. As an Afrikaner, he continued, he was painfully aware that his people were largely responsible. How does this happen to a people? He spoke briefly of the power of ideology to stifle reason and compassion and then of a concept of self-interest—which he said Scripture and history both refute—that safety lies in grabbing and keeping.

"Why does God allow it?" he asked, putting the question speculatively, then restating it directly: "Why, God, do you allow it?" Naudé didn't wait for an answer or pretend that he had one already. "I don't know," he said, sounding briskly conversational, "but I know that sooner or later the Supreme Being that we call God ordains there must be justice. Is that day of judgment approaching in our land? I don't know, but we must pray and strive for liberation, and in the meantime, we all have our responsibilities and duties." He then ended by praying for migrant laborers, their families, those who make the policies that control their lives, those who carry them out, those who don't understand, and those who do understand but whose lives are ruled by fear.

It was very nearly a perfect homiletic exercise, I thought. It was also, I imagined, what Christians call a witness. There was nothing in the sermon that could be described as incitement, scarcely anything that could be called political. Its preoccupation was with scriptural themes from start to finish; the sense of urgency had come from Beyers Naudé's exposition and example. "We all have our responsibilities and duties," this Christian had said. I was neither Christian nor South African, but I thought, if I were South African, the experience of hearing that sermon could have changed my life. In what amounted to a moral Rorschach test, he had left it to each of his listeners to supply content to the words "responsibilities" and "duties." Their answers would come from themselves, not him. I could not imagine what this tiny audience, made up largely of middle-aged white women, might be thinking. But in that brief instant, it occurred to me that younger and darker South Africans might come up with an answer that was neither explicit nor implicit in Beyers Naudé's presentation. It occurred to me that they might think of guns.

CHAPTER 11

—
W-Ā-R?

I t is possible to pinpoint an hour in which the Bastille might have been stormed in South Africa and wasn't. That prospect was raised, glimpsed, and extinguished on March 30, 1960, a day that saw the most impressive assertion of disciplined black political will the white regime has had to live through in this century. On that morning, a procession of at least 15,000 and possibly 30,000 blacks, most of them male migrant laborers, marched in ranks down a highway that winds around the lower slopes of Table Mountain in Cape Town, from the nearest of the black townships on a sandy expanse known as the Cape Flats to the basin where employees of the Dutch East India Company gained a toehold in Africa 308 years earlier, now the heart of the city. The route most of the marchers followed took them a little way up the mountain so they could look out to the shimmering expanse of the bay, then plunged them down into the city, bringing the bulk of them to within three blocks of the Parliament Building itself and the offices of the white government. By the time the vanguard got that far, a distance of 8 miles, an air force helicopter was hovering overhead and armored cars with police and army units were massing in the side streets. White troops with fixed bayonets arrayed themselves in front of Parliament, and machine-gun emplacements were established on its grounds. Only nine days earlier but 900 miles away, a confrontation between a crowd of unarmed Africans and nervous white policemen in an obscure black township called Sharpeville had ended with gunfire, the deaths of 68 blacks, and a crisis that, for a long moment, left white power with a giddy feeling that it was rocking on its foundations. No one could calculate the possible repercussions of another Sharpeville at the portal of white power. If it did not amount to the fall of the Bastille, it could hardly have been a lesser moment in the nation's history than the storming of the Winter Palace in 1905 was in prerevolutionary Russia.

Instead, as a result of what might variously be described as the good faith and essential moderation of the marchers or their innocence and gullibility, it proved to be an episode and, over the years, now decades, that followed, a small bone of contention for radical and liberal white academics, who debated whether a "revolutionary moment" might have been squandered that distant morning and, if so, whether white liberals could be held responsible in some way for the apparent failure of will on the part of the black masses. According to the assumptions of this debate, if the masses were not ready to make a bid for power, or if white liberals had little or nothing to do with the course of events, then the march of the black migrants would seem to be diminished in its significance. Even so, the march is generally acknowledged to have represented a turning point, the moment at which black leaders were finally forced to see the inadequacy of nonviolent tactics in the South African context.

Yet the nature of that turning point also remains open to question, for violent tactics have proved to be at least as inadequate, and white power has never been quite as unsure of itself as it was for a few moments at midday on March 30, 1960. I first set foot in South Africa five years after the event, but I came eventually to sense that the particulars of what actually happened that day, of what went right and wrong for blacks and what happened in the minds of white power wielders, contained essential clues to a whole epoch of racial struggle. What first set me thinking about it was a conversation in Cape Town with a young colored woman who described the feeling of awe that gripped her when, as a schoolgirl, she watched from a sidewalk as the marchers made their way into the city. Nothing in their demeanor was menacing; they were not yelling threats or brandishing fists. ("A notable feature of the march," the *Cape Times* reported the next morning, "was the almost complete absence of ill feeling.") Yet to her young eyes the black marchers looked as unthwartable and dangerous as destiny itself. School had been dismissed early on account of the presumed menace that the marchers represented, and she had rushed home. "I had only one more street to cross," she said, "but that was the street the kaffirs were marching down. I was afraid to cross. I stood inside one of the shops and prayed to God that no one would say something that would make them mad. The next morning in school, some of the boys said they hoped the kaffirs burned the whole of Cape Town down, just to show the whites. I told them not to talk like that."

Where did the feelings of inevitability that the marchers obviously felt and inspired come from? And more to the point, where did they go? The answers turn, in part, on the relationship between that huge throng and its leader, who wielded an authority that seemed absolute over thousands who might have been expected to dismiss him as a boy. Philip Kgosana was slighty built, twenty-three years old, and only six years out of primary school. "When I told them to sit down, they sat down," he later testified when summoned as a witness before a white commission of inquiry. "When I told them to stand up, they stood up. When I ordered them to go back quietly, they went back quietly." Every contemporary account agrees that this was the truth. For a period that can be measured in minutes rather than hours, Philip Kgosana appears to have held the fate of his country in his hand as no other black man has before or since. There can be no doubt that if he had ordered the crowd to march the final few blocks to Parliament, it would have marched, whatever the consequences. Was that, I wondered, a possibility he considered at the time? Was it one he had considered retrospectively in all the years that followed?

It took me several months after leaving South Africa at the end of my last tour there to locate Kgosana in exile. One source told me he was in Stockholm; another mentioned Ethiopia. Next I heard he was in Uganda, then Botswana. Eventually someone in Botswana said he appeared to be working for UNICEF. A check with UNICEF revealed that he had been living in Sri Lanka for three years. (He was not the first South African to wind up there. In the Boer War the British set up camps across the Indian Ocean, in what was then the colony of Ceylon, for their Boer prisoners of war.) Finally, one morning, a call came through in London from Philip Kgosana in Colombo. I was not heading for Asia, and he was not due to visit Europe, so we agreed to communicate by mail and phone. I sent a long list of questions; some weeks later I opened my mail box to find a cassette recording with Philip Kgosana's answers in the form of a meditation on the events of March 30, 1960. By then, I calculated, he had passed half his life in exile.

The recording was a poor substitute for meeting him, just as meeting him after all those years would have been a poor substitute for having been on the scene. But listening to the somber, sad cadences of the exile jarred my imagination in ways that yellowing newspaper clippings and meticulously researched historical narratives, even conversations with witnesses, had failed to do. For instance, I had never fully appreciated just how extraordinary the fact of young Kgosana's leadership actually was. Not only was he a youth, but he was practically brand-new to politics; and not only was he new to politics, but he was of the wrong ethnic background for the role he played, if the usual white assumptions about the influence of tribal identity in black politics are to be taken even as half-truths. Of the black men who marched in that column behind him, 98 or 99 percent must have been identified as Xhosas in their passbooks (which, as an essential part of their defiance of white authority, they were *not* carrying that morning)—that is, as members of tribal clans that inhabit the regions where the Xhosa dialects are most widely spoken. But Philip Kgosana, who had come to Cape Town on scholarship to study economics at the university there, hailed from the other end of the country, from a hamlet northeast of Pretoria. If he had to count, Xhosa would have rated as his fifth language, after Sesotho, Setswana, English, and Afrikaans. Yet when he said, "Sit," they sat.

Then there was the matter of his short pants. Practically every onlooker who later recorded his impressions was struck by the fact that the vanguard leader of the roughhewn masculine crowd was dressed like a schoolboy. The explanation in several accounts is that the march had started without its young leader, who rushed out without properly dressing and hitched a ride with an American correspondent to catch up with his supposed followers. Nearly a quarter of a century after the fact, Philip Kgosana, sitting in front of a cassette recorder in Colombo, was sensitive to the implication that he was even momentarily out of step with the masses on what was probably the most important morning of his life. It was true that he had grabbed a ride with a correspondent—the man was from *The Christian Science Monitor,* * he remembered—but if he was not at the front of the column from the start, that was not because he had been caught unawares. The white authorities were on a rampage that morning, rounding up anyone, black or white, who could be regarded as a radical or militant opponent of the regime.

*The name had slipped from Kgosana's memory, but *The Monitor's* correspondent in Cape Town on the day of the march was John Hughes, who more than two decades later, in his capacity as State Department spokesman, was called on to explain the Reagan administration's policy of "constructive engagement" with South Africa. However, Hughes has no recollection of giving the young leader a lift.

Leaders of the movement in which Kgosana had enlisted, the Pan-Africanist Congress, were obviously vulnerable, for it was the PAC that had launched the nationwide protest against the pass laws, producing within five hours the Sharpeville confrontation and the national crisis. The arrests in Cape Town had already left young Philip Kgosana the ranking leader there. His appearance at the head of the march, he said on the cassette, had to be carefully timed. "I was evading arrest and therefore would not present myself openly like that except on a strategic move. I wanted to make sure there was no confusion in case the people hit against the police."

Whatever the reason for his late appearance, his short pants had another, more important meaning, which went part of the way to explaining Philip Kgosana's standing with the migrants who followed him. He had come to the University of Cape Town as a result of an unlikely stroke of luck, bringing little more than the clothes on his back, and those garments had come to him as charity. The son of a poor rural pastor in the Church of Christ, which had been transplanted to South Africa by American missionaries, he was past seventeen when he started high school in a segregated township of Pretoria called Lady Selborne that has since been removed as a blemish on the "white area." It was in Lady Selborne that he became aware of the political currents moving other blacks. In 1956, when 20,000 black women marched on the prime minister's office to present petitions protesting the extension of the pass laws to women, Philip Kgosana was an onlooker. Then a collision with the system concentrated his political will. He thought he would become a pharmacist, only to discover that blacks were barred from that field. Instead of absorbing rejection fatalistically, he carried his grievance to a black patriarch, who could only refer him to an agency of white philanthropy. There his assertiveness and obvious intelligence made such an impression that arrangements were made for him to go to the University of Cape Town, South Africa's Cambridge, on a scholarship. Just before he left Pretoria, Kgosana went to a midnight meeting in an unlit church in Lady Selborne, where he heard Robert Sobukwe, who was then, after a break with the African National Congress, about to launch his as yet unnamed Pan-Africanist movement. "I thought I followed him well and had instant admiration of the man," he said. A year later, when Sobukwe came to Cape Town to lay the groundwork for his campaign, the undergraduate from Pretoria was there to offer his services.

Sitting in Colombo, across the gulf of miles and years, he could still

respond to my question about the short pants by recalling the prove-
nance of virtually every garment he wore on the day of the march. The
jacket had been a gift from the headmaster of his high school, "who
pitied me as I was going down to Cape Town." So were his shoes; he
wore no socks, for he had none, he recalled, in his days at the university.
His sweater and shirt were hand-me-downs from an older Pan-Africanist leader who had left the country to represent the movement abroad.
"There was no magic about the shorts," Kgosana said, "except that
they tell an untold story that at that time I did not have many clothes
to wear."

There was no magic about the shorts, but they point to this student's
extreme indigence, which was as severe as that of the masses he led,
so severe that he had moved into the barracks for migrant laborers in
Langa township when he arrived in Cape Town and even then had no
money for the rent until, with the same gumption that led him to recoil
against exclusion from pharmacy, he scrounged a handout from a
prominent white liberal named Patrick Duncan, the son of a former
governor-general. In Langa, he shared a tiny cubicle with an illiterate
migrant who worked in a canning factory and brought his pals into the
room to drink and sing, mostly drink, while the first-year student was
trying to apply his mind to economic theories, none of which accounted for the conditions of industrial serfdom in which his neighbors
were ensnared. One of the questions on my list was whether he had
moved in with the migrant laborers to organize them. "It was simple
deprivation that took me there," Kgosana replied, "and I had to live
with my people because there was no way out. But as things turned out,
I found myself among my own people and had to lead them when the
critical moment came."

Kgosana's propinquity to the migrants was not only unplanned but
a circumstance that, when he compared his lot to that of white university students, he regarded as a grievance. It does not by itself stand as
a total explanation for the fact that Sobukwe's antipass campaign
touched a nerve in Cape Town, drawing a quicker, deeper response
from the black masses there than any agitation had elicited in South
Africa until then. But it is the beginning of an explanation: A connection had been made. The African National Congress had experimented
with a range of nonviolent tactics over the previous decade, attempting
first to highlight the injustices of apartheid so that white voters would
be moved to change course; then, when that goal was finally recognized

as quixotic, seeking with mixed results to stage protests that would build its organizational strength. Sobukwe, who was still little known when he resolved to use his fledgling organization to engineer a national confrontation with white power, felt there was a force and courage latent in the black masses that the older movement—with its traditional moderation and emphasis on "multiracialism"—feared to tap. The ANC had experimented with nonviolent resistance in the fifties as a way of mobilizing mass support. The authorities replied by banning and jailing its leaders. By 1960, the ANC was in a defensive posture, with neither a strategy nor a hope of achieving immediate results. Sobukwe's reading of the lessons of the fifties was that the ANC had not dared enough. His idea was that Africans would stop carrying passes, present themselves for mass arrests, fill the jails, and deny their labor to the system until the pass laws—their foremost grievance— were abolished. Stop carrying them not merely as a gesture but as the beginning of the end of the system. That, he promised, would be the first step to an early triumph for black nationalism.

It is not clear how widely he was heard, so it is not clear how widely he was discounted or disbelieved. Seasoned organizers in the African National Congress were sure he was overpromising, inviting a fiasco. By and large that has been the verdict of most historians of the period, who, reasonably and inevitably, tend to read their knowledge of the outcome into the flux of the moment. An intellectual, Sobukwe was true to his conviction that a leader should not ask the people to do anything he would not do himself. So he offered himself as the catalyst for the whole campaign in its very first hour when, presenting himself for arrest at the Orlando police station in what is now Soweto, he effectively ended his political career. Nine years were to pass before he was released from detention, and never again, tragically, was he free to speak in public before his death in 1978. The immediate effect of the leader's arrest was that he was not available to adjust his tactics when, just five hours later, the situation was transformed by the shootings at Sharpeville. In itself Sobukwe's arrest appears to have been a catalyst for nothing; it ended as well as began the antipass agitation in Soweto, where the movement had failed to connect with the migrants in the Johannesburg area. Yet what happened in Cape Town went far to justifying his belief that there was a bedrock militancy in the black masses that was only waiting to be mined. Within a week of the start of Sobukwe's campaign, this was sufficiently apparent that Albert

Lutuli, the Methodist lay preacher and future Nobel laureate who was president of the older and more cautious congress, raised the bidding in the confrontation with the apartheid state by publicly incinerating his passbook and urging all blacks to do the same.

Kgosana, the student in secondhand clothes who lived with the migrants, carried Sobukwe's banner in Cape Town, where most Pan-Africanist activists were laborers. For eleven crucial days he was the link between the intellectual who led—then vanished behind bars—and the masses in whom the leader believed. What he managed to convey was a youthful conviction that this was not just another protest but the start of a new South Africa, in which blacks would finally unite to compel change. Every African, he told a mass meeting in Langa the day before the campaign started, had to promise himself that he would never again carry a pass. He called it the crossroads, the Rubicon, and, if that was lost on his audience, "the hour for service, sacrifice, and suffering." About half that speech, his keynote for the campaign, was made up of Sobukwe's final instructions. It was the last time the leader's words could legally be read in public in South Africa, and those words became the basis for Sobukwe's eventual conviction for incitement. Yet what he was inciting to was ABSOLUTE NON-VIOLENCE. The words were capitalized in Sobukwe's text. Allowing the campaign to degenerate into violence would be to alienate the masses by using them as cannon fodder, he said. "After a few days, when we have buried our dead and made moving graveside speeches and our emotions have settled again, the police will round up a few people and the rest will go back to their passes." What Sobukwe promised instead was "a never-ending stream" of nonviolent campaigns until a goal he defined as "independence" had been reached. "We are not leading corpses to a new Africa," he vowed.

Answering the questions I sent him in Colombo about the choices he made on the day of the great march, Philip Kgosana echoed some of the same phrases his younger self had read out in Langa. He spoke about not using the masses for cannon fodder, about moving graveside speeches, about not leading corpses. I looked again at the Langa speech; the explanation for the astonishing denouement of the march, eleven days later, was all there. Interpreting Sobukwe's instructions, Kgosana twice made it explicit that the command of "absolute nonviolence" meant that civil disobedience extended only to not carrying passes and staying away from work; it did not extend to disobeying a lawful order from the authorities to disperse and go home. "Not leading corpses to a new Africa" meant minimizing the opportunities for police violence. So he said, "If a police officer wants us to disperse, we shall disperse." And again, even if the leaders were arrested, he said, "The president's order is that you peacefully disperse without making any noise or interjections. You go home, sit in your houses, and paint the house or dig the garden or even play drafts." Then Cape Town and presumably the nation would remain paralyzed by a general strike of black laborers, which would be called off only when the leaders were released and the pass laws scrapped.

Sobukwe's tactical error wasn't to overestimate the potential militancy of the black masses. Where he went wrong was to underestimate both the weapon of nonviolent resistance and the ruthlessness of the state. He was not, in fact, a Gandhian; he did not believe in forcing the regime to show its violent face to itself and the world, possibly because he knew he had not adequately prepared his followers for what that would mean in South Africa. So he hoped for a miracle and took himself out of action, leaving instructions that were mute on the question of what to do if the authorities failed to follow his script.

Once the campaign was launched, they were shrewd enough to stop making arrests for violations of the pass laws in Cape Town. "Absolute nonviolence" broke down briefly on the first evening, when the police fired on a crowd, killing 2 and triggering a riot. Only on the fourth day did the PAC manage to get 100 of its volunteers arrested, but then, instead of filling the jails, the police released the same 100 in response to the next day's demonstration, at which Kgosana himself was picked up and after the intervention of his liberal friend Patrick Duncan, let go.* It is Duncan's mediating role on that one occasion that has given rise to the debate over whether white liberals deflected a revolution, but that was five days before the great march. On the cassette made in Colombo, Kgosana describes his anger on learning that his white friend had presumed to bargain on behalf of the Pan-Africanist Congress for a declaration that pass-law arrests would remain suspended for a month. "It was interference in a program which had been designed by us," he

---

*Three years later, as a white representative of the black PAC in exile, which had meantime expelled Philip Kgosana, Duncan went to Washington and interested Robert Kennedy in the idea of clandestine American support for a guerrilla effort, to the extent that Kennedy asked him for a memorandum on the movement's planning and requirements. But in 1960 Duncan's concern was to avert further bloodshed.

says, "and in any case we were not aiming at a suspension of the pass laws. We sought total abolition of the pass laws. I told Duncan in that furious mood that he should mind his business. He withdrew immediately and, later on, apologized."

By the morning of March 30th, no one was in jail for pass-law offenses in Cape Town, it seems, but the strike Sobukwe had promised had now paralyzed the port and those industrial sectors that were dependent on black labor. Across the nation the spirit of resistance among blacks still seemed to be on the rise. As was inevitable, the authorities now resolved to strike back. On March 28th a bill was introduced in the white Parliament to give the government arbitrary power to ban both black congresses. At the same time plans were drawn up to proclaim a state of emergency under existing laws, which meant that the police would be able to use preventive detention without reference to the courts or any obligation even to release the names of those detained. In fact, the first wave of mass arrests of black, brown, and white activists had occurred in the early hours of the thirtieth, before the proclamation had been made public. Shortly before daybreak, the police descended on Langa and Nyanga, another of Cape Town's ghettos, in an effort to break the black strike by beating the migrants out of their rooms and onto buses that would carry them back to work. The mass arrests and beatings were the immediate provocation of the great march that morning, which thus occurred on the spur of the moment, in a context that would more properly be described as counterrevolutionary than revolutionary. The commanding officer of Cape Town's police later said that he fell to his knees and prayed when he saw what was coming. Thanks not to his prayers but to the imprisoned Robert Sobukwe and his faithful young disciple Philip Kgosana, and to the deep hopes they had inspired, "absolute nonviolence" was still the order of the day.

PEACE IS
AIM,
NATIVE
SAYS

a headline declared over an interview with Kgosana in the first edition of the *Argus,* which was rolling off the presses as the marchers headed into the city. The interview was a day old, but having reached the head of the column, the young leader was urgently spreading the same message back through the ranks. At first it was assumed that this march would go to police headquarters, the destination of two smaller marches in the preceding week, but Kgosana decided that would be fruitless. "It was my own decision that the march need not go to a police station but we should march to Parliament in order to highlight the seriousness of our concern," he said on the cassette. "There was no point in going to seek for an answer in a place that provided no answer at all." But then he learned that troops were drawn up in front of Parliament, so, acting on his own, he decided to go to police headquarters after all. "I thought it was not wise to force my way to a Parliament surrounded by troops because otherwise an opportunity would have been presented to the racists to shoot, and that was not my purpose," he said, speaking into the recorder in Colombo twenty-four years after the fact. "Sobukwe used to tell us that if he wished us to resort to violence, he would first have to arm us."

Perhaps he could have sent the marchers ahead in small groups in defiance of the police, thus fulfilling his intention of filling the jails. Or perhaps he could have used mass civil disobedience as a weapon of confrontation. But such possibilities had not been discussed within his movement, and even if they had occurred to him on the spot, he would have been assuming a huge responsibility. Instead, remembering Sobukwe's instructions, he found himself negotiating with the same Afrikaner police commander who had released him five days earlier at Patrick Duncan's behest. The twenty-three-year-old black youth in short pants demanded to see the white minister of justice in order to register his protest and make his demands. A journalist who was within earshot recalls that he was told, "The minister is at lunch."

He could then have said, "We'll wait until he can see us." He might even have said, "We'll wait until our leaders are released and the government withdraws the bill to outlaw our party." Such possibilities seem more obvious after a quarter of a century than they must have then. On the spot, Philip Kgosana had to ask himself how long he could maintain his authority over a crowd of 15,000 or 30,000. He also had to wonder what his followers would do and what would happen to them if the police arrested him then and there. And he was obliged to take account of Sobukwe's order "that you peacefully disperse without making any noise or interjections." The Afrikaner commander was promising that Kgosana would see the minister if he sent his people home. He was speaking, the journalist who was within earshot recalls, of a "gentlemen's agreement." Kgosana debated with himself and bargained with the commander for twenty minutes. Cape Town seemed to be holding its breath. Eventually he agreed.

"Mr. Kgosana called for silence and the murmuring of thousands of voices stopped," the *Cape Times* reported the next morning. Then, as he later testified, "When I ordered them to go back quietly, they went back quietly." A police van led the way.

Politically literate South Africans, white and black, ought to know what happened then, but many don't. Only when history is rewritten from a black perspective will the arrest of Philip Kgosana be emphasized. It happened at four forty-five that afternoon, when he returned with four other members of the Pan-Africanist Congress for his appointment with the minister, but the emergency regulations forbade publication of that fact, so as far as his followers and newspaper readers were concerned, he simply vanished. A week later the minister of justice refused to answer when asked in Parliament whether Kgosana had been arrested. But later, when charges of betrayal and bad faith were aired, it was revealed that Kgosana had been briefly visited in his cell by a civil servant who was acting as a surrogate for the minister he had been promised he could meet. Calvinist consciences did not have to be troubled; there had been no betrayal, for he got his meeting and had never been promised, after all, that he would not be arrested. The policeman who made the promise was subsequently reported to have been denied promotion to brigadier for having presumed to negotiate with a black.

The emergency was proclaimed on the afternoon of Kgosana's arrest, and the Unlawful Organizations Act, which would be used shortly to ban the Pan-Africanist and African National congresses, was rushed through its second reading in Parliament. The *Cape Times* reported the next day that the headlights of cars passing the black townships that night "picked up the glint of bayonets at frequent intervals." Within two days Langa and Nyanga townships had been cordoned off by police, army, and even naval units. Water and electricity were cut off, and the troops were sent in to break the strike by force. "It took the police four days of continuous brutality to break the strike," Tom Lodge, a leading scholar on the period, has written. On the eighth day after Kgosana's detention, arrests under the pass laws were resumed in Cape Town. They have continued relentlessly, year after year, ever since. And of course, the Pan-Africanist and African National congresses remain unlawful organizations.

What happened on March 30, 1960, was not that the blacks lost faith in nonviolent resistance. What happened was that the authorities used the full power of the state to stifle any possibility of nonviolent resistance for a generation. Why has the march not been repeated? The simple answer is that the security police have effectively orchestrated black politics, mainly through repression but also through a selective lifting of the throttles and stops, so that the remarkable sense of opportunity and hope that existed on the eleventh day of Sobukwe's antipass campaign has not recurred. Frustration and anger, they have found, are easier to contain than hope. Today the authorities do not wait for a march on the white areas by the black masses to throw a military cordon around a seething township, nor do they negotiate with its leaders before detaining them. Black voices can be heard, but not when they threaten to establish the kind of rapport with a mass following that a twenty-three-year-old student had in that distant autumn of black discontent. South Africa was anything but an open society in March 1960, but it was not yet fully fledged as a police state; the formidable arsenal of arbitrary powers on which the white authorities have since relied was largely assembled in the five years following the crackdown on black politics at the time of the emergency. In March 1960 the white authorities were relying on the cumbersome tactic of entangling the black leadership in complicated legal proceedings and trials; thereafter the emergency powers were incorporated into the structure of criminal law and regularly expanded. In effect, the emergency became permanent, making it possible to lock up political suspects first and worry later, if at all, about framing charges.

The simple answer about why it has not happened again cannot be accepted, however, as the whole answer. There is the fact of repression, and there is the effect that repression has had, which has been to rob black nationalists who try to operate within the system of any legitimacy. For a generation blacks who are serious about politics have been conditioned to think that their real leaders are outside the country, gathering the force that will one day destroy apartheid, or in jail. Today a more sophisticated Afrikaner leadership might like to find black nationalists on whom it could force a deal the way it has managed to extract recognition and ransom from the former black nationalist revolutionaries who govern in neighboring states. But there could be no durable bargain that was not struck with the movements the government outlawed in 1960, in particular, the African National Congress, which may be one of the world's least effective "liberation movements" but, nevertheless, because of its heritage of more than seventy years and its ability to wage "armed struggle"—however desultory and feeble—has kept its grip on black loyalties, on that intangible quality of legitimacy that the Chinese know as the "mandate of heaven." Compromised by its readiness to condone repression anywhere in the Soviet sphere—in exchange for training and arms—it remains the broad, true church of black politics. And the ANC today is revolutionary in a sense it was only accused of being in 1960.

That year, toward the end of a four-year trial of ANC leaders on trumped-up charges of treason, Nelson Mandela envisioned the course of negotiations with the white government on which his movement might embark if its civil disobedience campaigns had the desired effect. Under cross-examination the alleged and future revolutionary dreamed aloud about a process of give-and-take after the government agreed to talk with the real leaders of the people:

> I would say, "Yes, let us talk" and the Government would say, "We think the Europeans at present are not ready for the type of government where there might be domination by non-Europeans. We think we should give you 60 seats, the African population to elect 60 Africans to represent them in Parliament. We will leave the matter over for five years and we will review at the end of five years." In my view, that would be a victory. ... I'd say we should accept it but, of course, I would not abandon the demands for the extension of the universal suffrage to all Africans. That's how I see it, my lords. Then at the end of the five year period we will have discussions and the Government says, "We will give you again 40 more seats," I might say, "That is quite sufficient, let's accept it," and still demand that the franchise would be extended, but for the agreed period we should suspend civil disobedience.

Instead, it was the authorities who suspended civil disobedience; they suspended the African National Congress, too, and Nelson Mandela finally went underground, then slipped out of the country and traveled to Algeria to take a course in revolutionary tactics. He had not been a revolutionary when he was accused of being one, but he did his best, when left with no other choice but submission, to fit the role in which the authorities had cast him. That became the pattern: official heavy-handedness and repression justifying official propaganda and establishing, in the process, a dynamic the logical conclusion of which would be the campaign of unrestrained "terrorism" that the authorities have forecast now for decades.

On August 5, 1962, only sixteen days after his reinfiltration into South Africa, Nelson Mandela was arrested and ultimately convicted of high treason in the second of two trials, then sentenced to life imprisonment. Now having spent more than half his adult life, nearly a quarter of a century, behind bars, he has become the living symbol of his movement and the personification of the bondage of his people, most of whom could never have seen or heard him. Yet, canonized as he has been as a result of his sacrifice, even Nelson Mandela would probably be unable to offer the responses he imagined back in 1960 in the event that today's Afrikaner government attempted to initiate the dialogue he sketched then. Mandela's 1960 dream of compromise sounds like a lesson in civics from another era, not only because of the regime's intransigence but because that intransigence has become a model for its enemies. A gradualist settlement would not be easy to sell to the exiles in Angola, Zambia, and Tanzania who have dedicated their lives to revolutionary struggle, even if it came blessed by Mandela and even if it promised swifter results than their seemingly suicidal assaults on the white bastion. The effect repression has had is to make the revolutionary stance and a revolutionary settlement the only stance and only settlement that most politically active blacks can imagine supporting so that when whites, at this late date, imply a possibility of compromise, it becomes hard for many blacks to imagine what that might mean.

Yet, for better or worse, most politically alert blacks are not revolutionaries. Thus the effect of repression and the political stalemate it has preserved has been to introduce a drastic split in black politics between the acceptable political style and the available means. The fear of seeming to have been co-opted, of compromising with apartheid, nullifies most black political efforts inside the country, making them seem either futile or fraudulent. A rocket attack on an isolated police station or the assassination of a black security cop can be accepted as a valid and authentic expression of the black struggle. But anyone who proposes using the Leninist tactic of infiltrating the state's institutions, such as the segregated local councils or the homelands, in order to destroy them instantly opens himself to the charge of selling out. Only in the new black trade unions is there a chance to build real organizational strength, and even there the most militant leaders have to be ready to fend off the accusation that they are working within the system, as, of course, they must every time they negotiate a contract, confront the police, or contemplate legal action to secure the rights of their members. By contrast, militant movements that vow to have no truck with apartheid in what remains the apartheid state tend to be reduced to debating societies—doomed, it sometimes seems, to re-enact perpetually the tactical and ideological disputes that divided the two congresses in the late 1950's. Or, in another guise, they become commemorative associations that often, in the drastically contracted arena of legal black politics, seem to function like patriotic and veter-ans' groups in more settled societies, ritualistically marking the anniver-saries of heroic efforts of past generations and the deaths of martyrs or organizing the funerals of loyalists to their cause. The perspective is retrospective and elegaic, in consonance with the veneration of ances-tors that has been traditional in the spiritual life of Africa. Here it is a political tradition that is being preserved. It is a matter of keeping faith until the miracle of "liberation."

This is necessary work. In view of the censorship that still puts most of the key texts of black political history beyond the reach of blacks, the cultivation of an oral tradition of resistance involves self-preserva-tion and self-respect. But the retrospective and elegaic slant also in-troduces a mawkish note, turning resistance into ritual in a manner that sometimes appears to demand little of the present generation beyond vigilance against traitors.

The black literary imagination strains to find a believable connection between the contradictory certainties that dominate its horizons, those of ultimate victory and present failure. So it finds the link in themes of betrayal, which help explain why heroic sacrifice is so often futile. In the militant faith there is an ambiguous note of fatalism, necessarily, perhaps because there can be little expectation of early success. The African National Congress, which was founded eight years before the Chinese Communist party, not to mention one year before the Na-tional party that now dominates South Africa, has little to celebrate beyond its survival. A revolutionary movement that finds itself in exile on its seventieth anniversary has to dig deep into its reserves of faith to overcome the pathos that attaches to millennial sects that guess wrong about the Second Coming. "Seventy years!" mused Mamphela Ramphele, Steve Biko's comrade, the last time I visited her clinic in the northern Transvaal. "We should hang our heads in shame rather than celebrate it."

She was not attacking the congress or questioning its standing as the national movement. She was simply pointing out that resistance can become an end in itself, a way of life detached from the objective of halting the suffering and injustice it talks about. She was lamenting a lack of urgency, which she attributed to the remoteness of the black leadership from the poorest blacks. "We have a problem of elitism," she said. Reasons can be sought in sociology and history for the isolation of the black political elites, but they are more easily found, of course, in the white security system and the white-run prisons. The isolation of potential leadership is a constant objective of the state.

The exile leaders stress the need to develop "secure areas" within the townships and homelands so training and organization can take place at the grass roots as well as in bush camps pushed back into Central Africa by the constant threat of retaliation by the South African military. Skillfully adapting tactics the Israelis pioneered in Lebanon, Pretoria sponsored insurgencies against neighboring black states to make border areas unsafe for its own rebels and the cost of backing them prohibitive for black governments, no matter how often and fervently they have sworn opposition to apartheid. But in the few cases where they have been shown to exist at all, the secure areas of which the exiles dream have never been more than a single township house or a dugout in the veld. Rebels can be infiltrated in tiny units of two, three, or five men, but as soon as they link up to an established political network, they run a high risk of stumbling across an informer's trip wire; that risk exists even if they keep to themselves because the resistance movement is also heavily infiltrated on its exile side by black and white agents. "I have them all the way to Moscow!" General Coetzee, the top security cop, boasted to me. The African National Congress, the general said, is crippled by the knowledge that any effort to recruit large numbers of blacks inside South Africa will heighten the risk.

Eventually I had an opportunity to repeat Coetzee's boast to Oliver Tambo, a former law partner in Johannesburg of Nelson Mandela, who became the president of the resistance movement in exile. "He was right! He was right!" Tambo said. "They've been giving us a rough time, making us work very hard. At one time there was a group of ten, and only one of them was genuine. We've developed the technique and method of screening, we've improved it a great deal, but it still means that it's awkward to have large groups because you can't be sure when they just come. Yes, it has given us a lot of work to screen them, and sometimes, when we have done it, at a later stage you discover that they went through the screen; they were that carefully prepared. Sometimes this has happened to people who were highly respected in our ranks, who had behaved very well, were disciplined and sounded very committed and certainly performed all their tasks very satisfactorily. Well, we've learned all that."

This was in the twenty-second year of "armed struggle." Learning all that meant making toughness, discipline, and security cardinal values; it meant unlearning the instinct for openness and trust. For its own preservation the movement is forced to become increasingly wary of outsiders. Organized in the 1950's as a mass movement, it had to reorganize itself in exile as a secret order, and now, it was noticeable, when it took in important black political figures after they had been forced to flee South Africa, it seldom seemed able to do more with them than honor them for their struggles and exploit them on the lecture circuit for their reputations. If Steve Biko had left South Africa and joined the African National Congress, one of his followers speculated, he might never have been heard from again. In an effort to be impenetrable to its adversaries in Pretoria, the movement runs the risk of becoming impenetrable to its supporters.

South African security men tirelessly spread the ancient allegation that the minuscule, antediluvian Communist party, which has dutifully followed Moscow's line on Czechoslovakia, Poland, and Afghanistan, dominates Umkhonto we Sizwe ("Spear of the Nation"), the underground's military arm. I have heard non-Communist sympathizers and members of the African National Congress wonder aloud whether that is true; a former member of the party assured me that it had been from the beginning. If this is so, then the effect for many blacks is not to lower the prestige of Umkhonto we Sizwe but to raise that of the Communist party. The immediate attraction is its supposed extremism —ideology comes later, if at all—because the choice for blacks between "moderate" and "radical," as it is defined by whites in South Africa, is a choice between reaching some accommodation with apartheid and insisting on full citizenship. The official propaganda organs constantly imply that it is only radicals and Communists who refuse to resign themselves to the idea that the Group Areas Act, influx control, and racial hegemony will have to remain part of any reasonable settlement. Young blacks are thus taught that only radicals and Communists are dependable. In a troubled township outside Durban called Lamontville, where they clashed repeatedly with the police during my last months in South Africa, the favorite "freedom song" extolled a white

Communist exile known to the singers only through government propaganda, which portrayed him as the evil genius of the underground's
bombing campaign. "We shall follow our Slovo," the lyric went, referring to Joe Slovo, a former Johannesburg attorney. "Even if we are
detained, even if we are hung."

The song didn't mention following him to victory, only to the gallows. It was a revolutionary dirge. In fact, a high proportion of the
young men who go this route—infiltrating South Africa on sabotage
missions after having been trained as soldiers in the "struggle"—wind
up in the hands of the security police, who squeeze them for information, select those who seem to have potential as double agents, and run
the rest through the constantly grinding mill of political trials. The
testimony in those trials then furnishes a record of the slow, painful
development of a revolutionary culture among young blacks. Here is
Simon Mogoerane, a young man who grew up in a dingy township
called Vosloorus near Boksburg, explaining what it meant to come of
age there to an Afrikaner judge in Pretoria who has just found him
guilty of treason:

> We have hostels in the township where migrant laborers stay,
> people who stay away from their families for a very long time and
> are quite inclined to become a nuisance in the township, commit-
> ting rapes, fights and such things. Another thing is, we stay in very
> small houses and . . . even if one has a girlfriend, he has just
> nowhere to take her to. There is just no comfort in the township
> whatsoever.

Part of his formal plea for mercy, it comes across as the cry of a
frustrated lover and consumer. He is talking about inconvenience and
"comfort" rather than liberty, equality, fraternity. The migrants are
not his abused brothers, or the sons and brothers of the marchers Philip
Kgosana led, but "a nuisance in the township." Very simply, the courtroom spectator infers, he believes that blacks should have what whites
have, that he, specifically, should have it. On this basis a political
consciousness is gradually formed, and when the 1976 disturbances
broke out in Soweto, he now testifies, "I thought at that time that the
war had started and that freedom was near. . . . I thought I had to take
part as an oppressed person."

The Afrikaner judge cannot believe he has heard right. "I'm sorry,"
he intervenes, "did you say you thought the war was near? W-A-R?"

The young man has been testifying in Sesotho, so the question and response have to be filtered through an interpreter. "Yes," he tells the red-robed judge, he meant war. "This was because of the riots."

The judge still doesn't get it. "What war?" he asks.

"What I mean is, immediately the uprisings had started, I thought this was the war which would eventually lead to freedom and I, as one of the oppressed people, also had to take part."

"I was just wondering whether the word war was used." The judge persists. "W-A-R?"

"Yes."

"Can I just get clear? You understand English?"

"Yes, I understand."

"Is the word war the correct word to use?"

"I mean a fight between groups of people. I do not know how one defines a war."

The young man is saying that he wanted to fight for his country. The judge, who conceives of it as *his* country even as he finds the young man guilty of treason, appears to consider the concept ridiculously overblown for a black from Vosloorus. Marcus Motaung, another defendant in the trial, simplifies it when it is his turn to plead in mitigation. "In South Africa," he testifies, "I was so hardened that I decided that all whites should be killed." He then left the country to get military training, but before sending him back to attack a series of police stations, the resistance movement refined his political understanding. "I was taught that the whites and the blacks in South Africa have got to live together. That was the greatest thing I received in the A.N.C. teachings," he tells the court. "Also I learned that the struggle of the black man inside South Africa is internationally supported." His lawyer then asks what he conceived his role to be when he returned to his country. "I took myself to be a soldier, a freedom fighter," he says.

The judge took him to be a criminal. On the day of sentencing, the courtroom was crowded, as it always is in political cases in which the maximum sentence may be applied, with security policemen in plain clothes and white secretaries from the offices of the prosecutor, their faces shining with piety and triumph, horror, and even a little pity. On June 9, 1983, Simon Mogoerane and Marcus Motaung both were hanged, H-A-N-G-E-D, in Pretoria along with a third member of the African National Congress named Jerry Mosoloi. In explaining its reasons for lengthening the roll of black martyrs, the government noted that four policemen, all blacks, had been killed in the raids in which they took part.

"We take them as mere militants," an ANC official in Lusaka later explained, "and we turn them into revolutionaries." The "mere militants" come out with a political consciousness that has been shaped on the wheel of apartheid; in many cases, of which Marcus Motaung's was one, this amounts to nothing more theoretical than an urge to reclaim the land by killing whites. Later, when they make their way back to South Africa as "revolutionaries," accepting risks that are at least as awesome as those most battlefield soldiers experience, they presumably carry a proper ideological fix on their place in the "struggle" and the place of their struggle among all the struggles in a suffering world. But then, the facts of these cases indicate, they often wind up killing blacks —informers, policemen, but also bystanders—or risking their lives to put bombs in empty government buildings, or missing their assigned targets altogether as a result of being betrayed by comrades who broke under interrogation or turned out to have been agents. The ones who come to trial, it must be acknowledged, are only those who get caught, but the level of mishap and misadventure seems grotesquely high. In the first ANC trial I went to in Pretoria, two of the accused had been arrested at a secret rendezvous with an underground contact who led sixty policemen to the meeting. Two others, having been instructed to make their way back to Mozambique if anything went wrong, abandoned their unfired rockets in the veld after the first misfired in an attack on a gasoline depot, then were caught stealing a car. The final two, including one supposedly given advanced training in East Germany, drank too much, had their Russian-made weapon stolen, and, in a desperate effort to recover it, announced that they were on an important mission for the underground.

In the next ANC trial I attended, a young man who had apparently broken under interrogation took the stand to repeat the testimony he had given to the police. Presumably he had received very specific descriptions of the consequences if, under cross-examination, he gave some hint of what had induced him to give his comrades away, so now, sparring with a barrister from Johannesburg, the youth felt he had to try to deny that there was anything strange or contradictory about his having decided first to flee the country to fight for his people and his readiness, afterward, to testify for the state. Beginning his probe for the motivation behind the young man's testimony, the lawyer asked whether he had resented having to carry a pass. "I did not have any attitude to that," the witness said. Was he aware that the standard of education for blacks was inferior to that for whites? "I did not know anything about that" came the response. Was he aware that in South Africa and the world there were many people critical of apartheid? "No, I never read about that in the newspapers." Had he ever discussed it with a friend? "Never." Then, since he enjoyed such innocence, what on earth had motivated him to leave his family and friends and flee the country, undergo military training, and return on an immensely dangerous mission? "I belonged to an orchestra," the young man replied, "and I wanted to play for a nonracial audience." Was that the only reason? "Yes," he persisted, "because I did not know about the other things."

But then why, having undergone training, did he put aside his loyalty to the ANC and divulge to the police the details of his mission? "Well," he said, "you see, in fact, I am not a person who is used to telling lies. I just decided to tell them the truth, which is what I did."

"And how long did this interrogation last?"

"Weeks."

"And why did it have to take weeks to describe what had taken place?"

"Well, I do not know what the reason is. I am not a policeman."

By this time, of course, every black and white in the courtroom thought he knew the reason. The blacks, it usually seemed, reacted with more pity than contempt for those who let down their cause under heavy pressure; with the whites, or so I guessed, it was normally the other way around. But why, after so many years of preparing, theorizing, plotting, and training, were so many young men sent into the country on underground missions found to be so woefully ill-prepared for the dangers they would confront? I could only speculate because the exile movement's suspicion of outsiders prevented any conversations with its young fighters, even after Oliver Tambo had promised that I could meet some. For three days I sat in a small hotel room in Lusaka, where I was visited periodically by a middle-aged middle-level official who wanted to know what it was, exactly, that I hoped to learn. I said that after three years in South Africa, I thought I knew something about their history and the justice of their cause, that I wasn't so much interested in hearing their arguments again as in learning about their experience, what exile and struggle had come to mean. I was after a feeling, not information, a sense of the layered realities of hope and despair. But what, after all, could my sense of their realities have to do with their precious "liberation"? And how do you explain such a cock-amamy need to an organization man who is supposed to be eating, drinking, and breathing the revolution? I didn't do it well.

The official would look dubious but say he understood; then he would advise me to wait in my room for a call. When the call didn't come, I would phone him and he would re-appear, after some hours, to ask all over again what it was that I really wanted to know. Finally he brought a colleague, who sat knee to knee with me and fed me a party line, explaining in the voice of a bored catechist what Winnie Mandela must really have meant to say the last time I saw her when she said something that plainly deviated from his line, until we were each so thoroughly bored and mistrustful of the other that I agreed to do the only thing I could possibly do to afford him some gratification, which was to say I had finished rapping at their door and planned to leave Lusaka.

So I was left with my own intuitions, reflections, and questions. The blacks were obviously outclassed in technology and firepower; they were also, it seemed, insufficiently ruthless. Why? The reason was certainly not racial, nor was it cultural, I thought; it was inherent in the situation. I do not believe that whites are really meaner or smarter than blacks, but starting from a base of power enables them to imagine that they are. An army or police unit patrolling the standard infiltration routes in the eastern Transvaal has radio contact with a headquarters or camp; if it stumbles on trouble, it knows it can summon helicopters or armored troop carriers or even, if the trouble is bigger than anything seen so far, Mirage jets. A few insurgents trying to swim like Mao's fish in the boundless sea of black South Africa have only their wits and the camouflage of their skins; if they stumble on trouble, they are on their own. By the time they have drawn close to their target, they have probably had to evade several roadblocks; now several hundred miles distant from their base, they know that the way back is likely to be as hazardous as the way forward. These "freedom fighters" may be trained as soldiers, but they are called on to perform as saboteurs and espionage agents; they are not marching in formation, striding forward in the footsteps of the man in front, except perhaps metaphorically. They must make their lonely way. The worst thing they can do is to succumb to the temptation to seek out sympathizers or friends, because then the fact of their return can become known to the police, compromising their mission, if it hasn't already been flashed to Pretoria through the informer networks. In fact, their friends and loved ones are likely to be under surveillance already.

So they are home, among their own people for the first time in four or five years, hearing their own language but knowing they will be at risk every time they use it. Maybe they notice that the standard of living has improved, that it is much higher than what they have seen in the Angolan bush or the various African market towns and capitals through which they have been whisked. Suddenly the townships look inviting: If only they could call a halt. . . . The "freedom fighter" needs a very firm idea of the freedom for which he is fighting when these contrasts and emotions well up; an even stronger idea if something goes wrong and he finds himself in an interrogation room, where, before he is maltreated, he may be invited with every appearance of politeness and even sympathy to consider why he has been required to run such terrible risks. Isn't he being used, it may be suggested, as cannon fodder, sent out to leave a bomb whose only purpose is not to undermine white power—he can see for himself, he will be told, how far removed he is from being able to do that—but to advertise the presence of the banned organization? He will be told that his life is cheap to the white Communists who manipulate his movement. Maybe his experience, training, and convictions will enable him to withstand the wheedling and insinuations of the interrogators, in which case he is probably in for worse. Maybe, in isolation and fear, he is now thoroughly disoriented.

Slowly, painstakingly, the movement attempts to build an internal network that could be capable of providing some cover to at least some of its operatives; and it waits for opportunities, for the kind of luck that a world war represented for Lenin, or a Japanese invasion for Mao, or the collapse of a regime in Lisbon represented to the insurgents in Mozambique, Angola, and, eventually, Zimbabwe. What that could be in the context of South Africa no one seems to know. The smart guys in the Western think tanks seem sure it doesn't exist. Guerrillas can never be more than a "serious nuisance" in South Africa, according to Lewis Gann and Peter Duignan, two unsentimental analysts from the Hoover Institution at Stanford. It is "military fantasy" and a "political fable" to imagine that the regime can be brought down by the forces of resistance. Its police and army are not subject to "revolutionary infiltration." White control will last, apparently indefinitely. The regime's opponents live in a "dream world." Of course they do. Perhaps if they resided in Palo Alto rather than Soweto or Ciskei or Lusaka, they would come to a reasonable appreciation of their own impotence and put their faith in the white "moderates" in Pretoria as these foreign, white analysts do.

Yet even if the experts at the Hoover Institution could demonstrate scientifically that it is hopeless, the struggle would not terminate itself. And the old debates about whose revolution it really is and what it is fighting for would still go on. Strangely, despite censorship, prohibitions on meetings, and close police surveillance, these debates are carried on more vigorously inside South Africa than in exile. Nearly a quarter of a century of exile has failed to produce a South African *What Is to Be Done?* or *The Wretched of the Earth.* If the African National Congress has had a fresh thought about the social order for which it is fighting since the Freedom Charter or Nelson Mandela's splendid final statement* before the judge who sentenced him to life imprisonment, it has studiously kept it to itself. It thus demonstates its maturity and prudence, one of its supporters retorted when I ventured this criticism, because it has kept its focus on the struggle to end apartheid and avoided the pitfalls of ideological sectarianism or utopianism.

The movement's black nationalist rivals, which have failed so far to pose any kind of insurgent threat to the regime, charge that this evasiveness masks an unholy yearning for accommodation with white power. Meanwhile, the major theoretical contribution of the Pan-Africanist Congress, in an exile phase marked conspicuously by schisms, intrigue, and internecine murder, has been the suggestion of a new name for the country to replace the geographical designation by which it has been known throughout this century. Azania is a historical and cultural misnomer, but now that it has been chiseled into Steve Biko's tombstone, it has taken on an undeniable authenticity for a generation of South African blacks. Neither Xhosa nor Zulu, Sotho nor Tswana, the term in its origins is a Hellenized version of an Arabic designation for East Africa. There is no evidence that it was ever applied to South Africa before the early 1960's, when an exile member

*"I have always regarded myself, in the first place, as an African patriot," Mandela said. "I have fought against white domination, and I have fought against black domination. I have cherished the ideal of a democratic and free society."

of the Pan-Africanist Congress, which was then casting around for a new name that could be used to forge a sense of national identity among blacks, was inspired to write from Algiers to Evelyn Waugh in Somerset to inquire where he got the name he used for the African kingdom in his novel *Black Mischief.* If Waugh had known, as he presumably did not, that he was assisting in the christening of a post-revolutionary black-ruled South Africa, he would have recognized an irony equal to any he had imagined for his Azania. But Waugh did write back. With only a touch of his customary churlishness, he replied, "As you should know, it is the name of an ancient East African kingdom."*

It is unclear whether it was because or in spite of that response, but henceforth, for the Pan-Africanist Congress and many other black South Africans, the promised land became Azania. Shortly before I left the country, the political grouping that traces its lineage to Sobukwe and Biko attempted to articulate its vision of an Azanian People's Republic in which "racial capitalism" would be replaced by "worker control of the means of production, distribution and exchange." I suggested to one of the theorists who had been involved in shaping this vision that the dubious origins of the name might be a handicap. Did it really matter that America was named after Amerigo Vespucci? he asked. Where did the name Argentina come from? Who cared why Brazil was Brazil? The etymology of a national name was less important, he argued, than the meaning that was given to it by its inhabitants. South Africa was a perfectly neutral name initially, but now it had acquired a meaning that was poisonous, so obviously there was a need for a new name in order to advance a new vision; the formation of a national consciousness was an essential part of the liberation of the land. Liberation couldn't be allowed to mean merely the integration of the brown and black middle classes into the white oligarchy. It wouldn't come and shouldn't come, he insisted, until it represented the hopes of the black masses. And if it was to do that, it had to junk all the old racial and ethnic appellations that the whites used to divide and rule—all, that is, except those of black and white. A struggle in the name of the black working classes could not enlist supposedly well-intentioned whites because, as I heard one speaker at a Cape Town rally

*The exchange with Waugh, reported by Patrick Duncan in a letter to a friend, is recounted in C. J. Driver's biography of Duncan.

argue, the best of these were merely "the most far-seeing agents of apartheid capitalism."

In other words, whites need not apply to become Azanians until after the revolution. It was the old debate of the 1940's, as replayed in the 1950's, as replayed in the 1970's (having been largely suppressed in the 1960's), and it seemed to have no greater appeal now to the black working classes in whose name the fight was being waged than it had in the past. The evasiveness of the African National Congress on basic questions, such as whether more than one party would be able to operate legitimately in the democracy it promised, sometimes seemed to me ominous; other times I thought it enfeebling. But every land mine and bomb the movement placed was effective as an argument against those who only talked of the struggle against apartheid, belittling it as a preliminary and relatively insignificant phase of some grander revolution that would somehow achieve for a socialist Azania everything that revolutions in the name of socialism had failed to provide in other lands. On one of my last evenings in Cape Town, I sat with three brown-skinned friends who were debating the questions of what the struggle was really about and whose struggle it really was; rather, two of my friends were debating, while the third, a well-to-do businessman who was our host, bestowed benign, noncommittal smiles on each of them. "*You* want to get rid of apartheid and exploitation," said the one who was skeptical of the need for an ideological purification of the movement. "*He* only wants to get rid of apartheid," the speaker continued, pointing to the businessman, who kept his smile. "So, naturally," he concluded with pointed sarcasm, "*you* can't have anything to do with *him.*"

The truth, it seemed to me, was that most blacks were ready to embrace any movement or ideology that promised results. At any given moment the movement that dared most, sacrificed most, and compromised least was the one that had the strongest claim to legitimacy in their eyes. Most blacks were able to applaud both sides of the argument about whether whites might belong to their revolution—that is, they believed with the Freedom Charter that "South Africa belongs to all who live in it, black and white," and they believed with Sobukwe and Biko that the struggle was for the restoration of African land to a self-reliant African people. Every June 16th in Regina Mundi, the largest church in Soweto, they managed at the commemorative service held to mark the first deaths in the 1976 troubles to use the slogans of the rival factions interchangeably and to cheer successive speakers who contradicted one another on these issues. The young blacks who identified themselves with the Black Consciousness Movement in the 1970's seemed to experience no contradiction when they joined the African National Congress in exile, even though this meant stepping across an ideological line. Beyond the debates there was a tradition of free-floating resistance that the rival political elites succeeded in mobilizing, it seemed, about once in a generation.

In between, the debate over revolutionary tactics, values, and participation was occasionally settled with fists and clubs.* At a segregated medical college in Natal, a follower of the Black Consciousness tendency was kicked and battered by other young blacks until he agreed to repeat a five-word invocation: "Nelson Mandela is my leader." Aggrey Klaaste, a black columnist who could be sharply independent on political issues without ever falling into the trap of sounding "moderate" to whites, wrote of the incident in a mood of despair. "It is going to be a long haul," he concluded, "and there are some among us who even have the dare to say that come Uhuru, we will be on the first planes out of Azania!"

As night was falling, I took a stroll on the piebald grassy expanse that stretched along the seafront near my Colombo hotel. When I returned, Philip Kgosana was just parking his Datsun. It wasn't hard to recognize him: An African in Colombo is nearly as rare as a Sri Lankan in Pretoria, and besides, the broad, slightly fretted features of the middle-aged international civil servant retained some of the glow of the young firebrand that shone even in fading Wirephotos, now nearly a quarter of a century old. My first reporting assignment after South Africa had carried me to India. Colombo, which I had given up any thought of visiting while Kgosana lived there, was then, all of a sudden, too close to bypass.

He drove me to one of the newest tourist hotels on the seafront, where we settled into a corner of a cocktail lounge that was otherwise populated by American and French tourists. Feeling my way conversationally, I checked out small random points that hadn't been clear to me when I listened to the cassette with his narration of the events of

---

*More recently, fire bombs. The involvement of police provocateurs is always a possibility in these conflicts, but Pretoria cannot claim all the credit for black dissension.

March 1960. The headmaster who gave him the jacket was black, not white as I had assumed. (These days, he had heard, the man was lecturing at a homeland university.) On the night before the great march, Kgosana had stayed in a house in the township, not in his room in the hostel; that, finally, was the explanation for the short pants—there hadn't been time to run back for trousers.

The voice that furnished these responses was lighter, younger-seeming than the heavy, meditative voice on the cassette, still ardent for the lost land but not adjusted in pitch for history's echo chambers. I wanted narrative, and he let me have it, first in conversation and then, at the end of a long evening, in the form of a 111-page autobiography he had written several years earlier. Usually, he said, he avoided conversations about South Africa. The people he met, in Africa as well as Asia, seldom had any sense of his life or the rigidity of the situation there. Implicitly or explicitly their uninformed conversation usually carried the questions "Why don't you resist? Why do you stand for it?" Trying to make them see that "we did" or "we don't" meant picking at old wounds for what then, more often than not, came to seem a futile performance: The audience was not really engaged. But I wouldn't require those explanations, he said; besides, I brought a relatively fresh sense of the place. Maybe I could tell him what to make of the recent changes. Would they make any difference? Did I see any hope?

He had written his autobiography for his children when they were old enough to startle him by asking the same questions that strangers and foreigners asked. In a real sense, of course, they were foreigners themselves, for they had been born and entirely reared in exile, never once setting foot in the land he claimed for them. "Can it be," he said, recounting his reaction, "that we have never explained to our children the situation in South Africa or why we're here?" So he wrote about Sobukwe and the march into Cape Town and his own arrest that afternoon, which he said he had anticipated. About how, nine months later, he was let out on bail by an Afrikaner prosecutor who had seemed not unfriendly, perhaps sensing in Philip Kgosana strengths he would have admired in a young white and not quite repressing his wonder at this discovery. And then how he was persuaded by his older brother that it wasn't his duty to go back to jail for eventual cold storage on Robben Island, that he should cross the border while he could. Once in Swaziland, then still a British protectorate, the young Pan-Africanist sent a telegram to Julius Nyerere in what was still Tanganyika, asking for help to enable him to go farther. Philip Kgosana simply assumed his name would count for something in Dar-es-Salaam, and it did.

His extraction from southern Africa was a celluloid adventure story in itself, with narrow escapes, car chases, even a love angle. Nyerere's lieutenants arranged to send a plane to pick him up, but the charter pilots advised they would have an easier time landing in Basutoland, later Lesotho, so arrangements had to be made for him to be airlifted back across South Africa into that landlocked state. Then, just as the plane from Dar was finally due, Basutoland was suddenly aswarm with South African agents hunting the fugitive. Kgosana, hidden in a house near the one landing strip, could see Nyerere's charter plane circle and land, but he could also see a security cop he recognized from Cape Town parked on the runway. That night he was spirited back into South Africa by friends and driven at breakneck speed through the Orange Free State and Transvaal to Bechuanaland, now Botswana, where he finally made his connection with Nyerere's pilot. Although he missed the plane in Basutoland, that still proved to be the most important station on his roundabout dash into exile, for in the house where he was hiding he met a slender student nurse named Alice Moruri with a radiant, unforgettable smile, who, a full six years later, followed him all the way to the Horn of Africa to become his wife.

Nyerere saw him his first evening in Dar-es-Salaam. Then Kwame Nkrumah received and lectured him in Accra. Kgosana's celebrity ruffled the exile leadership of the Pan-Africanist Congress, and there was a falling-out. Subsequently, having been flown to Ethiopia as a state guest, he was ushered into the presence of the King of Kings, Elect of God, His Most Puissant Majesty Haile Selassie, who mumbled an edict to his attentive minister of the pen, which led to Kgosana's being enrolled in the Ethiopian military academy at Harar, in a class of future officers who would figure prominently—some of them perishing—in the revolution. Graduated after three years with a paracommando's wings, he offered his services to an exile leader of the Pan-Africanist Congress, who agreed it was time for Kgosana's estrangement to end but then left the movement's former hero waiting in Addis for a summons that never came. "They couldn't welcome the size of fellow I had become, someone with notions of his own," he said, in a tone that sounded ruminative rather than boastful. So, promised a job as a training officer by Holden Roberto, the leader of one of Angola's three rebel movements, he next moved with his new family to Lubumbashi in Zaire.

In effect, he became a black mercenary. I asked if he thought that by joining Roberto he was contributing to a revolutionary upsurge in southern Africa. No, he said, the attraction was not so theoretical. He just wanted the experience of military command because that was something a black man in his country could never have. "It was curiosity," he said. "I sometimes say to myself that if I had six hundred different lives, I would do six hundred different things. Do them all because they were all denied me." But Roberto's army, which Kgosana joined at a bush camp near Kolwezi, proved to be a half-starved, disorganized rabble. This was not his cause, and Zaire was definitely not his country. The young Pan-Africanist, who had once embraced Nkrumah's vision of a United States of Africa, wanted out within half a year.

Resuming his exile's odyssey, he then moved unwittingly into an even more sinister heart of darkness. He had completed his undergraduate studies in economics and statistics in Addis Ababa; now he thought he would pursue public administration at the university in Kampala. So he arrived in Uganda shortly after Idi Amin's coup, in time to live through the entire nine-year terror, which pulverized what remained of the Pan-Africanist dream. There were Ugandan friends dragged into cars in broad daylight, never to be seen again; terrifying encounters with terrified soldiers at army roadblocks; gunfire outside his house at night, and his youngest son, Uganda-born Motlotlegi, drawing pictures at the age of five that showed gunmen blazing away at the windows of his parents' bedroom. The nightmare to which his white countrymen clung as a justification for their system and their lives— as if Amin, the black psychotic, had been sent to them as a divine sign —furnished the context of his daily existence. He knew more about it than any living South African, and in his mind it justified nothing. He still wanted to be free in his land.

At the end of the terrible decade that had started for him in Zaire and ended in Uganda, Philip Kgosana was acting head of whatever remained of the UNICEF operation in Kampala, an international civil servant entitled to "home leave." This took him back to Botswana and Swaziland, where his aged parents, closely monitored all these years by the South African security police, could be brought to meet him, the wife they had seen only once and the grandchildren they had never met. So it happened that in a Swazi resort area known as Happy Valley, he found himself soaking one afternoon in a hot mineral spring with two white undergraduates from Pretoria University who were speaking Afrikaans. He had not used the language for two decades, but he could still follow it. Introducing himself as a Kenyan, he asked them in English what they were speaking. Then, having struck up a conversation, he baited them with assumed innocence, asking how they could allow themselves to soak with him in a hot pool but insist on living apart from their countrymen, how they could justify their system and how long they thought it could last. The young Afrikaners, he was amazed to discover, were only too eager to unburden themselves to a Kenyan. "Don't you think it oppresses us, too?" one of them asked. Kgosana still refrained from introducing himself properly, but he was moved.

On my last evening in Colombo, I sat with Philip and Alice Kgosana on their veranda, looking out on their garden, which was graced by a spreading frangipani tree. Inside, Motlotlegi, now eleven, was taking a recorder lesson. As a tropical port, I remarked, Colombo with its lineup of new luxury hotels was slightly reminiscent of Durban. They didn't know, the two exiles said sadly; they had never seen Durban. Philip had a music lesson following Motlotlegi on a Japanese-made electronic keyboard instrument. Then we all moved inside, talking about present-day South Africa and whether they would ever be able to go home. I speculated that the authorities would be only too glad to welcome them back, especially if they could be persuaded to fit themselves into a square on the tribal checkerboard as Lebowans or Bophuthatswanans. I then described the showcase homeland capitals, where those who made this compromise lived on their own little islands of privilege. I spoke about their servants and cars, their rationalizations and frustrated anger. Philip Kgosana shook his head from side to side, seeming to acknowledge, in that instant, that from the vantage point of his twenty-three-year exile he could see the temptation as well as the deceit. Alice Kgosana's reaction was less complicated, mixed only in the sense that it mixed anger and disgust. "It's not their things we want," she said, her eyes blazing with feeling, "it's our freedom. They can never understand that. Oh, no, they can't. Living their life, that's not freedom. They don't know what freedom means."

Disillusioned by exile politics and Africa as well, Philip had ceased to believe that this freedom could be brought to South Africa from outside. It would have to have its own spontaneous growth there, he now said. Being outside himself, he could only watch and wait. At forty-seven, he sometimes had a thought that would have been unthinkable ten or twenty years earlier—that he might have to wait for the rest of his days.

When the conversation came around to this point, I asked one last time whether he had ever regretted his decision on March 30, 1960, to divert the Langa marchers from Parliament. "They would mow you down," he said, reliving that moment again, which meant acknowledging the fact of white power, then and now. "And they would walk on your blood. And the world would scream, it would scream its protests. And then Verwoerd would emerge with bullets in his head, and he would say, 'This is survival. We are fighting for our survival.'"

CHAPTER 12

■

PROLOGUE TO AZANIA

So we switch lights off in order
to knock over a stool.
All talk about the future
is the same old man's drool.
       —Joseph Brodsky

It is just barely possible that the gold-bearing reefs of the Witwatersrand will be mined out and exhausted in their subterranean depths before South Africa finally runs out of solutions on paper, designed exclusively by whites in order to get around, meet halfway, or vent off black demands. Inventing intricate, incomprehensible constitutional models and reinventing the map of South Africa in order to preserve most whites from the ignominy and presumed menace of equal citizenship with blacks are industrial operations in their own right, with their own rules of supply and demand. After a spasm of black resistance, culminating in acts of official gruesomeness such as the shooting of nonviolent protesters at Sharpeville in 1960 or of students in Soweto in 1976, the output of blueprints and maps suddenly soars. For a little while significant elements in the white power elite seem to be steeling themselves to address the central issue of black political rights. But then, like a high-board diver who suddenly loses his nerve, they substitute a simple jackknife for the triple back somersault that would require. Not now but later, they say; maybe in another generation. It is what they have been saying since 1908, when imperial Britain allowed its four South African colonies—the Cape, Natal, the Transvaal, and the Orange Free State—to design a constitution limiting membership in a new national parliament to persons of "European descent" and excluding even educated Africans from the vote in every province but the Cape. "I sympathize entirely with the Native races of South Africa," Jan Christiaan Smuts claimed in 1906, "but I don't believe in politics for them." Smuts was several generations ahead of his fellow "Afrikanders," as he was still calling them, for at least he acknowledged that there was a problem.

"Perhaps at bottom," he went on, clearing his lungs with a meta-physical sigh, "I do not believe in politics at all as a means for the attainment of the highest ends." Seen in a cosmic perspective, the question was really quite trivial; the trouble was, Smuts knew, it would not go away. "When I consider the future of the Natives in South Africa, I must say that I look into shadows and darkness," he admitted, "and then I feel inclined to shift the intolerable burden of solving that sphinx problem to the ampler shoulders and stronger brains of the future."

And that is where it remains. Here again we find that Jan Smuts has returned, more than thirty years after his rejection by white voters and his death, as the presiding, though unacknowledged, genius of an epoch that is presumably, but by no means surely, the last for white South Africa as a ruling caste. No one claims him, no one thinks about him. It is a position he gains by default. There is a vague awareness that his posturings as a philosopher and international statesman have not worn well. But those posturings provide clues to the present, for they repre-sent a willful obtuseness and indifference to contradiction, which is what white South Africa is left with now that it has backed off from the absolutist racial ideology of Verwoerd. Smuts tried neither to justify the racial order nor to reform it in any fundamental way. Instead, he offered a combination of finesse and force and a tremendous show of his own high-mindedness, as if he could demonstrate how to surmount the problem of racial conflict by placing himself above it.

The "sphinx problem" was too difficult, so he set out instead to solve the mystery of human existence and the problems of the world. The custodian of a decadent social order based on segregation, he wrote a treatise called *Holism and Evolution* that presumed to reveal that integration and synthesis, what he termed holistic assimilation, com-posed the basic force that shapes the physical and moral order of the universe, including all human history, culture, and society as well as their apotheosis in personality. His tract, written six years after he had lobbied Woodrow Wilson at Versailles, elevated "self-determination" from a principle for the new world order to a principle for the cosmos. "Free holistic self-determination" promised the "ever-widening reign of freedom." South Africa, along with the rest of the universe, was presumably tending toward the formation of "more composite holistic groups," but Smuts was preoccupied with bigger questions than that of South Africa and never got around to explaining how the cosmic laws he had revealed might apply to his own country. Between world wars he managed to establish himself as the Pericles of the British Commonwealth, a visionary who foresaw the holistic evolution of a new world order. The elfin field marshal with his snowy vandyke and steely blue eyes parlayed his role in the Commonwealth into a position of eminence among the Allies when the world order collapsed, turning up with Winston Churchill at Cairo in 1942 and then at San Francisco in 1945 for the founding of the United Nations. Amazingly it was this white South African, unmindful of the platform he was providing to enemies of his regime, who wrote the concept of "fundamental human rights" into the Preamble to the UN Charter. When, finally, he was rejected by his own people because he had no vision of their future, holistic or otherwise, his long life and many works seemed to add up to a mock-heroic evasion, punctuated by acts of repression.

Yet history has not passed him by. South African whites have worked their way back to 1948, the year they spurned Smuts for apartheid. Once again coloreds have the vote, and there is talk of compensating blacks for being excluded from the franchise by allowing them to elect a toothless national council, an exercise in diversionary tactics that Smuts promoted nearly half a century ago. He did not assert the principle of white supremacy; he merely practiced it. He was serving "civilization," epitomized by himself, and believed it was in everyone's interest that he should continue to do so. Smuts played down the old Afrikaans-English antagonism among whites; justified white rule on grounds that it was necessary for economic development, which in turn was necessary so blacks could progress; allied himself with business interests, even when that meant antagonizing the white working classes; and fobbed off black political aspirations by changing the subject, changing the time scale, waxing philosophic, or promising "practical social policy away from politics." In a nutshell, that became the policy of P. W. Botha, who back in 1948 had been a young Nationalist firebrand for whom Jan Smuts and all his works were anathema. Thirty-five years later, when he introduced a new constitution giving browns but not blacks a subordinate role in a multicolored government, Botha successfully resurrected the platform on which Smuts went down to defeat. The Botha way, white voters were told, was the middle way between extremes of left and right; they were voting for "human dignity" and against international isolation if they supported him. "No generation," Botha said when I interviewed him, "can say that the next generation won't take further steps. A country and its people are living organisms, and while there is life there must be movement."

Movement in a circle: The intolerable burden of the "sphinx problem" was still being shifted to the ampler shoulders and stronger brains of the future. It will remain there, it seems safe to predict, until the sphinx imposes its own answer in Xhosa or Zulu or the demotic linguistic combinations of the townships. However long that takes, the white elite's would-be "modernizers" will continue to turn out blueprints and updated partition plans from their think tanks and universities, as if their failure to evoke black consent so far has resulted from a failure of ingenuity that perseverance and time can overcome. Yet black consent has no real place, no function in their schemes. Now and then white academics bemoan the dearth of black leaders, meaning black leaders who might be interested in their plans. Black leaders with plans of their own, such as those who are presently in jail or exile, cannot easily be factored into their calculations. The consent of such leaders cannot be sought, the white planners know, because it cannot be gained without conceding on most of the major points in dispute: common citizenship, open schools, an end to resettlement and the pass laws, the scrapping of all racial statutes. This black sine qua non doesn't begin to address the distribution of political power or the economic arrangements in a society in which the white 15 percent sops up 60 percent of all income, yet it is rejected as radical by all but a tiny liberal minority among whites. Conceding on these points would mean relinquishing dominance, the feeling of control, that whites know as their way of life. ("Can any white man who wants change really be all there?" a Nadine Gordimer character wryly wonders in *The Late Bourgeois World.*) So the black sine qua non stands in its simplicity, its stark rectitude, in contrast with the self-deluding subtleties of the white models and maps, which gather dust on the shelf in between seminars, like military contingency plans, of which they are basically a part.

It is a strategic stockpile of solutions, to be rendered operational in an emergency. If the present table d'hôte won't do, we are assured, there are still many choices on the à la carte for those who can't stomach black rule. Under the various schemes that have been floated as academic trial balloons, the transition to what is called consensus comes in two stages or six stages, resulting in a government or governments with three, four, or six tiers. The country can be divided into two, three, five, six, ten, twelve, thirteen, or eighteen parts. These parts can be left separate, or they can be knitted together again in a federation or confederation, a constellation or common market, a commonwealth or condominium; or, possibly, a confederation between a white-dominated federal state and a black federation; or any other combination of the above. The last Nigerian federal system is one model; the Swiss cantonal system, another. After the "territorial pluralism" or "race federation" produced by any such "power deployment," the resulting state or states can be governed by a consociational, interparliamentary, or confederal council in which different communities or states may or may not exercise vetoes. There may be federative partition, something called demotomic partition, or radical partition. A professor named Gavin Maasdorp proposed a surgical solution that would slice the present South Africa into two states, Capeland and Capricornia. In Capeland—which would get most of the south and west of the country—there would be marginally more whites than blacks, at least at first, but whites would still amount to less than 30 percent of the population and coloreds would predominate. Even then, more than half the whites would be left in black-dominated Capricornia, which would have most of the industry, most of the mines, and the financial resources centered on Johannesburg.

The problem of Johannesburg—how to divide, share out, or set it apart—eventually defeats most of the mapmakers who try to devise a solution based on partition. It is the unholy Jerusalem that no one can relinquish, not because of its history or its saints but because of its wealth. Already blacks account for more than 60 percent of the 2.8 million persons in metropolitan Johannesburg. Holding the black share of the population down to that level requires more than 120,000 arrests a year under the pass laws within forty miles of the city center—120,000 arrests so that whites, who account for less than one-third of the metropolitan area's population, can have the continued comfort of imagining that they live in a "white area." Those whites are more than 20 percent of *all* South African whites; in fact, about 40 percent of all white South Africans live within sixty miles of Jo'burg, in the industrial belt that has the city as its core. Rather than contemplate abandoning them in a radical partition, such as the Capeland-Capricornia scheme, most planners look for devices to make the present racial checkerboard more acceptable to most blacks without spreading panic among most whites. In their schemes, what are called open areas, or "grey areas," or multiracial zones are interspersed among black ghettos and segregated white areas. In the segregated areas, so the theory goes, different groups would have "communal autonomy." Local government could then be segregated outside the open areas but multiracial at the regional level. Planning thus seeks to achieve a situation similar to that produced by civil war in Belfast or Beirut. If there weren't too many bombings along the way, that could be construed as progress in South Africa.

Viewed from inside, the conundrum seems almost impossible to resolve without setting fires that would rage out of control. If they are smoldering already in the basement, the solution of enlightened whites is to refurbish and redecorate and maybe build on another wing or floor to the house of apartheid. I asked a thoughtful member of the governing party in the white chamber of Parliament how long it would take to resolve the basic conflict and establish a regime that most whites and most blacks could accept. "Four, five, or six decades," the politician replied. He was relatively youthful, but he was giving essentially the same answer that Jan Smuts gave in 1906; he was saying, in effect, "Not in my lifetime." Four, five, or six decades meant 2023, 2033, or 2043. The white proportion of the population, which was more than 20 percent at the start of the century, could be less than 10 percent by the earliest of these dates. According to a conservative demographic projection, the black population then is likely to have reached 46 million, double what it is now. Using another set of assumptions about fertility rates, demographers say the black population could be as high as 55 million then. By 2053 it will be anywhere between 60 million and 100 million; the number of whites will not be much more than 7 million then if fertility remains constant and immigration continues; if neither of those assumptions holds true, it could be as low as or lower than now.

These projections explain the efforts being made by Afrikaners especially to forge alliances across the color line with coloreds (most of whom at least speak Afrikaans) and Indians (traditionally viewed by Afrikaners as foreigners). The idea is to shift the racial boundary from white versus nonwhite to black versus "nonblack," a term that was actually introduced into the most recent and exhaustive official study of *Demographic Trends in South Africa.* The absurdity of being defined by what you are not—the condition nonwhite South Africans have known—is one the whites are ready now to take on themselves but only, since the Population Registration Act and Group Areas Act will

remain in force, as camouflage. Cunning and altruism are both re-
fracted through this adaptation of ideology, but it is hard to see how
the citadel of power can be opened a bit for browns and kept shut for
blacks, or even if it can—even if 6 or 7 million whites are still able to
exert a measure of the dominance over 46 or 60 or 100 million blacks
that 4.7 million now have over 23 million—how the apartheid structure
and present division of land can survive under the weight of such
numbers. White constitutional thinkers call this "the numbers problem," for it is no longer respectable for scholars to talk about the
problem of blacks. It is Smuts's old "sphinx problem" renamed, the
question of black rights and how these can be reconciled with white
power; a question no self-respecting black can acknowledge, no matter
how conservative he is in his political or social values, except as an
aspect of white pathology. But most whites cannot address, for in their
abiding self-regard they cannot see, a white problem.

In fact, it is commonplace now for white Cabinet ministers to run
through a litany of the drastic demographic changes the country will
see in the coming decades—the swelling black numbers, the rising
demand for jobs, the pace of urbanization—as an argument for the
perpetuation of white dominance. The racial argument is usually, but
not always, implicit. A country facing such turbulence, it is contended,
would soon founder with less experienced hands at the helm. South
Africa with all its resources and productive capacity would return to the
African bush under black rule, if the Russians didn't gobble it up first.
The proof of black inadequacy to govern as a cultural trait is in the rest
of Africa or nearer to hand in the homelands. Ergo, as the transport
minister, an amiable bigot named Hendrik Schoeman, tactlessly put it,
"In this country four million whites must think and plan for twenty-five
million people. It is a question of the protection of the minority with
whom the brain power lies." South Africa can reform, but reform must
come from the top and only on the initiative of those with brainpower.
The whites represent order; the blacks, chaos. There are many in South
Africa who imagine themselves to be saying something new and urgent,
once they have learned to express that thought in the American
managerial idiom, when actually they are giving voice to their own
tribal ethos, their most primitive chant.

"The revolutionary movement was being born," Edward Crankshaw
notes in his narrative of the decline and fall of czarist autocracy, "at

the very moment that devoted reformers were making an impact on the system."

Can this have any meaning for South Africa today? It is difficult, given the overwhelming reality of white power, to imagine that it can; equally difficult, given the inexorable reality of black numbers, to imagine that it cannot. The analogy to nineteenth-century Russia is appealing on various levels: The paradoxical mixture of contempt for the West and slavish imitation that marked the aristocracy there is characteristic also of the racial oligarchy; the forms of revolutionary idealism and violence, of literary expression and penitential self-sacrifice by the children of the elite—all have their conspicuous parallels. But there are obvious limitations to the analogy. The racial and ethnic hostility is deeper than any cleavage of classes, which helps explain why the czar's ministers were more determined reformers than Afrikaner power wielders of today. They at least managed to summon the nerve to abolish serfdom, while South Africa's racial oligarchy has yet to contemplate seriously the abolition of the pass laws, a reform that could be similarly far-reaching. Nevertheless, at the very moment that devoted reformers were trying to make an impact on the South African system, I found myself in Potchefstroom, the first Afrikaner capital in the Transvaal and the seat now of an Afrikaans university that still forbids social dancing. On campus *Drie Susters (Three Sisters)* by "A. Tsjechof" had just completed a run. Others, it seemed, were groping for analogies.

My visit happened to coincide with the referendum for white voters on the Botha constitutional plan to give South Africa its first nonblack government that wouldn't be exclusively white. In Potchefstroom the political struggle had been an all-Afrikaans affair, a *broedertwis* ("fight among brothers") between those who supported the prime minister, even though they didn't quite understand where he was taking them or why, and those who assailed him and his plan from the extreme right for opening the door to "mixed government." Festooned across the façade of the Potchefstroom town hall, the opposition's posters featured a warning that went right to the point. *'n Bont Regering* ("A Multicolored Government"), it sneered. The governing party's organizers, looking prim and a little nervous, tried with only limited success to intercept voters outside the building. Their opponents were exuberant, sometimes raucous; they knew they would probably lose, but bucking the machine, they could still say out loud what most Afrikaners had been reared to believe. When an army chaplain attempted to march a platoon of white troopies in formation to the booths of the governing party, a rightist law professor from the university named Fanie Jacobs cut him down like a Cossack, using the law as his saber; the stunned dominee was informed that he would be formally charged with abuse of authority and interference at the polls. At a safe distance, across the street in front of a Caltex station, blacks in small groups of three or four stood watching, exchanging nods and occasional remarks in Tswana; every now and then they laughed. The brown nonblacks, the coloreds and Indians who were the supposed beneficiaries of the supposed reform, seemed to be keeping far out of sight so that neither blacks nor whites could study their faces for clues to their real sentiments.

There were four Potchefstrooms. I left the white town and went to look for the other three. I found them by following a black bus, which headed west out of town, passing the Dutch Reformed church and adjacent dominee's residence, where Beyers Naudé lived when he went through his private agony of soul-searching, and then to the highway, where, at the edge of the white town, the bus turned left on a cloverleaf that took it past the headquarters of the white army reserve unit and brought it to the outskirts of a small industrial area dominated by a fertilizer plant. At the far end of the industrial area, beyond the fertilizer plant, there was a wire-mesh fence and a stucco structure that looked like a toll booth or a factory gate. On its front, facing oncoming traffic, there was a large stop sign. This was the entrance to Ikageng, the black township; in human terms, the largest of the Potchefstrooms. In the 1920's and 1930's the Communist party had successfully organized a series of protests and strikes among Potchefstroom's blacks. Perhaps at this very instant, more than half a century later, the revolution was being born behind the wire-mesh fence, but on what might have been a politically charged occasion, the township looked absolutely cut off and contained.

Having no permit to enter, I didn't try to pass through the gate but drove along the perimeter, following a road that wound around a huge slime dam where the waste from the fertilizer plant rose as a physical barrier between the black township and the remaining two Potchefstrooms, one Indian and the other colored. At a fork in the road, I had a choice between turning left to Mohadin or right to Promosa. A pond lay between these two segregated townships, another barrier or moat, preventing brown nonblacks from undue mixing with other brown nonblacks. I turned left to Mohadin, the tiny Indian enclave, which was distinguished by its mosque and a half dozen large homes for the extended families of wealthy merchants, overshadowing the typical township matchboxes on tiny plots. Because there was so little of it, land in practically every Indian township in the country was at a premium, worth more than a similar plot in nearby white suburban developments, where there was usually a plenitude of space. The ironical, faintly sinister result was that well-to-do Indians, like well-to-do coloreds and blacks, could not avoid having a small stake in apartheid, for their incongruous ghetto palaces would automatically plummet in value on the day they were free to move out. I had once asked an Indian merchant in Durban whether, given these circumstances, he really wanted to see the repeal of the Group Areas Act. "Of course," he replied, "but not all at once." In crowded little Mohadin, I speculated, the calculations had to be similar. Promosa, the colored township to which I then circled back before crossing the several racial borders again on my return to white Potchefstroom and the polling station, was a little larger and a little poorer, more of an encampment; the sterile result of white racial planning, a sorry sight.

This short, superficial tour served to restore perspective. I wondered what proportion of the white nonblack voters had ever driven around the slime dam and actually glimpsed Mohadin and Promosa. Officials, the police, and perhaps some electricians or other artisans might have done so, but it seemed a reasonable guess, since these places were on the way to nowhere whites normally went, that more than 80 percent of the voters in this small town had never so much as seen the enclaves where their supposed new allies would wait to hear their verdict. The brown nonblacks might be invited to align themselves with the white nonblacks, but they would continue to reside out of sight, apart from each other and everyone else, on the wrong side of the slime dam.

So what were the whites fighting about? Only the timing of the white retreat, it seemed. The right-wingers, who struck me as more forthright and slightly less calculating than the prime minister's backers, thought he was breaking up the *laager* (circle of wagons) sooner than necessary. His supporters accepted the explanation that he was only trying to enlarge it. Perhaps they recalled, some of them, as a matter of historical fact, that when the trekkers lashed their wagons together for protection against looming Africa, whites were seldom in the majority on the inside of the circle.

As I nipped from side to side in the Potchefstroom *broedertwis*, I became the recipient of successive innuendos about the loyalty to the land of the players in the opposing camps. For the first time, after having spent a total of nearly four years in South Africa on my two tours, I was hearing Afrikaners talk openly about the possibility of emigration. It was not a new impulse, I knew. Some trekkers made it to the highlands of Angola in the nineteenth century; one doughty pioneer went as far as Cairo in hopes of finding a Zion where his people would not have to battle dusky trespassers. After their Boer War defeat, another lot took off for Patagonia. Their latest Zions seemed to be Paraguay or Ronald Reagan's America, or so each side said of the other. "Some of the people who are leading the campaign for a no vote are already buying property," a Botha supporter said, "so they will have a place to go when their policies land us all in a mess." A leader on the no side, the son of a former Cabinet minister, made a point of telling me he would stay in South Africa whatever happened, insinuating that this was not the case with those who were pushing for a yes. He also made a show of fond nostalgia for the mixed couple that had lived next door to his family in Madison, Wisconsin. "They adopted four children, two blacks and two whites," he said.

Another Afrikaner, a young lecturer who was not active in the campaign, privately acknowledged that black rule might be the only solution for South Africa but said he saw no way for it to be achieved peacefully. He thought rural America might be a safe and congenial place to rear his children. "I also liked Seattle," he said. Yet another faculty member confided that some of his relatives were talking of leaving. "They say, 'Our calling is over,' " he said.

"We can hold it for another ten years," said a man at a *braaivleis* ("barbecue") held that night on the lawn of the town hall, after the polls closed, for the poll watchers and party workers of the Conservative party, the right-wing faction.

"We can be like the Israelis," said a businessman, who kept a beady eye on my plate and beer can to make sure that I was not running low on steak, chops, *boerewors,* or any other essential commodity. "We can be like the Israelis and tell the world to get stuffed. *Fuck the world!"* His voice rose several decibels to add these sentiments to the general conviviality. A few appreciative chortles came back in echo. "Twenty years from now," he went on in a conspiratorial but still jolly tone, "the world will be so near nuclear war that the question of black rule in South Africa will seem trivial." Speaking mainly to myself, I agreed there was always that hope.

"You've got to battle for everything in this country," said a Colonel Kloppers, who had earned his rank in the prisons service, I was told, and then become wealthy as a contractor. "We've fought for everything we've got."

"The more you knock people down, the more they come up," added a man with a straw boater decorated with stickers that said *Stem Nee* ("Vote No"). He was referring to the Afrikaner will to resist, but I was befuddled, for never having seen any Afrikaners knocked down in South Africa, I had taken his meaning in a more obvious and opposite sense. Annette Jacobs, the vivacious wife of the law professor who had vanquished the chaplain, said her grandfather had spent six months in jail after the 1914 rebellion. "I'll fight if there's a yes," she promised. It felt like Texas; this was Alamo talk, I thought.

Then Ben van den Bergh, a local party figure who taught German at the university, interrupted this flow of pleasantries and social chitchat with a terse, pointed question. I thought he was taking my political temperature, to see if I was another of those soft, wishy-washy liberals who had almost brought America to its knees. "What do *you* think is really going to happen?" he asked.

Like a soft, wishy-washy liberal, I smothered my reply in platitudes and qualifications about how hard it was for anyone, especially a foreigner, to read the future. Then I offered it up in three words. "Plenty of conflict," I said sagely.

"It has to come," he answered, turning away.

"It has started in Johannesburg," the man said when he lurched to within speaking distance. I was supposed to know what "it" was.

This was Harare, Zimbabwe, the former Salisbury, Rhodesia, and I was through the looking glass, at the other end of my journalistic beat. Here, when the authorities warned of an evil conspiracy aimed at the nation's hard-won freedom, they were referring not to blacks, Marxists, and Moscow but to whites, racists, and Pretoria. Depending on your point of view, which in southern Africa normally can be deduced from your pigmentation, Zimbabwe was either the gaping abyss toward which South Africa was skidding or the heavenly fulfillment at the end of a long ascent. Either way, as seen from south of the Limpopo River, Zimbabwe could never be allowed to be a relatively small country stumbling or maybe careening through a difficult transition of its own, after an era of white dominance lasting less than a century and culminating in a ruinous bush war. In South African minds, Zimbabwe had no reality except as a symbol of South Africa's own future, black or white, in the same way that South Africa—since negative and mirror images prevailed—could be viewed from north of the Limpopo only as a symbol of Zimbabwe's past.

I had been walking to Meikles Hotel after filing a story when he entered my myopic field of vision, weaving toward me. I sensed immediately that he would attempt to deliver a message. Perhaps that fantasy made me look a little expectant, perhaps that provoked him. When the distance between us vanished, we were half a block from the small, meticulously kept park where jacarandas brilliantly bloom every October and where British television crews recorded the listless, oblivious reaction of Rhodesia's blacks to Ian Smith's fatuous parody of Jefferson when he declared the colony's independence in November 1965. In those days, as a comment on the seeming absence of black resistance, I used to say that Soweto's blacks would have set the torch to Johannesburg had they been given such a provocation and opportunity. Now with Robert Mugabe, who was then unknown and in jail, installed in the office nearby where I had once interviewed Smith, I was a little less quick on the draw when it came to interpreting appearances. Otherwise Harare looked and felt just like the Salisbury I remembered. The evening was still florid and fragrant. The man, a white with thick gray hair and a wild gaze, was florid and fragrant, too.

"What?" I asked, stopping because he blocked my path.

"Didn't you hear?" he said. "A bomb went off in the Carlton Center this morning at ten-thirty. Three people were killed, twenty-five injured." Thinking only of getting to a phone, I unlocked myself from his gaze and started to walk quickly away. "And I think this guy is making a mess of things, too," he shouted after me in a disjointed, paranoid style that was near enough to what often passes for normal discourse in southern Africa not to wrench my attention back from the news I had just received to its bearer.

A jumble of questions raced through my mind as I hurried past the Harare Club, formerly the Salisbury Club and still the preserve of the white business elite, where I had lunched that day with a diplomat: How many of the dead and injured were blacks? If this is the start of urban terrorism, do I continue to park at the Carlton? Will it still be safe to go to the shopping centers in Killarney and Rosebank? Where else can we shop? Do we need to phone our families to keep them from worrying? Can I still phone Air Zimbabwe? Is there a flight in the morning? Is this really "it"?

It wasn't. My secretary, when I got her on the phone minutes later, was still at the office, across the street from the Carlton Center. She had heard no explosion, no sirens. There was nothing on the wire. It had been a quiet day. Of course, I now said to myself, the guy was on a bender. I knew perfectly well, I now reminded myself, that the underground was unlikely to start a campaign of urban terrorism, which could alienate blacks as well as foreign sympathy for its cause, or that even if there was such an attempt, it was unlikely, at this stage, to be able to sustain it. I knew the essential data and probabilities, yet I had instinctively cast them aside. Whatever "it" was—urban terrorism, strikes and mass defiance, crowds in the streets—it seemed improbable only beforehand. Maybe "it" would never come, but if it did, few people, blacks or whites, would really be surprised. Instead, claiming foreknowledge, they would ask, "What took 'it' so long?"

Many months later that was the reaction among many blacks and some whites when a car bomb in front of the air force headquarters in Pretoria propelled glass and lethal hunks of metal through a downtown intersection, leaving nineteen dead, ten times as many injured. The word "finally" recurred in many of the answers I got when I gathered reactions, especially from blacks. As a matter of political tact, I tried to put my questions indirectly so that people could speak more easily in the tense aftermath, as if they were merely assessing public opinion rather than expressing their own feelings. "People are jubilant," said a black man with wide contacts in political circles. "What they are saying is that the African National Congress is finally hitting real targets." A mother who had seen two sons go into exile to join the "struggle" threw circumlocution to the winds. "The boys have finally struck where it hurts most!" she exclaimed.

More than a year then passed without a recurrence on the scale of the Pretoria bombing, an apparent indication that the underground was unable or unwilling to cause such high civilian casualties again. So that wasn't "it" either. "It" then receded, presumably to lurk in the future.

And then, years later, in ways that were not really foreseen, the future becomes the past, as has now happened in Zimbabwe. "We said we'd leave this country the way we found it in 1890," Cornelius Hoffman, known as Kas, told me the first time I visited him at his farm outside of Enkeldoorn, the only predominantly Afrikaans-speaking community in the old Rhodesia that had just vanished forever. The do-or-die promise of a scorched-earth retreat across the high veld to the Limpopo was a slight embarrassment now for those, like Kas, who had stayed on and still intended to remain. *"Ach,"* he said with a helpless shrug and a laugh, "we're Zimbabweans now, but what's in a name? We thought it would kill us to become Zimbabweans."

Cornelius Hoffman was a hulking, larger-than-life anachronism, not just in black-ruled Zimbabwe but in the whole region and whole era through which he had lived. In appearance as well as in thinking, he could have been reasonably presented as the last surviving *voortrekker,* for he wore the full, untrimmed beard of the Afrikaner pioneers from whom he was directly descended. His great-grandfather, Josias Hoffman, had been the first president of the Orange Free State when it proclaimed its republican sovereignty in the mid-nineteenth century (a position from which that patriarch was shortly ousted for seeming too dovish in his negotiations with Moshweshwe, king of the Sothos). His father had trekked to Central Africa in response to a newspaper advertisement placed by Cecil Rhodes, who rewarded him with 6,000 acres at Enkeldoorn. The first Hoffman to come into the country had his first crop there in 1895, then the next year rode off to aid in the suppression of a rebellion in Mashonaland. In 1947, when King George VI visited the self-governing colony of Rhodesia, the old Boer was summoned into the royal presence to show off the medal he had received for his role in the Mashonaland campaign. He lived on until 1954 and then, on his death at eighty-six after threescore years in the land, was buried in a small family plot across the road from his homestead—the destination to which he would have to be carried when the time came that he could no longer farm in Zimbabwe, Kas Hoffman now regularly insisted, pointing through the heavy protective mesh he had placed over the windows of his modest tin-roofed bungalow during the recent war.

The image of the old Boer showing off his medal to his sovereign, a photo to which the son called my attention on every visit with a stubby finger, helped to explain the time warp in which he had grown up. The father had escaped the Boer War, the son its sour heritage, and that gave the white tribal feeling he expressed its fixed, primordial quality—a seeming innocence, not without sweetness, which helped explain also how more worldly and cynical English-speaking colonists fell into the habit of calling Afrikaners childlike. It was at the Hoffman homestead in what was already Robert Mugabe's Zimbabwe, and not in some Transvaal *dorp* (hamlet), that I heard the story of Dingane and

Piet Retief told as living history, the way Paul Kruger might have told it, rather than as an attenuated parable on the theme of "plural relations" or "ethnic mobilization." Moments after we first introduced ourselves, Kas Hoffman grabbed me by the arm and hauled me to a screened veranda that doubled as a gallery for a framed sequence of now yellowing prints illustrating "Die Moord von Piet Retief" ("The Murder of Piet Retief"). The leap from that saga to that of the war just ended in Zimbabwe—or, to his mind, the one that was just getting under way in South Africa—was no leap at all. The events were separated by a century and a half, it was true, but the conflict was one and ineluctable.

I mean to portray Kas Hoffman respectfully as a primitive—in the sense of authentic or uncorrupted—Afrikaner and also as a reasonably unambiguous symbol of hope. For as the behavior-modeling psychologists are always eager to explain, individuals find it easier to adapt their conduct than their opinions. This individual Afrikaner was so rooted in his particular piece of Africa that he could remain a Zimbabwean even after many of his white neighbors had fled across the Limpopo. He had experienced no epiphany, no blinding conversion or remorse, but he had adapted, drawing on the same inheritance of perseverance and values that had put him at the extreme right of the white Rhodesian political spectrum. Expatriation was unimaginable to him, even under circumstances that had been unimaginable all through the first fifty-three years of his life, before the menace of black rule had become the surprising reality that, even more surprising, he found he could accept. This was not entirely a happy ending, all egalitarian sweetness and light suitable to one of those sinister revolutionary fairy tales of "re-education," in which the hereditary exploiter is made to see the wickedness of his ways. But it suggested to me that the ending in South Africa, however it came, did not have to be apocalyptic; that if there were to be an Azania, there would be untold thousands of white Afrikaans-speaking Azanians who would manage to find ways of their own to reinterpret and thus to preserve a heritage that had always held death to be a kinder fate. It suggested also that those who succeeded in such an adaptation would not necessarily be those who now presumed to call themselves "enlightened," arrogating to themselves alone the responsibility of saying how the society might be transformed.

Of course, there was no time for such speculation on that first visit when Kas hauled me back from his veranda to the living room where his wife, Cornelia, known as Corrie, was serving tea. Cornelius and Cornelia, an endearing matched set. Their experiences of war had been nothing compared to that of Afrikaans-speaking farmers who lived on Rhodesia's eastern frontier, next to Mozambique, where the guerrillas had been based. The Hoffman farm was never attacked, and there were no serious cattle thefts. But there were ambushes on the roads, sons of their neighbors were killed or crippled in combat, and there was the daily sense, weighing especially heavily on Cornelia, who became an insomniac, that the conflict was drawing nearer their home and their own son. Yet all the while Kas's whole heritage was insisting that the fight must go on, that compromise was unthinkable in Africa. Each stage of the white retreat came too soon for him. He felt let down when Ian Smith gave up the premiership in hopes, at the eleventh hour, of forming a multiracial regime that might begin to compete with the guerrilla movements for black popular support; and when finally there was an election under British auspices that gave sovereign power to the least compromised and most effective guerrilla faction, black Marxist ogres as far as he was concerned, he was completely unprepared and uncomprehending.

Robert Mugabe was hard to swallow but less so than the thought of parting with land that his family had farmed for nearly nine decades. He was never in any real doubt that he wanted to stay or that South Africa was simply not his country even if it was the only one in the whole world where his language was widely spoken, but he needed a new set of words to explain that feeling to himself and others. These he got from his dominee, a young South African from Natal named Johan Wasserman who had lately been called to the Dutch Reformed church in Enkeldoorn. In a sermon after the election results had been announced, the dominee responded to the sense of bewilderment and abandonment that had settled on Enkeldoorn's Afrikaner remnant, which felt, for the first time really, that its prayers had been rejected. Even the omnipotent God might have had difficulty answering those prayers, he pointed out, for they contained an absolute contradiction. On the one hand, they had prayed for peace; on the other, they had implored the Lord to see to the defeat of Robert Mugabe. Yet everyone knew, the clergyman said, that the defeat of the guerrilla factions at the polls was likely to lead to renewed war. They had been praying for peace for years; they had been praying for Mugabe's defeat for only five or six months. Therefore, if they thought about it, they would see that

God had weighed their prayers and had fulfilled their deepest, longest-standing need after all: He had blessed them with peace.

Kas Hoffman was then able to take the argument a step further. Black government, he reasoned, had to be acknowledged as the will of God. "I respect it as such," he said. It was a stunning discovery, and it made him wonder what else might lie in store. He still could not believe that it was divine will that he should live under "communism." Perhaps, after all, God would give him a sign to leave as a penniless refugee. "My whole life is in his hands," he said, "but at the moment there has been no sign at all. I only pray that the spirit will come down and work on these leaders and turn them away from communism and make Christians of them."

Until that had manifestly happened, he went on, adapting the traditional view of his people's history to his new conditions, how could Afrikaners allow themselves to feel that they had completed the mission for which they had been called to Africa? Tradition could be adapted even further, for if God now preferred black government for his people, wasn't it obvious that he was punishing them for their willfulness? And if that was the case, who was more likely to be punished now than the whites of South Africa? "They are so independent," Kas said, speaking with a sharpness I could not have anticipated, "they no longer rely on God almighty. Everything is their own creation. They're so independent, they're just concerned about themselves. They're not concerned about their next-door neighbor. I don't think I could fit in there. I just don't feel at home."

Besides, if God still intended to punish white South Africa for its pride, it would be crazy for Cornelius and Cornelia to join the exodus as if they thought it to be the promised land. That would be like praying for another plague. He said as much to a nephew who had come to gather up his mother, Kas's own sister, and take her to what he assumed to be safe refuge across the Limpopo. "You people are sitting on top of a time bomb," he told him. "When that thing explodes, you won't know what hit you." For the time being, at least, even the Calvinist's conviction that salvation and divine will show themselves in the worldly circumstances of believers seemed to be borne out in his life. In Zimbabwe he had his farm, which was rapidly being enlarged with prime grazing land bought from departing neighbors, who now found themselves in cramped apartments in Durban and Port Elizabeth, depending on the charity of relatives.

It struck him as strange, he confessed, that his sense of his place in the divine order had been so easily restored. "There has been an absolute revolution but I can't realize it," he said. "I don't feel it." Most things hadn't changed. There was still, to take the most obvious example, the everlasting problem of the blacks. He allowed himself to be impressed by Mugabe when the prime minister addressed the white commercial farmers in his district, but the "boys" on his farm were still "boys," capable of carrying out a fairly complicated task but only one at a time, not two in sequence, and only if he oversaw them with a strong hand. It was the old story of treating them as you treat your own children, trying to be Christian, but knowing what they are and therefore not expecting too much. Then, as he was spelling it out to me patiently on that first visit, as if I as a foreigner could not be expected to grasp all at once his good intentions and the obstacles he faced, Cornelius Hoffman interrupted himself to recount a disconcerting experience in the new Zimbabwe that he had not yet fully digested.

It had just happened, on the previous weekend. A well-spoken black man, dressed with casual stylishness, had driven up to the farm and introduced himself as Comrade Noshonga, or some such name, the local representative of Mugabe's party, known as ZANU. The man's manner couldn't have been more polite, but he made a request that Cornelius Hoffman, the son of a pioneer and great-grandson of the first president of the Orange Free State, had to regard as appalling and indecent: He said he would like to meet with the laborers on the farm. "You can see how I felt about that," Kas said, dropping his voice and speaking gravely. "If there are any problems on this farm, I can sort them out myself. I don't need any help. We've never stood for outsiders interfering with our boys."

"What did you do?" I asked.

"Well, he was from the party," Kas replied, his voice dropping lower. "What could I do? I let him speak to them."

That was not to be the end of his humiliation. A few days later, while he was having his tank filled at the gas station in Enkeldoorn, the ZANU man drove up. Of course, he instantly recognized Farmer Hoffman with his voortrekker beard, recognized him with pleasure, it seemed, as a progressive Afrikaner who had readily accepted the full implications of the Mugabe policy of "reconciliation" in the new Zimbabwe, for the ZANU man could not have known the private thoughts and sense of shame that gripped the farmer after he had given way without even a tiny demur at their first encounter. Now, to his astonishment, Kas saw something he had never seen or dreamed of seeing in his first fifty-three years in Enkeldoorn: His new friend from ZANU, this black man, was advancing on him with a wide smile and an outstretched hand.

"You know, I never shook a black man's hand," Kas said. "We don't mix with them at all."

"What did you do?" I asked again.

His eyes were downcast and his voice was practically a whisper when he made his confession. "I shook it," he said.

I saw Cornelius Hoffman twice in the following year. The first time I bumped into him in South Africa, at the airport in Port Elizabeth. Had God, I wondered, been so quick to give him a sign to join the white exodus from Zimbabwe? Not at all, he hurried to explain. He was there for the funeral of a brother. Just as lost as he had told me he always was when he came to South Africa, he overflowed with gratitude the moment I offered to locate his hotel and drop him off there. In the sterile vacancy of the new terminal at the Hendrik F. Verwoerd Airport, with its Avis, Hertz, and National car rental booths, this white Zimbabwean was an apparition, an African Rip Van Winkle stepping out of some grade-school storybook. Heads spun, eyes darted; outwardly, at least, he was more foreign in those surroundings than I was.

The next time I saw him he was back on his farm, to which I made a detour while driving through Zimbabwe with my wife. The protective mesh was still in place over the windows in the homestead, but Cornelius and Cornelia seemed more at ease in Zimbabwe. Conversation went the way of most conversations with whites in the country in that period when adjustments to the new order were still being made, which is to say, it dwelt on the deterioration of services for whites at hospitals that were no longer for whites only. But there was little of the contempt and resentment that seemed almost to choke many English-speaking whites when they went off on this tack. The Hoffmans sounded genial and indulgent, as if there weren't anything surprising about the adjustments whites were having to make, given the unchangeable fact of black rule. Kas himself didn't feel threatened but voiced sympathy for widows and pensioners. "It's hard to be an old Afrikaner woman," he said.

Their indulgence had little to do with a realization that the hospitals were now serving a much wider community, and a great deal to do with their low expectations of blacks, who remained "Afs" (a dismissive settler word for Africans) and "houts" (from *houtkop*, which is Afrikaans for "blockhead") in this conversation. At the same time those low expectations were mixed with sympathy, which was not all affectation. Many white farmers had halted the practice of paying their workers in kind with food as soon as the Mugabe government established a minimum cash wage for farm laborers, but the Hoffmans still supplied milk to the families on the farm. "It wouldn't have been Christian to stop giving them that," said Corrie, who then, to illustrate the point that blacks often took advantage of one another—as if that were a distinctive cultural trait—recounted the tribulations of the most hapless laborer on the farm who regularly gambled away his wages, his food, and sometimes even the shirt on his back. "Poor little Af," she said. This was in the second year of Zimbabwe's independence.

The third year was just running out when I stopped by the farm for the last time. Enkeldoorn had gone the way of Salisbury by then, changing its name to Chivu. Cornelius and Cornelia said they had found it hard at first to think of themselves as members of the Nederduitse Gereformeerde Kerk (Dutch Reformed Church) of *Chivu,* but they were now able to mix Afrikaans and Shona in this way without wincing, almost without self-consciousness. Kas had now found that the result of the ZANU man's single visit to the farm had been to bolster the ruling party's organization at the grass roots without diminishing, as yet, the authority that he had customarily regarded as God-given. Now he had a workers' committee, linked to the party organization, that had to give its approval before he could apply to the authorities to discharge an employee for cause. But the system worked smoothly and to his advantage, he assured me, pulling out a thick file as he got down to cases.

The first chairman of the committee, his records showed, had been Mambo Muchireripi, the storekeeper at the little shop the Hoffmans ran on their farm, where they reclaimed most of the cash wages they paid out, as white farmers have customarily done in their part of the world. When Comrade Mambo was caught in a profit-sharing scheme of his own devising, Kas Hoffman summoned the workers' committee, which readily agreed to unseat its chairman and authorized the farmer to apply to the Ministry of Labor and Social Services for permission to discharge him. The letter was sent on May 19th, and the authorization came back on July 30th. "The Minister of Labor and Social Services has agreed to accede to your request to dismiss Mambo Muchireripi," it said. On the bottom of the letter, the farmer himself had then written, "I have read the above letter and understand fully what my employer has stated." There Comrade Mambo had signed his name, in exchange for a promise that he would not face criminal prosecution. The deputy chairman, a certain Comrade Kefas, who was in charge of the work gang at the piggery, had by then taken Comrade Mambo's place at the helm of the committee.

"He was the next to go," Farmer Hoffman said with great good humor. The pigs had been neglected, and the committee had blamed its chairman. Now it was on its third chairman, and the farmer, far from grumbling about Marxist interference, as other whites were then doing, showed every sign of deriving a sportsman's satisfaction from his ability to play by the new rules.

The protective screens were still over the windows, for there had been some wild shooting in the neighborhood one day, when 200 soldiers gave chase to a couple of "dissidents," black deserters from the new national army who were ethnically and politically at a disadvantage in the new order. "Didn't I tell you that the Matabeles would never submit to the Mashonas?" Kas asked. He had indeed; practically every white I had met in Zimbabwe in the months after independence had predicted a tribal showdown, and Robert Mugabe had not disappointed them in that respect. Kas was unsurprised but not given to sounding snide. If anything, there was a new source of relief in the discovery that as a white, he was no longer involved in the country's political conflicts. He had been back to South Africa recently to visit some relatives, but he still didn't like the place, and the ex-Rhodesians there, he found, "have nothing they can call their own." It was good to come home to Chivu, Zimbabwe.

"It's sad what's going on between the Mashonas and the Matabeles," the last voortrekker said, "but this is still a darn good country to live in. Let them fight it out, if they have to, as long as we don't come into the crossfire." He no longer felt responsible for history, in either Zimbabwe or South Africa. "We've had our war," he said.

In an Afrikaner's scheme of things, this amounted to stoicism and acceptance, a kind of tolerance that could co-exist, oddly enough, with the old racial feelings. In the Bronx there are things that an Italian may say about Puerto Ricans to another Italian but not to any Puerto Rican. Kas Hoffman had come that far at least. For him it was a belated realization that the best is the enemy of the good. His best had been racial dominance, but he was learning that he could settle for less, so long as he could retain his personal sense of independence and his farm. "As Christians we are only tenants in this world," he said, quoting a sermon by Dominee Wasserman's successor, which had consoled him. "Our permanent home is in heaven. We're only here for a short time."

A copper plaque on the wall of the Hoffmans' living room, around the corner from "Die Moord von Piet Retief," expressed Kas Hoffman's revised and more humble sense of his place in Africa in the form of a prayer:

> Grant me the serenity
> To accept the things I cannot change,
> Courage to change the things I can
> And wisdom to know the difference.

The plaque had caught my eye the first time I visited Cornelius and Cornelia. Afterward I noticed that it seemed to be a staple in the souvenir shops of Salisbury and Bulawayo, embellished usually by a relief modeled after Dürer's praying hands. Then, it seemed to me, I started seeing it almost anywhere I went in southern Africa. North of the Limpopo the prayer was usually in the homes of those who had supported the fallen white regime; south of the border it popped up in the offices and homes of those who opposed the existing racial order. It was, I learned, a version of what is called "The Serenity Prayer," which Reinhold Niebuhr, the American theologian, wrote during World War II for a service in a small Congregational church in the Berkshires. Eventually I started to keep a rough record of the places I saw it. I found it hanging in one of Soweto's most popular shebeens, within sight of the Protea police station, where some of the nastiest interrogations have taken place. I found it in an Indian township that some white official had been inspired to name Nirvana, in the home of a white South African who had left the country in order to marry a young woman who happened to be brown-skinned and of Indian descent and then (after a letter-writing campaign lasting fifteen years and in spite of the racial laws forbidding mixed marriage, interracial sex, and mixed habitation) received permission directly from the prime minister's office to bring his family home. I found it in Cape Town, in the residence of an Afrikaner clergyman who had joined the colored church and participated in a march on Parliament on behalf of black squatters; in Manzini, Swaziland, in the home of a physician who had campaigned unsuccessfully for constitutional democracy in the kingdom. And in an obscure township called Lenyenye, I found it in the independent clinic that had been opened by Dr. Mamphela Ramphele, the mother of Steve Biko's child, who was also the keeper of his legacy.

"The Serenity Prayer" didn't suggest, in the uses to which it was put in southern Africa, that anyone was caving in or that there was a middle way of compromise that blacks and whites were yearning to take. Only the State Department in Washington pretended to believe that. I never saw the prayer in the home or office of any of the white regime's supporters—it was too soon for that—and in Mamphela Ramphele's clinic it was less conspicuous than a poster emblazoned with the battle cry "Forward to Azania!" The number of serenity prayers in circulation was nowhere near the number of guns. But remembering where I had first seen it, in the home of an Afrikaner Zimbabwean, I got a tiny charge of hope every time I came on it again. It was a reminder that most individuals, white and black, were basically sane, that they could rise above their inheritance or, at least, adapt it when left with no other choice; that, finally, it was the inheritance and the situation it produced that were deranged.

That helped make life bearable on a day-to-day basis in South Africa, but it was not much comfort in the long run, for I also accepted the truism about violence and what it begets. The question, it seemed to me, was not whether there would be violence in South Africa but whether there would ever be an end to it. There are lots of ugly possibilities of what could happen along the way to make self-fulfilling the whites' prophecies of disaster after power slips from their hands. There could be an Argentine-style junta, possibly with a brown or black front man, to bid for Western support. Eventually the whole society could implode on itself as in Northern Ireland or Lebanon. Or, worst of all for the present ruling minority, blacks could govern according to the values that whites have displayed. It is also possible to fantasize a reasonably open and stable society that, having removed the cancer of racial law, begins to fulfill the country's enormous promise as a model for Africa and the world. Those who now hold power have been hearing about that dreamy possibility from blacks, wayward whites, and interfering do-gooders from outside for decades, and occasionally now, to flatter the outsiders and themselves, they pretend to believe in it. But they don't, not for a moment. That is why apartheid existed in the first place and why it still survives.

Beyond all the fatuous theorizing and scenarios, there is the reality of what actually happens, day after day. Those I admired most, blacks and whites, were those who really looked. I don't mean those who snatched a glimpse in order to draw support for some tribal suspicion or inherited fear but those who, in stepping across a forbidden frontier, managed to shed their armor and arguments and take in the larger truth of what these had achieved.

The two kinds of looking were displayed on the single worst morning I passed in southern Africa, at the end of the single worst week. The sequence of events started for me at a dinner in Cape Town at which all the other guests, besides my wife and myself, were supporters of the governing party. Inevitably the discussion came around to Zimbabwe, which had been independent for less than a year, and how in black hands it was rapidly regressing into an era of tribal warfare. Of the eight persons at the table, I was the only one who had set foot in the country since the end of white rule. Without meaning to be provocative, I mentioned that I had recently made several visits there after an absence of fifteen years and that my strongest impression of the new Zimbabwe, notwithstanding the legacy of war and the advent of majority rule, was that it very much resembled the old Rhodesia. I suggested they might be surprised, or at least moved to reserve judgment, if they looked for themselves. I should have been ready for an argument, but I wasn't when one of the guests, a lawyer, let loose with a furious barrage at point-blank range across the table. "There will be a bloodbath in Zimbabwe," the lawyer promised, "within six months."

He was too cautious. Within forty-eight hours I was back in Zimbabwe, looking at the results of a bloodbath. Perhaps it was not large enough in scale to match the Uganda-style cataclysm that my adversary in Cape Town had been anticipating, but it was big enough to silence me for a while. Tribal suspicion between the two rival guerrilla factions that struggled against white rule had ignited a chain reaction of murderous clashes within the new national army and taken the country back to the brink of civil war. I drove into an army camp at a place called Connemara where a battalion trained by British officers had disintegrated overnight and 50 men from one tribal group had been massacred by members of another group only because they believed they would be slaughtered themselves if they didn't act first. Those who did the massacring had then fled to the bush and now were trickling back, looking bruised and sullen or, some of them, frozen in stark terror over the danger of reprisals. Altogether more than 300 were dead in the senseless killing, and the rival guerrilla factions were still confronting each other with mortars and automatic weapons in the most densely populated townships of Bulawayo. It was not amusing to be in Bulawayo that weekend, but it was preferable, I thought, to another encounter in Cape Town with the lawyer. Perhaps unfairly, I imagined I could hear him and most of white South Africa cackling over the Zimbabwean dead.

On the Sunday morning of that week, I forced myself to go to the railyard in Bulawayo, where the authorities had established a makeshift mortuary in three refrigerated freight cars so that families could search for missing brothers and sons in the aftermath of the fighting. On the outside of the first of these cars, a handwritten sign identified their contents. "Corpses," it said. Inside, the bodies were stacked crossways like cords of wood, so that all the faces, where faces remained, could be seen. A white army physician on duty in the railyard pursued me in the self-appointed role of Greek chorus, speaking on behalf of the subcontinent's whites. "The irony is," he said, "that the European in this country was *right!* And the European in this country has been branded as a racialist by the whole world!"

I knew the answering argument, but my ardor for disputation was still at a low level. So I didn't point out that there had been no guerrilla armies in the country when 250,000 whites asserted their sovereignty over more than twenty times as many blacks in 1965, that this harvest had been sown then. I didn't say anything. The black relatives, standing stiffly in the hot morning sun, were also not saying much as they prepared themselves for the ordeal of searching through the corpses. They seemed too preoccupied to allow the gloating of the whites to register, even that of a beefy white policeman who unzipped his orange Adidas running jacket to flaunt the T-shirt he was wearing underneath. The T-shirt showed a Halloween ghoul and a tombstone. "R.I.P.," it said. Also, "I Want Your Body." The physician still hadn't finished with me. "Facts are facts," he was saying.

I had heard enough and walked away. The relatives were now filing through the first of the refrigerator cars. The black bodies inside were lightly coated with frost, but the stench of death was no figure of speech. An elderly woman collapsed, moaning. She had not found her son, but she had seen bodies that were beyond identification because of mortar fire. "This is our independence," said a merchant who had failed to find a brother and a cousin in the first refrigerator car and was now waiting for his turn to enter the second. "It's ridiculous, our independence. It's pathetic."

At just that point I saw a scene that left me choking on the accumulated horrors of those days. For a long moment I was overcome with an urge to get out of Bulawayo, out of Zimbabwe, and out of Africa. None of this has anything to do with me, I thought. It was the sight of a white man leading two white adolescent boys in the file of black relatives into the chill of the first car on the siding. The man was dressed in his casual Sunday best, in powder blue shorts and matching knee socks. With blond hair slicked back and pomaded, he fitted the caricature of a white African. He looked stony and determined, the kids looked scared. At a glance I thought I read the meaning of this little tableau. The man was providing a racial lesson, I thought, showing the boys what blacks do to each other, cultivating their sense that black means death, negation, ruin. Why, I wondered, couldn't the lunatic do that at home?

A little while later, by which time I had remembered I was there as a reporter, I looked up and saw the man walking in my general direction. He had a pleasant face, and although I had already convicted him of first-degree racism, I returned his lopsided half smile and fell into conversation. Piet Marais worked for Zimbabwe Railways. He was there with his sons, Paul and Darin, ages thirteen and fifteen. "Kids is cruel, kids is cruel really," he said when I asked what had possessed him to bring his boys to the railyard on this morning. They had heard about the killings in the army camps and townships at their school, and full of high spirits, they had come home every evening with another batch of wisecracks and crude jokes.

"To them it's just a lot of dead kaffirs," Piet Marais said. "I bring my sons here to see firsthand what they are speaking. I don't want them to speak secondhand."

And now that they had seen it, I asked, what did he expect them to say?

"I hope they say nothing really," the railway man replied. "I just want themselves to feel, 'Hell, this is terrible.' I don't want them to talk about it. I want them to stop talking about it really."

If I understood him right, Piet Marais was speaking about letting live. He was also speaking about common humanity and peace. Maybe he had seen too much war. He said that morning that he didn't know whether he would stay in Zimbabwe. He thought all governments were basically the same and wanted to remain, he said, but felt he might have to leave if the events of that week kept being repeated. I learned nothing about his politics, never saw him again, and don't know what he finally did. But I hope he found serenity, for he had, I thought, the wisdom that knows the difference, that could make the difference if anything can.

Author's Note

■

This book cannot appear without some accounting of my debt to the many South Africans who were generous, open, and available—often without stint—to an inquisitive foreigner. Some friends may feel that I have paid inadequate tribute to their struggle. Others, also friends, are likely to be disappointed, even angered by these pages and what they may dismiss as my easy judgments. No apologies in an afterword can make amends for such hurts. There are dozens of South Africans whom I would like to thank by name. I refrain from doing so because some who are under surveillance and pressure on account of their political commitments might not want attention drawn to them here, while others might be distressed to find themselves associated with what I have written. Except then to say that I am grateful to Sue Sparks and Phillip van Niekerk, who checked some facts for me long after I left the country, I will rely on private communications and telepathy to convey my thanks, admiration, and fond feelings to friends in South Africa.

I can be more explicit about help I received from colleagues, friends, and family in other places. A. M. Rosenthal of *The New York Times* understood my compulsion to return to South Africa. So did Robert Semple. James Greenfield, reading my mind better than I have ever managed to do, stood by me at every turn. Our publisher, Arthur Ochs Sulzberger, provided vital encouragement, both during my long wait for a South African visa and later, at the end of my tour. Mary Benson, William Connolly, Richard Eder, and Anthony Lewis read the manuscript and made valuable suggestions. So did Toby Lelyveld, who dealt severely with her son's punctuation, and Nita Lelyveld, who cleaned up her father's atrocious spelling. Her sister, Amy, rescued him from a couple of silly errors. Carl Brandt and Jonathan Segal did everything possible to enable me to write the book I thought I had to write. The John Simon Guggenheim Memorial Foundation found reason to support the efforts of a journalist as it does those of scholars and artists.

Carolyn Lelyveld, whose experience of South Africa was distinct from mine and in some respects deeper and more important, discovered this book's title and much else. I'll abstain, nevertheless, from the formal spousal encomia that are standard on pages such as this. Fortunately—it's the greatest fortune I have—I don't need a typewriter or word processor to send her a message.

Essentially this is a book of personal experience and observation, but I have foraged freely in the scholarship of others and plundered their research to suit my purposes. Such sources are mostly obvious to anyone familiar with serious writing on the subject, and some are acknowledged in the text. A full bibliography of the many books that kept me company in South Africa and afterward, while I was organizing my thoughts, would serve no purpose. But I feel impelled to mention some that are especially obscure, especially exploited here, or simply sources for quotes and facts I have lifted:

Biko, Steve. *I Write What I Like.* Edited by Aelred Stubbs. London, 1978.

Churchill, Lord Randolph S. *Men, Mines and Animals in South Africa.* Reprint. Bulawayo, 1979.

Crankshaw, Edward. *The Shadow of the Winter Palace.* Hamondsworth, Middlesex, 1978.

Davis, Richard Harding. *With Both Armies in South Africa.* New York, 1900.

Driver, C. J. *Patrick Duncan, South African and Pan-African.* London, 1980.

Du Toit, André and Gilomee, Hermann. *Afrikaner Political Thought: Analysis and Documents, 1780–1850.* Cape Town, 1983.

Frederickson, George M. *White Supremacy.* New York, 1981.

Gandhi, Mahatma. *Collected Works,* Volume V (1905–1906). New Delhi, 1961.

Gann, L. H., and Duignan, Peter. *South Africa: War? Revolution? Peace?* Cape Town, 1979.

Gould, Stephen Jay. *The Mismeasure of Man.* New York, 1981.

Gregory, Sir Theodor. *Ernest Oppenheimer and the Economic Development of Southern Africa.* Cape Town, 1962.

Hancock, W. K. *Smuts.* 2 volumes. London, 1962 and 1968.

Horne, Alistair. *A Savage War of Peace: Algeria 1954–1962.* New York, 1979.

Kane-Berman, John. *Soweto: Black Revolt, White Reaction.* Johannesburg, 1978.

Karis, Thomas; Carter, Gwendolen M.; and Gerhart, Gail M., editors. *From Protest to Challenge: A Documentary History of African Politics in South Africa,* Volumes 1 and 3. Stanford, 1972 and 1977.

Kgosana, Philip Ata. *Lest We Forget: An Autobiography,* Privately published. Kampala, 1979.

La Hause, Paul. "Drinking in a Cage: The Durban System and the 1929 Riots." *Africa Perspective* 20 (1982).

Lodge, Tom. *Black Politics in South Africa Since 1945.* Johannesburg, 1983.

Macmillan, Harold. *Pointing the Way.* London, 1972.

Milton, John. *The Edges of War: A History of Frontier Wars, 1702–1878.* Cape Town, 1983.

Mutwa, Credo Vusa' Mazulu. *My People: The Incredible Writings of a Zulu Witch-Doctor.* Hamondsworth, Middlesex, 1971.

Neto, Agostinho. *Sacred Hope.* Translated by Marga Holness. Dar-es-Salaam, 1974.

Noer, Thomas J. *Briton, Boer and Yankee: The United States and South Africa, 1870–1914.* Kent, Ohio, 1978.

Rabie, Pieter Jacobus, chairman. *Report of the Commission of Inquiry into Security Legislation.* Pretoria, 1981.

Simkins, Charles. *Four Essays on the Past, Present and Possible Future Distribution of the Black Population in South Africa.* Cape Town, 1983.

Smith, Edwin W. *The Life and Times of Daniel Lindley.* London, 1949.

Smuts, J. C. *Africa and Some World Problems.* Oxford, 1930.

———. *Holism and Evolution.* London, 1926.

Steyn, Martinus T., chairman. *Report of the Commission of Inquiry into the Mass Media.* 4 volumes. Cape Town, 1981.

Streak, Michael. *The Afrikaner as Viewed by the English.* Cape Town, 1974.

Surplus People Project. *Forced Removals in South Africa.* 5 volumes. Cape Town, 1983.

A Survey of the Proposals for the Constitutional Development of South Africa. Unpublished study for Chatham House, London, 1980.

Themba, Can. *The Will to Die.* London, 1972.

Van Onselen, Charles. *New Babylon, New Nineveh: Studies in the Social and Economic History of the Witwatersrand, 1886–1914.* 2 volumes. Johannesburg, 1982.

Walker, Eric A. *The Great Trek.* London, 1934.

Welsh, David. *The Roots of Segregation.* Cape Town, 1971.

Worrall, Denis, chairman. *First Report of the Constitutional Committee of the President's Council.* Cape Town, 1981.

—*J. L.*
London and Cutler, Maine
November, 1984

INDEX

ACKNOWLEDGMENTS

—

Grateful acknowledgment is made to the following for permission to reprint previously published materials:

Ad Donker (Pty.) Ltd.: Excerpts from the poem "Time Has Run Out" by Mongane Serote. Used by permission of Mongane Serote and Ad Donker (Pty.) Ltd., South Africa.

Farrar, Straus and Giroux, Inc.: Excerpt from "Strophes" from *A Part of Speech* by Joseph Brodsky. Translation copyright © 1980 by Farrar, Straus and Giroux, Inc. Used by permission.

Jobete Music Company, Inc.: Lyrics from "Master Blaster," words and music by Stevie Wonder. Copyright © 1980 by Jobete Music Co., Inc./Black Bull Music. Used by permission. International copyright secured. All rights reserved.

Eugenia Neto: Excerpts from "Reconquest" by Agostinho Neto. Reprinted by permission of Eugenia Neto.

Staffrider Magazine: Excerpt from "Friday Night" by Monyele Matome. Used by permission of Staffrider Magazine, South Africa.

TRO-Ludlow Music, Inc.: Lyrics from "Gonna Build a Mountain" from the Musical Production *Stop the World—I Want to Get Off*. Words and music by Leslie Bricusse and Anthony Newley. Copyright © 1961 TRO Essex Music Ltd., London, England. TRO-Ludlow Music, Inc., New York, controls all publication rights for the U.S.A. and Canada. Used by permission.

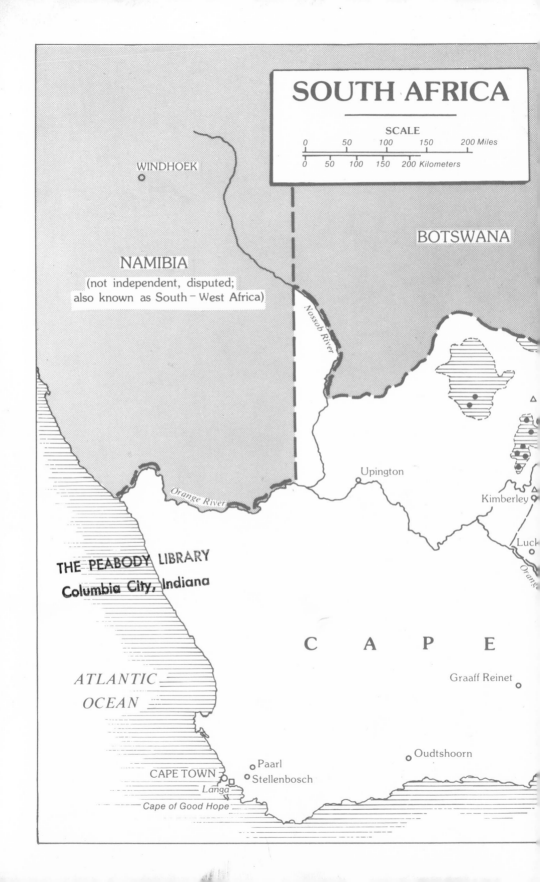

SOUTH AFRICA

SCALE

0   50   100   150   200 Miles

0   50   100   150   200 Kilometers

WINDHOEK

BOTSWANA

NAMIBIA

(not independent, disputed;
also known as South – West Africa)

Nossob River

Orange River

Upington

Kimberley

Luck

Oran

THE PEABODY LIBRARY
Columbia City, Indiana

C A P E

Graaff Reinet

ATLANTIC
OCEAN

Oudtshoorn

CAPE TOWN   Paarl
                   Stellenbosch
Langa
Cape of Good Hope